VLUCHT UIT SPARTA

Karen Sergeant

Vlucht uit Sparta

UITGEVERIJ

DE EENHOORN

CIP-gegevens: Koninklijke Bibliotheek Albert I
© Tekst: Karen Sergeant
© Omslagtekening en binnentekeningen: Erik Bongers
Druk: Oranje, Sint-Baafs-Vijve

© 2008 Uitgeverij De Eenhoorn bvba, Vlasstraat 17, B-8710 Wielsbeke

D/2008/6048/26
NUR 284
ISBN 978-90-5838-484-3

www.eenhoorn.be

Tussen Sparta en Athene

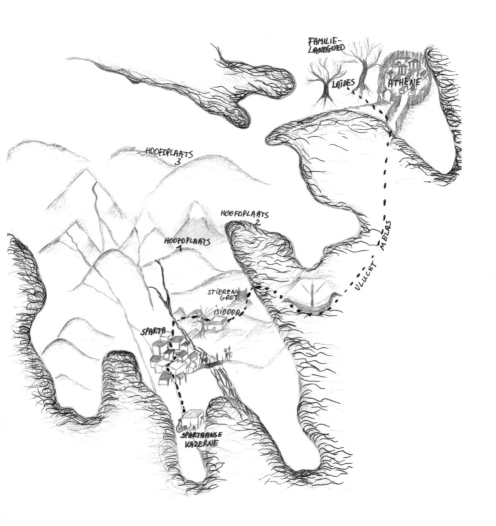

Mijn tweelingbroer

De dag waarop soldaten me weghaalden uit het huis van mijn moeder, scheerden vogels laag boven de olijfbomen.

'Melas.' Mijn moeders ogen wilden mij iets duidelijk maken. Iets van belang. Een soldaat met een haviksneus klemde haar mond dicht met zijn hand.

'Waar is die andere?' gromde een soldaat die wijdbeens de deuropening versperde. Ze zochten Laïdes, mijn tweelingbroer.

'Ik weet het niet.' Mijn stem klonk schor. 's Ochtends had de strozak waarop mijn broer sliep, koud aangevoeld. Ik had hem die dag niet gezien. Ook niet aan het ontbijt. Dat was vreemd. Meestal week hij niet van mijn zijde, ik was zijn sterke broer.

'Verstopt!' snauwde de soldaat met de haviksneus. 'Jij hebt die jongen verstopt!' Hij schopte tegen de kruik. Het water liep over de vloer als een donkere bloedvlek.

'Jij bent geen Spartaanse. Jij bent een verraadster!' Hij sloeg mijn moeder in het gezicht. 'Die nutteloze zoon van jou is alleen maar in leven gebleven omdat jouw man raadslid van de koning is!'

Moeder wankelde en viel. De soldaat gaf haar een trap in de

buik. Ze kreunde: 'Help ons, machtige Zeus.'

De soldaat liep door ons huis, keek in spleten en gaten, en gooide alle banken omver. De haviksneus hield me vast bij mijn nekvel. Ik kon nauwelijks ademen.

'Waar is die slappeling, dan maken we een soldaat van hem!'

'Rustig maar, Trifonas,' zei de andere soldaat. Hij plantte zijn speer dwars in de deuropening. Ze waren gestuurd door de koning. Zo ging dat in Sparta. Alle jongens van zeven moesten het leger in. De soldaat in de deuropening droeg een prachtige rode mantel, zijn lange zwarte haren hingen tot op zijn schouders.

Ondanks mijn angst en ellende bewonderde ik hem.

'Waar is die kleine mislukkeling?' Trifonas spuugde vol verachting op de grond. Hij gooide moeders aardewerk aan scherven. Moeder zweeg. Ik beet op mijn tanden. Tranen zouden het alleen maar erger maken. En ik was al zeven, te oud om te huilen.

'Genoeg Trifonas!' zei de man met de speer. Trifonas duwde me het huis uit. Ik zocht de ogen van mijn moeder. Tevergeefs. Roerloos lag ze op de grond.

'Dit jong krijgt slaag voor twee.' Trifonas duwde me het tuinpad op. 'Tot die ander opduikt.'

Ik wierp een laatste blik op ons tuintje waar de lavendel was uitgebloeid. Misschien was het beter zo. Ik hoopte dat ze mijn broer nooit zouden vinden.

'Je broer is een lafaard.' De buurjongens schreeuwden om het hardst. Mijn tweelingbroertje werd vaak uitgelachen omdat hij zo mager is. Laïdes bleef meestal dicht bij mij, ik was groot en sterk en beschermde hem.

We liepen door nauwe steegjes, richting kazerne. Trifonas grijnsde. Het droge zand van de weg prikte in mijn neus. Mijn keel deed pijn. Ik slikte. En nog eens. Maar ik hield het hoofd recht en de tanden stijf op elkaar.

In de verte lag het legerkamp. Toen we dichterbij waren gekomen, zag ik nog andere jongens van mijn leeftijd. Niemand huilde. Niemand keek op. Ze zaten netjes op een rij. Trifonas wees me mijn plaats aan: naast de andere jongens, op de kale bank. Elke spier in mijn lichaam was gespannen, mijn handen waren gebald tot vuisten. Uitgeput zakte ik neer op de bank.

Trifonas hield een lange toespraak over alles wat niet mocht en alles wat moest. Eindelijk was het tijd om te eten. We sprongen overeind en renden kriskras door elkaar naar de eetruimte.

'Stop!' We bleven stokstijf staan. 'Opnieuw,' brulde Trifonas. 'En deze keer in een rechte rij.' Geschrokken gingen we netjes weer op de bank zitten. De eerste jongen stond aarzelend op, de anderen volgden één na één.

'Hoofd recht. Borst vooruit.' Trifonas tikte met zijn stok tegen het achterwerk van de jongen voor me in de rij. De jongen rilde, strekte zijn hals om het hoofd nog rechter te houden. Langzaam kwam de rij in beweging.

9

'Jij niet.' Trifonas trok me uit de rij. 'Jij krijgt pas iets te eten als je zegt waar je broer is.' Trifonas sloot me op in een hok, zonder eten. Mijn ogen wenden geleidelijk aan het duister. Ik duwde tegen de planken. Alles zat muurvast. Ik liep naar een andere hoek. Er kleefde spinrag aan mijn handen en gezicht. Nergens vond ik een kiertje om naar buiten te kijken. Ik hoopte dat Alexius met de speer me zou vrijlaten. Uiteindelijk ging ik op de harde bank liggen. Ik wou aan mooie dingen denken: aan de lavendel in de tuin van mijn moeder en al haar kruiden die ze thuis liet drogen in manden, op de tafel.

De volgende ochtend liet Alexius me mee aan tafel schuiven. Zo onopvallend mogelijk keek ik om me heen. Mijn broer was nergens te zien. We aten een dikke soep. Ik moest mijn ogen sluiten en mijn neus dichtknijpen om een hap naar binnen te krijgen. Het beestenbloed kleurde de soep zwart. De stukjes groenten slikte ik door zonder te proeven. Trifonas klopte me kameraadschappelijk op de schouder. Ik wendde mijn hoofd af.

'Kijk,' zei hij en hij hield zijn beide handen gesloten naar mij uitgestrekt. 'Kies een hand.' Ik wees zijn linkerhand aan. Daarin lagen twee vijgen; ik was dol op de zoete smaak. Thuis kregen we vijgen als nagerecht.

'Eet,' zei Trifonas. Ik stak mijn hand uit.

'Wacht,' zei hij kordaat terwijl hij zijn hand wegtrok. 'Eerst vertel je me waar ik moet zoeken.'

Ik hield mijn ogen op zijn handen gericht. Ik wist niet of mijn moeder mijn broer had verstopt, niemand had me iets verteld. Laïdes evenmin. Maar Trifonas ging ervan uit dat ik loog, dat ik mijn broer probeerde te beschermen. Hij pakte me in mijn nekvel en sleurde me naar het hok. Hij duwde me ruw naar binnen en vergrendelde de deur. Ik had het koud, hoewel het zomer was. Mijn magere lijf deed pijn toen ik op de bank ging liggen om te slapen. De volgende ochtend kwam Trifonas terug, in zijn hand hield hij versgebakken brood en olijven. Mijn maag gromde. Trifonas at smakkend, boerde en vroeg tussen twee happen door: 'Iets te vertellen?' 'Ik weet niets!' Het klonk bozer dan ik bedoelde. Trifonas trok de rode tuniek van mijn rug en hield een zweep van buigzame takken klaar. De eerste slag deed me wankelen. Bij de tweede klap zakte ik door mijn knieën. Daarna stopte ik met tellen.

Om niet aan de zweepslagen te denken, dacht ik aan vroeger: mijn blik gleed langs de openstaande deur, ver over de heuvels, tot waar de bergrivier moest zijn. Enkele weken geleden hadden mijn broer en ik een lange tocht gemaakt om kruidenaftreksels van mijn moeder te brengen naar een man die in de bergen woonde. Op een van zijn handelsreizen had hij de pest gekregen. De huisbediende van de man nam onze medicijnen aan. Er stond een meisje naast hem.

'Ik heet Kallista,' zei ze. 'Ik ben de dochter van Isidoor.' Isidoor was ongetwijfeld de zieke man. Kallista droeg mooie kleren en om haar hals hing een snoer van parels die schitterden in de zon.

'Ik kom later naar huis,' zei Kallista tegen de huisbediende. De hele namiddag speelden we bij de rivier. We zochten klei in de rivierbedding en boetseerden beelden. Kallista bewonderde Laïdes' fijne handen die zonder moeite haar gezicht boetseerden. Ik vroeg Kallista of ze mee wilde gaan duiken maar ze speelde liever met Laïdes. Isidoor was een rijk man. Op de berghellingen rond Sparta liet hij druiven groeien. Schepen brachten zijn wijn tot in de landen aan de Zwarte Zee. Hij was geen Spartaan, maar hij was rijk genoeg om gerespecteerd te worden. Op verzoek van de Spartanen importeerde hij graan of ijzer. Van het ijzer werden speerpunten gemaakt.

Ik zocht nog andere dingen om aan te denken maar het hielp niet, de zweep deed pijn. Trifonas liet zijn zweep een laatste keer knallen, ondertussen kauwde hij luidruchtig op zijn brood. Mijn gedachten keerden terug naar mijn lichaam. Ik had veel pijn maar ik gaf geen kik. Dat gunde ik hem niet. Hij sleepte me uit de donkere hut. Mijn ogen knipperden en traanden door het plotse, felle daglicht. De andere jongens waren aan het hardlopen alsof hun leven ervan afhing. Ze waren bang voor de zweep. En nog banger om uitgelachen te worden. Als je niet kon volgen, werd je uitgelachen. 'Komaan Melas,' zei Trifonas en hij duwde me de looppiste op. 'Laat eens zien wat je waard bent.' Ik voegde me bij de anderen. Na het derde rondje werd het zwart voor mijn ogen. Mijn benen voelden slap aan. Volhouden, dreunde het in mijn hoofd. Even later viel ik voorover in het hete zand. Trifonas liet de zweep naast me neerkomen. 'Opstaan,' zei hij. Ik was blij dat mijn broer hier niet was. Je leerde hier gehoorzamen zonder te morren, pijn verdragen zonder een kik te geven. Dat was goed voor soldaten maar niet voor mijn broer.

'Sta op!' beval Trifonas. En ik rende verder terwijl ik de zon op mijn huid voelde branden. Ik voelde mijn hart kloppen in de striemen op mijn rug. Eén van de jongens liep opzettelijk tegen me aan en schopte tegen mijn scheenbeen. De pijn schoot door me heen. De jongen grijnsde en wilde me een tweede trap geven. Een jongen met een donkere huid ging voor me staan en ving de klap op. Ik haalde opgelucht adem. Zijn grote bruine ogen gaven me vertrouwen. De pijn trok weg.

's Avonds werd ik weer zonder eten naar het hok gebracht. Als een blok viel ik in slaap. Midden in de nacht werd ik wakker omdat iemand mijn naam fluisterde.

Leander

Ik kreeg mijn ogen nauwelijks open. Opnieuw trok iemand aan mijn mouw.

'Ssst. Ik ben het, Leander.' Hij waste mijn gezicht met koud water en gaf me brood met olijven.

'Je mag niet wachten tot Trifonas of Alexius je eten geven,' zei hij. 'Je moet eten, desnoods voedsel stelen zodat je niet verzwakt. Stelen mag. Je krijgt alleen straf als ze je betrappen.' Ik kwam te weten dat nog meer jongens werden behandeld zoals ik. Het was een oefening om te wennen aan het leven in de kazerne. Ze zonderden me af en lieten me honger en kou lijden om te zien of ik in staat was voor mezelf te zorgen: niet passief afwachten dus maar 's nachts rondsluipen en eten stelen.

'Kom mee,' zei Leander. Buiten was het fris. In het kamp kregen we maar één kledingstuk. Kou en hitte moesten we verdragen. Leanders huid was veel donkerder dan de mijne. Hem zouden ze niet gemakkelijk zien in het donker.

'Hoe heb je de deur open gekregen?'

'De deur zat met een touw op slot,' antwoordde hij. 'Ik zal je laten zien hoe je hun knopen loskrijgt. Kom!' Plots hoorde ik stemmen en ik dook in het gras.

'Slaven probeerden te ontsnappen,' zei Leander. We zagen hoe een slaaf werd vastgebonden en meegevoerd. Spartanen waren hard voor zichzelf en nog veel harder voor hun slaven. Een slaaf die probeerde te ontsnappen, werd zonder pardon naar de gevangenis gebracht en vaak doodgemarteld.

Ik dacht terug aan Androcles, onze huisslaaf. Wanneer vader niet thuis was, behandelde moeder Androcles als een vriend. Hij mocht met ons mee aan tafel. Hij was de vriendelijkste man die ik kende. Hij hielp mijn moeder bij het drogen van lavendel en tijm. Daarna maakten ze er zalven en aftreksels van. Mijn moeder leerde hem hoe hij een verzwikte enkel of gebroken been moest verzorgen. Om de drie weken kwam mijn vader een paar dagen thuis, dan veranderde het leven van Androcles helemaal.

'Ga water halen, snel!' snauwde mijn vader vaak. Mijn vader liep rond in zijn rode soldatenmantel en tussen zijn riem zat een dolk. We waren bang voor hem.

Androcles bediende mijn vader op zijn wenken, het hoofd gebogen.

'Bij ons eten slaven gewoon mee aan tafel,' vertelde ik Leander. 'Tenminste, als mijn vader niet thuis is.'

'Zeg dat maar niet aan Trifonas of Alexius,' zei Leander. 'Want dat is tegen de Spartaanse wetten.'

'Slaven zijn ook mensen,' protesteerde ik. 'Ze behoren alleen tot een ander volk.'

'Zeg zulke dingen niet,' siste Leander. We liepen naar een plek met veel olijfbomen. Leander klom in een boom. De olijven waren rijp door de zon van de laatste dagen.

'Ik wil naar huis,' zei ik. 'Ik houd niet van het legerkamp en de trainingen.'

'Je hebt geen keuze, vriend,' zei Leander. 'De eerste weken zijn moeilijk, maar het went.'

Dat kon ik nauwelijks geloven, maar het was waar.

Na enkele weken leerde ik eten stelen waar Trifonas bij stond. Leander zorgde ervoor dat Trifonas werd afgeleid en ik stal ondertussen brood uit de voorraadkamer. Daar hadden we veel plezier om.

De jaren gingen voorbij. Leander en ik werden twaalf jaar. Van de zweep had ik geen schrik meer. Ik zou een dappere soldaat kunnen worden zoals mijn vader en Alexius. Maar vrienden had ik niet, op Leander na. Ik bleef een buitenstaander. Soms was ik jaloers op de pret die de andere jongens maakten, maar ik hoorde er niet bij.

'Tempo houden,' snauwde Trifonas. We moesten alweer hardlopen. Mijn gedachten dwaalden af naar vroeger toen ik met Laïdes en Kallista bij de rivier speelde. Door mijn dagdromen struikelde ik over een steen. Trifonas hield zijn zweep al in de lucht om me te bestraffen voor mijn onoplettendheid, maar Leander sprong op het laatste nippertje tussen ons in. De klap was hevig, Leander wankelde en viel.

'Idioot!' riep Trifonas. 'Sta op en ga water halen, ik heb dorst.'

'Wij zijn geen slaven!' Ik balde mijn vuisten. 'Je bent zelf een idioot!' Mijn spieren spanden zich als bogen. Ik wilde Trifonas naar de keel vliegen, maar Leander sprong overeind en hield me tegen.

Trifonas grijnsde. De andere jongens lachten heimelijk want ik zou weer eens gestraft worden.

Mijn plan

Trifonas liet me allerlei smerige karweitjes opknappen en gaf me geen eten meer.

Op een dag speelden de jongens een sluipspel. Ze hadden zichzelf in twee groepen verdeeld. Ze probeerden de andere groep gevangen te nemen en hun eigen gevangenen te bevrijden. Leander mocht meedoen. Maar toen ik door de struiken sloop, nam niemand me gevangen. Toen ik de anderen uit de gevangenis bevrijdde, deden ze alsof ik niet bestond. Leander juichten ze toe toen hij erin slaagde de gevangenen te bevrijden.

Elke nacht trokken Leander en ik eropuit om voedsel te stelen. De jongens uit onze groep wilden dat Leander met hen mee zou gaan. Ze prezen hem om zijn kracht en gaven hem gestolen stukken vlees. Dat was iets waar Leander en ik niet in slaagden: vlees stelen. Wij aten bessen, brood en groenten. Ik wist niet eens waar je vlees kon vinden, laat staan stelen. Als iemand uit de groep mij tegenkwam, liep hij met een grote bocht om me heen, alsof ik een besmettelijke ziekte had.

'Waar wil je vannacht naartoe?' vroeg mijn vriend.

'De graanvallei?' stelde ik aarzelend voor. Ik was bang dat ook hij me op een dag in de steek zou laten.

'Goed idee.' Hij klopte me bemoedigend op de schouder.

'Je mag ook met de anderen meegaan, dan kan je vlees eten.'

'Neen,' zei Leander. 'Trouwens, ze krijgen het vlees van Trifonas.'

Dat zat me niet lekker. Trifonas gaf de anderen dus vlees in de hoop dat Leander zich bij hen zou aansluiten. Maar Leander speelde dat spel niet mee. Hij was vriendelijk tegen de andere jongens, hij vergaf hen hun valsheid maar sloot geen vriendschap met hen. We stapten stevig door naar de graanvallei. Onderweg stilden we onze honger met bramen en olijven.

Het gerucht ging dat mijn moeder ziek was, maar Trifonas stond niet toe dat ik haar opzocht. Ik moest haar zien en vroeg Leander om mee naar het huis van mijn moeder te gaan.

'Te ver,' zei Leander. 'De kans is groot dat we onderweg ontdekt worden.'

Ik knikte en zei dat ik het erop wilde wagen. Leander probeerde me dit uit het hoofd te praten.

'Het is te gevaarlijk,' zei hij nadrukkelijk en zijn ogen werden donker.

'Ik moet!'

Leander schudde zijn hoofd en zuchtte: 'Wacht in elk geval op een nacht zonder maan.'

Eindelijk was het zover. Leander omhelsde me en zei: 'Moge Zeus je op je pad begeleiden.'

Ik volgde de bedding van de rivier om geen sporen achter te laten. Takken en doornen schramden mijn benen. Ik zocht in de verte, naar de berg met de eeuwige sneeuw. Daar keek ik vaak naar toen ik nog in het voortuintje van mijn moeders huis speelde. Maar het was te donker om iets te zien. Een uur later kwam ik bij het zijriviertje dat door de stad stroomde. Het houten bootje waarmee Laïdes en ik vaak hadden gespeeld, was verdwenen. Ik rook weer de geur van vroeger: gedroogde tijm en lavendel. De geur vermengde zich met rook. Het leek of iemand een vuurtje had gestookt. Ik was nu dicht bij ons huis en ik werd ongerust. Hoe dichter ik het huis van mijn moeder naderde, hoe indringender de geur werd. Verbrand stro of hout? Het gebeurde wel eens dat ze bij een ernstige ziekte persoonlijke spullen verbrandden. Ik liep steeds sneller en mijn hart klopte in mijn keel toen ik vaag de omtrek van mijn ouderlijke huis zag. Hier was de geur van verkoolde spullen nog sterker. Er was geen licht in huis. De deuren en ramen waren gesloten. Ik rammelde aan de voordeur. Binnen bleef het stil. Ik opende het luik van het raam aan de voorkant en kroop naar binnen. Alle spullen stonden op hun plek. De schaal met vijgen op de bovenste plank en de kruik met water naast het aanrecht. Ik werd er helemaal stil van. Hier voelde ik me vroeger zo thuis. In de slaapkamer zag ik een zwak kaarsvlammetje.

'Hallo!' riep ik enkele keren. Maar ik hoorde enkel de galm van mijn stem. In huis bleef het volkomen stil. De houten planken kraakten onder mijn voeten toen ik naar het slaapvertrek liep. Daar lag moeder, languit op bed. Haar ogen waren niet gesloten. Maar het leek alsof ze niets zag en naar een bepaalde plek op het plafond staarde. 'Moeder,' fluisterde ik, bang dat ik haar zou laten schrikken. Ze hoorde me niet.

'Halt! Halt!' riep een bekende stem. Androcles wilde me bij de arm wegtrekken.

'Wat is er?' vroeg ik verbaasd. 'Ik ben het maar.'

Androcles' handen trilden nog na en zijn ogen waren donker van woede.

'Melas,' zei Androcles verbaasd. 'Ik dacht dat je een overvaller was. Ze blijven je moeder pesten,' zuchtte hij. 'Zeker nu ze zwak is. En nog steeds om Laïdes die verdween op het moment dat zijn militaire opleiding begon. De Spartanen vergeven het haar niet. Elke nacht verzinnen ze wel wat. Ze kan er niet meer tegen. Laatst hebben ze het huis in brand gestoken.'

Ik legde mijn hand op moeders voorhoofd dat warm aanvoelde. Ze rilde. Het begon tot me door te dringen waarom ik maar geen vrienden maakte in de kazerne. Mijn familie had een wet overtreden en dat zou men ons blijven aanwrijven. Dit was niet vol te houden, dit was geen leven.

'Heb je pijn?' vroeg ik haar.

'Het is de angst,' zei ze met een zwakke stem. 'Ik voel me hier een vreemdeling. Sinds Laïdes is verdwenen, mag niemand nog met me spreken. Ze laten me leven want ze vrezen jouw vader. Ik zou liever sterven. Mijn kruiden helpen niet meer.' Naast haar bed stonden talloze mandjes met kruiden. Mijn hart klopte in mijn keel. Ik had de deur willen uitlopen om luid uit te schreeuwen hoe onrechtvaardig ik dit vond. Mijn moeder stond altijd klaar voor iedereen. En nu was niemand bereid haar te helpen.

'Kan vader je dan niet helpen?' vroeg ik hoopvol.

'Hij mag... hij wil niet met me praten zolang ik niets zeg over Laïdes. Voor hem is de Spartaanse wet heilig.'

'Ik wil weg uit dit vervloekte land,' zei ik. 'Ik neem jou en Androcles mee. Wanneer de maan is gegroeid en weer afgenomen, moeten jullie klaar staan.' Mijn moeder wilde me waarschuwen voor alle gevaren die me te wachten stonden, maar ik legde mijn vinger op haar mond. In haar ogen zag ik een sprankje hoop.

'Jij wilde toch soldaat worden?' vroeg mijn moeder. Dat was waar, soldaten kregen respect in Sparta. Maar hoe kon ik respect hebben voor de Spartanen? En waarom deed mijn vader niets aan onze ellende? Hij kon ervoor zorgen dat mijn moeder en ik een beter leven hadden. Als staatsman had hij het recht alle kazernes te bezoeken. Maar ik had hem nog niet gezien.

'We gaan hier weg, dat staat vast,' zei ik kordaat en ik voelde dat dit de juiste beslissing was. Ik vroeg Androcles of hij samen met mij over een ontsnappingsplan wilde nadenken. We

22

spraken af dat hij naar Isidoor zou gaan met een pakket medicijnen. Dat had hij wel vaker gedaan. Ik wist dat ik Isidoor en Androcles kon vertrouwen, ze hadden geen van beiden Spartaans bloed. Voor hen was het geen probleem als iemand Sparta wilde verlaten. Androcles zou Isidoor vragen ervoor te zorgen dat er een schip klaar lag in een rustige baai. We zouden ook een dag in Isidoors huis doorbrengen. Androcles wilde alles regelen. Hij was als een vader voor me, hij wel. De ochtendschemering brak al door toen ik uitgeput op mijn bed in de kazerne neerviel. Leander haalde opgelucht adem. Hij had de hele nacht tot de goden gebeden.

De daaropvolgende dagen kregen we intensieve trainingen. Alexius en Trifonas organiseerden een vijfkamp. Eerst moesten we hardlopen, daarna discuswerpen, verspringen, speerwerpen en worstelen. Ik was de beste in hardlopen. Trifonas zei alleen iets over mijn slechte resultaten in het discuswerpen. Zijn haviksblik was op mij gericht als ik de discus probeerde weg te slingeren. Het lukte me nog steeds niet. Er haperde iets aan mijn techniek.
'Je werpt als een vrouw,' spotte Trifonas. Hij nam de discus en wierp die met gemak tot voorbij de streep die hij voor ons getrokken had. Leander zat aan de kant en keek toe. Naast hem zat een duif op het gras. Hij gaf het diertje wat broodkruimels. Spijtig dat ik Leander niets kon zeggen. Ik vreesde dat ze hem zouden ondervragen op het moment dat ik verdwe-

nen was. Het was beter dat hij niets wist. Ik zag dat hij best
wel zin had om ook met de andere jongens om te gaan. Maar
dat kon alleen als hij mij liet vallen. Misschien kreeg Leander
het wel makkelijker als ik weg was.

Leander was gespierd als een echte soldaat, maar de duif liet
zich door hem strelen. Ze leek helemaal niet bang. Hij bracht
zelfs de dieren tot rust. Ze kwamen spontaan naar hem toe.
Ik zou hem missen. Zonder hem had ik die kazernejaren niet
overleefd.

'Waarom kijk je zo vreemd?' Leander keek me bezorgd aan.
'Is er iets?'

'Ik ben moe,' loog ik. 'Vannacht trek ik er niet op uit, ik heb
mijn slaap nodig.'

Leander knikte en zei dat hij iets lekkers voor me zou mee-
brengen.

Ik deed alsof ik sliep terwijl Leander geruisloos in de nacht
verdween. Ik legde de duivenveer, die ik voor hem had be-
waard, op zijn bed. Het was alles wat ik hem kon nalaten.
Deze keer had ik geen tijd om de langere maar veilige weg
langs de rivier te nemen. Het moest snel gaan. Moeder en ik
moesten in Isidoors huis zijn voordat het weer licht werd,
voordat Trifonas doorhad dat ik gevlucht was. Ik had stukken
schapenvacht om mijn voeten gebonden, zodat het geluid
van mijn voetstappen werd gedempt en mijn voetsporen on-
herkenbaar waren. Af en toe hoorde ik geritsel of voetstap-

pen die zich snel verwijderden. Iedereen die 's nachts in Sparta ronddoolde, had iets te verbergen. Behalve de Spartaanse wachters. Maar die maakten vaak lawaai en hadden brandende toortsen, zodat ik me makkelijk voor hen kon verbergen.

'Moeder,' fluisterde ik, toen ik eindelijk het huis had bereikt en naar binnen was gegaan. Ik kreeg geen antwoord. Het was aardedonker in huis. Ik moest even stil blijven staan om weer een beetje op adem te komen. Met mijn handen tastte ik de bedden af. Ze waren leeg en voelden koud aan. Wat was er gebeurd? Mijn knieën trilden. Ik zonk neer op de bank.

Ezeltje

'Melas, hier!' klonk moeders stem vanuit de tuin. Ik hoorde de ademhaling van een dier. Ze leidde een ezeltje aan haar hand, beladen met dekens, voedsel en leren zakken gevuld met water.

'Die kunnen we niet meenemen,' protesteerde ik. 'Zo vallen we te veel op. Stel dat de ezel lawaai gaat maken!' Mijn moeder nam een poot van de ezel met haar beide handen vast en liet zien hoe ze repen zacht leder onder zijn hoeven had gebonden. Tot mijn verbazing liet de ezel moeder begaan.

'Niemand zal iets horen,' zei ze en ze stapte kordaat de weg op, de ezel aan een touw leidend.

'Waar is Androcles?' vroeg ik.

'Hij is al bij Isidoor en bereidt onze tocht voor,' antwoordde moeder. De smalle, donkere steegjes leken kleiner dan ik me herinnerde. Pas na een poosje merkte ik dat mijn moeder mannenkleren droeg. Ze leek wel een schapenhoeder.

'Jij zou ook beter je lange haren verbergen en zeker je rode tuniek. Moeder wilde iets uit een mand halen maar toen bleef de ezel staan, hij wilde geen stap meer vooruit.

'Zie je nu wel,' fluisterde ik. 'Je hebt altijd problemen met zo'n beest.'

Moeder lette niet op wat ik zei en volgde een ander pad waarlangs de ezel wel verder wilde. Op de weg die we net verlaten hadden, zag ik opeens een stel bewakers aankomen. Ze hadden een slaaf opgepakt. Ik bleef als verlamd staan. Even hield een bewaker een toorts in onze richting. Hij hield zijn hand boven zijn ogen. Maar de nacht was inktzwart en ze kwamen niet langs het pad dat de ezel voor ons had gekozen. Moeder haalde een kalebas uit een van de draagzakken.

'Drink,' zei ze. 'Om rustig te blijven.'

'Ik ben rustig.'

'Wil je een stukje suikerwortel om te kauwen, dat helpt.'

'Nee!'

Ze knikte en zette de kalebas aan haar lippen.

We konden Sparta niet verlaten langs de hoofdbrug; die werd dag en nacht bewaakt. Maar ik kende een ondiepe plek in de rivier. Om die plek te bereiken, moesten we een stukje hoger de bergen in en dat betekende een omweg, maar ik wist niets beters. Ik betwijfelde of de ezel de steile helling op zou willen. Maar het ergste was dat er maar één weg liep. Als de wachters die controleerden, zaten we in de val.

'Ze zullen ons voor herders houden,' zei moeder en ze haalde een muts en een wollen jak voor me uit de draagtas van de ezel. 'Androcles heeft alles geregeld.' Ik stopte mijn lange haar onder de muts en trok het jak over mijn kleed.

'Nu de schapen nog ophalen bij de hoeve van Gregorius,' zei moeder rustig.

'Wat!' riep ik gevaarlijk luid. 'Weet die familie van onze vlucht?'

'Dat weet ik niet,' zei moeder. 'Androcles heeft hun gevraagd drie schapen voor ons klaar te zetten in de weide achter de hoeve.'

'Moeder, je bent te goedgelovig. Hoe weet je dat het geen valstrik is? Androcles is al jaren jouw slaaf. Dit is de gelegenheid voor hem om zich te wreken en een betere positie te verwerven, bijvoorbeeld in het paleis, bij vader,' zei ik woedend. 'En als Androcles ons niet verraadt dan zal Gregorius dat wel doen.'

'Rustig,' zei moeder en ze legde een hand op mijn schouder. 'Het heeft geen zin om nu driftig te worden.' Ik kon haar hand niet verdragen en maakte me los. Ik beet op mijn lip en was kwaad omdat mijn lot in de handen van anderen lag. Inademen, uitademen. Als ik naar mijn adem luisterde, werd ik weer rustig. Met het hoofd gebogen liep ik achter moeder aan, het pad volgend dat naar de hoeve liep. Het was aardedonker achter de hoeve waar de schapen stonden. Moeder aaide de schapen. Mijn spieren werden hard als steen, ik was erop voorbereid om elk moment in elkaar geslagen te worden. Maar het bleef volkomen stil. De schapen volgden ons gewillig. We waren al verder dan ik had durven dromen; hoe had Androcles dit voor elkaar gekregen? Het steile pad kronkelde omhoog langs een afgrond, waar je onmogelijk kon wegvluchten. We gedroegen ons als twee herders die hun ver-

28

dwaalde schapen gingen zoeken. De wachters kenden dit pad maar al te goed. Het was dé weg om uit Sparta te vluchten. De vraag was of ze ook vannacht dit pad bewaakten. De meeste slaven kwamen niet zo ver en werden al opgepakt nog voor ze Sparta uit waren. Ik spitste mijn oren. Daar was het weer, het geluid van voetstappen. De ezel rukte aan de teugels. Ik wilde weglopen maar de ezel trok ons mee, een holte in, aan de kant van de weg. Moeder en ik kropen zo ver mogelijk weg in het gat. Erg diep was het niet. De schapen kropen tegen ons aan.

De voetstappen kwamen dichterbij. Ik wist zeker dat het wilde bonzen van mijn hart hoorbaar was. 'Hier zit wat,' lalde een stem en hikte. Ik herkende het Spartaanse accent.

'Het zijn maar beesten,' zei de ander. 'Je hebt te veel op.'
'Ik hou van beesten,' zei zijn collega en hij liep naar de schapen toe. Ik perste de lucht uit mijn longen, in de hoop nog kleiner te worden. Moeder hield haar hoofd gebogen, roerloos. De ezel begon jammerlijk te balken en zette zich schrap tussen ons en de twee mannen in.
'Jij houdt dan wel van beesten,' lachte de Spartaan luid. 'Maar dit beest houdt duidelijk niet van jou.' De dronken man greep de ander bij de kraag, gaf hem een duw en riep: 'Die beesten houden wel van mij!' Hun toortsen gaven veel licht. Te veel. Ik zag hun metalen beenbeschermers glimmen. De nuchtere soldaat gaf zijn collega ook een duw. De toorts viel

29

met een smak op de grond, lichtte nog even op en doofde ten slotte uit. Zwarter kon de nacht niet zijn. De mannen vervloekten elkaar. Ik sloop de weg op. Moeder volgde. De schapen bleven liggen in de rotsspleet, met de ezel naast hen. De mannen maakten behoorlijk wat lawaai. Hun stemmen echoden tegen de rotshelling.

'Hoor jij ook iets?'

'Het is je eigen gelal.'

'Niet waar. Stil, ik hoorde iemand weglopen!'

Na honderd stappen durfde ik achterom te kijken. De mannen hoorde ik niet meer.

'Dank je Zeus, machtigste der goden,' fluisterde ik.

'Leerde je in het kamp bidden?' Moeders stem klonk verbaasd.

'Niet echt,' zei ik verlegen. 'Vooral vechten, maar ik ken de gebeden nog die je me hebt geleerd.'

Ik kon moeder niet zien, maar ik voelde dat ze glimlachte. We liepen zwijgend verder. Sparta was steeds verder weg, dieper in het dal. Het was nog opletten bij de koopmanshuizen die hier en daar langs de weg stonden. Een koopman kon in aanzien stijgen als hij een vluchtende slaaf of Spartaan aangaf.

'Wacht even,' fluisterde ik en ik spitste mijn oren. Moeder hoorde het ook. Geritsel en gesnuif. Ik beet op mijn lip. Ik trok moeder mee, het pad af. Het was ongetwijfeld de Spartaanse wachter die versterking was gaan halen en nu met andere soldaten achter ons aankwam. Net op tijd zonken we neer in een greppel. Het gesnuif was vlakbij.

'De ezel,' zei moeder en ze sprong uit de greppel. De schapen kwamen mekkerend achter de ezel aan. Moeder gaf hem een kus op zijn kop en streelde zijn nek. Ze wilde haar mand openmaken om de dieren iets lekkers te geven.

'Geen tijd,' siste ik. We liepen verder en weldra hoorden we het ruisen van de rivier. De rivier was hier ondiep, maar zeer breed. Ik trok mijn kleren uit. Het water stroomde van de besneeuwde bergtoppen, waar de goden leefden, naar beneden. Om mijn spieren niet te laten verkrampen, masseerde ik ze stevig, dat had ik in de kazerne geleerd. Het water was dieper dan ik dacht. Halverwege de rivier reikte het al tot aan mijn middel.

'Jullie moeten hier blijven,' zei moeder tegen de schapen. 'Gregorius komt jullie halen.' Moeder ging op de rug van het ezeltje zitten. Ik zag haar lippen bewegen tegen het oor van de ezel en het dier bereikte zonder aarzelen de rotsachtige overkant. De meeste ezels die ik kende, waren koppiger. Ik rilde van de kou terwijl ik mijn tuniek over mijn hoofd trok. Moeder wilde me warm wrijven maar ik hield haar tegen. 'We moeten verder.' Ik moest me inspannen om mijn ijskoude ledematen te bewegen.

'Drink hiervan,' zei ze en ze reikte me een kalebas aan. 'Het zal je verwarmen.'

'Ik heb geen hulp nodig.'

Moeder begreep me niet. 'Je bent veranderd,' fluisterde ze.

31

Langzaam lukte het me mijn gevoelloze benen weer in een normaal tempo te bewegen.

'Hier groeit gember,' zei moeder. 'Het is een uitstekend middel om het weer warm te krijgen.' Moeder begon zenuwachtig gemberplantjes uit te trekken.

'Laat dat, we moeten verder.'

'Maar...'

'Nee,' zei ik en ik trok haar overeind.

'Vroeger was je dol op mijn kruiden.'

'We moeten verder.'

Het schemerde al, ik kon de silhouetten van bomen en rotsen onderscheiden. Het pad dat naar Isidoors huis leidde, liep langs een afgrond. Overal lagen losse stenen. Ik lette op waar ik mijn voeten neerzette. Links van ons stonden bomen. Na lang klimmen zag ik Isidoors huis. De dag brak aan. Elk moment konden we mensen tegenkomen die water gingen halen of hout sprokkelen. Als ook maar één Spartaan een vermoeden had van waar we waren, als ook maar één mens wist welke weg we volgden, dan waren we verloren. Dan zou ik de rest van mijn leven boeten voor mijn verraad.

'We moeten ons vermommen als kooplieden,' zei moeder. 'Die krijgt Isidoor vaak over de vloer.' Uit de tas die over de rug van de ezel hing, haalde ze een lange mantel en een hoed. Achter een boom kleedde ik me om. Ik legde mijn tuniek in een kuil en gooide er zand over. Niet veel later kruisten Isidoors houthakkers onze weg. Mijn hart bonsde.

'Goeie morgen,' zeiden de houthakkers vriendelijk. De mensen waren hier anders dan in Sparta, vriendelijker. De houthakkers waren slaven van Isidoor maar ze zagen er gezond en gelukkig uit. Ze kregen vast goed te eten. De druivenvelden reikten zo ver als mijn oog kon zien.

Isidoor kwam ons tegemoet, schudde ons de hand en behandelde ons alsof we zakenpartners van hem waren. We kregen een rijkelijke maaltijd. Een vrouw legde een kleurig kleed op de tafel en zette volle schalen neer. Ze bewoog lenig en geruisloos door het huis. Iets in haar stap kwam me bekend voor. Ze had prachtig glanzend, lang zwart haar. Opeens herkende ik haar.

'Kallista?' fluisterde ik. Ze keek me aan en knikte bijna onmerkbaar. Ik deed mijn mond open, en weer toe. Er waren te veel onbekenden in het vertrek. Keurig veegde ik mijn mondhoeken af aan het servet, in een poging om me als koopman te gedragen. Heel even keek Kallista me aan. Wist zij iets over mijn tweelingbroer? Ik schuifelde ongedurig heen en weer op mijn stoel. Ik sloeg mijn ogen neer toen ik opeens besefte dat ik Kallista zat aan te staren. Een slaaf bracht moeder en mij naar de logeervertrekken. Toen we over de binnenplaats liepen, voelde ik de zonnestralen op mijn huid. Ik was doodop van de reis en vooral van de spanning. Ik verlangde naar rust. Mijn aandacht werd getrokken door een rij beelden die uit klei waren gemaakt. Heel de binnenplaats stond vol beelden: goden, een houthakker, een koopman. Eén beeld viel bijzon-

der op: een mooie, jonge man die over een zieke stond gebogen. Zijn smalle handen rusten op het hoofd van de zieke.
Moeder was al gaan slapen. Ik voelde dat iemand naar me
keek en daarna hoorde ik een zachte stem: 'Wat vind je ervan?' Achter me stond Kallista. Ik knikte kort en dacht aan
mijn broer.
'Kan ik je ergens anders spreken?' fluisterde ik. Maar ze was
al verdwenen.

De schuilplaats

De schemering viel over het bergachtige landschap. In het donker van de nacht klopte mijn hart rustiger. Het was te gevaarlijk om hier lang te blijven. We moesten verder. Na onze zware tocht van Sparta naar het huis van Isidoor hadden we een dag gerust. De soldaten zouden nu al massaal naar mij op zoek zijn. Tenzij ze dachten dat ik verdronken was. Alleen Leander had ik een teken van leven achtergelaten. Ik wilde mijn koopmanshoed opzetten om mijn lange haren te verbergen.

'Melas, wacht even.' Kallista stond weer achter me. 'Je haar moet korter.' Ze haalde een mes, nam een lok in haar handen en sneed die met een forse haal af.

'Niet doen!' zei ik en ik hield haar hand tegen. 'Ik ben een solda...' De woorden stolden in mijn mond. Ze keek me geschrokken aan en hield een vinger tegen haar lippen.

'Nou goed, doe dan maar,' zei ik nors. Ik was fier op mijn lange haar. Ik slikte een paar keer toen de ene lok na de andere op de grond viel.

'Het spijt me,' fluisterde Kallista. Ze stond nu heel dicht tegen me aan, haar mond raakte bijna mijn oor. 'Wil je mijn groeten overbrengen aan Laïdes?' Verbaasd keek ik haar aan. Ze duwde me een scherf in de hand, er stonden tekens op die ik niet herkende.

'Voor hem,' fluisterde ze. Kallista zag mijn verbazing maar ze maakte me met een korte knik duidelijk dat we nu niet konden praten. We werden in de gaten gehouden. Ze ging door met mijn haar korter te knippen. Voortdurend liepen slaven af en aan. Ze waste mijn haar dat nu kort en stekelig was.

'Zo is het wel goed.' Ik duwde haar hand met het mes weg.

'Ik wil het nog even bijwerken.' En ze ging vlijtig door.

'Stilzitten!'

'Ja, nee.' Ik wist niet dat ze zo vervelend kon zijn. In mijn dromen was ze een stuk meegaander.

'In welke taal heb je op de scherf geschreven?'

'Gewoon,' zei ze. 'In het Grieks.' Dat verbaasde me, want ik had lang niet alle tekens herkend. Kallista had leren schrijven en boetseren in de tijd dat ik in de kazerne zat. Ik had leren hardlopen en pijn verdragen. Ik begon me zorgen te maken. Zou ik buiten Sparta ook een buitenstaander zijn? Wat kon ik eigenlijk? Ik was alleen maar opgeleid tot soldaat.

'Zit stil!'

'Genoeg.' Ik voelde even aan mijn haar. Het was niet overal gelijk geknipt, maar ik had er schoon genoeg van.

Moeder beladdde de ezel met eten en drinken en deed hem weer de lederen pantoffeltjes aan.

'Androcles!' Ik was verbaasd en blij hem weer te zien.

'Kan ik u van dienst zijn?' antwoordde hij onderdanig zoals

slaven dat doen, maar hij knipoogde even toen niemand keek.

'Ga je met ons mee?' vroeg ik. Maar dat wilde hij niet. Om de een of andere reden wilde hij Sparta niet verlaten.

De weg leek lang. Met elke stap nam ik weer een stukje meer afscheid van mijn land. Het land waar ik geen voet meer kon zetten zonder het gevaar ontdekt en gedood te worden. Mijn prachtige land met hoge bergketens en diepe dalen met koele riviertjes. Op de hoge toppen met eeuwige sneeuw woonden de goden en ik bad dat ze ons ook op de rest van onze tocht zouden bijstaan.

'Volg het pad tot aan de rots die de weg lijkt te versperren,' had Isidoor gezegd. In de verte leek die rots op de kop van een stier die me elk moment op zijn horens kon nemen en de lucht in zwieren.

'Daar zal je Helena ontmoeten,' had hij ook gezegd. 'Ze zit in het verzet en zal je het geheime pad naar het schip wijzen.'

'Welk verzet?' Ik had nog nooit iets over het verzet gehoord. Maar Isidoor was niet ingegaan op mijn vraag en wees in de richting van de weg. Ik moest vertrekken. Zo snel mogelijk.

Een jonge vrouw wachtte ons op in de rotsholte. Ze gaf ons met een hoofdknikje te kennen dat we haar moesten volgen. Ze droeg een wijde, groene mantel maar ik kon zien dat ze slank was. Het leek alsof ze mijn blik voelde. Ze draaide zich plotseling om en keek me vijandig aan.

'Doorlopen,' zei ze koel. 'Altijd rechtdoor!' Zelf liep ze nu achter moeder en mij aan. Af en toe keek ik om. Haar gezicht leek van marmer in het licht van de toorts. Nadat we een poosje hadden gelopen, zagen we dat de gang uitkwam op een soort binnenplaats.

'Hier moeten jullie wachten,' zei de vrouw die ongetwijfeld Helena was en ze gaf moeder en mij een deken.

'Waarom doe je dit voor ons?' vroeg ik. 'Het kan je het leven kosten. Mensen helpen ontsnappen is verboden.' Ze drukte me een rol papyrus in de handen.

Op het blad voelde ik kleine klodders kaarsvet, harde stipjes. In het licht van de toorts kon ik getekende bergketens en rivieren zien.

'Is dat het geheime pad dat we moeten volgen?' Moeder volgde met haar vinger de stippen op de papyrusrol.

'Jullie moeten voorlopig hier blijven,' zei de vrouw schijnbaar rustig. 'Spartaanse soldaten doorkruisen het kustgebied waar jullie schip ligt.' Even trilden mijn handen maar ik vermande me snel en vroeg: 'En wat als de soldaten hier binnenvallen?'

'Deze plek kennen ze niet,' antwoordde Helena kalm. Ze wees naar een donker gat. 'Langs daar kunnen jullie weg als er gevaar dreigt. Kallista traint haar paarden in de omgeving. Ze stuurt ons een boodschap als jullie hier weg moeten.'

'Zit zij ook in het verzet?'

'Je stelt lastige vragen.'

Mijn moeder glimlachte en zei: 'Hij was gisteren nog soldaat. Het leven buiten de kazerne is hem vreemd.' Die opmerking maakte me onzeker. En het wachten in de grot zenuwachtig. 'Melas, probeer even stil te zitten.' Moeder sprak me zacht maar streng toe. De toorts doofde, het was stikdonker. Ik rommelde wat aan de toorts en wilde richting uitgang lopen. 'Blijf hier!' Helena's stem klonk vlak. Ik was verbaasd dat ze me gehoord had, ik liep op de toppen van mijn tenen. Tegen mijn zin ging ik weer zitten. Mijn ogen wenden een beetje aan het duister. Vaag zag ik het silhouet van Helena. Waarom koos een jong meisje voor zo'n gevaarlijk werk?

'Waar is je familie?' vroeg ik aarzelend. Misschien was ook dit een verkeerde vraag. Het bleef een hele tijd stil.

'Ik heb geen familie meer,' zei ze ten slotte, toonloos. 'Mijn vader is vermoord door Spartaanse soldaten.' Ik liet mijn hoofd zakken. Ik was blij dat Kallista mijn Spartaanse lokken had afgesneden.

Helena

'Ik stam af van de Agaeërs, het volk dat op de plek woonde waar later de Spartanen binnenvielen en hun stad Sparta stichtten,' zei Helena. 'Mijn grootvader was koning. Voor de ogen van zijn volk maakten de Spartanen van hem een slaaf. Elke dag van zonsopgang tot zonsondergang moest hij een rotsachtige lap grond omspitten. Zijn vrouw werd huismeid bij een rijke familie. En de kinderen moesten hout sprokkelen of water halen. Ze mochten niet naar school.' Helena's stem werd hees. 'Mijn vader vluchtte naar de bergen. Hij hakte er met zijn houweel een woning in de rotsen, vlak naast de rivier. Al snel vertelden de slaven dit nieuws aan elkaar door. Velen waagden hun kans en vluchtten. Maar de Spartaanse bewakers grepen in. Elke slaaf die ze betrapten op zijn vlucht, martelden ze. Velen stierven. De Spartanen vreesden een opstand. Ze wilden de alleenheersers blijven en ze hadden hun slaven nodig. De wet was heilig, ze zorgden ervoor, desnoods met geweld, dat iedereen hun regels naleefde. Toch kon mijn moeder vluchten. Ze hield zich dagen schuil, leed honger en kou maar vond de plaats waar mijn vader woonde. Al snel ontstond er een kleine gemeenschap van bergbewoners. Daar werd ik geboren. Ik leerde met pijl en boog voedsel verzame-

40

len. Ik was gelukkig tot de Spartanen ons kamp ontdekten. Mijn vader bracht moeder en mij naar een veilige plaats. Hij redde vele stamleden. Voor hem was het te laat, hij werd omsingeld door Spartanen, ze doodden hem met hun speren. Zijn kreten galmden over de bergen. Toen heb ik gezworen zijn werk verder te zetten: mensen uit Sparta helpen vluchten. In mijn dromen hoor ik zijn hulpgeroep nog steeds.' Helena zweeg en keek me aan.

'Ik ben geen slaaf en ik stam ook niet af van jouw volk,' zei ik.

'Waarom help je me dan vluchten?'

'Ben je een zuivere Spartaan?' vroeg ze. Ze keek me nadenkend aan.

'Je helpt je vijand ontsnappen,' probeerde ik nog eens. 'Ik ben opgeleid tot Spartaans soldaat.'

'Sparta zal je vlucht niet goedkeuren. Je bent een banneling net als ik,' zei ze koel.

'Mijn vader is raadslid van de Spartaanse koning,' antwoordde ik.

'Maar je moeder is Atheense,' zei Helena. 'Ook jij hebt die lichte ogen.'

'Athene?' vroeg ik verbaasd en ik keek vertwijfeld naar mijn moeder. 'Dat is onze vijand.'

'Nu wel,' antwoordde moeder. 'Maar vroeger waren Spartanen en Atheners vrienden.' Dat kon ik nauwelijks geloven. In de kazerne hoorde ik dat Atheners lui waren en te laf om te vechten.

41

Een pestkop riep eens: 'Jij bent net een Athener, altijd maar nadenken over het leven en verwarring veroorzaken.' Hij had dus nog gelijk ook. Wisten Trifonas en Alexius iets van de afkomst van mijn moeder? Sloten ze me daarom buiten?

Mijn ledematen voelden stram aan. Ik voelde mijn ruggengraat ijskoud worden. Vlak daarop kreeg ik het broeierig heet, alsof een bol van woede zich door mijn lichaam verspreidde. Mijn ideeën over Atheners waren niet zo fraai, ik vond ze egoïstisch en arrogant.

'Ik ben geen Athener,' gromde ik.

Moeder begon onhandig in haar mand te rommelen. 'Ik heb lindeblaadjes voor je.'

'Nee,' siste ik. 'Laat me met rust.'

'Wat is er met Laïdes gebeurd?' vroeg ik woedend. Maar Helena trok aan mijn mouw en zei dat ik stiller moest spreken.

'Je hebt Laïdes geholpen en mij aan mijn lot overgelaten.' Zweetdruppels liepen langs mijn slapen en ik was misselijk. 'Besef je niet dat de Spartaanse soldaten me haatten?'

'Ik hield veel van je vader,' zei moeder. 'Hij kon toen niet weten dat de Spartanen de aartsvijanden zouden worden van de Atheners.'

Ik schudde mijn hoofd. Al die jaren van haat en afwijzing... Had ik het makkelijker gehad als ik had geweten waarom men mij haatte? Moeder stamelde een gebed om de hulp van Zeus af te smeken.

'Blijf alsjeblieft kalm,' zei Helena. Per ongeluk raakte ik even haar hand aan. Die was ijskoud. Ik deed mijn mantel uit en legde die over haar schouders. Nu ik haar verhaal had gehoord, schaamde ik me ervoor dat ik me had beklaagd over mijn lot. Mijn woede was weer een beetje tot bedaren gekomen.

'Slapen jullie maar,' zei ik. 'Ik hou de wacht.'

'Ik slaap niet als ik werk,' antwoordde Helena.

'Maar je kan toch geen nachten achter elkaar zonder slaap?'

'Sinds mijn vader dood is, kan ik veel. Ik kan trouwens overdag rusten.' Haar stem had weer die harde klank. Misschien had ik haar bang gemaakt. Haar magere, pezige gestalte ontroerde me. Voorzichtig legde ik mijn hand op haar arm. Maar ze verstijfde en deinsde terug. Ze trok de mantel wat strakker om zich heen.

'Ik kan nuttige informatie geven over het Spartaanse leger, over de wachtrondes, de ligging van de kazernes, de bergwegen die de soldaten bewaken, de aanvalstactiek van het leger,' zei ik, in de hoop dat ze weer met me zou praten. Ze knikte. Ik vertelde haar dat ik altijd bevriend was geweest met Androcles die ook een slaaf was, dat ik vond dat alle mensen gelijkwaardig waren. Eigenlijk was ik daar niet zeker van, maar ik wilde een brug slaan tussen haar en mezelf.

'Wil je nog meer weten?'

Ze knikte. Fluisterend vertelde ik haar over het Spartaanse leger. Helena luisterde roerloos naar alles wat ik vertelde. Als een spons zoog ze elk woord in zich op.

Ik keek over moeders schouder mee naar de ontsnappingsroute die op de papyrusrol stond. Dat stuk papier had Helena ons gegeven. Het verzet gaf elke vluchteling een vluchtroute mee, het kon gebeuren dat leden van het verzet niet meereisden tot aan de eindbestemming. Een belangrijke taak van het verzet was het gebergte rond Sparta in kaart brengen, zodat vluchtelingen zelf de weg konden vinden.

'Verbrand dit vel als je het niet meer nodig hebt,' zei Helena streng.

'Weet ik,' antwoordde ik. 'Isidoor vertelde me hetzelfde.'

'Het is belangrijk.'

'Waarom?'

'Na jullie gebruiken ook anderen dezelfde geheime vluchtwegen. Als de Spartanen onze vluchtwegen kennen, moeten wij nieuwe zoeken.'

'Klopt,' zei ik rustig. 'Maar je weet dat Spartanen niet geneigd zijn om te lezen. In Sparta heb ik geen kaart leren lezen.'

'Dat valt mee, je zou nog vreemd opkijken,' zei Helena. Ik dacht daar anders over, maar ik wilde haar liever niet tegenspreken. Na een vluchtige blik op het plan leek het alsof Helena de weg in haar geheugen had geprent. De sterren en de maan verbleekten, we hadden geen tijd om te treuzelen.

'Kom,' zei Helena en ze leidde ons langs een pad dat werd afgezoomd door struikgewas. Niets ontging aan haar donkere ogen. Ze wees op losliggende stenen en verraderlijke kuilen. Het pad liep steil omlaag. Ik droeg moeder soms op mijn rug.

Na een tijdje zag ik de zee die er in de ochtendnevel grijs-blauw uitzag. In een baai lag een schip. Elke stap dichter bij het schip was er een verder weg van Helena...

'Ga mee,' zei ik haar. 'Het is hier veel te gevaarlijk.'

Helena glimlachte. 'Ik moet de taak van mijn vader afmaken.' Mijn moeder zegende haar, kuste haar hand en zei dat de go-den haar zouden belonen voor zoveel goedheid.

'Drink dit als je moe bent,' zei moeder en ze drukte Helena een kruikje in de handen. 'Een drankje met veel ijzer.' De woorden bleven in mijn keel steken. Ik gaf Helena een hand, draaide me om en liep naar het schip. Ze was al verdwenen nog voor we de touwen hadden losgemaakt. Ik rilde. Noch de knoestige olijfbomen noch de rotsen lieten vermoeden dat ze een vrouw als Helena herbergden, een teer wezen tussen de wilde dieren en het grillige gebergte.

Athene

De schipper loodste zijn schip tussen de klippen door naar de volle zee. Daar liet hij de zeilen hijsen en we voeren richting Athene, mijn moeders geboortestad. Al snel gingen de roodbruine zeilen bol staan in de wind en maakten we snelheid. Terwijl ik naar het diepe water keek, dacht ik aan Helena. Ik schrok toen ik de stuurlui hoorde roepen. In de verte naderde een oorlogsschip. Sprakeloos bleef ik kijken naar de ontelbare roeispanen die het reusachtige schip aan een duizelingwekkende snelheid voortdreven. De witte zeilen reikten hoger dan de onze. Ze kwamen recht op ons af.

'Haal het zeil neer!' riep de schipper. Eén van de matrozen klom in de mast maar halfweg bleef zijn voet haken in het touw.

De schipper die tot dan toe rustig leek, riep: 'Opschieten!' De zweetdruppels parelden op zijn voorhoofd en zijn blik gleed onrustig van de een naar de ander.

'Haal het zeil neer!' bulderde hij. 'Ik kan het roer niet loslaten.' Het oorlogsschip was op een honderdtal armlengtes genaderd, als we niet uit zijn vaarwater gingen, zou het ons rammen. Snel greep ik een mes en ik klom de mast in. Ik sneed het touw door dat rond de voet van de matroos gedraaid zat. Even later haalde hij de zeilen neer. Onze snelheid nam af. Een andere matroos duwde me een roeispaan in de handen.

'Stuurboord roeien!' riep hij. Ik ging naar de andere kant van het schip, liet de roeispaan zakken in het water en roeide met grote slagen, zonder stoppen. Ook moeder hielp. Ik durfde niet te kijken naar het oorlogsschip dat nu vlakbij moest zijn. Bij elke slag keek ik diep in het zeewater en bad tot Poseidon. 'God van de zee,' bad ik hardop. 'Laat ons niet verdrinken.' Toen kraakte het schip, ik kreeg een ontzettende dreun en sloeg overboord. Het zeewater sloot zich boven mijn hoofd. Ik trapte met mijn voeten en hapte naar adem. Eindelijk kwam ik weer boven, mijn longen deden pijn, ik was buiten adem en hoestte zeewater op.

Het oorlogsschip gleed rakelings langs. Eén mast van ons schip was afgebroken en dreef naast mij in het water.

'Pak aan!' riep een matroos en hij gooide me een touw toe. Ik zwom naar het touw en greep het beet. Moeder stond aan boord, de handen gevouwen. De schipper ademde diep in en wiste het zweet van zijn voorhoofd. Met het touw hesen ze me weer aan boord. De matrozen gingen er even bij zitten om van de schrik te bekomen. Het schip raakte moeizaam vooruit zonder groot zeil.

Na een paar dagen zagen we in de verte de haven van Athene liggen. Op de kade spraken we een voerman aan.

'Mijnheer!' riep ik de man toe. 'Kunt u ons naar het markt-plein brengen?' Hij wendde zijn paard en kwam met de mooie, houten kar naar ons toe gereden. Zijn kleed was kleurrijk en hij keek me aandachtig aan. Zijn ogen waren op-vallend licht.

'Weet u zeker dat u naar Athene wilt?' Ik knikte.

'Dan zal je een andere voerman moeten zoeken, mij krijg je daar niet heen,' zei de man. 'De pest is uitgebroken in de stad.' Moeder verstijfde. Ze wist hoe ernstig dit was. Instinctief hield ze haar tuniek voor de mond. Ze was bang voor die ziekte waardoor je overal etterende builen op je lichaam kreeg. Meestal stierf je aan de pest. Het was haar gelukt om Isidoor van de pest te genezen maar het had haar heel wat moeite gekost. Het was beter die ziekte te vermijden.

'We hoeven niet naar de stad,' zei mijn moeder kordaat. 'We gaan naar het platteland, ik zal u de weg wijzen.'

'Stapt u maar in.' Het viel me op dat de tuniek van onze voer-man van een fijne stof gemaakt was, afgezoomd met zilveren stiksels. De vrouwen in de straten droegen om hun polsen armbanden die glinsterden in de zon. In hun haren staken haarspelden met schitterende stenen. Al snel verlieten we de haven en we bereikten niet lang daarna het platteland waar hier en daar een boerderij te zien was. De boeren waren op het land, het was oogsttijd. De gewassen zagen er uitge-droogd uit. De koeien en schapen graasden in dorre weiden. De mensen hadden een lichtere huidskleur en waren lang niet zo gespierd als ik. Mijn moeder aarzelde geen enkele keer over de weg die we moesten nemen.

'Zijn jullie kooplieden uit het zuiden?' vroeg de voerman en hij keek nieuwsgierig naar onze kleren.

'Ja, we zijn op weg naar mijn zus, we hebben geneesmiddelen voor haar,' antwoordde mijn moeder. 'Ze helpt vrouwen bij de bevalling. Haar naam is Arthyssa.'

'Arthyssa weet ik wonen,' zei de man blij. 'Ze heeft mijn zuster gered toen ze van een tweeling moest bevallen. Arthyssa heeft de zegen van de goden, dat weet iedereen. Als zij bij de bevalling aanwezig is, gaat er niets mis. Men verwacht dat haar zoon een groot arts zal worden. Hij volgt les bij de beroemde Hippocrates.'

Arthyssa kwam vroeger regelmatig bij ons logeren. Maar ik wist niet dat ze een zoon had. Voor zover ik wist, was ze niet getrouwd.

'Hoe oud is haar zoon?'

'Een jaar of dertien, schat ik,' zei de voerman nadenkend. Ik kon aan mijn moeders gezicht zien dat ze liever had dat ik dit gesprek niet voortzette, maar daar trok ik me niets van aan.

'Hoe heet hij?'

'Ze noemen hem Laïdes.'

Weerzien

'Hier wonen Arthyssa en Laïdes,' zei de man. Moeder gaf de man een paar muntstukken. We liepen door een prachtige, oude olijfboomgaard. De grijsgroene blaadjes aan de takken en de talloze gele bloemetjes onder de bomen maakten me rustig. Hier en daar stonden lege, rieten manden en ladders tegen de bomen. Iedereen was druk bezig met oogsten. De zon brandde. Waarschijnlijk hield iedereen nu zijn middagrust. Naast de boomgaard lagen moestuinen waar uien, sla, bonen en rozen groeiden. Keurig in rijtjes naast elkaar. Een lemen huis stond in de zon, de luiken gesloten. Alles straalde rust uit.

'Hier woont je broer,' zei moeder ontroerd. 'Het is het huis waar je grootouders woonden. Ik woonde hier tot je vader kwam.' Op de binnenplaats hingen kleurige hangmatten en het rook er fris, naar citroen. In de deuropening stond een jonge man. Hij was klein. Zijn haar was kort en stekelig, zijn tuniek hing los om zijn schouders, hij was erg mager.

'Laïdes?' vroeg ik onzeker. Mijn broer keek me verbaasd aan. Op zijn gezicht verscheen een glimlach. We omhelsden elkaar.

'Je ziet er gezond uit,' zei mijn broer.

50

Mijn broer was verstandig. Hij stelde me met een paar woorden op mijn gemak.

'Hoe ben je uit Sparta ontsnapt?' vroeg ik hem. Hij nam me mee naar de tuin en we gingen in de schaduw van een olijfboom zitten. 'Ik moet vanmiddag weer naar de stad om zieken te verplegen. Daarna vertel ik je alles.'

'Als voorzorg tegen de pest zou het goed zijn als je dit op je huid smeerde.' Hij haalde een potje met zalf uit zijn tas en wilde het me aanreiken.

'Nee, dank je.' zei ik. 'Daar doe ik niet aan mee.'

Maar moeder nam het dankbaar aan en smeerde zich onmiddellijk van kop tot teen in met rozenolie. Ik hield niet van dat kleverige spul.

'De pest is een ernstige ziekte,' zei Laïdes. 'Maar weinig mensen overleven haar.'

'En jij?' vroeg ik. 'Wat doe jij ertegen?'

'Ik smeer me in,' zei hij. 'En ik houd me aan strenge voorschriften. De rozen beschermen je tegen de ziekte, maar je moet je elke dag insmeren.'

'Als jij het zegt, zal het wel helpen,' antwoordde ik. Het stoorde me dat mijn broer het allemaal zo goed wist.

'Ben je ondertussen al getrouwd?' vroeg ik nonchalant om van onderwerp te veranderen. Mijn broer bloosde, net zoals vroeger. Mijn humeur werd er meteen een stuk beter op. Ik dacht ineens aan wat Kallista me had gegeven en doorzocht zenuwachtig mijn beurs.

'Hier,' zei ik en ik gaf hem de scherf waar een boodschap op stond. 'Je hebt de groeten van Kallista.' Nu werden de wangen van mijn broer vuurrood.

'Hoe gaat het met haar?' vroeg hij. Het deed hem zichtbaar genoegen toen hij hoorde dat ze beelden uit klei maakte. Maar lang konden we niet met elkaar praten, want hij moest naar de stad.

'Het spijt me Melas, ik kom zo snel mogelijk terug en dan praten we echt bij,' zei hij. Ik knikte. Hij gaf me een broederlijk schouderklopje.

Rond het vuur

Het schemerde al toen Laïdes doodmoe terugkwam van Athene. Hij waste zich grondig en smeerde zich in met rozenzalf. Een huisbediende roosterde kastanjes die we aten terwijl we rond het vuur zaten.

'Je was opeens uit moeders huis verdwenen. De Spartaanse soldaten hebben overal naar je gezocht.'

Mijn broer keek naar de vlammen. Het bleef stil.

'Jij was in alles beter dan ik,' zei mijn broer. 'Hardlopen, verspringen.'

Ik knikte en keek naar zijn slanke vingers.

'Op den duur ging ik liever met moeder kruiden plukken. Ik leerde planten kennen en zij leerde me de remedies tegen allerlei ziektes. Je herinnert je misschien nog dat Arthyssa vaak langskwam, om mama te helpen bij bevallingen. Dat was niet toevallig, mama had een plan. Ze liet me vaak lang alleen met Arthyssa. Ik kreeg een hechte band met haar. De dagen dat vader thuis was, waren ellendig. Op een nacht hoorde ik onze ouders ruzie maken. Vader zei dat moeder me verwende en belette dat ik een goede Spartaanse soldaat zou worden. Moeder vertelde hem over mijn talent voor geneeskunde, maar daar wilde vader niets van weten. "We hadden hem bij

53

zijn geboorte van de rotsen moeten gooien. Hij is waardeloos, een schande voor de Spartaanse samenleving. Waarschijnlijk overleeft hij de trainingskampen niet eens, maar hij moet en zal erheen!" brulde vader. Moeder huilde en ik kroop diep onder mijn schapenvacht. Enkele dagen later beladde moeder ons ezeltje en zei dat we Isidoor gingen bezoeken. Hij had een dienstbode gezonden en gevraagd of moeder bij hem wilde langskomen. Kallista was daar ook. Ze liet me prachtige schelpen zien die haar vader voor haar had meegebracht.'

'Kallista was gek op jou,' zei ik. 'Ze wilde dat je haar leerde boetseren. Weet je dat nog?'

Laïdes glimlachte.

'Mama gaf me medicijnen mee voor Kallista's vader. Ik speelde bijna de hele dag met Kallista bij de rivier, waar we een kamp hadden opgeslagen. Daarna vertrok ze met de medicijnen naar huis.'

'Wat gebeurde er daarna?' vroeg ik ongeduldig terwijl ik het vuur aanwakkerde.

'Heel vaag herinner ik me dat moeder me 's nachts wakker maakte en me iets te drinken gaf. Ik voelde hoe mijn ledematen slap werden en ik viel in een droomloze slaap. Toen ik ontwaakte, lag ik in Arthyssa's armen. Ze streelde mijn haar en zei dat ik moest eten. Toen merkte ik dat ik in Isidoors huis was. Kallista bracht een schaal met druiven en een bord met vis. Omdat ik nog wat duizelig was, hielp Arthyssa me.

Ze zei dat we een lange reis zouden maken. Ik wilde naar huis maar door het drankje was ik te suf om weg te lopen.

"Na het eten mag je even met Kallista spelen," zei Arthyssa. We boetseerden met de klei die ze had meegebracht van de rivier. Daarna gaf Arthyssa me weer een lepel van dat slaapverwekkende drankje,' vervolgde Laïdes.

'Toen ik weer wakker werd, waren we in Arthyssa's huis in Athene. Ze vertelde me dat ik vanaf nu elke dag les zou krijgen. Ik miste jou en moeder. Ik vroeg haar vaak om over jou en mama te vertellen. Dat deed ze niet graag. Ik denk dat ze bang was dat ik heimwee zou krijgen en weg zou lopen, terug naar jullie. Ze zei dat er voor mij geen leven was in Sparta. Mijn leraar was streng. Stap voor stap leerde ik het alfabet en daarna spellen en lezen. Arthyssa hielp me met mijn huistaken. In mijn vrije tijd plukte ik wilde planten, nam ze mee naar huis en leerde van elke plant de naam kennen. Als ik met planten bezig was, was het alsof mama dichtbij was en al snel wist ik dat ik zieke mensen wilde genezen, net zoals zij. Dankzij Arthyssa kreeg ik les van Hippocrates. Je kan je geen betere leraar wensen.'

Ik gooide nog een blok hout op het vuur. Het gezicht van mijn broer stond gespannen. Boven ons fonkelden de sterren in een heldere hemel. Het was al laat. Maar ik had geen zin om te slapen. We moesten elkaar zoveel vertellen. Het moeilijkste moest nog komen.

'Arthyssa heeft me gezegd dat ik jullie niet mocht gaan zoeken,' zei mijn broer. 'Er ging geen dag voorbij dat ik niet aan je dacht. Ik heb alle goden gevraagd je bij te staan. Ik wist dat zelfs een sterke jongen als jij het niet makkelijk zou hebben in de kazerne.' Laïdes kuchte. Hij had een krop in zijn keel. 'Neem nog een slok,' zei ik zacht en ik gaf hem de beker wijn. 'Ik moest mijn hand op de heilige steen leggen en beloven dat ik jullie niet zou opzoeken. Arthyssa vertelde dat mijn moeder me had afgestaan om me te redden. Ik vond het vreselijk. Ik dacht dat ze mij niet meer wilde. Ik dacht dat ze meer van jou hield omdat jij het perfecte Spartaanse kind was.' Hij zweeg. Even raakte ik zijn hand aan.

'Wat heeft Arthyssa nog meer verteld?'

'Moeder is op deze plaats opgegroeid,' ging mijn broer verder. 'Mama en Arthyssa leefden hier met hun ouders op een boerderij. Mama was erg mooi en uit de hele streek kwamen mannen om haar hand vragen. Maar haar vader wilde dat zijn kinderen bij hem bleven om op de boerderij te helpen. Mama maakte meestal het eten klaar, samen met haar moeder. Ze wist van een handvol graan en wat olijven een ware lekkernij te maken. Het waren moeilijke tijden. Verjaagde volkeren en soldaten trokken door het land. Velen overnachtten in het lemen bijhuis, een opslagplaats voor de gewassen. Op een avond stonden er drie mannen voor de deur. Te paard en met een schild. Arthyssa vertelde me dat ze zich de metalen plaatjes die over het paard hingen, nog goed herinnerde. Een deken van metalen schelpen, daar leek het op. Later begreep ze dat het een harnas voor een paard was. En zij en mama waren diep onder de indruk van de man met het leeuwenschild.

'Ga door,' zei ik ongeduldig terwijl ik ervoor zorgde dat het houtvuur niet doofde. Ik begreep niet waarom mijn broer zo diep inging op details. Ik werd er onrustig van, ik had het gevoel dat hij op het punt stond me iets verschrikkelijks te vertellen.

'Die drie jonge mannen waren soldaten. Ze hadden een speer en droegen een helm. Grootvader zag dat zijn dochters hun ogen niet van deze jonge mannen konden afhouden en stuurde hen naar bed. 's Nachts merkte Arthyssa dat mama niet meer naast haar lag. Ze ging naar haar op zoek. Ze vond mama in het bijhuis in de armen van de jongen die het schild met het leeuwenteken droeg. Tante trok aan mama's haren, schreeuwde dat ze terug moest komen. Maar mama wilde de vreemde soldaat volgen, waar hij ook naartoe ging. Arthyssa huilde toen ze afscheid nam van haar zus. De jongen met het leeuwenschild was Hector.' Laïdes zag er doodmoe uit. Hij had donkere schaduwen onder zijn ogen, maar ik kon het niet over mijn hart krijgen om hem welterusten te wensen. Ik wou alles weten.

'Veel later,' ging mijn broer verder, 'toen ze allang in Sparta woonde en wij al geboren waren, liet moeder Androcles, onze huisbediende, naar Arthyssa op zoek gaan. Tante woonde toen in Athene en hielp daar vrouwen bevallen. Androcles haalde haar over om mee te gaan naar mama in Sparta. En omdat tante geen Spartaanse was, moest mama een smoes bedenken om haar zus over de grens te krijgen. Moeder vertelde dat Arthyssa een belangrijke buitenlandse genezeres was. Ze bezocht ons in die tijd regelmatig en werkte samen met mama. Weet je dat nog?' vroeg Laïdes me. Natuurlijk kon ik me die heerlijke tijd dat wij bij moeder woonden nog herinneren; het was de leukste tijd van mijn leven. Ik zou ervoor zorgen dat mijn eigen kinderen veel langer bij hun moeder konden blijven.

'Mama vertelde haar zus dat ze een van de tweelingbroers moest redden en dat ze daarbij hulp nodig had.'

'Wist vader daarvan?' vroeg ik.

'Natuurlijk niet,' antwoordde Laïdes. 'Je kent zijn opvattingen toch wel. Als het aan hem had gelegen, had ik dezelfde militaire opvoeding gekregen als jij, ook al had ik dat niet overleefd.' Hij klonk opeens opgewonden. 'Toch heeft vader één keer de wet overtreden.'

Ik keek mijn broer ongelovig aan. Ik kon zijn gezicht niet meer zo goed onderscheiden; het vuur flakkerde nog eenmaal op, daarna smeulde het alleen nog maar.

'Het was bij mijn geboorte,' zei mijn broer. 'Ik was een kleine en zwakke baby. Vader was ervan overtuigd dat de Spartaanse raad zou oordelen dat ik van de rotsen geworpen moest worden. Als ik bleef leven, zou ik alleen maar een last voor mezelf en de maatschappij zijn.' Mijn broer staarde naar het zacht smeulende vuur. Het moet vreselijk zijn als mensen je alleen als een last zien.

'Heeft vader de Spartaanse raad omgekocht?' vroeg ik ongelovig.

'Nee,' zei Laïdes. 'Onze ouders bedachten een list. Ze vertelden niet dat ze een tweeling hadden gekregen. Ze lieten jou keuren door de raad. De volgende dag vertelde papa opgewekt dat er een tweede kind was geboren en hij liet jou een tweede keer keuren. De Spartaanse raad feliciteerde moeder met de twee stevige kinderen die ze op de wereld had gezet. "We zitten in de val," zei mama toen. "Dit kind kan de Spartaanse opvoeding niet aan."

"Dat kan wel," zei Hector. "Je hebt zeven jaar de tijd om dit kind gezond te maken. Met de juiste voeding zal hij sterk zijn en een goede Spartaanse soldaat worden." Vanaf toen droeg moeder haar zorgen alleen. Ze vertelde niet aan vader dat ik een zwak kind bleef, dat ik niet kon hardlopen en hoogspringen zoals de anderen. Moeder ontdekte dat ik net als zijzelf geïnteresseerd was in planten en kruiden. Bang zag ze mijn zevende verjaardag naderen, ze wist dat ik geen militair kon worden. Ze moest me uit Sparta laten verdwijnen, maar ze wist dat Hector dit niet zou goedkeuren. Tante zegt dat mama lang in tweestrijd was. Ze hield van vader en begreep zijn idealen. Sparta was een stadstaat met veel aanzien en ze had waardering voor de goede organisatie van de staat. De mensen waren gelukkig. Maar zij had, jammer genoeg, een kind dat niet in dat systeem paste,' zei Laïdes. 'Vaak had ik nare dromen over wat moeder en jou kon overkomen. Maar ik had op de heilige steen gezworen niet terug te keren naar Sparta. Ik besefte dat moeder zich voor mij had opgeofferd. Daarom stortte ik me op mijn werk en mijn studie.' Het vuur was bijna uit. Laïdes en ik vielen naast elkaar in slaap, zoals vroeger.

Wonen in Athene

In de olijfboomgaard hingen hangmatten. Ik rustte uit terwijl een huisbediende heerlijke visgerechten opdiende. Ik vond het nog steeds een wonder dat ik in alle rust van mijn eten kon genieten. Laïdes was zelden thuis. Als hij er was, maakte hij een bezorgde indruk. Hij at weinig en wees alle luxe af. Ik niet. Ik vond het heerlijk om verwend te worden. Ik nam elke dag een lavendelbad, klaargemaakt door huisbedienden.

'Het gaat niet goed met Athene,' zei Laïdes op een avond. 'Steeds meer mensen zoeken bescherming binnen de muren van de stad. De geruchten gaan dat zwaarbewapende Spartaanse troepen in de buurt rondzwerven. Dit familiegoed zal geplunderd worden, daar ben ik van overtuigd. Jullie kunnen hier niet blijven. Ik weet een plek in de stad waar jullie veilig zijn.'

Het dagenlange suffen in de hangmat en het vele eten waren me gaan vervelen. Ik wilde niet op de kosten van mijn broer leven. Ik werd rusteloos en kon mijn draai niet vinden. Ik ging in de leer bij een klompenmaker en hielp oogsten bij een boer. Dat was niets voor mij. Ik probeerde het ambacht van pottenbakker te leren, maar ik kon me niet concentreren. De potten die ik maakte, waren waardeloos.

'Ik wil dit landgoed bewaken,' zei ik zelfverzekerd. 'Dat is tenminste iets waar ik voor opgeleid ben!'

'Dat is geen goed idee, Melas,' zei moeder.

Mijn broer knikte instemmend en zei: 'Tegen een leger kan je in je eentje niets beginnen.'

'In dat geval ga ik terug naar Sparta, me aansluiten bij het verzet,' zei ik. 'Slaven helpen ontsnappen.' Mijn broer en moeder zwegen. Ze keken naar de grond.

'Ik wil nuttig werk doen,' zei ik. 'Ik kan goed hardlopen, zware spullen tillen, ik ben getraind om bij het verzet te gaan.'

'Je bent een soldaat. Je bent getraind om te gehoorzamen. Als je je aansluit bij het verzet, zal je geen rust kennen!' riep mijn moeder uit.

'Alsof ik de afgelopen jaren rust heb gehad.' Het was duidelijk dat ze geen van beiden beseften hoe moeilijk ik het had gehad. Ze waren er gewoon van uit gegaan dat ik me wel zou redden, in alle omstandigheden. Gewoon omdat ik een sterk lichaam had. Alsof dat genoeg was. Alsof dat een garantie was voor geluk en vriendschap.

Mijn moeder keek me aan en zuchtte. Ze begreep dat ik mijn besluit al genomen had.

'Je zal de zegen van de goden nodig hebben om te overleven.' Moeder gaf me de schelp die ze altijd aan een lederen touw om haar hals droeg.

'Raak deze schelp aan als je in levensgevaar bent,' zei ze kort en ze gaf me een zoen op het voorhoofd. Mijn broer en moeder gingen met de mensenstroom mee; iedereen zocht bescherming binnen de stadsmuren van Athene, uit vrees voor de Spartaanse legers. Ik liep de andere kant uit. Ik drukte moeders schelp tegen mijn borst. Laïdes omhelsde me stevig en drukte me een papyruskokertje in de handen.

'Een brief voor Kallista,' fluisterde hij verlegen. 'Mocht je haar toevallig tegenkomen...'

'Je kan op me rekenen,' zei ik en ik knipoogde. Ik had in Sparta niet leren schrijven. Dat zouden ze in Athene raar vinden: een volwassen man die niet kan schrijven. Hopelijk was dat voor het verzet geen probleem.

'Neem dit ook nog mee,' zei moeder en ze nam een kruikje uit haar mand.

Voor één keer nam ik haar spul aan.

'Iets om te kalmeren,' zei ze. 'Dat kan wel eens van pas komen.' Even later verdwenen ze in de menigte. Laïdes keek een laatste keer om en zwaaide.

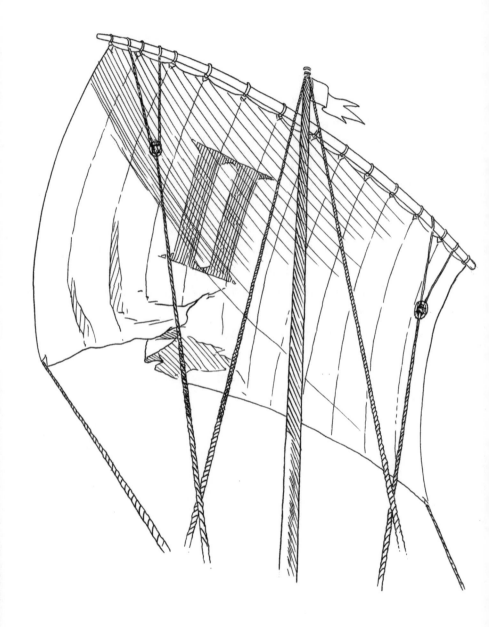

De terugreis

Na twee nachten op zee kregen we stormachtig weer. Ik zag een muur van water op me afkomen. Met beide handen greep ik de reling vast. De roerganger lachte en zei dat het ergste nog moest komen. Ik maakte de schelp en het kokertje stevig vast rond mijn hals. Een aantal matrozen liet de zeilen neer. Anderen hoosden water. Ik nam een leeg vat, schepte water op en kieperde het overboord. De schipper riep bevelen. De juiste koers aanhouden, was nu de minste van zijn zorgen. Hij wilde vooral voorkomen dat de mast brak of dat er een gat werd geslagen in de boeg. Met moeite schepte ik water uit de buik van het schip. Het viel niet mee om bij dit weer overeind te blijven.

Tegen de ochtend ging de storm liggen. De zeilen waren gescheurd en de matrozen repareerden ze. Met de storm was ook de wind gaan liggen. De schipper beval te roeien. De matrozen knoopten de roeispanen los.

'Geef hier,' zei ik tegen een matroos. Ik trok de roeispaan uit zijn handen. Al snel merkten ze dat ik roeide voor twee, ik genoot van hun bewonderende blikken. Een paar uur later stak de wind weer op en werden de zeilen gehesen. Ik zocht een rustig plekje op en viel uitgeput in slaap.

Toen de schipper me heftig door elkaar schudde, had ik ongetwijfeld al een paar uur geslapen. 'Opstaan,' zei hij. 'We naderen de Spartaanse kust.' Ik had de schipper beloofd dat ik op vijf boogscheuten voor de kust van boord zou springen, zo liep hij geen gevaar. De schipper wees waar ik heen moest zwemmen.

Het water was koud maar dat deed me goed. Met elke slag kwam ik dichter bij het vasteland, dichter bij Helena. Naarmate ik de kust naderde, zag ik de rotswanden groeien. Hoe kon ik daar aan land geraken? Door de sterke stroming dreef ik voorbij het strandje. Ik zwom langs een muur van rotsen. Om mij heen dreven stukken hout en vuil. Ongetwijfeld van een schip dat was vergaan tijdens de storm. Ik greep me vast aan een stuk drijfhout en rustte even uit. Daarna speurde ik in de verte. Er zat een bocht in de rotswand. Ik hoopte dat daarachter een strand was of een inham met bomen, en ik begon weer te zwemmen. Achter de rots was niets te zien behalve water en een volgende bocht. Ik zwom door. Uiteindelijk bereikte ik een klein strand. Moe liet ik me neerzakken op het warme zand en ik viel meteen in slaap. Vaag herinnerde ik me dat ik moest opletten, dat ik niet veilig was op Spartaanse bodem. In gedachten sleepte ik me nog tot onder het struikgewas. In werkelijkheid bleef ik midden op het strand liggen, een donkere vlek op wit zand.

Kallista

'Waarom ben je teruggekomen?' Kreunend opende ik mijn ogen en knipperde tegen het felle licht.

'Jouw vader laat dit huis bewaken.' Ik herkende Isidoors stem die harder klonk dan normaal. 'Ik sta op slechte voet met de Spartanen sinds jullie verdwijning. Voorlopig mag ik hier nog wonen. In ruil verlangt de Spartaanse raad dat mijn dochter met Jaron, de zoon van de Spartaanse familie Nikè, huwt.'

Ik schrok en sprong op van het draagbed waarmee bedienden me van het strand hadden weggedragen. Dat Isidoor zijn dochter aan zo'n man moest uithuwelijken! Jaron kende ik van de kazerne. Hij was de lieveling van Trifonas. Hij was een tijger die zonder genade zijn prooi verscheurde.

'Je mag haar niet met hem laten trouwen!' riep ik geschokt.

'Ik heb geen keuze, vriend,' gromde Isidoor.

Na het eten wilde Isidoor me spreken in zijn kamer. Hij vroeg of ik Kallista wilde overhalen de huwelijksregeling te aanvaarden.

'Je moet haar uitleggen hoe belangrijk dit huwelijk is!'

Ik zat in de val. Isidoor had me zo vaak geholpen en nu vroeg hij mij om hulp.

'Ze zal niet van hem houden,' zei ik voorzichtig.

'Natuurlijk niet,' zei Isidoor kortaf. 'Ze zal niet de eerste zijn die een huwelijk zonder liefde kent. En ook niet de laatste. Maar het is een goede overeenkomst. Ze zal goed verzorgd worden.'

'Ze kan weigeren,' zei ik.

'Dat kan ze niet,' zei Isidoor. Hij stond op en liep de kamer uit.

Kallista keerde terug van de rivier waar ze haar kleren had gewassen. Ze slofte lusteloos naar de binnenplaats. Ze droeg een zwarte hoofddoek, ik herkende haar bijna niet. Met een bons zette ze de wasmand neer en ze begon het wasgoed op te hangen. Me verschuilend achter een laken, stopte ik haar het kokertje van Laïdes toe.

'Hoe gaat het met hem? Ik moet volgende maand trouwen met een soldaat.' Haar ogen stonden verdrietig. 'Dit is mijn enige hoop.' Ze drukte Laïdes' kokertje tegen haar hart en liep snel weg.

's Avonds zat ze met gebogen hoofd op mijn slaapbank. 'Je moet me naar Laïdes brengen.'

'Ik vrees dat ik je niet kan helpen.'

'Vind je dat ik moet trouwen om mijn vader en het verzet te steunen?'

Ik schudde mijn hoofd en zei: 'Ik ga niet terug naar Athene.'

'Wat ben je dan van plan?'

'Het verzet helpen.' Mijn stem klonk onvast.

Ze keek me onderzoekend aan. 'Helena,' zei ze en er klonk minachting in haar stem. 'Jij dus ook. Sinds Helena in het verzet zit, is er geen tekort aan mannen.' Ze snoof.

Ik was van mijn stuk gebracht. Was Helena's glimlach echt geweest? Of had ze me gewoon voor het verzet willen winnen? Ze kon onmogelijk weten dat ik terug zou keren. 'Heeft ze een man?'

'Ze wil alleen maar zoveel mogelijk slaven uit Sparta redden. Ze is bikkelhard. Ze is de nieuwe aanvoerster.'

'Waar kan ik haar ontmoeten?' Mijn stem was schor van de spanning.

'Dat weet niemand. Ze kent de Griekse bergen als haar eigen tuin en verblijft niet langer dan twaalf uur op dezelfde plek. Maar ik ken iemand die met haar samenwerkt.'

Tijdens het ontbijt duwde Kallista me een opgerold vel papyrus in de handen. Snel stopte ik het onder mijn tuniek. Tijdens het opdienen van het eten kwam ze naast me staan. Met haar mond vormde ze woorden zonder klank: 'Help mij.' Haar ogen hadden een donkere glans. Ze raakte de lekkere gerechten niet aan.

Op proef

In een grot bestudeerde ik de landkaart die Kallista me had gegeven. De stippen op de kaart liepen over een bergtop. Pas toen ik geen hand voor ogen meer zag, ging ik naar buiten. Ik had de reisroute in mijn hoofd geprent en nam het pad dat naar de hoge bergen leidde. Ik schrok van een vogel die uit het struikgewas opvloog. Na een poosje vond ik het bergriviertje dat op de kaart stond. Ik moest het volgen en dat betekende steil omhoog. Af en toe bleef ik stilstaan en luisterde of ik het geluid van een waterval hoorde. Daar, zo stond op het plan aangegeven, moest ik de opening van een grot zoeken. Voorbij de volgende bocht hoorde ik opeens geklater. Met mijn handen tastte ik de rotswand af tot ik een opening vond. Ik kroop naar binnen en zocht mijn weg in de duisternis.

'Halt!' Twee paar sterke armen grepen me beet en fouilleerden me.

'Heb je wapens?'

'Nee.'

'Wachtwoord?'

'Ken ik niet.' De twee hadden een toorts in de hand en waren gemaskerd.

'Wat kom je hier zoeken?' Ze lieten me niet los. Ik voelde me niet prettig, kreeg klamme handen. Ik ademde diep in en vroeg: 'Kan ik Helena spreken?' Bij het horen van haar naam werd hun greep iets minder stevig.

'Hoe heet je?'

'Melas.' Mijn stem klonk kordaat. De mannen fluisterden even onder elkaar.

'Blijf hier,' zei een van hen. Ik knikte. Meer uitleg gaven ze niet en ze verdwenen geruisloos. De zon was al op toen een van hen terugkeerde en me meenam naar een grot in de omgeving. Een lange gang kwam uit op een grote ruimte met tafels en banken. De grot werd verlicht met toortsen. Een man zat aan een tafel en tekende een plattegrond op een vel papyrus. Ook hij droeg een masker. Hoewel hij me vriendelijk begroette, voelde ik me niet erg op mijn gemak. Hij gaf me eten en wees naar een plek waar een aantal strozakken lag. Doodmoe viel ik in slaap.

Ik werd wakker en hoorde een ruisend geluid. Ik zag een gedaante in een lange, groene mantel. Helena! Op slag was ik klaarwakker. Ze negeerde me compleet en praatte verder met de man aan tafel. In het toortslicht zag ik haar mooie mond, haar fonkelende zwarte ogen. Toen ze uitgepraat leek, gaf ze met een hoofdgebaar te kennen dat ik haar moest volgen. In een zijgang stond een aantal banken. We gingen tegenover elkaar zitten.

'Zo,' zei ze koel. 'Je wil je dus inzetten voor het verzet.' Ik knikte.

'Je zal zoals iedereen een proefperiode moeten doorlopen.'

'Hoe werkt het verzet?'

'Het enige wat je voorlopig moet weten, is ons wachtwoord.' Ze tekende een cirkel in het zand dat op de vloer lag en zei: 'Teken er een kruis overheen.' Daarna duidde zij vier punten aan.

'Teken nu een slang.' Met haar hand maakte ze een beweging in de lucht. Ik tekende de slang in het rulle zand. Ze knikte.

'Nu ken je het wachtwoord.'

'Maar hoe...'

Helena snoerde me de mond en zei dat ik verder niets hoefde te weten.

'Hermes?' riep Helena. De man met de vriendelijke ogen kwam aangesneld.

'Hij is je nieuwe hulp.' Helena liet me achter bij de man die Hermes heette. Ik klemde mijn tanden op elkaar, woede kolkte in me op. Ze had niet eens mijn naam genoemd.

'Ik heet Melas.' De man knikte, maar zei verder niets. Helena keek niet meer om.

'Kom mee,' zei Hermes. 'We hebben degelijk schoeisel nodig. Ken jij iets van handwerk?'

'Hoe bedoel je?'

'Leder bewerken of omgaan met naald en draad?'

'Nee,' stamelde ik. 'Hardlopen en sluipen, daar ben ik goed

in. Ik wil mensen ophalen in Sparta.'

'Rustig maar,' zei Hermes en hij klopte me vriendschappelijk op de rug. 'Dat soort taken is voor na je proefperiode. Jij zal voorlopig in het atelier werken.' Ik slikte mijn teleurstelling moeizaam weg.

'Dat kan ik helemaal niet, ik ben toch geen schoenmaker!' riep ik kwaad.

'Hier,' zei Hermes en hij drukte me een bezem in de handen. 'Begin met de vloer te vegen. En verzamel daarna fijne takjes om toortsen van te maken.'

Met tegenzin gehoorzaamde ik.

'Prima,' zei Hermes. 'Flinterdunne takjes. Bovendien merk ik dat je je geruisloos door het struikgewas kan bewegen.' Hermes deed me voor hoe ik met touw de takjes bij elkaar moest binden. De dagen gingen voorbij en ik ving geen glimp meer op van Helena. Ik ontmoette nog een aantal verzetslieden. Sommigen hielden zich bezig met het maken van voedzame graankoeken voor vluchtelingen die door het hooggebergte moesten. Anderen stippelden nieuwe vluchtwegen uit en tekenden kaarten. Ook zag ik een ploeg die kleren maakte en schoenen, vooral schoenen. Schoenen voor in de bergen, schoenen om door de rivier te waden, enzovoort. Overdag waren de ateliers en werkplaatsen meestal leeg, dan maakte ik schoon: opruimen en vegen. 's Avonds laat kwamen de mannen terug.

'Waarom dragen de verzetsstrijders een masker?'

'Ze willen niet herkend worden,' antwoordde Hermes. 'Ze hebben vrouw, kinderen en werk in Sparta. Als iemand een van onze mensen oppakt en martelt, kan hij de anderen niet verraden, want ze kennen elkaar helemaal niet.'

'Waarom heeft Helena mij dan geen masker gegeven?'

Hermes schokschouderde en zei dat hij dat niet wist. Helena droeg ook geen masker. Het was idioot, maar het gaf me het gevoel dat we daardoor een soort band hadden. Ik keek met veel ongeduld uit naar de eerste vergadering. Dan zou ik haar eindelijk terugzien. Midden in de nacht riep iemand mijn naam. Ik wreef slaperig mijn ogen uit en probeerde overeind te komen.

'Helena vraagt naar je.' Ik sprong overeind en botste bijna tegen de rotswand op.

'Hierlangs!' Ik hoorde een lach in zijn stem.

'Was je gezicht even met koud water,' zei Hermes en hij reikte me zijn waterzak aan. Hij leidde me langs een pad dat volledig aan het gezichtsveld onttrokken was. Ik was er nooit eerder geweest.

Een nieuw leven

Al van ver zag ik haar golvend haar in het toortslicht glanzen. Haar gezicht stond strak, ze keek streng. Ze wenkte me ongeduldig.

'Melas,' zei ze koel, 'een aantal verzetsstrijders is in handen van de Spartaanse wacht gevallen. Ik zoek iemand om een gevaarlijke opdracht over te nemen. Het is een noodsituatie. Ken je de weg van hier tot aan de grotten waar Isidoor woont?'

'Natuurlijk!' zei ik kortaf. Ze was blijkbaar vergeten dat ik haar daar voor het eerst had ontmoet.

'Je moet daar morgennacht een man ophalen, dat betekent dat je vannacht nog moet vertrekken. Je hebt tot overmorgenochtend de tijd om hem naar een schip aan de kust te brengen, veel tijd is dat niet.' Ze gaf me twee landkaarten en een toorts.

'Je mag alleen maar 's nachts reizen. Heb je verder nog vragen?' Ik was nerveus en had niet verwacht dat ik alleen op pad zou moeten gaan. Maar ik schudde mijn hoofd, ik had geen vragen.

'Wacht even,' zei ze en ze verdween in een aangrenzende ruimte. Ze gaf me schoenen, gemaakt van zacht schapenleder. Ze raadde me aan donkere kleren te dragen en gaf me ook een tas met eten en drinken mee.

'Breng niemand hiernaartoe. Alles mag als schuilplaats dienen, behalve deze plek. Zorg ervoor dat je de weg hierheen terugvindt. Hij staat op geen enkele kaart, het is onze hoofdplaats.'

Ik knikte. Ik was sprakeloos, mijn positie binnen de organisatie was in een paar uur tijd drastisch veranderd.

'Veel geluk,' zei ze en ze verdween. Ik was teleurgesteld. Ze had met geen woord gerept over vroeger, geen enkel teken van herkenning gegeven. Ik had niet verwacht dat ze zo afstandelijk zou doen. Ik had haar willen vragen waarom ze mij geen masker gaf. Onwennig keek ik rond. Ik voelde me erg alleen. Nog voor middernacht verliet ik de hoofdplaats. Ik trok mijn donkere tuniek aan, de kleur van de nacht. Even later liep ik door het bos tot aan een veld met bloemen, die zilverachtig glinsterden in het maanlicht.

Het was nog steeds donker toen ik de stierenrots bereikte. Hoezeer ik ook probeerde, het lukte me niet daar stil te blijven zitten en te rusten. Ten slotte stond ik op en ik ging naar de rivier waar Kallista altijd de was deed. Na lang wachten zag ik een van haar bedienden.

'Kan ik Kallista spreken?' vroeg ik zo beleefd mogelijk.

Het meisje bekeek me van top tot teen en knikte langzaam. Ze verwijderde zich om haar meesteres mijn aanwezigheid te melden. Kallista kwam meteen.

'Ik kan je op een schip naar Attica zetten,' zei ik. 'Maar je moet snel beslissen, vannacht gaat er een schip. Wanneer het volgende gaat, weet ik niet.'

'Ik ga mee,' zei Kallista.

'Het is gevaarlijk,' waarschuwde ik haar. 'En het leven in Athene is geen pretje, zeker nu niet. De pest is er uitgebroken.'

'Weet ik,' zei ze kortaf.

'Zorg dat je tijdig, vóór zonsopgang, in de grot bij de stierenrots bent.'

'Ik zal er zijn.'

De schoenen die Helena me gegeven had, waren even soepel als mijn eigen huid. Ze maakten geen enkel geluid, zelfs de vogels bleven gewoon zingen wanneer ik langskwam. Geen aparte fluittoon om gevaar aan te kondigen, het was net of ik een van hen was.

Toen de zon helemaal onder was, liep ik tot aan de rand van het bos en ik wachtte. Na een tijdje hoorde ik driemaal het geluid van een duif. Ik antwoordde met dezelfde roep. En even later vroeg een man mij om het teken te maken. Ik trok een cirkel in het zand en verlichtte de plek met mijn toorts. De man trok zonder aarzelen een kruis over de cirkel. Daarna zette ik de vier stippen. Hij tekende de slang en veegde daarna alles weer uit. Hij haalde de slaaf en vertrouwde hem aan me toe. In het licht van mijn toorts zag ik dat zijn polsen gezwollen waren. Zijn handen zaten vol wonden.

'Gaat het?' vroeg ik toen we in de grot aankwamen, en ik wees naar zijn polsen.

'Mijn handen doen pijn,' antwoordde hij vriendelijk. 'Door het trekken van de ploeg. Ik heb mijn hele leven akkers geploegd.'

'Rust wat,' zei ik en ik wees naar de dekens die in een hoekje lagen.

'Dank u,' zei hij nederig en hij boog zijn hoofd. Ik merkte dat hij geleerd had te gehoorzamen. Hij wist ook niet beter.

'Ik ga even weg maar jij moet in de grot blijven,' zei ik hem. Hij knikte. Buiten zocht ik in het licht van mijn toorts naar lavendel. Van mijn moeder wist ik dat je met lavendel wonden kan ontsmetten. Ik plukte een hele bos en ging weer naar binnen. Met een steen plette ik de lavendel fijn. Het sap smeerde ik over de handen van de man. Helena had me niets gezegd over wel of geen vragen stellen aan vluchtelingen. Ik was zo nieuwsgierig dat ik het er maar op waagde.

'Waarom wilde je weg uit Sparta?'

'Mijn vrouw,' zei de man zacht. 'Ze is overleden.'

'Het spijt me,' zei ik onhandig en ik wist niet meer wat te zeggen.

'Ik moest weg,' ging de man spontaan verder. 'Het kon me niet meer schelen of ik doodgemarteld werd of kon ontsnappen.'

'Was het leven in Sparta dan zo erg?'

'Niet altijd,' zei hij. 'Maar wel sinds mijn vrouw ziek werd.

Zelfs toen moest ze doorgaan met werken. Met wat rust had ze misschien kunnen genezen.'

Ik was blij dat ik hem naar een ander leven kon leiden.

Kallista kwam tegen de ochtend. Ze droeg een eenvoudige tuniek en had weinig spullen bij zich. Zonder namen te noemen stelde ik de slaaf en Kallista aan elkaar voor. Ik gaf de slaaf de koopmanskleren. Hij trok ze dankbaar aan. Voor de ochtendschemering begonnen we aan de tocht naar de boot. Daar aangekomen legde ik Kallista uit hoe ze bij mijn broer moest geraken. De slaaf gaf ik een bemoedigend schouderklopje. Kallista omhelsde me.

'Hou je goed, Melas,' fluisterde ze. Net zoals Helena de vorige keer, bleef ik niet op het strand. Ik vertrok nog voor de matrozen de touwen hadden losgemaakt. Voordat ik naar de hoofdplaats ging, waste ik me in een klein bergriviertje. Ik sneed een paar wilde rozen af en wreef die over mijn huid. Dat had ik mijn moeder zo vaak zien doen. Ik drukte de schelp die ze me had gegeven, tegen mijn borst.

Het verzet

Ik was tevreden over mijn eerste opdracht, alles was vlekke-
loos verlopen. Ik glimlachte toen ik bij de hoofdplaats aankwam. Helena leidde de vergadering die blijkbaar al een hele tijd aan de gang was. Ze zag er bleker uit dan anders. Even
dacht ik dat ze me zou vragen verslag uit te brengen over
mijn eerste opdracht, maar ik vergiste me. Ze keek me nauwelijks aan.
'Missie volbracht,' zei ik fier toen ze de vergadering afsloot.
Helena keek me koel aan. 'Ik heb gehoord dat de schipper
twee vluchtelingen moest vervoeren. Dat was niet afgesproken. Hij was betaald voor één persoon. Kan je dat verklaren?'
'Het was een noodgeval,' stamelde ik.
'Impulsief gedrag is levensgevaarlijk!'
'Maar, ik kan alles uitleggen...'
'Liever niet!' Helena stond haastig op. Ik keek naar haar ge-
zicht. Koud marmer, er stond geen gevoel op te lezen.
'Hermes moet je beter opleiden. Als dit jouw manier van
werken is, ben je nutteloos voor ons.' Ze beende weg.
Verslagen bleef ik achter. Nutteloos! Ze vond me nutteloos.
'Kom, Melas.' Hermes tikte me geruststellend op de schou-
der. Moedeloos slofte ik achter hem aan.

Elke dag nam ik stof af en veegde ik vloeren. Door de fakkels die ook 's nachts bleven branden, werden de ateliers snel smerig. Het voelde aan alsof ik van nul moest beginnen. Alsof ik een nul was. Ik bad tot de goden dat Helena me snel een andere taak zou geven. Het vrat aan me dat ze niet eens de moeite had genomen om naar mijn verhaal te luisteren. Ik verlangde naar een glimlach van haar, een teken van begrip. Ik wist zeker dat ze lief en gevoelig kon zijn. Of vergiste ik me? De dagen kropen voorbij. Ik probeerde gesprekken af te luisteren in de hoop iets meer te weten te komen over Helena. Alleen haar geraffineerde tactiek en doortastende leiding kwamen ter sprake. Hermes vroeg me vaak hem op zijn tochten te vergezellen. Zo leerde ik veel: nieuwe wegen ontdekken, nieuwe codes, dierengeluiden nabootsen en nieuwe schuilplaatsen voor vluchtelingen vinden.

'Weet Helena dat ik met je meega?'

'Niet altijd.'

'Vindt ze het goed?'

'Ik moet ervoor zorgen dat je een goede opleiding krijgt.'

Ik leerde vluchtelingen begeleiden. Maar geen enkele keer mocht ik mee tot in Sparta om daar iemand op te halen. Op een keer zagen we mannen van de Spartaanse wacht in de buurt van het huis van Isidoor. Het verzet liet geen mensen meer bij Isidoor overnachten, zijn huis was voortdurend omsingeld door Spartaanse wachters.

Toen het weer bijna volle maan was, werd ik bij Helena geroepen. Ik wreef me in met rozenbladeren en kamde mijn haar. Helena zat op de bank in het hoofdkwartier. Ik schrok toen ik haar zag. Ze leek nog breekbaarder dan toen ik haar leerde kennen. Snel sloeg ze haar lange mantel om haar tengere lichaam.

'Morgen moet iemand via een gevaarlijke bergpas vluchten,' zei Helena. 'Ik wil dat je meegaat, dan leer je meteen de bergen kennen. Iemand die het hooggebergte niet kent, verdwaalt of sterft. Het zal een zware nacht worden. Rust voldoende.'

Haar woorden overrompelden me. Ik gluurde naar de andere verzetsstrijders. Deden die ook alles wat Helena vroeg? Kallista had gelijk. Helena leefde uitsluitend voor het verzet. Ze gedroeg zich als een man. Ze aanvaardde hulp, maar een band met haar opbouwen, lukte niet. Ik vond dat Helena leek op de bolster van een kastanje die met haar stekelige uiterlijk de binnenkant beschermt.

Ik had energie voor drie. Al fluitend zocht ik voedzame graankoeken, twee toortsen en andere spullen bij elkaar. Toen ging ik rusten op mijn vertrouwde plek, onder een struik.

Tocht over een besneeuwde bergrug

Ik opende mijn ogen, iemand trok ruw aan mijn schouder.
Loom draaide ik me om, mijn huid was warm van de zon.
'Opstaan,' zei Helena. 'We moeten de tocht voorbereiden.'
'Ben je uitgerust?' vroeg ik haar. Ze zag eruit als een eerste
klas soldaat.
'Gaat wel,' antwoordde ze. 'Help me met de touwen.'
Ik volgde haar, langs de gang die uitkwam in het midden van
de hoofdplaats. In de wand zaten haken waar touwen van
verschillende afmetingen aan hingen. Ze nam een korte voor
zichzelf en bond die om haar middel.
'Deze is voor jou.' Ze gaf me een lang touw. Ze vroeg me ook
een touw voor de vluchteling mee te nemen. In het atelier
nam ze een paar bergschoenen van de onderste plank.
'Trek deze aan,' zei ze, een beetje kortaf. 'In de bergen kom je
niet ver met de schoenen die je draagt.' Ik ruilde van schoenen. Mijn schoenen van soepel leder maakten plaats voor
stevige bergschoenen. De zolen waren ruw en oneffen om te
voorkomen dat je uitgleed op natte stenen of ijs.
'We hebben ook drie schapenvachten nodig,' zei ze. 'Het
vriest in de bergen.'
'Waar kan ik die vinden?'

'Vraag dat aan de kleermaker.' Zelf liep ze naar Hermes toe en begon hem instructies te geven. In het naaiatelier bond ik de schapenvachten samen tot een bundel en hing die over mijn schouder. Ik stond klaar, maar Helena die blijkbaar zoveel haast had om te vertrekken, was er nog niet. Eindelijk kwam ze opdagen, druk gebarend. Enkele verzetsmensen liepen naast haar en verzekerden haar dat ze alles zouden voorbereiden. Maar wat precies, dat kwam ik niet te weten.

De zon ging onder, maar Helena's ogen waren ongetwijfeld gewend aan de duisternis, want ze struikelde over geen enkele steen. Toen we een hele poos hadden gelopen, verscheen een sikkelvormige maan van achter de wolken.
'Hier moeten we op de vluchteling wachten,' zei ze. We gingen zitten op een rotsblok onder een boom. Ze zat op een armlengte van mij vandaan. In het donker aten we stilzwijgend onze graankoeken. Ik keek haar onopvallend aan. Haar blik spiedde onrustig in het rond, alsof de vijand elk moment uit het struikgewas kon opspringen.
'Is er iets?' vroeg ik tussen twee happen door.
Ze knikte en antwoordde: 'Er wordt gefluisterd dat de Spartaanse wacht een tip heeft gekregen over de ligging van onze hoofdplaats.'
'De hoofdplaats is goed te verdedigen!'
'Nee,' zei ze moe, 'dat gevecht kunnen we niet winnen.'
'Wat gaan we dan doen?'

'Morgen verhuizen we.'

'Waarheen?'

'Nu niet,' zei ze en ze keek onrustig om zich heen.

Het bekende geluid van een duif klonk in de verte. We volgden het hele ritueel en de slaaf werd opgehaald.

We passeerden de boomgrens. De lucht werd ijler. Ik zag hoe Helena's kuitspieren zich spanden. We stopten af en toe om op adem te komen. Het pad dat hier en daar spiegelglad was, liep steil omhoog. De slaaf gleed uit, het touw waarmee hij aan Helena en mij vastzat, was strak gespannen. We trokken hem overeind. Ik zei de slaaf dat hij zijn voeten schuin moest plaatsen om niet uit te glijden op steile stukken. Om ons te beschermen tegen de gure wind, hulden we ons in een schapenvacht. Helena knoopte de touwen nog eens stevig vast. Als een van ons uitgleed, zou hij niet in het ravijn vallen. Boven op de berg stond een kleine hut waar we even rustten. Helena gaf de man de kaart die ze had getekend. Van mij kreeg hij de tas met eten en ik bond zijn touw weer om mijn middel. Het pad voorbij de bergpas was minder glad. De slaaf kon nu alleen verder.

'Dat de goden jullie zegenen,' zei hij en hij vertrok. Ik keek naar de hoge bergtoppen die in het licht van de maan blonken. Daar woonden de goden die regeerden over de mensen. De lucht was er te ijl voor een gewone sterveling.

Op de terugtocht hadden we de wind pal in het gezicht. Hier en daar veranderde de sneeuw in spiegelglad ijs. We moesten op stokken steunen om niet uit te glijden.

'Wil je even rusten?' vroeg ik.

'Dan bevriezen we,' zei Helena bars. Stap voor stap daalden we af. De een stond stil terwijl de ander voorzichtig verder liep op het verraderlijke ijs. Naast ons gaapte een ravijn. Opeens gilde Helena. Ze gleed uit, schoof over de rand. Ik zette me schrap. Mijn hart sloeg een tel over.

'Helena?' riep ik. Het bleef stil.

'Ik hou me vast aan een rotspunt, probeer omhoog te klimmen!' riep ik zo luid als ik kon. Ze gaf geen antwoord. Ik kon haar niet zien, maar aan het touw hing een zwaar gewicht. Ik kon onmogelijk gaan kijken, dan zou ik te pletter vallen. Ze moest zich tegen de ravijnwand afzetten en naar boven zien te klimmen. Maar ik voelde geen enkele beweging. Het touw stond strak. Ik zette mijn tanden op elkaar en trok met één hand aan het touw. Met de andere hand hield ik me vast aan de rotspunt. Ondanks de kou brak het zweet me uit. Hoe hard ik ook trok, ik kreeg Helena niet naar boven. Nog steeds voelde ik geen beweging in het touw. Enkele meters verderop zag ik een stevige rotspunt, naast het pad. Ik probeerde een stap te verzetten, het ging moeizaam, het touw kraakte. Eindelijk bereikte ik mijn doel en ik bond haar touw vast aan de rotspunt. Ik nam het tweede touw, dat van de slaaf, en bond ook mezelf vast aan de rotspunt. Ik liep voorzichtig tot aan de rand van het ravijn, ging op mijn buik liggen en keek naar beneden. Daar hing ze, met bebloed hoofd, de ogen gesloten.

Ze leek wel dood. Haar rechterslaap vertoonde een diepe hoofdwond waaruit bloed sijpelde. Het kostte me heel wat moeite, maar ik slaagde erin haar omhoog te hijsen. Ik greep haar arm, trok haar over de rand en legde haar voorzichtig neer. Ik scheurde een stuk van mijn tuniek en bond het rond haar hoofd. Al snel zag ik het bloed er doorheen kleuren. Ik scheurde nog een stuk af en drukte dit tegen de wond.

'Helena?' Ze zag lijkbleek. Zenuwachtig nam ik haar pols. Die klopte zwak. Ik kon daar niet blijven, we zouden bevriezen. Ik deed mijn schapenvacht uit, bond Helena met het touw vast tegen mijn lichaam en wikkelde ons beiden in de schapenvacht. Stap voor stap schuifelde ik verder. Geleidelijk aan schoot ik sneller op; de sneeuw werd dunner om ten slotte helemaal te verdwijnen. Aan de rand van het bos legde ik haar neer. Ik luisterde naar haar hartslag. Die klonk ver weg, erg zwak. Haar lichaam voelde koud aan. Ik wreef haar warm, drukte haar dicht tegen me aan.

'Helena!' Ze bleef bewusteloos. Misschien kan ik iemand van het verzet bereiken, dacht ik. Ik imiteerde een luid koerende duif en hield mijn oren gespitst. Tevergeefs. We waren op twee uur lopen van de hoofdplaats. Toen zag ik haar lippen bewegen.

'Water,' klonk het flauwtjes. Haar ogen bleven gesloten. Ik nam de leren waterzak en bevochtigde haar mond. Ze likte aan haar gebarsten lippen. Ik gaf haar druppel voor druppel te drinken.

'Slaaf... bergen...,' mompelde ze.

'Dat is voorbij,' zei ik. 'Je bent gevallen.' Helena verloor weer het bewustzijn. Ze had verzorging nodig, ik moest hulp zien te vinden, anders zou ze sterven. Ik droeg haar in mijn armen tot aan de hoofdplaats. Geen enkele keer zag ik haar lippen bewegen. Ze was lijkbleek.

Hermes snelde op me toe toen hij zag dat ik Helena in mijn armen droeg.

'Leg haar hier neer,' zei hij bezorgd. Ik legde haar op een stel dekens. Hermes maakte omzichtig het verband om haar hoofd los, bekeek de wond aandachtig, ontsmette die, luisterde naar haar hartslag en nam haar hand in zijn handen. 'Helena, kindje,' zei hij zacht. Als door een wonder opende ze even haar ogen. Ze glimlachte flauw.

'Ga jij maar rusten, Melas,' zei Hermes. 'Je bent uitgeput. Ik doe alles wat ik kan voor haar.' Hermes tilde Helena op en verdween naar haar kamer. Toen pas merkte ik hoe ik er zelf aan toe was. Mijn handen lagen open van het trekken aan het touw, mijn knieën knikten. Maar ik dacht alleen maar aan Helena en bad vurig dat ze zou genezen. Even kwam de gedachte in me op dat Hermes wel héél erg lief voor haar was, ze hadden zo te zien een innige band met elkaar. Ik hoopte dat hij een goede dokter voor haar vond. Ondanks mijn vermoeidheid was ik te onrustig om te slapen. Ik liep naar de ateliers om mijn volgende tocht voor te bereiden: drie vluchtelingen begeleiden langs een pad dat alleen Hermes kende.

Hermes

'Stilte!' Hermes probeerde de vergadering te leiden maar die verliep zeer rommelig. Helena verkeerde nog steeds in levensgevaar.

'Ontruimen we de hoofdplaats?' vroeg iemand nadat Hermes dat al twee keer had gezegd.

'Ja, maar we kunnen niet alles meenemen.'

'We kunnen onze minst belangrijke spullen achterlaten,' zei een andere man.

'Dat is gevaarlijk,' zei Hermes. 'Onze spullen bevatten heel wat nuttige informatie.'

'Laten we die dan verbranden,' stelde iemand voor.

'Een rookpluim kan je al van heel ver zien,' zei ik. 'Het kan ons verraden.' Er werd instemmend gemompeld.

'We moeten een valse rotswand maken,' zei Hermes. 'Daarachter kunnen we spullen verbergen. En later, als de Spartanen hier niet meer komen, kunnen wij onze spullen komen ophalen.' Een geroezemoes brak los.

'Stilte!' riep ik streng. Ik wilde dat alles ook zonder Helena's aanwezigheid goed verliep. 'Wie wil me een handje toesteken?' Een aantal mannen stak de hand omhoog. Ik koos vijf sterke kerels uit om me te helpen met de valse rotswand. We sleepten hout, steen en lood aan. Ik wees waar ze alles moesten neerzetten. We bewerkten hout met lood waardoor er stukken rots aan bleven kleven. Achter de rotswand borgen we schrijfgereedschap, toortsen, schoenen, touwen en houwelen op.

Een ander groepje maakte een inventaris op van wat er in de ateliers stond, en pakte spullen in manden en tassen. Sommigen vertrokken meteen al naar de nieuwe hoofdplaats.

Terwijl mijn mensen verder gingen met de valse rotswand, ging ik op zoek naar Hermes.

'De vluchtelingen van deze nacht?' vroeg ik. Hermes knikte en vroeg op zijn beurt: 'Heb je waterdichte schoenen?' Hij keek naar mijn voeten.

'Is dat nodig?'

'Jazeker. De vluchtweg die we vannacht nemen loopt door een rivier. En natte voeten in de vrieskou zijn gevaarlijk. Ze worden zwart en vriezen af. Pak aan.' Hij drukte me twee blinkende laarzen in de armen. Met een hand streelde ik over het ingevette leder. De zon ging onder en een kille mist kwam opzetten.

'Hierlangs,' zei Hermes en hij wipte over de omheining. De geiten staarden ons aan. Het verzet hield enkele geiten voor de melk.

'Je manier van lopen kwam me meteen vertrouwd voor,' zei ik.

Hermes hield abrupt de pas in. Zijn ogen keken me geamu-

seerd aan. Het was niet ver lopen naar de afgesproken plek.
Ik vond het vreemd, slaven op te halen zo dicht bij de hoofdplaats. Maar nood breekt wet.

'Wie haalt de slaven op in Sparta?' vroeg ik Hermes die naast
me op de schapenvacht kwam zitten.

'Diegene die de slaaf kent. Iemand over de rivier brengen,
buiten Sparta, is de zwaarste opgave.'

'Worden er dan veel opgepakt?'

'We hebben informatie over de wachtrondes van de Spartaanse wacht. En ook over hun onverwachte patrouilles.'

'Heeft het verzet spionnen in het leger?'

'We hebben zowat overal spionnen.'

'Zitten er ook hooggeplaatste mensen in het verzet?' Ik
schoof een beetje ongedurig heen en weer op de vacht.

'Het is beter dat je niet te veel weet.'

'Ik heb het gevoel dat ik je ken,' zei ik en ik keek hem recht in
de ogen.

Hij draaide zich om.

'Wie weet,' zei hij zacht. Mijn vermoeden werd sterker maar
ik durfde zijn naam niet te noemen. Stel dat ik me vergiste.
Op hetzelfde moment hoorde ik het afgesproken geluid, het
gekoer van een duif. Ik beantwoordde het signaal en even later kwamen een paar mannen onze richting uit. De vluchtelingen leken doodmoe. We lieten hen even uitrusten en gaven
hun geroosterde noten om nieuwe energie op te doen. We
moesten onder struikgewas door kruipen en bereikten even

later een rivier. Hermes haalde een tas uit een greppel en gaf de vluchtelingen waterdichte laarzen en een toorts. Vanaf hier moesten we door het water waden. De rotswanden aan weerszijden van de rivier werden steeds hoger. De kloof ging over in een grot. Daar lag een houten bootje te dobberen op de rustige stroming van de ondergrondse rivier. Hermes en ik roeiden. De slaven zaten onrustig op het houten bankje. Ze voelden zich duidelijk niet op hun gemak. Vanaf de uitgang van de grot gingen de vluchtelingen alleen verder. Ik gaf hun de kaart met daarop de uitgestippelde route. Als ze die bleven volgen, bereikten ze uiteindelijk een dorp waar veel gevluchte slaven woonden.

Hermes en ik moesten terug met het bootje, tegen de stroom in.

'Laat het roeien maar aan mij over.' Hermes keek bewonderend naar mijn gespierde armen. Het belangrijkste werk was achter de rug. We moesten nu alleen nog tijdig ons kamp bereiken, zodat we konden helpen bij de verhuizing.

'Eerst even rusten', zei Hermes. Toen we in het gras gingen liggen, voelde ik de vermoeidheid toeslaan. Mijn ogen vielen dicht, al wist ik dat het geen goed moment was om te slapen. Ik schrok wakker van enkele regendruppels op mijn gezicht. Aan de hemel pakten donkere wolken samen. 'Opstaan Hermes! We moeten naar de hoofdplaats.' In gedachten zag ik Helena gewond in de hoofdplaats liggen, omsingeld door de vijand. Ik trok aan Hermes' tuniek. Toen pas zag ik zijn gezicht heel duidelijk. Ik schrok van zijn gelaatstrekken die me maar al te bekend voorkwamen. Mijn vermoeden klopte. Daarom wilde hij niet met ons vluchten. Een warm gevoel ging door me heen terwijl ik keek naar onze vroegere huis-slaaf.

'Wakker worden, Androcles,' zei ik zacht. 'We moeten verder.' Hij draaide zich om en wilde snel zijn masker opzetten.

'Ik heb je herkend,' zei ik. 'Maar ik zal je niet verraden. Nooit. Ook al martelen de Spartanen me dood.'

'Je zou er vroeg of laat toch achtergekomen zijn,' zei hij glimlachend. 'Het verbaasde me zelfs dat je me niet onmiddellijk herkende.'

'De verhuizing,' zei ik. 'En Helena...'

'Heb je je voor haar bij het verzet aangesloten?' vroeg Hermes op de man af. Ik bloosde.

'Je bent niet de enige die haar op handen draagt. Ze heeft tegelijk iets teers en strijdlustigs. Heel wat mannen zijn diep onder de indruk van haar.'

'En jij?' vroeg ik. 'Ben jij ook onder de indruk van Helena?' Ik wilde graag te weten komen of Helena's vader zijn dochter misschien aan Hermes had beloofd. Ik herinnerde me opeens weer hoe zorgzaam Hermes voor haar was.

'Ik mag haar heel erg. Ze is talentvol, een fantastische leider. Ik zou het niet kunnen zoals zij het doet.'

'Ben je verliefd op haar?' Tot mijn verbazing barstte Hermes in een klaterend lachen uit.

'Verliefd?' vroeg hij en hij hikte weer van het lachen, de tranen sprongen in zijn ogen. 'Mijn beste Melas, ik ben niet verliefd op haar. Hoe kom je daar bij? Ik ben haar oom. Helena's vader was mijn broer. Toen hij naar de bergen vluchtte en daar een gemeenschap oprichtte, bleef ik bij jullie om jouw moeder te helpen. Dat heeft me het leven gered.'

Androcles was voor mij altijd een beetje een vader geweest en daarom durfde ik het aan hem nog één vraag te stellen.

'Denk je dat Helena iemand heeft?'

'Dat denk ik niet,' antwoordde hij. 'Daar heeft ze geen tijd voor. Al haar energie gaat naar het voortzetten van haar vaders werk. Toch hoop ik dat ze op een dag zal trouwen zoals het bij ons volk de gewoonte is.'

'Zou je het goed vinden als ze met mij trouwde?' Androcles' ogen twinkelden. Hij deed moeite om zijn lach in te houden. 'Probeer je met mij te onderhandelen zoals dat gebruikelijk is in Sparta?'

Ik voelde me verlegen worden. Ik was het niet gewend dat Androcles zo tegen me sprak. Als bediende sprak hij op een andere toon.

'Bij ons volk gaat dat niet zo,' vervolgde hij. 'Vrouwen kiezen zelf hun partner. Ik hoop dat ze binnenkort weer helemaal genezen is,' veranderde hij van onderwerp. Ik knikte heftig.

'En nu moeten we er als de bliksem vandoor,' zei Hermes en hij wees naar de loodgrijze wolken.

Toen we in de buurt van onze hoofdplaats waren gekomen,

bleven we staan. Op het eerste zicht leek de plaats verlaten. Geen beweging te bespeuren. Toen zag ik dat iemand op de uitkijk stond. Of liever gezegd: op de uitkijk zat, in een boom. Hij droeg geen masker. Ik herkende maar al te goed de rode mantel die hij droeg.

'Onze hoofdplaats is ontdekt,' zei ik geschrokken tegen Hermes. De kerel wenkte iemand in de verte.

'Kom,' fluisterde Hermes. 'Volg mij.' Tot mijn verbazing sloop Hermes recht naar onze hoofdplaats. In de verte zag ik de veren op de Spartaanse helmen dansen in de wind.

Ontsnapping

In ons kamp was de vloer bezaaid met landkaarten en andere spullen. Daaruit leidde ik af dat onze mensen in allerijl gevlucht waren. Dat kon niet lang geleden gebeurd zijn, waarschijnlijk hadden ze de Spartanen zien aankomen. Hermes keek om zich heen en legde alle belangrijke papieren achter de valse rotswand, in de geheime bergplaats. Hij gooide een heleboel spullen op een hoop en stak die in brand. Ik keek zenuwachtig naar buiten. De hevige regen belette me veel te zien.

'Schiet op, Hermes, daar is geen tijd meer voor! Laten we gaan!' zei ik. Maar Hermes bleef kalm, drukte me een toorts in de hand en wees naar het atelier. Ik wist niet of het verstandig was, maar ik ging er toch maar heen en stak zoveel mogelijk spullen in brand. Ik struikelde over mijn tuniek toen ik naar Hermes rende. Hij pookte in het vuur. De vlammen likten al aan de zoldering.

'Laten we gaan! Ze zijn vlakbij, ik heb ze horen roepen. Ze komen eraan!' Hermes greep snel zijn tas. Tot mijn verbazing liep hij niet naar de uitgang van de grot, maar ging de grot nog verder in. Spoedig zouden de vlammen de uitgang van de grot versperren. Er was geen weg meer terug, we moesten wel verder de grot in. De gang liep steeds steiler naar beneden. In het licht van mijn toorts zag ik een bootje dobberen op een onderaardse rivier. Hermes sprong behendig in het bootje. Ik maakte het touw los en ging naast hem staan. We lieten ons meevoeren op de stroom, langs de bochtige gangen die de rivier in het kalkgebergte had gegraven. Niemand had me verteld over deze weg onder de hoofdplaats. Ik ging voorzichtig op de rand van het bootje zitten. Soms was de gang zo smal dat we ons moesten bukken. Duizenden druppeltjes druipten van de rotswand in het riviertje. Het plenzende geluid maakte me onrustig.

'Denk je dat de Spartanen ons achtervolgen?' vroeg ik. Hermes knikte en duwde zich met zijn handen tegen de rotswanden af waardoor het bootje sneller vooruitging. Ik keek achterom, ik zag niets maar ik hoorde hen wel. De gang splitste zich. Misschien konden we de Spartanen hier van ons afschudden. We konden duidelijk horen dat de Spartanen bleven staan om te zien welke gang we waren ingevaren. Een paar tellen later zetten ze de achtervolging weer in. Ze naderden pijlsnel, naar het lawaai te oordelen. Opeens greep Hermes met beide handen een uitsteeksel in de rotswand vast. Het bootje kwam tot stilstand. Behendig knoopte Hermes een touw om een houten paal.

'Het is een stut,' zei hij. 'Die moeten we onderuit zien te trekken.'

'Daar zijn ze!' Ik zag hun triomfantelijke blikken in het

toortslicht. Mijn hart hamerde, ik kon nog nauwelijks ademen. De stroom voerde ons weg van de stut. Ik hield het touw stevig in handen.

'Een, twee,...' Met een enorm geraas kwamen er stenen en zand naar beneden. De Spartanen vloekten. Maar jammer genoeg was de doorgang niet versperd. Toen splitste de gang zich weer. Hermes twijfelde even.

'Daar!' wees ik hem. 'Nog een stut.' Razendsnel knoopte Hermes een touw om de stut en deze keer stortte het gewelf helemaal in. Ons bootje kantelde bijna door het opspattende water.

Hoe meer we de uitgang naderden, hoe vaker de gang zich vertakte. De Spartanen zaten ons niet meer op de hielen. We hoorden hen in elk geval niet meer. Door de instorting hadden ze blijkbaar geen idee waar we ons bevonden. Ik ging er even bij zitten, om uit te blazen.

'De stroom voert ons wel mee,' zei ik.

'Niet waar,' zei Hermes paniekerig en hij roeide uit alle macht. 'De rivier stijgt. De talloze riviertjes voeren regenwater aan van buiten waardoor het waterpeil gaat stijgen. Als we niet opschieten, verdrinken we.' Ik begon uit alle macht te duwen. Het bootje wankelde en ik sloeg bijna overboord. Toen ik even stopte om op adem te komen, voelde ik de deining van de aanzwellende rivier. Verschillende waterlopen vloeiden samen op die plaats en het water kolkte angstaanjagend. De puntige rotsen boven ons waren vlijmscherp. Ik haalde mijn handen open. Hoe ver was het nog en hoe snel steeg het water? Ook Hermes duwde zich af tegen de rotswand die al glibberig begon te worden van het opspattende water.

'Daar, licht!' zei Hermes. 'Deze rivier mondt uit in zee. We moeten het bootje achterlaten en naar zee zwemmen, anders halen we het niet. Zwem achter mij aan en klem je vast aan de rotsen als de golven je terug naar binnen duwen.' Hermes gooide zijn toorts weg en dook het water in. Hij begon te zwemmen, naar de rotsopening die we in de verte zagen. Ik zwom hem achterna. Halverwege moest ik me vastgrijpen aan de rotsen, de stroming van het water was zo krachtig dat ik me nauwelijks kon vasthouden. Ik zag hoe Hermes' handen over de stenen gleden en loslieten toen er een golf aan kwam rollen.

'Grijp mijn been!' riep ik hem toe. Gelukkig was de golf inmiddels weer voorbij en konden we verder zwemmen. De ruimte boven onze hoofden werd steeds kleiner, het water steeg nu heel snel. Het werd lichter in de grot maar de uitgang was nog niet te zien.

'We moeten onder water zwemmen,' zei Hermes, 'daar is de stroming minder sterk.' Ik dook achter hem aan. Ik hield mijn ogen open en zag zeewier. De zee kon niet meer ver weg zijn. Toen we weer boven kwamen, hadden we net genoeg ruimte om adem te halen. Maar de volgende golf overspoelde ons helemaal en we moesten ons snel weer vastklampen aan de rotsen. Toen de golf weer weg ebde, konden we weer even naar adem happen.

'Ik denk dat we nu in één keer naar buiten kunnen zwemmen,' zei Hermes. 'Pomp je longen vol lucht.'

Even later waren we uit de grot, maar een golf dreigde ons mee te sleuren. Snel dook Hermes weer onder. Ik greep me vast aan een tak die boven het water hing, maar de stroming was te sterk en sleurde me mee. Ik dook naar beneden, waar de stroming minder was en zwom een eind. Toen ik weer boven kwam, hapte ik naar lucht. Hermes zag ik niet meer. Ik was te uitgeput om hem te roepen. De stroom voerde me mee in de richting van het strand. Ik liet me drijven. Nog nahijgend kroop ik uit het water en ik liet me uitgeput neervallen in het zand. Ik vocht tegen de uitputting. Mijn oogleden voelden aan als lood en de geluiden om me heen werden steeds zachter. Nog even probeerde ik me te verzetten, ik moest wakker blijven. Tevergeefs. Uren later kwam ik weer bij door de kou. Ik lag op het strand, vlak bij het water. Het was donker, de maan scheen. Ik stond op om Hermes te zoeken.

Een nieuwe hoofdplaats

Mijn stem stierf weg tussen de bomen, ik riep Hermes tot ik helemaal schor geschreeuwd was. Ik zocht hem overal. Zonder resultaat. Ik hoorde of zag niets of niemand.

Moe nestelde ik me in een holle boom en viel weer in slaap. 's Ochtends verzamelde ik noten, bessen en wilde olijven om mijn honger te stillen. Waar was de nieuwe hoofdplaats van het verzet? Ik wilde Isidoor opzoeken, maar hoezeer ik ook mijn best deed, ik kon me absoluut niet oriënteren. Ik had geen flauw idee waar ik me bevond, geen enkel pad kwam me bekend voor. En ik kwam ook niemand tegen die me misschien had kunnen helpen. Tegen de middag stond ik weer op het strand. Ik ging op zoek naar de onderaardse rivier langs waar Hermes en ik gevlucht waren. Ik schrok toen ik opeens mensen zag lopen op het strand. Snel dook ik weg achter een boomstam. Gespannen tuurde ik in de verte. De mensen liepen verspreid over het strand. Ze zochten onder struiken, zetten hun handen aan hun mond en riepen iets. Gebukt sloop ik wat dichterbij, van struik naar struik. Toen zag ik vlakbij een meisje met lang, zwart haar. Haar alerte blik speurde in het rond en ze riep af en toe mijn naam.

'Helena!' riep ik terug. Ze kwam naar me toe. Haar hoofd zat nog in een verband, maar ze zag er beter uit.

'Eindelijk, daar ben je,' zei ze ongerust. 'Hermes is gisteren aangekomen. Hij was je kwijt. Kom mee, ik wijs je de nieuwe hoofdplaats.'

Helena heeft zich zorgen om me gemaakt, jubelde het in me. Ze was ongerust! Ze voelt dus toch iets voor mij!

De nieuwe hoofdplaats was een ruime plek, onzichtbaar vanuit de verte want verscholen achter varens en bomen. Je hoorde er de golven tegen de rotsen slaan. Daar moest ik aan wennen.

'Hier is geen vluchtgang zoals in de vorige hoofdplaats,' stelde ik vast. Ik probeerde een gang maar die liep dood.

'We moeten een vluchtgang hakken,' antwoordde Helena.

'Door de rotsen?'

'Met houwelen,' zei Helena. 'Dat hebben we al vaker gedaan.'

'Waar zijn jullie dan aan het hakken?'

'We hebben geen gereedschap. Alle houwelen liggen in de oude hoofdplaats. Voorlopig kunnen we daar niet heen. De Spartanen houden er de wacht.'

'Dat valt tegen,' zei ik. 'Ik wil het hier zo snel mogelijk in orde maken.'

Ik barstte van de energie. Helena had naar me gezocht. Ze was ongerust geweest. Of was het angst? Angst dat de Spartanen mij te pakken hadden gekregen en me zouden doen praten? Ik was meteen een stuk rustiger.

'Geduld, vanavond zien we de anderen op de plek van de drie

heuvels. Daar verzamelen de verzetsstrijders als we een hoofdplaats hebben moeten opgeven.'

's Avonds gidsten we een aantal verzetslieden van de plek van de drie heuvels naar onze nieuwe hoofdplaats. Helena vroeg hen om tegen de volgende nacht gereedschap mee te brengen om een doorgang in de rotsen te hakken. Ik hoorde van anderen dat zo'n gang uithakken een zware klus was. Maar hier zouden we vrijwel ongestoord kunnen doorwerken. Door het klotsen van de golven kon je de houwelen niet horen. Er wachtte ons veel werk. Eerst en vooral was er de vluchtgang die zo snel mogelijk af moest zijn. Maar er moest van alles gebeuren: bergschoenen maken, touwen vlechten, voedsel bereiden en nieuwe vluchtwegen zoeken en in kaart brengen. Aan al die dingen had ik niet gedacht en ik vervloekte de Spartanen. Het zou weken duren voor we weer slaven konden helpen.

'Als we de spullen ophalen die we achter de valse rotswand hebben verborgen, hoeven we niet zoveel kostbare tijd te verliezen,' zei ik.

'Zet dat maar uit je hoofd,' zei Helena. 'Het kleinste kind begrijpt dat het dom is om daar nu heen te gaan.' Ik schrok van haar harde toon; ze was een harde leider en duldde geen tegenspraak.

De volgende nacht brachten de verzetsstrijders gereedschap mee, maar geen houwelen. Ik wist niets van leer snijden en naaien. Ik weigerde naald en draad vast te nemen. Ik zocht

Hermes op, en zei dat ik enkele dagen weg ging maar terug zou komen om met de anderen aan de vluchtgang te werken. Het was fijn om door het bos te lopen. Ik liep in de richting van de vorige hoofdplaats. 's Nachts sliep ik in een boom. De volgende ochtend klom ik tot in de top. Van daaruit kon ik heel goed onze oude schuilplaats in de gaten houden. Ik zag geen rookpluimen, blijkbaar waren de vuurtjes die we in onze schuilplaats hadden gestookt, al uit. Terwijl ik zocht naar eetbare paddenstoelen, dacht ik na over de spullen achter de wand: de bergschoenen, de landkaarten, de touwen en vooral de houwelen. Ik was nu vlakbij de verlaten hoofdplaats. Ik zag geen Spartaanse soldaten. Wel geiten. Ze mekkerden, ze moesten gemolken worden. Alles lag er vredig bij. In een opwelling drong ik zonder verder na te denken de oude hoofdplaats binnen. Mijn zintuigen stonden op scherp, maar er was niets te horen of te zien. Voor ik naar binnen ging, brulde ik de Spartaanse strijdkreet om te zien of daar reactie op kwam. Nee dus. De Spartanen wisten ook wel dat we ons nu niet op deze plek zouden durven vertonen. Ik was nog maar een tiental stappen van de valse rotswand verwijderd. Ik liep er snel heen en nam twee houwelen. Ook bond ik een rij schoenen aan een touw en hing het om mijn nek. Ik draaide me om, om me snel uit de voeten te maken. En keek recht in het gezicht van een Spartaan! Ik was verloren. Ik zou Helena niet meer terugzien. Elke spier in mijn lichaam was gespannen. In een tweegevecht zou ik hem aankunnen, maar ik wilde niet vechten. Hij was vast niet alleen. In de verte hoorde ik al het geluid van voetstappen. Voor ik het goed en wel besefte, had de Spartaan me achter de valse rotswand geduwd. Het was er aardedonker. Ik viel met mijn dijbeen op een houweel. Ik probeerde mijn pijn te verbijten. Ik greep naar mijn been en voelde iets kleverigs. Bloed.

'Is hier iets te zien, Leander?' vroeg iemand met een Spartaans accent.

'Niets,' antwoordde Leander rustig. 'Ik denk niet dat ze hier nog terugkeren.'

'Wat was die kreet dan? Hoorde jij die ook?'

'Dat was ik,' zei Leander. 'Ik dacht dat ik iets zag bewegen. Vals alarm.'

'Hier ligt as,' zei de ander. 'Misschien vinden we nog spullen.'

'Ik denk van niet,' antwoordde Leander. 'Ze hebben alles verbrand.'

'Wanneer worden we afgelost?' vroeg de ander.

'Als de zon in het Westen staat.' Ik kreeg het benauwd en begon te zweten. Ze waren blijkbaar van plan hier de wacht te houden. Het vooruitzicht hier nog uren in het donker te moeten zitten zonder eten of drinken, beviel me niet. Bovendien had ik behoorlijk veel pijn in mijn dij en de wonde bleef maar bloeden.

'Ik ben moe,' zei de andere Spartaan en hij geeuwde luid.

'Laten we nog éénmaal onze ronde doen en dan hier wat rusten,' stelde Leander voor. 'Ik neem de eerste wachtronde voor mijn rekening.' Ik hoorde hoe ze ieder een andere kant uit liepen. Dit was het moment om ervandoor te gaan. Ik nam twee houwelen mee, anders had ik al die ellende voor niets doorstaan. Hinkend bereikte ik het struikgewas. Een tijd later hoorde ik iemand het bos in komen.

'Melas, waar ben je?' Leander! Was hij alleen? Ik ritselde in het struikgewas zodat hij wist waar ik zat. Als dit maar geen valstrik was, bedacht ik opeens. Misschien lagen de andere soldaten op de loer en gebruikten ze Leander als lokaas. Toen hij de rand van het bos bereikt had, hield ik me nog steeds verborgen achter een dikke boom.

'Leander, ben je alleen?' fluisterde ik.

'Wees gerust,' zei hij. 'Ik zal je niet verraden. Pas over een uur word ik afgelost.' Aarzelend verliet ik mijn schuilplaats.

'Je hebt me gered,' zei ik terwijl we elkaar de hand schudden. We gingen zitten achter een dikke struik en praatten op fluistertoon. Terwijl hij mijn been verzorgde, vertelde hij dat zijn leven makkelijker werd na mijn vertrek.

'Tegenover jou gedroegen ze zich echt smerig, maar voor mij zijn ze oké. Ik zou me thuis kunnen voelen in Sparta, als...' Hij zweeg abrupt en zijn ogen kregen een trieste uitdrukking. .

'Als wat?'

'Ik ben verliefd,' zei hij zacht. 'Op Jasmina. Ze werkt als slavin aan het hof. In Sparta kan ze mijn vrouw niet worden. We kunnen hier niet blijven.'

'Ik help je!' Een warmte vulde mij. 'Ga met me mee!'

'Nee,' zei Leander. 'Ik wil samen met Jasmina vluchten.'

'Als je wil vluchten, laat dan hier een teken achter.' Hij knikte en vertelde dat het geen eenvoudige beslissing was. Hij had inmiddels promotie gemaakt en voerde het bevel over twintig soldaten.

'Wist je dat Trifonas haast gek werd toen jij verdween?' vroeg Leander. 'Hij begon zonder reden zomaar op iedereen in te slaan. Ze hebben hem een tijdlang moeten opsluiten.'

Ik huiverde. Trifonas was gek. Gek, maar ook wreed en levensgevaarlijk...

'Ga nu maar en wees gerust. Ik verraad je niet. Vroeger niet. Nu ook niet.' Leander omhelsde me en liep toen langzaam terug.

Verdriet

Toen ik bij het kamp kwam, schemerde het al.

'Waar kom jij vandaan?' vroeg Helena. Toen zag ze de houwelen. Haar ogen schoten vuur en ze gaf me een stevige duw. 'Je hebt ons allemaal in gevaar gebracht!'

'Dat denk ik niet.'

Helena kreeg rode vlekken in de hals, draaide zich om en wilde weglopen.

'Luister,' zei ik en ik hield haar tegen.

'Ga uit de weg!' riep ze woedend. 'Wat leren ze jullie eigenlijk in het leger? Om als een kip zonder kop te handelen? Om anderen in gevaar te brengen? Verwijderen ze jullie hersenen, zodat jullie zonder nadenken mensen kunnen afslachten? Mannen, vrouwen en... kinderen. Smeerlappen!'

Ze rukte zich los en liep weg. Ik rende haar achterna en hield haar vast. Ze liet zich op de grond zakken. Ze huilde met diepe, lange uithalen. Haar schouders schokten. Ik wist niet wat ik moest doen. Dit verdriet ging mijn krachten te boven. Ik liet haar los en liep weg.

Twee dagen lang sprak ze geen woord tegen me. De derde dag ging ik naar haar toe.

'Het spijt me,' zei ik. Ik vertelde haar over Leander. Dat hij te vertrouwen was en dat we dus niet bang hoefden te zijn. Daarna werd het erg druk. We moesten nieuwe vluchtroutes uitstippelen en daar kwam heel wat bij kijken. Onvermoeibaar bracht Helena bij het licht van een toorts de nieuwe wegen in kaart. Anderen kopieerden haar kaarten. Ze was goed in haar werk. Met moeite tekende ik een route uit op een vel papyrus. Binnen de kortste keren zat mijn blad vol vegen en vlekken. Helena grinnikte. Ik kon er nog steeds niet tegen om uitgelachen te worden en probeerde het vel te verbergen.

'Wie heeft jou zo goed leren tekenen?' vroeg ik haar.

'Mijn vader.' Ze toonde me hoe ik het stuk houtskool fijn moest slijpen en tussen duim en wijsvinger vasthouden. Ik waagde nog een poging, maar ook nu bracht ik er niets van terecht. Helena vertelde over haar vader.

'Zo hield mijn vader mijn hand vast,' zei ze en ze nam mijn hand vast om samen de lijnen te tekenen. Ik glimlachte. Het bleef lange tijd stil terwijl we verder tekenden. Toen legde ze haar houtskool neer, keek me aan en zei: 'Melas, ik wil het verzet verlaten.'

Ik staarde haar aan. 'Dat meen je toch niet?'

'Ik heb er lang over nagedacht en zal niet meer van mening veranderen. Het wordt tijd voor een nieuw leven. Ik heb mijn vaders missie zo goed mogelijk voortgezet. Ik wil een ander leven. Hermes weet ervan. Hij neemt de leiding over.'

'Helena,' stamelde ik. Ze keek me aan en vroeg of ik wilde

111

vertellen over Athene. Ik zocht moeizaam naar woorden.

'Helena,' zei ik weer. 'Zonder jou heeft wat ik hier doe geen betekenis.'

'Ga met me mee. We hebben genoeg ellende meegemaakt voor tien mensenlevens. Nu is het tijd om gelukkig te zijn,' zei Helena.

Ze verbaasde me. Al die tijd had ze zich als een bikkelharde leider gedragen en nu wilde ze er zo maar mee kappen. Ik zweeg een hele poos.

'We kunnen niet naar Athene,' zei ik ten slotte. 'Daar gaan mensen dood aan de pest. Maar we kunnen naar het familie-landgoed.'

Helena straalde. Ik nam haar hand. Lange tijd bleven we zo zwijgend zitten.

'Voor we gaan, moet ik nog iets doen,' zei ik. Ik vertelde Helena over Jasmina, de vriendin van Leander.

'Ik begrijp het,' knikte Helena. 'We zullen hen helpen.'

Vriendschap

Op zijn typische, bescheiden manier zette Hermes zich in voor het verzet. Ik was blijer dan ooit dat hij er was, hij was een rots in de branding. Helena gaf al haar taken aan hem door.

Eigenlijk was ik bang om het verzet te verlaten. In Athene zou ik nutteloos zijn. Wat kon ik nu helemaal? Vechten, eten zoeken en rennen. Wat heb je daar aan in vredestijd?

'Ik weet niet of ik een gezin kan onderhouden,' bekende ik.

'Dat zijn zorgen voor later,' zei Helena.

Bijna elke dag gingen we zwemmen in zee. We werkten vaak samen en praatten veel over het landgoed dat mijn moeder had geërfd. We maakten toekomstplannen en Helena bloeide helemaal open. Ze werd zachter en mooier. Haar gezicht dat me vaak aan koud marmer had doen denken, zag er nu warm en levendig uit.

'Je bent mooi,' zei ik.

Ze bloosde, mijn stoere heldin bloosde. Ik grinnikte, want ik besefte maar al te goed dat ze me nog steeds de stuipen op het lijf kon jagen als ze boos werd. Maar steeds vaker was er die zachte blik in haar ogen. Ik smolt weg. Ik vroeg of ze met me wilde trouwen. Ze knikte. Heel lang bleven we dicht tegen elkaar zitten terwijl we naar de ondergaande zon keken.

Die nacht vroegen we Hermes of hij ons kon trouwen.

'Ik ben geen priester,' antwoordde hij. 'Maar als jullie mij kiezen, wil ik jullie huwelijk wel inzegenen.'

Tijdens een van de vergaderingen van het verzet, trouwde ik met Helena. Ze had haar haren gevlochten en een lange, witte jurk aangetrokken. Om haar duim droeg ze een ring die ik nooit eerder had gezien. In stilte baden we tot de goden. Ik had een kaars voor Helena aangestoken. Uit mijn tuniek haalde ik een ketting die ik voor haar had gemaakt en ik vroeg: 'Aanvaard je mijn vriendschap en liefde?'

Ze boog haar hoofd en ik deed de ketting om haar hals. Toen keek ze me in de ogen en schoof de ring van haar duim.

'Aanvaard je mijn vriendschap en liefde?' Teder schoof ze de ring om mijn ringvinger. Haar ogen blonken in het kaarslicht. Helena en ik deelden gedroogde vruchten uit aan iedereen die getuige was van ons huwelijk. Onze kameraden klapten in de handen en juichten ons toe. Ik voelde een warme vriendschap voor hen, want ik wist dat ze net als ik vooral voor haar waren gekomen. Maar ze gunden mij mijn geluk.

We maakten één groot bed voor ons beiden.

Hubris

We bleven langer dan de bedoeling was. Het was niet makkelijk om de vlucht van Leander en Jasmina te regelen. Ik vond dat niet erg. Ik voelde me gelukkig. De hoofdplaats was een thuis voor Helena en mij. Ons bed van takken en mos was een nest. Het gevaar was onderdeel van mijn leven. Als ik mensen kon helpen ontsnappen, als ik de Spartaanse wacht te slim af kon zijn, voelde ik mijn bloed warm door mijn aders stromen. Hier hoorde ik erbij, hier betekende ik iets. Maar Helena werd ongedurig.

'Morgen vertrekken we. Ik zal deze plek missen,' zei ik.

'Ik niet,' zei Helena. Ze streelde over haar buik. Die werd een beetje boller en haar humeur werd erg onvoorspelbaar.

'Overmorgen zijn we veilig in Attica,' zei ik en ik tilde haar op, legde haar op bed en zei dat ze moest rusten tot ik terugkwam met Leander en Jasmina.

Het had de hele dag geregend maar ik kende de vluchtroute op mijn duimpje. Ik wachtte Leander op in de stierengrot. Hermes zou Jasmina brengen. Een schip van Isidoor ging naar Klein-Azië via de haven van Athene. We zouden ons verbergen tussen de wijnvaten.

Bij zonsondergang begon ik onrustig van het ene been op het andere te wippen. Mijn ogen deden pijn van het turen naar het struikgewas. Ik spitste mijn oren om de afgesproken kreet te horen. De wegen waren glibberig door de aanhoudende regen maar het was niet normaal dat de tocht zo lang duurde. Ik besloot een kijkje te gaan nemen. Het was koud in het bos. De ondergaande zon verdween achter een dik pak wolken. De avondschemer was blauwgrijs in plaats van roze. Na een tijdje hoorde ik voetstappen. Dit klopte niet. Ik klom in een boom en wachtte roerloos af.

Even later zag ik een gedaante. Het was Hermes. Hij was gewond aan zijn been en kon nauwelijks lopen.

'De wacht heeft Leander opgepakt,' zei Hermes, nadat ik me uit de boom had laten zakken. 'Jasmina werd betrapt toen ze wou vluchten. Ze hebben haar gemarteld en vermoord. Ze waren op de hoogte van mijn komst. Ik ben ternauwernood kunnen ontsnappen.'

'Ik moet Leander helpen.'

'Niemand kan nu iets doen,' antwoordde Hermes. Ik wuifde zijn woorden weg en zei: 'Breng Helena naar het schip. Ik wil dat ze veilig is. Vraag haar zonder mij naar het landgoed van mijn familie te vertrekken.'

'Maar...'

Ik hoorde niet meer wat hij zei, ik rende richting Sparta. Ik lette niet op de gevaren, nam de makkelijkste weg tot ik de rivier had bereikt en stak die wadend over. Tijd om het geluid van mijn voetstappen te dempen of mezelf te vermommen, gunde ik me niet. Het was donker toen ik in Sparta aankwam. In de kazerne brandden toortsen. Het schijnsel wierp grillige schaduwen over de vlakte. Ik sloop naderbij, het licht ontwijkend. Ik hoorde het slaan van de zweep. Ik hoorde onderdrukte kreten. Dat moest Leander zijn. Na een tijdje werd het stil. Ik vond blindelings mijn weg naar de houten hut. Leander zat vastgebonden aan een paal, zijn rug bloedde. Mijn adem stokte. Paniek sloeg mij om het hart. Ik moest iets doen. De bewakers dronken wijn. Als ik nog even wachtte, zou hun aandacht afnemen.

'Leander deugt niet.' De haartjes op mijn armen gingen rechtop staan toen ik de stem van Trifonas herkende. 'Hij is een verrader, net als Melas.' Hij schaterde het uit. En draaide zich om.

Ik probeerde weg te duiken. Maar ik voelde de speerpunten in mijn rug. Ik zou zwaar betalen voor mijn onvoorzichtigheid.

In de val

Ik werd wakker van een vuistslag in het gezicht. Mijn ledematen wogen als lood. Onder mij knarsten wielen, houten wielen op zand. Elke hobbel in de weg rammelde mijn lichaam door elkaar. Ik voelde me kotsmisselijk.

'Wakker worden.' Het geluid deed pijn aan mijn oren. Iemand schudde me door elkaar en brulde: 'Wakker worden! Geniet van je laatste levensuurtjes.'

Pijnscheuten trokken door mijn hele lijf. Alles werd weer zwart voor mijn ogen, ik liet me wegzinken. Maar toen dacht ik aan Helena, en met alle moeite van de wereld opende ik mijn ogen.

'Hij komt bij,' zei een bekende stem. Trifonas! Zijn gezicht was getekend door littekens en zijn haar was grijs. De opsluiting had hem geen goed gedaan.

'Geef hem water,' zei Alexius. 'Voor hij sterft, moet hij praten.' Ze draaiden me op mijn rug en goten water in mijn gezicht. Ik opende even mijn ogen en keek recht in het gezicht van Leander. Zijn huid was asgrauw. Ik wilde naar hem toe kruipen, bundelde al mijn krachten om mijn arm in zijn richting te bewegen. Zijn hand was ijskoud.

'Dood!' triomfeerde Trifonas. 'Wat had je gedacht?' Hij

grijnsde en kauwde op een snee brood. 'Je hebt je vriend veel pijn bespaard door tijdig op te duiken. Ik wist wel dat jij hier achter zat. En als jij niet zoveel nuttige informatie had,' voegde hij eraan toe, 'was je ook al koud geweest.'

Uur na uur, dag na dag, week na week werd ik gefolterd en ondervraagd.

'Waar is de schuilplaats van het verzet?' Ze lieten me voedsel eten waar ik van moest braken, maar ik zweeg.

'Geef ons de vluchtroutes!' Ik klemde mijn lippen op elkaar. Urenlang lag ik doodziek en misselijk op de vloer. Af en toe werd ik wakker en het enige dat ik over mijn lippen kreeg, was: 'Leander, het spijt me zo.' Dan gaf Trifonas me een klap. Hij spotte met mijn verdriet. Het raakte me niet. Ik bad tot de goden voor diegenen die mij lief waren: Helena, Leander en zijn vriendin Jasmina. Telkens als ik bijkwam uit een donker, zwart gat, probeerde ik me in gedachten vast te klampen aan een van hen. Ik rilde. Ik wist niet of het dag of nacht was. Soms leek het of Leander me wenkte naar een zacht licht en dan schrok ik weer van Helena's angstige ogen die me terugriepen naar het hok waar ik op de koude vloer lag. Ze stopten niet met vragen: 'Wie werkt er voor het verzet? Hoe groot is jullie leger? Is Isidoor bij het verzet?' Zelfs als ze uit het hok waren verdwenen, bleven de vragen door mijn hoofd hameren. Ik zonk weg in een weldoende slaap. In mijn droom zag ik Helena lachend met een kind op haar arm. Het kind strekte zijn armpjes naar me uit. Ik werd glimlachend wakker.

Hector

Op een nacht kwam een man in een wit kleed me opzoeken. Eerst zag ik alleen maar zijn voeten, in sierlijk gevlochten sandalen. Hij was alleen, had geen soldaten meegenomen. De mannen met de speren lagen een eind verderop op de grond te rusten. De man betastte de schelp op mijn borst.

'Dit is de schelp van je moeder,' zei de man. Nu pas herkende ik Hector, mijn vader.

'Ik keur niet goed wat je hebt gedaan,' zei hij terwijl hij de schelp streelde. 'Het strekt mij niet tot eer, jou overigens ook niet. Hoe gaat het met haar?' Ik ging ervan uit dat hij mijn moeder bedoelde. Zijn ogen bleven aan de schelp gekluisterd.

'Ik heb haar deze schelp gegeven,' zei hij. 'Ze was de mooiste vrouw die ik ooit heb gekend. Is ze bij haar familie?'

Ik dacht aan het landgoed van mijn broer en aan Helena. Ik slikte.

'Ik ben te weten gekomen dat je getrouwd bent en een kind verwacht.' Verschrikt keek ik op.

'Je bent me veel verschuldigd,' zei Hector. 'Als je levend uit Sparta wil geraken, moet je mij jouw eerste zoon schenken.'

'Ik sterf liever.'

'Je bent gek,' zei mijn vader.

'Mijn leven in het Spartaanse kamp was een hel,' zei ik traag. 'Zoiets wil ik mijn kind niet aandoen.'

'Mannen dromen van de roem die jij had kunnen krijgen.' Hector spuugde de woorden bijna uit.

'Ze weten niet beter.'

'Ik heb twee mannen ingehuurd om je te helpen ontsnappen. De wachters slapen.' Mijn vader haalde een mes van tussen zijn riem.

'Ik kan je doden,' zei hij. 'Dan word ik volgens de Spartaanse wet de vader van je zoon.'

Het angstzweet brak me uit. Stel dat hij Helena zou vinden. Mijn plaats innemen. Haar schaken. Ik zakte door mijn knieën en keek verslagen in de verte. Mijn handen woelden door de losse aarde, op zoek naar houvast. Praten kostte mij moeite. 'Vader...' stamelde ik.

Hij liet het mes zakken.

'Vader,' herhaalde ik. 'Waarom heb je mij in de steek gelaten?' Ik keek in zijn ogen, zijn gezicht vol rimpels. Hij was een oude man.

'Ik had de raad beloofd niet met jullie te spreken zolang Laïdes niet terugkwam,' zei Hector. Zijn stem klonk zachter.

'Trouw aan de wet, maar niet aan je gezin,' gromde ik.

'Zwijg!' De aders op zijn slapen spanden zich. Hij hield zijn mes weer in de aanslag. 'Wordt het je zoon of je leven?'

Ik deed teken dat hij zijn mes moest wegdoen en liet het hoofd zakken.

'Ik zal je een bericht sturen als mijn eerste zoon zeven wordt.'
'Neem hem mee!' beval mijn vader. Zijn huurlingen kwamen aangerend. 'Laat hem uit Sparta verdwijnen.' Hij hield de schelp.

Bezinning

Zonder problemen bereikte ik het vasteland, een eind buiten de haven van Athene. Ik trok meteen verder, naar het landgoed van mijn broer. Het was bijna donker toen ik in de verte de oude boomgaard zag. Hier en daar lagen bomen omver. Andere bomen hadden dode takken of waren ziek. Het huis met de luiken leek vervallen. Een deel van het dak was ingestort, hier en daar zaten gaten in de muren. Toen ik de binnenplaats overstak, glipten ratten en muizen weg. In een klein kamertje achter in het huis brandde licht.

'Helena!' Mijn stem weerkaatste tegen de wanden. Verder bleef het stil. Ik ging het volgende vertrek binnen.

'Helena.' Mijn stem klonk onvast. Nu ik merkte dat Helena hier niet was, werd ik ongerust. In een hoek hing een oude hangmat, buiten het bereik van ongedierte. Ik rook eraan in de hoop iets van Helena te herkennen. In de verte zag ik iemand naderen. Ik ging naar buiten en kneep mijn ogen tot spleetjes om de silhouet in de avondschemer beter te onderscheiden.

'Helena!' Mijn stem sloeg over. Ik liep op de gedaante in de verte toe. Ik wist niet zeker of het Helena was, zo ver reikten mijn ogen niet.

De vrouw leek mij wel te herkennen. Even verstijfde ze en toen rende ze naar me toe.

'Melas.' Haar stem trilde. Mijn vermoeidheid verdween, ik tilde haar op en droeg haar naar het huis.

'Ik dacht dat ik je niet meer terug zou zien,' zei Helena en een traan rolde langs haar wang. Zachtjes streelde ik door haar haren. Later stond ik op om hout te zoeken en ik maakte vuur. Helena's buik was gegroeid. Ik legde er mijn oor tegen om naar het kind te luisteren.

'Je bent gewond!' zei Helena geschrokken. Opeens werd ik weer herinnerd aan het verdriet en de pijn van de afgelopen weken.

'Ze hebben je gemarteld,' jammerde Helena. Ze haalde water en waste de wonden uit. Ik kreunde.

'Vertel me maar niet wat ze met je hebben gedaan,' zei ze. De zon stond al hoog toen ik ontwaakte. Dagenlang moest ik het bed houden. Vaak doezelde ik weg en droomde ik dat ik weer in handen viel van de Spartanen. Ik moest Helena vertellen over mijn vader. Maar hoe? Ik durfde niet over ons kind te praten. We aten van de groenten uit het moestuintje dat Helena had aangelegd. Toen ik me beter voelde, knoopte ik een visnet en ik ging vissen. De belofte aan mijn vader vrat aan mij.

'Je bent onrustig,' zei Helena. 'Wat is er aan de hand?'

Ik duwde haar weg en zei dat ik mijn familie moest zoeken. Helena knikte, maar vroeg om haar niet te lang alleen te laten, de baby zou niet lang meer op zich laten wachten. Zelf wilde ze niet naar Athene gaan, uit angst voor de pest. In de buurt leende ik een paard van een boer en ik vertrok naar de stad. In Athene scheurde ik een lap van mijn onderkleding en bond die voor mond en neus. In een herberg kwam ik te weten dat Laïdes buiten de stad woonde. De volgende ochtend vertrok ik om hem te zoeken.

Familie

Even buiten de stad vond ik Laïdes' huis en trof er een stralende Kallista aan die haar baby voedde.

'Laïdes zal gelukkig zijn dat hij je ziet. Ga maar gauw naar hem toe.' Kallista duwde me lachend het huis in.

'Broer! Eindelijk!' Laïdes omhelsde me hartelijk. Nu pas voelde ik hoezeer ik hem had gemist.

Laïdes vertelde me dat de pest was verdwenen in Athene. De stad herleefde.

'Waar is moeder?' vroeg ik hem.

'Kom mee,' zei hij. 'Ik zal je haar rustplaats tonen. Ze is gestorven.'

Ik schrok. Mijn moeder zou haar kleinkinderen niet zien opgroeien. Zij die zoveel mensen had genezen, had zelf geen weerstand kunnen bieden aan die afschuwelijke ziekte. Ik slikte.

'Ze is gestorven terwijl ik bij haar waakte,' zei Laïdes. 'Kom, laten we naar haar graf gaan.'

Ik knielde bij haar graf neer en bad tot de goden. In stilte vertelde ik haar over de schelp terwijl mijn handen de bloemen op haar graf streelden. Laïdes had er tientallen kruiden geplant.

'Ze heeft jou het familielandgoed geschonken,' zei Laïdes.

'Dat landgoed is ook van jou.'

'Nee,' zei Laïdes. 'Arthyssa en ik willen dat het jouw thuis wordt, we respecteren moeders laatste wens.' Ik dankte moeder en beloofde haar dat ik van het familielandgoed een bijzondere plaats zou maken.

'Ik wil een gemeenschap oprichten voor gevluchte slaven,' vertelde ik Laïdes terwijl we weer naar zijn huis wandelden. Laïdes luisterde aandachtig naar al mijn plannen. Ik probeerde hem over vader te vertellen, maar de woorden bleven in mijn keel steken.

'Jammer dat moeder Helena niet kan helpen met de bevalling,' zei ik ten slotte.

'Vraag Arthyssa,' antwoordde Laïdes. 'Ze woont in de bergen, op een halve dagreis hier vandaan.' Toen ik afscheid nam, beloofde Laïdes dat hij spoedig langs zou komen op het landgoed.

Arthyssa was blij me terug te zien. Haastig verzamelde ze potten met kruiden en andere spullen. Netjes stapelde ze de spullen in haar kar die ik achter het paard spande.

'Het lijkt wel of je gaat verhuizen,' zei ik.

Onzeker keek ze me aan: 'Ik dacht, ik hoopte... Ik zou voor jullie kunnen koken, voor de kinderen zorgen, ik...'

'Je bent zeer welkom,' zei ik blij en ik tilde haar op de kar.

Alexander en Aneas

Ik snoeide de olijfboomgaard, wiedde de moestuin en zaaide graan. De gaten in het huis dichtte ik met leem. Helena's bevalling duurde een hele nacht. Toen ik eindelijk bij haar mocht komen, was ik vader van twee zoontjes: Alexander en Aneas. Het klikte meteen tussen Helena en Arthyssa die hun handen vol hadden met de baby's. De kinderen waren sterk en gezond. 's Avonds praatte ik vaak met Helena over de toekomst.

'Het wordt tijd dat je Hermes opzoekt. Vertel hem over je plannen. Zeg hem dat mijn vader een gemeenschap zoals jij die ziet ook gewild zou hebben,' zei Helena. Dankbaar omhelsde ik haar. Ik vulde een tas met voedsel, trok mijn bergschoenen en een warme mantel aan. Mijn kinderen groeiden snel. Het knaagde aan me dat Alexanders toekomst nu al vastlag. Ik hoopte vurig dat Hermes me raad kon geven.

Het was helder weer. De bergen met eeuwige sneeuw flonkerden in de zon. Het was barkoud, zelfs de dikke mantel gaf nauwelijks voldoende beschutting. 's Nachts sliep ik in een berghut. Er lagen droge takken die ik dankbaar aanstak. Na een paar dagen bereikte ik de hoofdplaats. Hermes had zorgenrimpels rond zijn mond en ogen maar zijn glimlach was even hartelijk als altijd. Toen hij hoorde van mijn plannen, klopte hij me op de schouder en zei: 'Ik kan over een paar dagen al een aantal mensen met je meesturen.' Vaak wisten vluchtelingen niet waar naartoe. Ze wisten alleen dat ze Sparta moesten verlaten. Maar zodra ze zich op onbekend terrein bevonden, liepen ze verloren.

'We gaan verhuizen,' zei Hermes. 'Het is tijd om een nieuwe hoofdplaats in te richten. Ik weet een plek vlak bij de bergpas om naar Athene te gaan. Dan kunnen slaven gemakkelijker jouw landgoed bereiken.'

Hermes en ik aten samen. Ik vertelde hem over Helena en onze kinderen. Hij hoorde de spanning in mijn stem en vroeg wat me kwelde. Met horten en stoten vertelde ik het hele verhaal.

Hermes keek me geschrokken aan. Hij streek door zijn grijze haar. 'We moeten een oplossing vinden,' was alles wat hij zei. We nestelden ons in een deken en vielen in slaap. De volgende avond leidde Hermes de vergadering. Daarna laadde men allerlei spullen over in manden en werd alles in gereedheid gebracht voor de verhuizing.

'Ga jij mee naar de nieuwe hoofdplaats?' vroeg iemand. Ik knikte en kreeg een grote zak meel in de handen gedrukt. De nieuwe hoofdplaats lag goed verborgen in een dal. 's Avonds besprak ik met Hermes de plannen om vluchtelingen naar mijn landgoed te brengen. We stippelden verschillende routes uit en spraken een wachtwoord af. Enkele dagen later vertrok ik met drie vluchtelingen weer naar huis. Hermes keek me in de ogen en zei: 'De tijd zal raad brengen.' We omhelsden elkaar. De vluchtelingen bleken afstammelingen van Helena's volk. Ze waren uitgeput door de lange reis, maar klaagden niet. Het was erg koud in de bergen en we rustten zo weinig mogelijk. In de graanschuur op het landgoed maakten we bedden van hooi. Doodmoe maar blij kropen de vluchtelingen onder de dekens.

Zo gingen jaren voorbij. Vele groepen vluchtelingen begeleidde ik over de bergpas tot in onze gemeenschap. Sommigen bleven bij ons wonen, anderen trokken verder. Ze hielpen in de tuin of in het huishouden: brood bakken, vis vangen, akkers ploegen en onkruid wieden. Onze kinderen waren inmiddels al zes jaar. Aneas was een vrolijke jongen, maar Alexander maakte het ons lastig. Hij stal vaak messen uit de keuken en sneed dolken en sabels uit hout.

'Oorlog is geen spel!' zei ik dan kwaad en nam het mes af. Ik begreep niet dat een kind van mij zo dol kon zijn op geweld. Ze werden dagelijks geconfronteerd met de gevolgen ervan. De vluchtelingen die hier onderdak zochten, waren erdoor getekend.

Soms verdween Alexander een hele dag. Dan hielp iedereen koortsachtig zoeken, behalve Helena die ziek van ongerustheid in bed bleef. Tot hij ver na zonsondergang glimlachend ons huis binnenstapte en zei: 'Ik heb gespeeld met soldaten in rode mantels.' Ik schrok. Misschien was mijn vader een van hen, klaar om zich mijn zoon toe te eigenen?

Op een dag bracht Alexander een Spartaan mee naar huis. Helena was gespannen toen ze vroeg waarvoor hij kwam. De vluchtelingen spoedden zich naar het bijhuis waar ze zich verstopten.

'Hij is mijn vriend,' zei Alexander fier, 'ik wil mee met hem om de vijfkamp te leren.' Alexander wilde beenbeschermers en een speer, net zoals een echte soldaat. De Spartaan kende ons niet. Tijdens de plundertochten had hij een meisje leren kennen in de omgeving. Af en toe verliet hij het Spartaanse leger om zijn geheime geliefde te bezoeken. We repten met geen woord over vluchtelingen of verzet en waren opgelucht toen hij eindelijk vertrok. We probeerden Alexander thuis te houden of met Aneas te laten spelen. Vaak vroegen meisjes van de boerderijen in de buurt of Aneas en Alexander met hen wilden spelen. Maar Alexander verveelde zich snel en sloop dan weg, op zoek naar avontuur. Helena probeerde hem af te leiden door hem te laten leerlooien, hout bewerken en muziek spelen, maar daar had hij geen geduld voor.

'Hij lijkt op jou en toch ook weer niet,' zei Helena dan. Alexander wilde met zijn Spartaanse vriend mee naar het leger. Ik had me nog zo voorgenomen om mijn kinderen lang bij hun moeder te laten en dan kreeg ik een zoon die zelf weg wou.

Ik begreep hem niet. Laïdes probeerde met hem te praten.

'Hij heeft vaders karakter,' zei Laïdes.

Die opmerking was als een vuistslag in mijn gezicht. Was dit een straf van de goden omdat ik mijn belofte aan vader niet wou houden?

'Ken je veel Spartanen?' vroeg ik mijn zoon op een dag.

'Nee, vader,' zei Alexander, maar hij keek me niet aan.

'Ken je een man met rode veren op zijn helm?' drong ik aan.

'Nee,' zei Alexander. Vrolijk huppelde hij door het landschap, op blote voeten. Hij had ergens een helm gevonden waar hij zelf veren op zette.

'Vader!' Alexander trok aan mijn mouw en toonde hoe hij met één pijl een vogel uit de lucht schoot. 'Dat heb ik van mijn Spartaanse vriend geleerd,' zei hij trots. Ik probeerde Alexander te volgen om te zien of hij misschien in het geheim werd opgeleid door mijn vader. Maar ik kon niets verdachts ontdekken.

Bode uit Sparta

Een maand voordat Alexander en Aneas zeven werden, klopte er een bode uit Sparta aan.

'Je vader laat weten dat hij van zijn wens afziet,' zei de bode.

Ik bracht de man een bord soep en vroeg hem om meer uitleg.

'Hector wil jou niet dwingen om je zoon af te staan,' legde de bode uit. 'Het heeft geen zin om je aan een belofte te houden die je niet wil nakomen.'

'Hoe gaat het met hem?' vroeg ik de bode.

'Hij is bij de raad van ouden,' sprak de man. 'Zijn gezondheid is goed hoewel hij het rustig aan moet doen. Hij heeft weinig familie en zelfs zijn slaaf heeft hem verlaten. Daarom zorg ik voor hem.'

'Mist hij zijn familie?'

'Ik denk het wel. Maar klagen doet hij niet.'

'Wil je bij ons de nacht doorbrengen?' vroeg ik de bode.

'Graag,' zei deze. 'Maar morgenvroeg moet ik weer naar Sparta. Ik kan je vader niet te lang alleen laten.'

'Is hij nog sterk genoeg om tot hier te reizen?' vroeg ik hem.

De bode keek me verbaasd aan en antwoordde: 'Ik denk van wel.'

'Wil je mijn vader vragen,' zei ik aarzelend, 'of hij over een maand naar de tempel aan de voet van de Olympus wil komen om zijn kleinzoon te ontmoeten?'

'Dat wil ik zeker.'

'Alexander droomt van een soldatenleven. Hij zal fier zijn op zijn grootvader.'

De volgende ochtend ging de bode al heel vroeg weer op pad. Ik keek hem na tot hij nog maar een klein stipje was in het weidse landschap.

'Wat heeft hij gezegd?' vroeg Helena.

'Vader komt langs,' zei ik. 'Om Alexander te zien.'

'Hier?' vroeg Helena geschrokken.

'Nee, wees maar niet bang. Hij komt naar de Olympus.'

'Alexander zal dol zijn op je vader,' zei Helena droef. 'Hij zal met hem mee willen naar Sparta.' Ik nam haar in mijn armen.

'Dat kan ik niet toestaan!' riep Helena kwaad en ze rukte zich los.

'Alexander moet zijn eigen bestemming volgen,' zei ik, maar ook mijn hart deed pijn.

Alexander

Ik sta aan de tempel aan de voet van de Olympus. Mijn zoon zit naast me op de bank. Hij is niet bang. En nu hij naar mijn verhaal luistert, naar de avonturen die ik meemaakte toen ik uit het Spartaanse leger ontsnapte, wordt hij stil. Met grote ogen kijkt hij me aan. Ik denk niet dat ik hem van zijn wens zal kunnen afbrengen. Hij wil hardlopen en speerwerpen. Hij zal een goede soldaat worden. Ik doe mijn best om wat vrolijker te zijn. Alexander springt op mijn rug en wil paardje rijden. We draven wat in het rond en vallen dan in het gras. Alexander hikt van het lachen en vraagt: 'Vader, waarom lach je niet?' Dan ziet hij in de verte een soldaat aankomen. Hij draagt een prachtige helm en zijn schild glinstert in de zon. Zijn rode mantel hangt tot op de rug van het paard. Ik zie mijn zoon vol bewondering kijken.

'Dat is je grootvader,' zeg ik.

Hector komt dichterbij. Zijn gezicht is verweerd maar zijn ogen zijn zacht. Hij drukt me de hand en zegt dat hij me tot niets wil dwingen. Ik knik, mijn keel zit dicht. Alexander toont mijn vader zijn pijl en boog.

'Hij wil soldaat worden,' zeg ik tegen Hector.

'Ik zal hem elke dag bezoeken,' antwoordt Hector. 'Daar mag je op rekenen.'

Ik knik. In de verte komt Helena aan. Dit gaat slecht aflopen, gaat het door mij heen. Ik bijt op mijn lip. Helena's haren zitten in de war. Haar ogen blinken van de tranen.

'Ik ga met u mee,' zegt Alexander tegen mijn vader. Mijn vader knikt. Helena kijkt haar zoon zwijgend aan.

'Ik zal elk jaar met hem naar deze plek komen,' zegt mijn vader. Hij steekt zijn hand naar Helena uit. De ogen neergeslagen, drukt ze hem aarzelend de hand en zegt: 'Ik zal altijd van mijn zoon blijven houden.'

Langzaam lopen we naar ons huis terug.

STUDIES IN THE LABOUR PROCESS

David Knights and Hugh Willmott (*editors*)
†GENDER AND THE LABOUR PROCESS
†MANAGING THE LABOUR PROCESS
*NEW TECHNOLOGY AND THE LABOUR PROCESS
*LABOUR PROCESS THEORY

David Knights, Hugh Willmott and D. Collison (*editors*)
†JOB REDESIGN

Derek Torrington, Trevor Hitner and David Knights
†MANAGING THE MULTINATIONAL WORKFORCE

Chris Smith, David Knights and Hugh Willmott (*editors*)
*WHITE-COLLAR WORK: The Non-Manual Labour Process

Published by Macmillan
†*Published by Gower*

Series Standing Order

If you would like to receive future titles in this series as they are
published, you can make use of our standing order facility. To place a
standing order please contact your bookseller or, in case of difficulty,
write to us at the address below with your name and address and the
name of the series. Please state with which title you wish to begin your
standing order. (If you live outside the United Kingdom we may not
have the rights for your area, in which case we will forward your order
to the publisher concerned.)

Customer Services Department, Macmillan Distribution Ltd,
Houndmills, Basingstoke, Hampshire, RG21 2XS, England.

White-Collar Work

The Non-Manual Labour Process

Edited by

Chris Smith
Lecturer in the Aston Business School
Aston University, Birmingham

David Knights
Reader in the Manchester School of Management,
UMIST, Manchester

and

Hugh Willmott
Lecturer in the Manchester School of Management,
UMIST, Manchester

MACMILLAN

First published 1991

Published by
MACMILLAN ACADEMIC AND PROFESSIONAL LTD
Houndmills, Basingstoke, Hampshire RG21 2XS
and London
Companies and representatives
throughout the world

Typeset by Footnote Graphics,
Warminster, Wiltshire

British Library Cataloguing in Publication Data
White-collar work: the non-manual labour
process.—Studies in the labour process
1. White-collar personnel
I. Smith, Chris. II. Knights, David, 1940–
III. Willmott, Hugh. IV. Series
331.792
ISBN 0–333–44040–4

Reprinted 1993 by
Antony Rowe Ltd
Chippenham, Wiltshire

Contents

v

vi   *Contents*

Notes on the Contributors

Peter Armstrong is a Lecturer in the School of Information Systems, University of East Anglia. He is co-author of *Workers Divided, Ideology and Shopfloor Relations* and *White-Collar Workers, Trade Unions and Class*. He has published numerous articles in sociology and management journals. He has been a visiting Principal Research Fellow at the Industrial Relations Research Unit, Warwick University, and his main research areas are currently management formation and the accounting profession, white-collar workers and the labour process.

Chris Baldry is a Senior Lecturer in Industrial Relations in the Department of Organisation Management and Employment Relations, University of Strathclyde. His current research interests are in technical change and the built environment. He is author of *Computers, Jobs and Skills: The Industrial Relations of Technical Change*.

Anne Connolly is a corporate planner in the Town Clerk's Department, City of Glasgow.

Rod Coombs is a Senior Lecturer in the Manchester School of Management, University of Manchester Institute of Science and Technology, and Director of its Centre for Research on Organisations, Management and Technical Change (CROMTEC). He has published widely on technological change; his most recent book is *Economics and Technological Change* (with P. Saviotti and V. Walsh).

Mike Dent is a Senior Lecturer in the Department of Sociology, Staffordshire Polytechnic. His current research, with colleagues within the Technology and Organisation Research Unit (TORU), concerns new technology and IT strategies and new organisational forms carried out under the NAB initiative. He has conducted research into IT developments within the NHS and has published articles on the subject.

Ola Jonsson is a researcher in the Development of Economic and Social Geography, Lund University, Sweden. He has worked extensively in the area of the spatial aspects of technological change.

David Knights is a Reader in the Manchester School of Management at the University of Manchester Institute of Science and Technology. He has conducted research into industrial relations, equal opportunities for ethnic minorities and sex discrimination in recruitment. He has published in sociology and management journals. He is co-author of *Managing the Multi-Racial Workforce* and co-editor of a number of books on the labour process.

Cliff Lockyer is a Senior Lecturer in Industrial Relations in the Department of Organisation Management and Employment Relations, University of Strathclyde. His current research interests are in Scottish labour market studies. He is author of *Industrial Relations in Britain*.

Henry Miller is a Lecturer in the Sociology of Education in the Business School at Aston University. He is currently researching on the first City Technology College and has published numerous papers on teachers, higher education, schools and the local state.

Glen Morgan is a Research Fellow in the Financial Services Research Centre, Manchester School of Management, University of Manchester Institute of Science and Technology. He is author of *Organizations in Society*, and a number of articles on aspects of work and management in various industries.

David Murphy is a Lecturer in the Manchester School of Management at the University of Manchester Institute of Science and Technology. He is an ex-journalist and has conducted research into the occupational formation and work of journalists. He is author of *Silent Watchdog* and *The Stalker Affair and the Press*.

Harvie Ramsay is a Senior Lecturer in Industrial Relations in the Department of Organisation Management and Employment Relations, University of Strathclyde, and is currently on secondment to the Industrial Relations Research Unit, Warwick University. He has published widely in the areas of worker participation, international capital and labour, profit sharing and on the impact of computerisation on work. His current research is on the impact of 1992 on trade unions, firms and workers. He is author of *Transnational Corporations in Australia*, and co-author of *Peoples' Capitalism, Socialist Construction and Marxist Theory* and *For Mao: Essays in Historical Materialism*.

Chris Smith is Lecturer in Industrial Relations in the Business School, Aston University. His main research interests are in white-collar workers (especially technical labour), management strategies and work restructuring, and white-collar unionism. He is author of *Technical Workers* and co-author of *White-Collar Workers, Trade Unions and Class* and *Reshaping Work: The Cadbury Experience*.

Hugh Willmott is Lecturer in the Manchester School of Management at the University of Manchester Institute of Science and Technology. He has researched the accounting profession and the strategic development of the personnel specialism. He has published in a wide range of social science and management journals and is co-editor of a number of books on the labour process.

Diane Winstanley is a Senior Lecturer in Organisational Behaviour and Personnel Management at Kingston Polytechnic. She has conducted research into the organisation and management of engineering design, and is currently writing a book on recruitment and retention in high tech industry, and researching into personnel management in Europe.

1 Introduction

Chris Smith, David Knights and Hugh Willmott

Historically our understanding of the labour process in capitalist societies has been identified with manual labour, the direct production of physical artifacts for sale on the market. In other words, the labour process is commonly seen as necessitating the production of material goods through work activities that are predominantly manual or physical in character. The title of this book may therefore appear something of a misnomer, a contradiction in terms. We can dispel this misconception by briefly examining the reality and appearance of productive work, and the way cultural and common-sense notions of work disguise its nature in modern society.

In Volume 1 of 'Capital', Marx (1976, p. 1040) makes two observations about productive work. Firstly, that with the advent of modern industry it was no longer a requirement to labour manually or directly upon a material commodity in order to be productive. The extended division of labour between different groups of wage-earners, he argues, made production a cooperative activity, where the collective labourer or aggregate worker was responsible for production. The collective labourer is composed of occupations both close to, and those at some distance from, the point of production or 'actual manual labour'. Therefore for Marx, the manual–non-manual division of the workforce does not correspond to productive and unproductive labour.

Secondly, workers could be engaged in a 'labour process' without necessarily producing a physical commodity. The materialisation of labour in a corporeal form was not necessary for exchange value to be generated. Workers who transport goods from one place to another do so without altering their form, but nevertheless add value to such goods. Also private sector service workers are engaged in non-manual employment but nevertheless contribute to the generation of profit from the services that they provide. Insofar as these workers receive less in wages than the exchange value of their services, then they can be seen as economically exploited; these are labour processes if they generate exchange and surplus value (Marx, 1969, pp. 171–2).

1

There are also many non-manual workers who work in the public sector. In general this sector has been neglected by labour process analysts, not least because of the difficulties in translating to the public arena a theory concerned with the extraction of surplus value for the purposes of private accumulation. By contrast, in the public sector the production of goods and services is often subsidised and non-profit criteria frequently condition the purpose and organisation of work. Despite the presence of four chapters which locate their research in this area, we do not claim to have resolved all the problems of developing a perspective in studying the public sector. Nonetheless their inclusion should stimulate a debate upon the strengths and limitations of labour process analysis in illuminating the organisation and control of the work of public sector employees.

Briefly, our argument is that the principles of organisation developed and legitimated within the private sector are presently being applied to 'restructure' the labour process of white-collar state workers. We recognise that the demand for their work is not directly promoted by a capitalist incentive to expand surplus value for private share-holders. In this sense, the public sector is not immediately involved in the exchange between capital and labour. But there are at least two senses in which the public sector connects with private industry. Firstly, public sector services are vital to the development of private capital since they provide essential services (for example, energy, water, communications, transport facilities) that are sometimes offered at a subsidised rate to industry but, in any event, are ultimately guaranteed by the taxpayer. Indirectly then, private capital may be seen to appropriate some of the surplus generated by public sector labour.

Secondly, the organisation and control of work is increasingly treated as if labour were there to generate profits. This is most obvious when public sector industries are being prepared for a privatised flotation, as has already been undertaken with British Telecom, Rover, British Gas, British Airways and the Airport Authorities. The impact is visible in the National Health Service, where centralisation, competitiveness and budgetary controls are transforming work processes in the name of cost effectiveness and value for money (see Dent in this volume). The likely effect of these changes upon the majority of non-manual workers in the NHS seems to be intensification, closer surveillance and a loss of autonomy in respect of medical decision making. However, because of the non-capitalist nature of some public sector organisations, capitalist

solutions must always be a half-measure, an approximate fit, contested and competing with a service ideology and wider political practices that go beyond the criteria of profitability. Just as studies of the labour process have identified the mediation of ideology and political processes to moderate earlier deterministic arguments about the inevitable 'logic of capital' in the deskilling of labour, so when examining the organisation and control of work within the public sector it is important to incorporate an awareness of its distinctive characteristics.

These observations also help to orient our approach to non-manual labour more generally within contemporary capitalism. We should expect the economic pressures to which manual workers are subjected to apply equally to non-manual labour, with the qualification that certain features may not precisely fit the model of the private appropriation of socialised labour. Equally though, the division of labour is not homogeneous in character, since technical, administrative, and supervisory as well as manual categories of labour are part of any large-scale production process. Braverman's (1974) analysis of the labour process has been timely in revealing the universality of the forces operating on wage labour irrespective of its specific character. In particular his analysis of clerical workers highlights how the application of technology, speed-up, Taylorism, fragmentation and routinisation strategies intensify labour, increase productivity and extend control of most non-manual occupations in ways which parallel the experience of manual workers. On the strength of such trends commentators such as Martin (1988) and others have claimed that 'the conventional distinction between manual and non-manual labour has become less salient both sociologically and amongst the population at large' (Newby, et al. 1986, p. 92). Or, as Duke and Edgell suggest, a 'mounting tide of criticism' into the meaning of the manul−non-manual boundary has challenged the utility of the distinction (Duke and Edgell, 1987, p. 448).

However it is one thing to suggest the long-term erosion or imminent demise of the division between manual and non-manual workers, it is quite another to create new categories which are pertinent to both common-sense categorisation of class and the theoretical analysis of class relations in advanced capitalism. Despite material changes in the division of labour, and the trend towards greater homogeneity between manual and non-manual work, many social scientists return to this traditional working class−middle class distinction as a predictor of, for example, voting behaviour, class

identity, and the career and class trajectory of persons occupying these positions (Marshall, 1988). Notwithstanding Martin's prognostication of its demise as a 'social category' the manual–non-manual divide continues to have meaning, value and significance for sociologists and the population at large. We cannot as yet talk about a single labour process, because of the persistence of a distinction which stems from deep-seated features of Western aristocratic culture that elevates mental over physical activity, the mind over the body (Sohn-Rethel, 1978). Even though the notion that any kind of work can be clearly separated, occupations are still classified by their proximity to direct production and the cultural structuring of occupational hierarchies along a broad and ill-defined mental–manual continuum. Hence technicians working with computers all day would still be classified as non-manual, although shop-floor engineers responsible for Computer Numerical Machine tools are seen as manual. Secretaries operating word processors are non-manual, while workers who install telephones or service washing machines are manual. The distinction is not a function of the physical qualities of the job, rather it derives from features such as conditions, location, relative degrees of supervision, and the traditional split between 'the shopfloor' and 'the office' in manufacture which is especially prominent in Britain. Hence there is a cultural determinant to the classificatory divide between manual and non-manual workers within industry that reflects as well as reinforces its structuring of the division of labour more generally.

Partly because earlier sociological studies of non-manual workers have concentrated upon lower hierarchy occupations, for example, clerks, (Lockwood, 1958; Crompton and Jones, 1984), the majority of the case-studies in this book are concerned with more privileged groups of workers. There are chapters on doctors, engineers and managers, as well as on occupations rarely studied within the labour process literature – academics, journalists and salespersons. In keeping with our concern to incorporate public sector work within labour process analysis, the first four empirical chapters involve studies in the field of local government, the health service (two chapters) and higher education. A central feature of these chapters is the question of the break-up of employment stability for non-manual workers in large bureaucracies, a theme employed further in cases drawn from the private manufacturing industry, such as Winstanley's chapter, (Chapter 7).

The book opens with a theoretical assessment of the alternative

perspectives on the class situation of non-manual workers. This provides a theoretical context to subsequent case study chapters by exploring the relationsthip between the main Weberian and Marxist positions within the debate. The authors suggest that a focus on the ✗ economic exploitation of white-collar workers is essential for understanding their labour process situation. In particular it is argued that 'skill' cannot be utilised to draw class boundaries; unfortunately debates about the proletarianisation of white-collar workers have frequently committed this error. The project of searching for 'pure' class models is also criticised; instead a perspective is favoured which situates the analysis within a wider relational context and theorises class as a process rather than as a position. The chapter consequently rejects the idea of artificially grouping white-collar, non-manual workers in a 'new' class. Rather, the authors suggest that the differentiated work situation of non-manual workers is best approached through examining the interaction between general and specific class zones as they impact on their labour process.

Chapter 3 examines the impact of new technology on clerical, technical and administrative workers within the local state. Locating computerisation of the work of different non-manual workers within the public service sector to wider debates on class, the authors note the 'limitations of *a priori* approaches which characterise many structuralist accounts of class in particular'. Important as structural factors, such as supervisory position, economic function and the performance of mental or manual labour are, the authors suggest that such forces only set parameters to social action – they do not determine that action. Key elements in their discussion of the labour process of workers in this sector are gender, the political context of local government, the multi-functional nature of work and the importance of a service ethos used by local authorites to combat the market ideology being imposed by central government. The chapter concludes that the introduction of Information Technology in local authorities will be mediated by a variety of forces, not simply those of capital and labour, and the impact on working conditions of white-collar workers, will equally vary with occupational position, gender and certain wider contextual factors within which the local authority is operating.

Dent's chapter (Chapter 4) on the medical profession also reveals the state, notably absent from discussions of the 'new middle class', to be a major force restructuring the employment status and working conditions of one section of professional labour – doctors. The

chapter explores the relationship between the occupational control policies pursued by the leadership of the medical profession and state administrators. Importantly it highlights the failure of state officials to restructure hospitals through incorporating consultants within the systems of organisational control in hospital management, and the rejection of bureaucratic controls by the Thatcher administration in favour of market mechanisms, which Dent believes have broken down the medical professions's resistance to clinical budgeting. This split between 'paternalist rationalisers' and 'market reformers' reveals the divergent strategies available to manage qualified state employees and the consequences these have on their experience and conditions of work. The case study emphasises the importance of examining management strategy formation over a long time-period, rather than isolating the labour process conditions of this section of qualified labour within a narrow time-frame which may misrepresent their changing employment status and working conditions.

Coombs and Jonsson, examining hospital workers in Chapter 5, also discuss the division between management and coordination carried out by hospital administrators and doctors. They suggest that in the long term Information Technology will offer senior doctors more direct forms of management and supervision of work organisation in hospitals. Against suggestions in the literature of a class or labour process polarisation between economic or technological forces operating in private and public spheres, the authors note that 'publicly funded organisations can exhibit similar managerial motivations to market-based organisations with respect to introducing new technology'. Their chapter also emphasises the centrality of the national or cultural context in evaluating the extent of managerial power in introducing new technology. The rights of a worker to 'hands-on' control of the introduction of new technology is deeply rooted in contemporary Swedish culture and the authors suggest that this situation attenuates unilateral management interventions.

Chapter 6 examines a group of public sector employees who are not normally associated with performing labour, let alone being subject to 'labour process' pressures like other workers. University academics, Miller suggests, are mental labourers whose work is undergoing considerable transformation as higher education is rationalised under state sponsorship. Miller highlights the way the 'academic labour process' is being fragmented, as the conception and management of academic work is 'concentrated in the hands of a relatively new and expanding strata of academic managers'. In this

context, university teachers are seen increasingly to be subject to more stringent bureaucratic controls over their employment conditions. As with other public sector employees, University teachers have experienced an erosion in their stable employment position, as market regulation and contract fragmentation and the influx of casual, contract and part-time labour has undermined their bureaucratic status. This, Miller suggests, has provided a more powerful and effective managerial control over the work of academics than direct controls through the monitoring and supervising of work tasks. Miller notes the segmentation between comparatively 'well' resourced institutions and other smaller technological universities where the new managerialism is most evident. Using the case of Aston University, he describes the centralisation of management control and the weakening of autonomy for this section of qualified, white-collar labour.

Chapter 7 explores the labour process of journalists who, according to Murphy, are very much wage-workers, and thereby part of the working class. This is because they have a direct involvement with production, represent a variable cost to their employer, exercise strategic power over newspaper production, are in a concentrated employment location and enjoy the benefits of a strong and cohesive unionised position. The chapter takes us through the evolution of mass circulation newspapers and changes in the labour process and labour market position of journalists, which he believes has transformed their conditions of employment towards those of mass-production workers. However one of the qualities of journalists (like academics) is their autonomy and creativity in generating 'unique' cultural products. This, it has been suggested, marks them out from manual workers who are not only subject to tight supervisory control in the performance of their work, but also to alienation from the product of their labour, which is appropriated by the employer for purposes of exchange. Murphy argues against what he terms this somewhat idealised portrait of the creativity of journalist's labour. He suggests the 'formularisation of story telling' for example, is a 'form of conceptual technology necessary to the mass production of news [which] controls workers in just the same way as machine production'. What distinguishes manual workers from journalists however, is the individualism and market ideology fostered by their labour market position and the competitive structure of newspaper ownership and production. Murphy discusses two case studies of cooperative news production, established especially to overcome the routinised and fragmented position of journalists in capitalist news

production. These studies reveal the limitations of such cooperatives in overcoming the ideology of journalism, which Murphy sees as premised on market individualism irrespective of the ownership or political content of news stories.

Winstanley, in her chapter on 'technological staff' workers (Chapter 8), reveals the importance that manipulating the labour market has in managing the labour process experience of workers. By examining the different labour market strategies used by employers in recruiting and utilising 'technological staff', she again challenges the equation between qualified white-collar workers and bureaucratic employment security and stability. Her case studies of hi-tech firms in the South West of England point to a growing use of casual employment contracts to fragment and manipulate the labour process of skilled technical workers. Subcontracting, for example, is not unusual amongst certain groups of technical workers, such as draughtsmen and women, but it has frequently been subjected to controls through union organisation. However Winstanley reveals that in the hi-tech sectors, unions increasingly 'lack the strength to impose conditions on employers'. While labour market mobility can be a sign of market power for some 'technological staff', she suggests this is not the case for all, and employers are having some success in eroding national conditions of employment in this sector.

Chapter 9 examines technical workers, only here the focus is on the role of engineers. Against mainstream labour process writing, which sees engineers as wedded to the managerial hierarchy, and the conditions of control that subordinate manual workers, Smith suggests a more contradictory relationship between engineers, capital and other workers. Within monopoly capitalism, craft and professional–scientific ideologies inform engineers' relations with other workers. Their perspectives on job design are conditioned by their employment concentration and the nature of the product and production process in which engineers are engaged. The chapter examines the contrasting ideology of engineers in designing jobs in a small batch, luxury production environment and a mass production setting. Smith's chapter also suggests that strong elements of Taylorism are enshrined in the occupational ideology of engineers, irrespective of the particular context or way in which their jobs are designed. Technological change, especially Computer Aided Design and Computer Aided Manufacturing, are altering the conditions of work of engineers and introducing elements of machine-pacing, extended hours, task fragmentation and loss of autonomy associated with

manual workers. However Smith suggests that engineers regard themselves as masters of such technology, a mastery which enables them to resist the deskilling and control pressures ordinarily imposed on other workers. His chapter argues that the bifurcation within technical labour, between graduate engineers and non-graduate technicians, will be amplified by computer technology.

The chapter by Knights and Morgan (Chapter 10) is concerned with developing theoretical arguments on subjectivity that have been generated or promoted in previous conferences and texts (Knights and Willmott, 1989; Knights, 1990; Willmott, 1990) and illustrate them in an empirical context. Drawing upon their fieldwork in an area that has been ignored by labour process theorists – the sale of life insurance – the authors focus on the ways in which the activity involves the production of certain kinds of identity or subjectivity that are crucial to the control of labour, both at managerial and direct sales level. Central to the argument is a view that the intensification of production and the realisation of surplus value cannot be fully understood in the absence of seeing how labour engages in its own self-discipline through becoming attached to specific conceptions or definitions of itself and its competence. Management control then, involves an exercise of power that stimulates labour to pursue an ideal sense of its own contribution to organisational 'progress' and productive competence. In short it is argued that power is exercised by management to transform sales staff into subjects whose meaning and sense of themselves (identity) is contingent on successfully achieving sales targets and winning the recognition of colleagues and superiors within the company. After a brief description of the company from which the empirical material is drawn, the paper proceeds to examine these disciplinary processes, first at the level of management and then in relation to field sales staff. Two modes of discipline are highlighted. Firstly, the external pressures of targets and commission incentives for productivity, and secondly, the use of social relations outside of work to stimulate success by involving salesmen's wives in performance celebration through foreign jamborees. In both cases managers and sales staff are controlled from without by the strategies of surveillance, and from within by the internal commitment that comes from assuming personal responsibility for their own future and fate. All in all this amounts to considerable pressure and one should not be surprised to find some resistance to it. However, the individualised and 'normalised' subjectivities that result from the various disciplines leave sales staff with little but

resigning from the job as a strategy. Nonetheless, with staff turnover at rates above 25 per cent per annum, this resistance has serious repercussions for management and indeed constitutes a pressure for those who have to maintain full staffing as well as productivity targets. The chapter concludes by commenting on the possibility that the subjectivity of financial self-discipline that informs and is produced by life insurance sales staff could become the target of deconstruction, so as to remove the illusion that our security can be purchased like a commodity in the market place rather than through the development of collective and communal relations.

The final chapter in the book is a theoretical treatment on the character of management in Britain. The divorce between productive and unproductive labour at the heart of some discussion of the relationship between manual and non-manual workers is not, suggests Armstrong, the same as the separation between management and workers. Neither, he argues, is the divorce between conception and execution at the core of Braverman's discussion of the labour process, the same as a split between labour and capital, or management and workers. Rather, Armstrong, with careful support from Marx, argues that management perform both productive and unproductive functions, and in their classic treatment by Taylor, are quite definitely a productive force in the labour process. From the work of Urwick onwards, Armstrong argues that management in Britain has been represented as a 'set of abstract practices divorced from the elements of productive management in the Taylorite heritage'. Such productive groups around management, such as costs and time study engineers, have been relegated to marginal, technical functions divorced from management status, while the core of management decision making is taken by an unproductive strata embedded in marketing and financial functions and divorced from productive activity. Armstrong claims that this division of labour within management has had a profound effect on the economic performance of British capitalism.

 The non-manual workers examined in the case studies in this book are increasingly experiencing their work as a form of wage labour. However their response to its various features, such as the intensification of production or increases in management control, are quite diverse. Theoretically we can put white-collar workers together in a heterogeneous working class or an equally divergent new middle class. But what comes across from the studies in this volume is the importance of the class process, not the isolated class position of

different occupations in the structure of social relations. In this regard more attention is given to the strength of forces, such as state policies, management strategy or national culture and how these condition the labour process experience of non-manual workers. In our view this focus avoids the limitations of the class placement literature, which tends to ignore the wider context and dynamics of class structuration – namely the nation, state, the international economy, gender, political culture and the specific productive or service sector of employment.

Taken together these case studies suggest that the secure employment conditions in stable bureaucracies, often characterised by Weberian theorists as a hallmark to differentiate non-manual from manual workers, are being eroded in the public and private sectors alike. Replacing or competing with bureaucratic modes of management control are strategies that have the effect of exposing managerial and non-managerial staff to market forms of regulation and uncertainty. This occurs as a result either of rendering employment contracts more flexible through workforce segmentation, or by introducing market forces into the task and work organisation structures within which these workers operate. Central to these changes has been a New Right political philosophy subscribed to by a number of contemporary Western governments.

In Britain especially, the 'de-regulation' of markets for labour, products and capital, combined with the privatisation of non-market spheres of the economy, have created a hostile environment for the public sector and forms of occupational regulation specific to the public sector, bureaucratic offices and professional activities. Clearly the privileges ordinarily associated with non-manual employment are vulnerable in these circumstances, revealing the historically contingent nature of Weberian models of class stratification. The question remains as to whether the economic forces of capitalism homogenise all forms of labour to the point at which status distinctions no longer undercut class solidarities. As the papers in this volume illustrate however, a diverse range of practices pull in several directions both to sustain established divisions but also to erode them, to constitute distinct groups of workers, but also to generate new functions and to block mobility opportunities for some whilst opening them up for others. These changes within non-manual work and their relationship to strategies of government and technologies of management are crucial topics for the study of the labour process and social transformations in contemporary capitalism.

References

Braverman, H. (1974) *Labor and Monopoly Capital* (New York: Monthly Review).

Crompton, R. and G. Jones (1984) *White Collar Proletairiat: Deskilling and Gender in Clerical Work* (London: Macmillan).

Duke, V. and S. Edgell, (1987) 'The Operationalisation of Class in British Sociology: Theoretical and Empirical Considerations' *British Journal of Sociology*, vol. XXXVIII, no. 4, December: pp. 445–63.

Lockwood, D. (1958) *The Blackcoated Worker* (London: Allen & Unwin).

Marshall, G., D. Rose, H. Newby and C. Vogler (1988) *Social Class in Modern Britain* (London: Hutchinson).

Marshall, G. (1988) 'Classes in Britain: Marxist and Official', *European Sociological Review*, vol. 4, no. 2, September: pp. 141–54.

Marshall, G. and D. Rose (1988) 'Proletarianisation in the British Class Structure', *British Journal of Sociology*, vol. XXXIX, no. 4, December: pp. 498–518.

Martin, R. (1988) 'Technological Change and Manual Work' in D. Gallie (ed.), *Employment in Britain* (Oxford: Basil Blackwell).

Marx, K. (1969) *Theories of Surplus Value, Part 1* (London: Lawrence and Wishart).

Marx, K. (1976) *Capital, Volume I* (Harmondsworth: Penguin).

Newby, H., C. Vogler, D. Rose and G. Marshall (1985) 'From Class structure to Class Action: British Working Class Politics in the 1980's, in B. Roberts, R. Finnegan and D. Gallie, *New Approaches to Economic Life* (Manchester University Press).

Sohn-Rethel, A. (1978) *Intellectual and Manual Labour* (London: Macmillan).

2 The New Middle Class and the Labour Process

Chris Smith and Hugh Willmott

INTRODUCTION

This chapter will explore the debates within the literature on class around what Braverman (1974) called 'intermediate employees' and what we call 'middle groupings'. In particular we will see how these debates conceptualise the *labour process* dimensions of class relations within the division of labour of advanced capitalist economies. Skill, so central to labour process theory, has also become a focal concern in theories of the class structure which pay attention to the divisive significance of knowledge-based qualifications or credentials. We argue strongly against the assumptions of these theories and in favour of a broad definition of the collective, working class, which contains within it diverse types of wage workers. But our argument is not simply about constructing or defending a model of the class structure. We strongly reject the classificatory myopia of much of the class literature, in particular the competitive wish to *identify* and *categorise* groups into closed class positions. We favour stressing the *relational* nature of class and importance of allowing the structure and context of the network of social relations, within which class identities are formed, to take dominance over the urge to isolate and classify individuals and groups into discrete categories.

At the outset, it is relevant to note the 'contested' meaning of 'class'. Differing background assumptions underpin the construction of alternative theoretical frameworks for identifying and analysing classes: knowledge of class is not generated independently of the values and interests that guide its identification, conceptualisation and analysis. As McLennan et al. (1984, p. 1) have observed

> there can be no simple value-free accounts of political or social phenomena because we have no access to a descriptive language of political and social phenomena about which we could all agree. For facts do not simply "speak for themselves", they are, and have to be interpreted; and the framework we bring to the process of

13

interpretation determines what we "see", what we notice and register as important.

Three competing frameworks for conceptualising class can be identified: 'static', 'dynamic' and 'critical'. (cf. Nichols, 1979) The first, 'static' approach represents class as a position within a stratified hierarchy based principally upon differences of income. In our view, this conception of class has no place in sociological analysis except as a focus for understanding how state calculations serve to constitute a consciousness of status based upon income differences. The second, 'dynamic' conception of class focusses attention upon the efforts of individuals to act strategically to secure and deploy resources in an effort to maintain and advance their social position. This approach dispels the suggestion, invited by the static approach, that the existence of a set of class positions is 'given', or that it is the product of impersonal forces – such as those of industrialisation (Garnsey, 1975). A third, 'critical' perspective argues that this focus upon individual or collective strategies of social mobility deflects attention from the *structure of relations* through which access to resources necessary for the pursuit of such strategies is distributed. Here class signifies the nature of the dominant principle through which *relations* between individuals are organised. In capitalist society the dominant principle is the private accumulation of wealth through the hiring of formally free wage-labour. Commenting upon its emergence from the prior era of feudal organisation, Marx and Engels (1970, p. 36) observed:

> The modern bourgeois society that has sprouted from the ruins of feudal society has not done away with class antagonisms. It has but established new classes, new conditions of oppression, new forms of struggle in place of the old ones.

Marx's analysis of the political economy of capitalism provides the basis for our examination of the 'middle class'. This, we shall argue, directs attention not towards abstract classification, but towards the material relations within which social class relations unfold.

MARX AND THE 'MIDDLE CLASS'

The dynamic structure of modern society is understood by Marx as a medium and outcome of an antagonistic relationship between

oppressive and oppressed classes. This relationship, he anticipated, would produce 'more and more splitting into two great hostile camps, into two great classes directly facing each other: Bourgeoisie and proletariat' (*ibid.*, p. 36), a schism which would eventually undermine and transform capitalist society. More specifically, in conjunction with the inherent instabilities of capitalism as an economic system, Marx believed that the socialisation of the productive process would foster the revolutionary organisation of the oppressed class of wage-labourers.

> The advance of industry, whose involuntary promoter is the bourgeoisie, replaces the isolation of the labourers, due to competition, by their revolutionry combination, due to association. . . . What the bourgeoisie, therefore produces, above all, is its own grave-diggers. Its fall and the victory of the proletariat are equally inevitable (ibid., p. 46).

As yet, Marx's prognosis has not been realised. However, it is perhaps a little too easy to reject his conceptualisation of class on the basis of unrealised predictions. Marx's account of the basic antagnostic structure of class relations may be sound even if his grasp of the *dynamics* of struggle may lack an adequate appreciation of the institutional possibilities for managing and massaging the instabilities of capitalism, including the buffering of its oppressive consequences for wage-labour.

As a manifestation of such possibilities, one may cite how the expansion of non-manual labour within both public and private sectors mediates the structural antagonism within capitalist society. Significantly Marx had comparatively little to say about clerical, technical, managerial and professional workers. However Rattansi (1985) has pieced together remarks scattered through his post-Manifesto writings to pinpoint Marx's identification of three occupational groups whose numbers are swelled with the development of capitalism: *guardians of the capitalist state*, such as civil servants, policemen and soldiers; *office workers* who are engaged in 'calculation, administration and sales'; and *managers* 'to whom administration and supervisory responsibilities are delegated' (Rattansi, 1985, p. 653, emphasis added). Rattansi stresses Marx's recognition of the divisive, fractionalising effects of technological innovations upon wage-labour – including the creation of new groups of technically qualified workers who maintain the productive machinery

(cf. Nicholaus, 1967; Przeworski, 1977). In our assessment, these scattered remarks simply elaborate and qualify, but do not fundamentally change the *Manifesto* conception of a structure of class relation whose dynamic moves relentlessly in the direction of polarisation and homogenisation. The problem, we suggest, is that Marx simply fails to theorise the historical role of the occupational groups which are not locatable unequivocally within either of 'the two great classes'.

Various terms have been devised to characterise the distinctive features of these middle groups. Amongst them have been 'the service class', 'the new class' and 'the new petty bourgeoisie'. For the purpose of this chapter, the descriptive content of the Ehrenreichs' (1979) characterisation of the middle class will be used. Within the middle groups are included 'technical workers, managerial workers, "culture" producers, etc.' (*ibid.*, p. 9), as well as teachers, social workers and entertainers, etcetera. Our image of the term 'middle grouping', and rejection of their term 'professional-managerial *class*', serves to highlight the heterogeneity of this population which, according to the Ehrenreichs (1979) can .be seen to stretch from registered nurses and those engineers in routine production and inspection jobs to the occupants of positions in the middle levels of corporate and state bureaucracies.[1] In opposition to the Ehrenreichs, it is doubted whether the characteristics of these workers are sufficiently distinctive or coherent to constitute it *analytically* as a class (cf. Crompton and Gubbay, 1977; Wuthnow and Shrum, 1983; Barbalet, 1986). Indeed we are inclined to support Draper's (1978, p. 626) highly quotable observations on the hetrogeneity of the elements which comprise the middle groupings:

> It is one thing to recognise the existence of increasing numbers of intermediate elements of various sorts, as Marx did; it is another thing to construct out of these elements an organic class that is meaningful enough to seriously affect social and political life. This requires a cohesiveness, a fund of common interests, an objective basis for solidarity and social unity, such as do not exist among the disparate elements of the ectoplastic class construct. C. Wright Mills called it an "occupational salad", but this may be too complimentary, since a good salad needs considerable togetherness; the "new middle class" is more like a dish of herring and strawberries.

The heterogeneity of the 'new middle class' is perhaps most clearly illustrated by reference to the contradictory position of junior and

middle managers. From a Marxist perspective, it can be argued that these employees perform the functions of controlling the workforce initially undertaken by the capitalist. In this *functional* light, they are seen to comprise a fundamental part of a bourgeoisie which is segmented into owning and controlling components. In contrast to the workers whom they supervise, it is argued that a large part of their effort is directed to the unproductive task of ensuring that a socially adequate surplus is appropriated from others. Noting the trend for all types of labour, including that of the professions, to become wage labour under capitalist production, Marx (1976, pp. 1041–2) cautions against the tendency to overlook the distinction between its 'productive' and 'unproductive' forms. This distinction is crucial, he argues, because it differentiates those whose labour directly produces the goods or service from those who are employed simply to secure and expand capitalist relations of production.

In response to this argument, on the other hand, it may be countered that the junior and middle ranks of management have become an integral part of the collective labourer, and therefore bear a much closer resemblance to that of their subordinates. They share an experience of insertion into a labour process over which they exercise very limited control. Referring specifically to managers, as well as engineers and technologists, Marx himself observes how

> An ever increasing number of types of labour are included in the immediate concept of *productive labour*, and those who perform it are classed as *productive workers, workers directly exploited by capital and subordinated to its process of production and expansion* (Marx, 1976, p. 1040, emphasis added).

This brief discussion is indicative of Marx's ambivalent treatment of what may be termed middle groupings in general, and of managers in particular. Elsewhere in Marx (1969, p. 573) members of these middle groupings are described as standing 'between the workman on the one hand and the capitalist and landlord on the other, thereby burdening the former whilst increasing the social security and power of the latter'. In the third volume of *Capital* Marx (1961, p. 294) appears to resolve this tension in his analysis by suggesting that workers engaged in unproductive, commercial operations – such as the calculation of prices, book-keeping and managing funds – are employed because the cost of their labour is less than their contribution to the process of accumulation. Despite undertaking the

functions of capital and burdening productive labour with the cost of their salaries, the exploitation of their labour appears to align them with the class position of other productive wage-labour. What this account marginalises however, is the extent to which the skills and employment of such workers depends upon the continued existence of the capitalist system. This may also be said of many 'productive' workers, given the extent to which they have been alienated from the means of production. Similarly many managers enjoy little autonomy, and in this respect their position is not so dissimilar to that of manual wage-labour.

A focus on the function and condition of junior managers within the capitalist enterprise reveals the structural source of their class ambiguity, it does not resolve the question of class identity. Indeed a purely functional account to class, which marginalises questions of process and relationship, uncovers the contradictory pressures upon middle groupings, rather than a fixed identity. Therefore functional analysis should also contain something of the context and process of class relations in order to be meaningful.

WEBERIAN RESPONSES TO MARX

An influential response to the limitations and ambiguities inherent in the Marxian conception of class has been constructed upon the role of the market in allocating different forms of property within society. Associated most closely with the work of Weber, the concept of class is used to describe populations who possess similar forms of property and therefore enjoy comparable life-chances. In this formulation, an emphasis upon ownership of the means of production is com-plemented (and diluted) by consideration of the qualifications and expertise which individuals bring to the labour market. In principle this definition of class allows an infinite number of class positions. Indeed, as Giddens (1973, p. 78) notes, if pushed to its logical conclusion, it would identify 'as many classes as there are concrete individuals participating in market relationships'.

This observation highlights the fundamental difference between the dynamic, Weberian conception of class and the third critical perspective on class advanced by Marx. Whereas Marx uses the concept of class to disclose the *relational structure of society*, Weber deploys it to differentiate *the position of individuals* according to their *opportunities for competing within* its dominant institutions. From a

Marxist standpoint, the weakness of the second Weberian perspective resides in its inability to account for the presence of institutions, notably the market, through which skills and opportunities are defined and organised. Johnson (1980, p. 345, emphasis added) makes this observation when he argues that

> the Marxian starting point – the social relations of production – eliminates the possibility of conceiving of the market as an arena of individualized 'capacities' or 'skills'. Skill is not a given individual capacity which endows a subject with power. . . . *Skill is a product of social power.* . . . In Weberian theory exchange is a relationship of equality which functions to create inequalities, only because individuals bring differential capacities to the relationship, while *Marxian theory attempts to explain why exchange is unequal.*

The central issue to be grasped is that in contrast to Weberian conceptions of class, in which the existence of class positions are explained by the differential capacities of individuals (for example wealth and skill), the Marxist formulation locates the conditions of their existence in the (capitalist) structure of society. The market, as well as the possessions and skills which it values, is understood as a consequence of this structure of antagonistic relations and not simply as a condition of its reproduction. A Weberian would interpret the class position of the middle groupings primarily as an outcome of their members shared market capacities. In contrast, Marxian analysis views it as a medium and outcome of a struggle between the powers of capital and the powers of labour, upon which the process of accumulating capital depends.

Given the focus upon the possession of similar forms of property, including qualifications relevant for competing in markets, it is not surprising that those working within the Weberian tradition have encountered comparatively little difficulty in identifying a 'middle class' boundary within the working class(es). Of these, Lockwood's (1958) conceptualistion of class as a fusion of market, work and status situations is perhaps the most widely known. From a Neo-Weberian perspective the class differentiation between white-collar and manual workers is quite readily identified in terms of their differential access to promotion and career opportunities; the ability to monopolise and/or close access to scarce skills; salaried pay systems with guaranteed increments; a cleaner, less noisy, more comfortable environment; more authority over their own and others' work; greater freedom of movement and less supervision than manual

workers, etcetera. Although the existence of such differences is not denied by Marxist analyses of class, they are seen to reduce class as an *analytical* concept for penetrating the structure of *society* to a *descriptive* concept for differentiating the life chances enjoyed by a plurality of groups.

In this and the previous section we have presented Weberian and Marxist approaches as fundamentally distinct, as differences between what we have called *dynamic* and *critical* perspectives. This does not mean that efforts to reconcile or merge the two have been absent in class analysis. However, sophisticated attempts at fusion, like that of Lockwood (1958), where the detailed historical development of clerical labour is discussed within a framework sensitive to authority, labour process and labour market transformations, are comparatively rare in the Weberian literature. More typical are case studies of particular occupations that utilise the concepts of income, status, and authority relations within a limited time-frame. Recently Marxist writers have attempted to examine the importance of social conditions, status and privileges in segmenting wage-labour, and as such have moved into Weberian territory.[2] It is to a consideration of their contribution that our attention now turns.

NEO-MARXIST APPROACHES TO THE 'NEW MIDDLE CLASS'

There are two broad reactions within Marxist literature to the differentiation between manual and non-manual labour. The first, orthodox, response sees the interests of white-collar workers converging with those of manual workers as similar economic forces operate upon their wage-labour condition. The second identifies permanent *class-based* barriers between groups of wage-workers, and the fragmentation of the capitalist class structure beyond the polarity of capital and labour suggested by Marx. In both camps the *particular quality* of wage-labour, rather than simply their formal non-ownership condition, are identified as significant criteria for redrawing the class structure. In this way there are strong echoes of Weber in both these theories.

The *first* response stresses the significance of the changing *historical conditions* of non-manual workers. Whatever minor status advantages they may possess, it is argued that these will be eroded as their numbers increase and they become subject to the same pressures of

market competition, deskilling and job routinisation as manual workers. The universal consequences of employment concentration, work rationalisation and competition will, in effect, *proletarianise* these positions. Against Neo-Weberian writers' insistence on the immutable barriers or boundaries between white-collar and manual conditions, orthodox Marxists emphasise how their common economic condition as wage-labour will expose them to the same pressures from capital and erode these historical privileges. Strict orthodox Marxist discussions on white-collar labour, such as Klingender's (1935) work on clerical labour, are comparatively rare, most writers making concessions to the persistent reproduction of 'middle groupings' or 'intermediate employees'. Braverman (1974), for example, adopts an equivocal stance towards Marxist orthodoxy, recognising the relative permanency of 'intermediate employees', while stressing the long-term effects that routinisation, deskilling and labour market 'massification' will have on the their conditions as privileged wage-workers. As we discuss below, such ambiguity frequently rests upon a very narrow view of the proletariat, and shares many elements of a Weberian definition of social class.

The *second* response suggests not a growing commonality between non-manual and manual workers, but rather a class divide between the two categories. White-collar workers in this scenario are considered a *new middle class*, combining work tasks, or objectives of capitalists and workers, but being the equivalent of neither. Such a perspective suggests that technicians, supervisors, and managers are expanding in late capitalism, gradually out-numbering those in working class positions. Far from proletarianisation being the main process in the class structure, the continual expansion of managers and others is the main tendency of the system. A recent study in the US claims to identify 'a decisive acceleration of the growth of managerial class locations in the 1970s and a clear *de*proletarianisation within and across economic sectors' (Wright and Martin, 1987, p. 1). Because both the orthodox proletarianisation position and versions of a new middle class position are central to a conceptual understanding of the non-manual labour process, we now examine them in turn.

THE CONFUSION OVER PROLETARIANISATION

As noted in our previous section, a major element of the debate over the social position of non-manual workers has revolved around the

concept and process of proletarianisation. In our view, this has confused rather than clarified what is at issue. Proletarianisation as constituted by Marx simply means shifts in the character of labour into a wage-labour form: the transition of a non-wage producer, such as peasant, slave, indentured labourer or petty bourgeois, to a wage-labourer. In other words it describes the dispossession of direct producers, such as peasant farmers, from the means of production, and their transformation into waged workers. In recent debates this definition has been unselfconsciously reconstituted to include changes *within* formal wage-labour positions, in particular changes in the conditions of work and social position experienced by white-collar workers. Marshall and Rose (1988, pp. 499–500), for example, construct from this recent literature four versions of 'proletarianisation', consisting of deskilling of particular jobs; sociopolitical radicalism amongst white-collar workers; changes in the composition of the class structure, with an expansion of working class positions; and reducing career opportunities or trajectories in white-collar jobs.

All four positions rest upon the assumption that the 'proletariat' is not the equivalent of wage-labourers, but a narrower, homogeneous category of labour composed of deskilled, routinised and supervised functions. From this perspective, if movement towards the *conditions* associated with this category can be demonstrated, through the de-skilling of clerical workers for example, then white-collar workers can be said to be 'proletarianised'. Conversely, if it can be empirically shown that the career opportunities, skills and political attitudes of non-manual workers remain distinct from manual workers then, using this *conditions*-based definition of the working class, these groups cannot be said to have been proletarianised or to be in the proletariat. By laying down these narrow job-related or attitudinal definitions of the working class – criteria largely derived from Weber not Marx – the majority of white-collar workers are excluded from a working class location. This point can be illustrated by reference to the question of skill. The assumption that 'skill' forms a basis for class distinction is central to Weberian analysis. However this thesis has been mistaken to be Marxist, due perhaps to the influence of Braverman and the 'deskilling debate' within Marxist circles. Yet, in common with arguments about the embourgoisement of manual workers through high levels of income or affluence, material difference or other distributional characteristics of the division of labour do not define class divisions in the Marxist sense. To disregard this

distinction is to confuse what we have called dynamic and critical definitions of class.

Weberian-inspired accounts of proletarianisation depend on narrow economic or market criteria, thereby marginalising questions of exploitation between capital and labour, and the pressures operating upon all wage-labour due to capitalist competition and accumulation forces. This is evident in Marshall's triumphant return to Weber via a critique of revisionist Marxist definitions of proletarianisation. By empirically demonstrating that clerical and other white-collar workers are not universally 'deskilled', he claims that 'there is no evidence here that clerical and administrative employees, no matter how routinised their particular work tasks, are uniformly "proletarianized" and therefore part of a large undifferentiated working class (1988, p. 148). What he forgets is that differentiation has always existed within the working class, and 'privileged, skilled autonomous workers are still wage-labourers, whose privileges, skills and autonomy are under constant threat of removal by capitalists' (Meiksins, 1985, p. 112). Elaborating this point Meiksins has remarked that:

> The various parts of the collective worker seem preoccupied with their internal differences, as this or that part claims entitlement to more rewards, and so on. It appears then that *status* rather than exploitation is the key to the actual pattern of stratification in capitalist societies. [However] in struggling over status, specific groups of workers are not trying to take something away from those below them in a kind of zero-sum game. They are trying to get more from their *employers*. The fact that they sometimes enter into competition with other employees is a result of the way in which employers structure the conflict, not of any necessary conflict of interest among themselves. There is a real sense in which status consciousness is a reaction to the experience of *class* exploitation. (Meiksins, 1985, p. 114).

Implicit within this analysis is the idea of class consciousness being 'segmented' by status divisions amongst the collective worker. The lack of correspondence between class position and class consciousness is due primarily to the intervention of capitalists in segmenting or dividing labour along status lines which act as an ideological barrier to class consciousness. Meiksins notes that the 'ideology of professionalism' is the most powerful status division in the workforce, placing formidable barriers between those occupations that define

themselves as 'professions' and other types of wage-labour' (Meiksins, 1985, p. 115). He also notes that status is especially strong amongst occupations for which self-employment is possible, such as doctors and lawyers. Hence professionalism and other white-collar occupational statuses are partly an ideology of protection 'from the worst effects of wage-labour . . . legitimating the profession's "right" to autonomy and high social reward'. But they are also the reflection of the 'ambiguous' class position that allows access to petty bourgeois class positions and hence the ideology of status, individualism and distinctiveness from wage-labour. Conversely '"deprofessionalisation" remains a constant danger', with all the associated loss of status and the sense of separation from other wage workers.

THE NEW MIDDLE CLASS AND THE END OF AMBIGUITY?

For orthodox Marxists like Meiksins, there is no 'new middle class' between the capitalist and working class, but rather a small capitalist class, and a large heterogeneous working class, within which certain positions are 'ambiguous' because they permit the occupants to enter the capitalist class or the petty bourgeoisie. Critics of this perspective argue that such ambiguous positions are in fact *new* structural class places, separate from the working class and capitalist class. That occupants of these places or positions are not merely 'ideologically' confused, stuck within 'false' consciousness where their 'true' identity as workers is obscured, but objectively in a different class, and hence their ideological and political consciousness is a genuine reflection of this different material reality.

Poulantzas (1975) and Carchedi (1977) have both advanced structural Marxist critiques of orthodox Marxism and suggested that the working class is becoming a progressively smaller section of society, outnumbered by a new middle class. In Britain, Carchedi has been used by such writers as Johnson (1980) and Carter (1985), to criticise theories of the inexorable proletarianisation of white-collar workers, professionals and other autonomous groups. They reject Weberianism for its concern with *individual* life chances and market properties without explaining the structural underpining of market inequalities. They also reject orthodox Marxism for a linear determination of class based on the possession and non-possession of capital, and its inability to explain the fragmentation of wage-labour other than through recourse to Weberian concepts of status or idealist definitions

of consciousness. They seek to resolve the 'ambiguity' within wage-labour, produced by the near universal nature of the wage-form within advanced capitalism and hence its non-discriminate nature in differentiating class relations, by creating a new class location defined not simply by ownership, but by the economic performance of dual functions within the division of labour. As we shall demonstrate however, Carchedi's model and Carter and Johnson's attempts to operationalise it, do not overcome the limitations of the theories they set out to reject.

Carchedi's theory of the new middle class rests upon the assumption that the function of labour and capital have been collectivised in capitalism, and are no longer attached to distinct, separate classes of workers and capitalists. Following Marx, he suggests that the separation of ownership from control has left the 'functioning' of capital to 'agents' of capital rather than the capitalist. Carter says 'the function of capital was collectivised and with that collectivisation grew the new middle class'. Why is this new class not simply part of the capitalist class, as they perform capitalist functions? It is because, like other wage-labourers, they lack ownership of the means of production. Moreover they perform 'functions' of labour, that is, create surplus value or surplus labour, in addition to coordinating and controlling the labour of others. Hence this *new middle class* performs *both* 'functions' of labour and functions of capital *simultaneously*. As Carter puts it:

> an increasing number of people perform jobs the composition of which is made up of part function of capital, part function of labour. People performing such jobs make up the new middle class. . . . There now exists a relatively large group of employees who share characteristics on both sides of the oppositions. (Carter, 1985, p. 65).

Does that imply that an increasing number of us are 'new middle class'? The boundary criteria for those in new middle class positions is the performance of collective labourer functions and capital functions. Yet, as Carter himself stresses, it is only *'analytically* possible to distinguish the function of capital and function of labour' in practice this may be impossible (Carter, 1985, p. 65, our emphasis). A further difficulty is that the 'new middle class' contains groups of occupations which differ from each other markedly in terms of economic power and authority, yet by Carchedi's functional criteria

they belong to an *undifferentiated* 'new middle class'. Middle management and junior technicians, for example, may both be involved in collective worker and global capitalist functions, although clearly to different degrees, something not measurable or relevant to a blanket concept of a new middle class. In accommodating this criticism, Carter introduces a bifurcation into the new middle class based on the *quantitative* performance of capital or labour functions. Does this mean some are *more* new middle class than others, or simply closer to either of the dominant classes without being workers or capitalists? Either way, the empirical measures for quantifying such polarisations lead him into major problems.

Similarly Johnson, describing the work of accountants, introduces the idea of a polarisation between two factions of the 'new middle class', those who mostly perform functions of capital or functions of labour. 'While part of the membership is incorporated into the labour process and its activities subject to routinisation and fragmentation, a dominant group partakes in the functions of capital' (Johnson, 1980, p. 261). Hence he introduces a bifurcation in the accountancy profession not dissimilar to Braverman's description of 'intermediate' workers being split between those closer to top management and those pushed into the working class through labour market, technological and labour process pressures. Again, while analytically it may be possible to make such a distinction, in practice finding it may be more troublesome. Indeed, for all his rigour in avoiding the taint of Weberianism, the only empirical basis for such a bifurcation is authority, which obviously draws such writers into a Weberian power framework.

To return to Carter, he too ends up emphasising authority relations, and thereby reproduces elements of the dualism of the orthodox Marxism he sets out to criticise. Taking the case of foremen as representative of new middle class workers, he rejects forecasts of their imminent proletarianisation because the 'proletarianisation process is a constant tendency, but only one side of a relationship. As authority is removed from certain personnel it is not simply abolished but reconstituted in the hands of others' (Carter, 1985, p. 68). This definition of proletarianisation is based on power relations and hence owes more to Weber than Marx. Leaving this aside however, Carter says there is a constant re-constituting of the new middle class, as some go into the working class, although this is increasingly hard to define, and others enter the capitalist class. Hence Carter rejects the linearity of the proletarianisation thesis, while not rejecting the

process of proletarianisation. In so doing, he reproduces the confusion around this concept discussed earlier.

Carter further muddies the analytical waters by identifying two separate economic foundations within the new middle class. Following Carchedi, he says this reconstitution of the new middle class can be indicated by the rise and fall of wage levels relative to average wages. The new middle class is paid out of variable capital, as part of its collective worker function, and revenue, as part of its global capital function. If wages fall relative to average wages this could be because of deskilling, fragmentation or other pressures on their labour function; or alternatively, loss of authority or capital functions and hence that portion of the wage made up from revenue.

Here it is relevant to refer to Marx's discussion of the wages of superintendance in Volume III of Capital, where he contends that managers and supervisors are paid out of variable capital 'just like the wages of other workers' and not out of revenue (Marx, 1981, p. 512). Marx strongly rejects the bourgeois claim that 'confuses the profit of enterprise with the wages of management' as this is used to justify exploitation by denying that profit has no equivalent, but results from surplus labour appropriated by the capitalist (Marx, *ibid.*, p. 514). It follows that if the wages of management and supervision are not linked to the profitability of the enterprise, then they are subject to labour market pressures 'just like every other wage'. Historically the transition from internal contracting to foreman systems of labour process control, as Clawson (1980) and Littler (1982) indicate, reflects changes in the class position of supervision from petty capitalists to wage workers. Hence 'just like the wages for skilled labour in general' the wages of supervision are affected by 'the general development that reduces the cost of production or labour-power with special training' (Marx, *ibid.*, p. 513). In a footnote Marx adds that such pressures are the general extension of education and training opportunities which reduce the scarcity of educated workers. So not only does Carter's application of Carchedi have no basis in Marxian economics – rather it resurrects bourgeois apologetics – but, in addition, the empirical problems of identifying the variable capital and revenue elements within the wages of supervision are formidable.

By way of illustration, let us consider again the example of foremen, the focus of Carter's work. Because of the dual functions performed by these workers, Carter suggests that management can devise dual strategies to enhance either their capital or labour

function. For example, foremen can be promoted into management proper and have their collective labour function reduced, or alternatively they can have their authority delegated to workers in autonomous work groups which displace the need for separate supervision. Carter notes that these two strategies 'would change the class position of foremen' (Carter, 1985, p. 118). But is this the case? Are foremen still foremen if they lack supervision? If autonomous work groups start to 'practice a degree of discretion previously the prerogative of the foremen' (p. 118) are the workers in these groups 'reconstituted' as new middle class? Arguably, as Hyman (1983, p. 36) has suggested, there are large numbers of skilled workers in authority positions over unskilled workers, and therefore perform some element, however small, of the functions of capital as defined by Carchedi. Indeed payment systems, such as individual piecework, have powerful commanding and controlling elements which are internalised by the workers under these systems, as Burawoy (1985) demonstrates but does not theorise in these class terms. Similarly French writing on neo-Fordism, Palloix (1976, p. 65) for example, suggests that the introduction of team and group work onto assembly lines is designed to internalise authority into self-discipline and control. Does this then constitute changing the class position of workers who experience these work organisation changes? We don't think so since, in Carter's example, the expansion of worker functions disappears in an absolute sense rather than have their 'class position' in production altered. Even if foremen are moved-up into line management and have their capital function enlarged, they would still be defined as new middle class, because by Carchedian analysis all those performing the dual functions of capital and labour belong to this class. Again there is no obvious change of class position, but rather modification in the *degree* of authority exercised by the two functions.

In sum, Carchedi's analysis fails to specify differences within the new middle class, and has the tendency to equate class identity to functional task performance. Moreover, because of the opacity surrounding capital and labour functions, it appears that the class structure of advanced capitalism is composed of an ever-growing, heterogeneous new middle class. Lines of economic conflict between capital and labour which affect all wage-labour positions are obscured, and the dualism and ambiguity of Weberian proletarianisation theories are not overcome. When operationalised, Carchedi's model uses authority as the basis of differentiation, therefore echoing Weber's, not Marx's, approach to class.

New middle class writing may have been useful in correcting the view that argued that the economic forces within capitalism are only ever moving in a linear direction towards deskilling, fragmentation and routinisation, and hence ignoring counter-movements towards up-skilling, qualifying and professionalisation of wage-labour. However they do not resolve the inherent ambiguities within wage-labour of middle groups by calling them a *new* class, they merely reintroduce the confusion of Weberian analysis under a different name. The problem remains however, over the question of whether we can constitute social classes from the functional performance of tasks in production, without wider social, ideological and political levels of determination. The exclusion of such dimensions in the interests of rigour or theoretical purity, paradoxically only serves to highlight the fruitlessness of such a project which, as the works of Johnson and Carter highlight, encounters major problems when applied to concrete labour processes of the middle groupings.

CONCLUSION: THE UTILITY OF THE NEW MIDDLE CLASS?

The difficulties encountered in developing an analysis of the social significance of what we have called 'middle groupings' are not new. For those who accept the force of Marx's thesis on the organising principles of capitalism as a mode of production, the question of their identity hinges upon an understanding of their involvement in the dynamic relationship between capital and labour. From this perspective, the reproduction of capital necessitates the routine exploitation of labour, a process which demands the harnessing and continuous revolutionising of labour's productive capacity. Within this process the collective labourer becomes an evermore complex totality, with divergent and heterogeneous elements, and not a homogeneous category consisting of essentially unskilled manual operations. Middle groupings within the collective labourer, experience ambiguous conditions and relations with both traditional labour and corporate capital, but these do not provide the basis for a *separate* and *exclusive* class identity. To assume this is to risk setting the dynamics of class relations in concrete, and to lose the sense of contradiction and uncertainty given by the complex network of relations involved within the collective labourer of advanced capitalism.

The literature which worries about the problematic identity of those who occupy an ambiguous, intermediate, middle position,

arises from a perspective in which principles and dynamics of social organisation are reduced to the personification of these principles in individuals and groups. If instead the focus is upon *class as a relationship* rather than the descriptions of functions undertaken by different occupations, it is possible to replace the analysis of the boundaries between places with an exploration of the dynamics through which places are constituted. In which case the challenge is not to identify the boundaries between classes, but rather to analyse how the processes of capitalism are practically organised within the sphere of work.

The rise of technical, administrative, managerial and supervisory groups is a consequence of capitalist development in which the division of labour is continuously revolutionised in the pursuit of capital accumulation. Or as Marx and Engels (1970, p. 38) put it:

> The bourgeoisie cannot exist without constantly revolutionising the instruments of production, and thereby the relations of production, and with them the whole relations of society. . . . Constant revolutionising of production, uninterrupted disturbance of all social conditions, everlasting uncertainty and agitation distinguish the bourgeois epoch from all others.

Within the collective labourer middle groupings are the principle agents of this continuous technical revolution, which affects authority relations, the length of managerial hierarchies, diverse control strategies and the size and number of intermediate workers. Internecine competition between these groups over their value to capital is a hallmark of their struggle within the capitalist division of labour. This in turn promotes a degree of rivalry and atomism that is less marked amongst most unskilled workers, although manual workers with mobile skills may endorse similar anti-collective values. Individualism and competition is, however, checked by the continual expansion of the costs of skilled labour to capital, and the necessity this creates for evaluating their worth and developing methods of cheapening the costs of their specialist labour. In other words, applying coercive pressures on their labour, which in turn stimulates an interest in defensive institutions, such as trade unions, which enable such specialists to organise and defend their interests, collectively and individually, against the less welcome demands and attentions of capital.

Because intermediate workers are wage-labourers, their utility to

capital can never be accepted at face value, but must be subject to the same conflicts, suspicions, doubts and antagonisms attached to all capital-labour relations. The ambiguous class position of such workers lies precisely in their *perceived* utility to capital, something which is always contested in three basic ways. First, as already noted, those occupying such positions seek to justify their own existence by asserting their own social and/or technical indispensibility. Second, manual workers seek to usurp their position by expanding their own sphere of autonomy. Third, the agents and guardians of capital facilitate or concede changes in the work of middle groupings, such as maintaining and developing hierarchies as buffers and barriers within the collective labourer, or alternatively by reducing specialist job structures in favour of using labour whose productivity is more easily quantified. The dynamics of this three-way interaction are what give shape and identity to the middle groupings. By labelling them a *new middle class*, analysis of these class dynamics is set aside in favour of a comparatively sterile, superficial analysis of membership and boundaries. In its place we have recommended that the concept of class is used as a concept to analyse the forces of change within advanced capitalist society, including the processes through which the positions occupied by the so-called intermediate strata are constituted and reproduced.

Notes

1. The Ehrenreichs' description is adopted because it usefully highlights some of the tensions inherent in developing a critical analysis of this ill-defined strata, and is more focused than more generalised descriptions such as the 'new middle class' (for example, Carchedi, 1977). That is it draws attention to groups whose employment is characterised by a significant measure of trust and integration into bureaucratic structures (that is, the 'service class'); those who are employed in state organisations as well as in commerce, banking, marketing etcetera (that is, the 'new petty bourgeoisie' described by Poulantzas, 1975); a small, but not insignificant, section of the 'new working class' – that is the 'professional' element of well qualified white-collar workers who undertake 'scientific' labour discussed by Mallet (1975); and finally, a large part of what Gouldner (1979) has termed the 'new class' of liberal–radical intellectual workers.
2. The debate between Marxists and Weberians frequently rests upon divergent time-frames, rather than theoretical or political differences.

Braverman, for example, has been particularly committed to a broad historical perspective on the consequences of occupational change, while his critics have tended to use the narrow vehicle of case-studies to insist that work degradation of white-collar workers cannot be historically demonstrated for their particular study group. In a vigorous defence of Braverman, Armstrong (1988) has highlighted the confusions within this methodological incompatibility.

References

Abercrombie, N. and J. Urry (1983) *Capital, Labour and the Middle Classes* (London: Allen & Unwin).

Armstrong, P. (1988) 'Labour and Monopoly Capital', in R. Hyman and W. Streeck (eds), *New Technology and Industrial Relations* (Oxford: Blackwell).

Barbalet, J. M. (1986) 'Disappearance of Class Theory and the Limitations of Status: the Problem of the New Middle Class', *Sociology*, vol. 20, no. 4: pp. 557–75.

Braverman, H. (1974) *Labor and Monopoly Capital* (New York: Monthly Review Press).

Burawoy, M. (1985) *The Politics of Production* (London: Verso).

Carchedi, G. (1977) *On the Economic Identification of Social Classes* (London: Routledge & Kegan Paul).

Carter, R. (1985) *Capitalism, Class Conflict and the New Middle Class* (London: Routledge & Kegan Paul).

Clawson, D. (1980) *Bureaucracy and the Labour Pracess: The Transformation of US Industry 1860–1920* (New York: Monthly Review Press).

Crompton, R. and Gubbay, J. (1977) *Economy and Class Structure* (London: Macmillan).

Crompton, R. and G. Jones (1984) *White-Collar Proletariat: Deskilling and Gender in Clerical Work* (London: Macmillan).

Draper, H. (1978) *Karl Marx's Theory of Revolution, Volume 2: The Politics of Social Classes* (New York: Monthly Review Press).

Duke, V. and S. Edgell, (1987) 'The Operationalisation of Class in British Sociology: Theoretical and Empirical Considerations', *British Journal of Sociology*, vol. XXVIII, no. 4: pp. 445–63.

Ehrenreich, B. and Ehrenreich, J. (1979) 'The Professional–Managerial Class', in P. Walker (ed.), *Between Labour and Capital* (Brighton: Harvester Press).

Garnsey, E. (1975) 'Occupational Structure in Industrial Societies; Some Comments on the Convergence Thesis in the Light of the Soviet Experience', *Sociology*, vol. 9, no. 3: pp. 438–58.

Giddens, A. (1973) *The Class Structure of Advanced Societies* (London: Hutchinson).

Gouldner, A. (1979) *The Future of Intellectuals and the Rise of the New Class* (New York: Seabury).

Hyman, R. (1983) 'White Collar Workers and Theories of Class', in R. Hyman and R. Price (eds), *The New Working Class? White-Collar Workers and their Organizations* (London: Macmillan).

Johnson, T. (1980) 'Work and Power' in G. Esland and G. Salaman (eds) *The Politics of Work and Occupations* (Milton Keynes: Open University Press).

Klingender, F. D. (1938) *The Condition of Clerical Labour in Great Britain* (London: Martin Lawrence).

Littler, C. R. (1982) *The Development of the Labour Process in Capitalist Societies* (London: Heinemann).

Lockwood, D. (1958) *The Blackcoated Worker* (London: Allen & Unwin).

Mallet, S. (1975) *The New Working Class* (Nottingham: Spokesman).

Marshall, G. (1988) 'Classes in Britain: Marxist and Official', *European Sociological Review*, vo. 4, no. 2: pp. 141–54.

Marshall, G. and D. Rose (1988) 'Proletarianisation in the British Class Structure', *British Journal of Sociology*, vol. XXXIX, no. 4: pp. 498–518.

Marshall, G., D. Rose, H. Newby and C. Vogler (1988) *Social Class in Modern Britain* (London: Hutchinson).

Martin, R. (1988) 'Technological Change and Manual Work' in D. Gallie (ed), *Employment in Britain* (Oxford: Basil Blackwell).

Marx, K. (1961) *Capital, Volume III* (London: Lawrence & Wishart).

Marx, K. (1969) *Theories of Surplus Value, Volume 2* (London: Lawrence & Wishart).

Marx, K. (1976) *Capital, Volume I* (Harmondsworth: Penguin in association with *New Left Review*).

Marx, K. (1981) *Capital, Volume III* (Harmondswroth: Penguin in assocation with *New Left Review*).

Marx, K. and Engels, F. (1970) 'The Communist Manifesto' in *Marx and Engels: Selected Works* (London: Lawrence & Wishart).

McLennan, G., Held, D. and Hall, S. (1984) *State and Society in Contemporary Britain* (Cambridge: Polity).

Meiksins, P. (1985) 'Beyond the Boundary Question', *New Left Review*, no. 157, May/June: pp. 101–20.

Nicholaus, M. (1967) 'Proletariat and Middle Class in Marx: Hegelian Choreography and the Capitalist Dialectic', *Studies on the Left*, 7: pp. 22–49.

Nichols, T. (1979) 'Social Class: Official, Sociological and Marxist', in J. Irvine, I. Miles and J. Evans (eds), *Demystifying Social Statistics* (London: Pluto Press).

Palloix, C. (1976) 'The Labour Process: From Fordism to neo-Fordism', in Conference of Socialist Economists (eds), *The Labour Process and Class Strategies* (London, Stage 1): pp. 46–67.

Poulantzas, N. (1975) *Classes in Contemporary Capitalism* (London: New Left Books).

Przeworski, A. (1977) 'Proletariat into a Class: The Process of Class Formation from Karl Kautsky's *The Class Struggle* to Recent Controversies', in *Politics and Society*, vol. 7, no. : pp. 343–401.

Rattansi, A. (1985) 'End of an Orthodoxy? The Critique of Sociology's View of Marx on Class', *Sociological Review*, vol. 36, no. 1: pp. 641–69.

Wright, E. O. and B. Martin (1987) 'The Transformation of the American Class Structure, 1960–1980', *American Journal of Sociology*, vol. 93, no. 1: pp. 1–29.

Wuthnow, R. and Shrum, W. (1983) 'Knowledge Workers and the "–New Class"', *Work and Occupations*, vol. 10, no. 4: pp. 471–87.

3 Municipal Microchips: The Computerised Labour Process in the Public Service Sector

Harvie Ramsay, Chris Baldry, Anne Connolly and Cliff Lockyer

The primary aim of this paper is to analyse the introduction of information technology into the labour process and work experience of white-collar staff in local government. To this end we shall draw on research carried out in a large Scottish local authority, with supporting reference to other research on the municipal sector. In pursuit of this objective, we have found it useful to reflect on both the extent and limitations of the insight provided for our analysis by existing work on information technology in the labour process tradition, and by accounts of white-collar class and gender structuration. Our deliberations suggest, however, the existing class theories in particular seem markedly inadequate in deciphering the processes under examination, and that a much greater contribution is gained from a consideration of the role of specific historical and current contingencies in shaping management and labour organisation strategy and response.

The interaction between information technology and the organisation and experience of work has generally been interpreted in one of two ways. The technological determinist approach, setting out to describe 'impacts' and 'effects' of technological change, has rightly been criticised as over-simplistic, mechanically unidirectional, and as reifying technology into a force in its own right. The main alternative in recent years has emerged within the 'labour process' perspective, but has tended to substitute an almost equally simplistic 'managerial determinism', in which technology is consciously designed and applied by management in pursuit of a coherent strategy of deskilling and enhanced management control.

However, an examination of the emerging research work on new

35

technology shows that when specific examples are considered, such variables as the nature of the product market, the immediate context of introduction, the nature of effectiveness of union organisation, and the pattern of power relations within the workforce and between employees and management at workplace level, can emerge as pivotal. As a result a more fluid and flexible analytical approach is required, which attends to these sorts of variables empirically, and does not presume them to be merely dependent on, or changing in reflex to, technology or management strategy. Our approach in this paper is therefore to describe the salient features of the introduction of information technology in a local authority, and to relate our understanding of the processes involved to the contextual factors discussed in the following sections.

WHITE-COLLAR WORKERS IN CLASS ANALYSIS

As the contours of capitalism have repeatedly shifted and altered over the years, social analysis has witnessed periodic bursts of extensive debate over the nature of social class and the construction and application of classificatory systems. Recent work in this area has begun to pay particular attention to the classification of the 'middle groups' as a litmus test of differing approaches to class, and in consequence a number of contributions have focused on white-collar workers in far more detail than afforded by most previous work (Armstrong et al., 1986).

The approach to classification advocated by the structuralist Marxists, such as Carchedi and Poulantzas who made the pace in the 1970s, emphasised the largely abstracted analysis of place or function stressing whether the labour carried out by a given category is productive or unproductive,whether any supervision of other labour is carried out, the mental or manual character of the work, as well as the extent of any legal or real ownership of the means of production.

Wright, like Carchedi, emphasised relationship to the means of production, and made his classification according to an assessment of the location of categories capital, and over labour power.

When these differing structuralist approaches have been applied to the position of white-collar workers, their conclusions have varied dramatically. For Poulantzas, all non-manual workers are objectively members of the 'new petty bourgeoisie', even where their work is deskilled and their income low, due to their unproductive nature. For

Carchedi, the judgement is less final, since a duality is recognised for the 'new middle class' entailing that they may be both exploiters and oppressed, and the balance of functions performed (respectively, capital and labour) may change in a way entailing proletarianisation. For Wright, the determinate analysis becomes even more qualified as the category of 'petty bourgeoisie' is recreated, as in addition are 'contradictory class locations' including managers and supervisors (between capitalist and working class) and 'semi-autonomous employees', supposedly including groups such as technicians between the working class and petty bourgeoisie. His subsequent affiliation to a more market-based definition produces an even more bewildering list of stratified groups, hard to distinguish in principle from the layering constructed by census officials.

This confusion suggests that the structuralist approach on its own therefore becomes at best a filing system for elitist academics, or at worst a stigmatisation and exclusion of many from political movements on grounds of their class classification.

Critics of this entire approach argue that class is not essentially merely an objective or abstract category, and that to have any political or even sociological meaning, any consideration of a group needs to investigate aspects of their condition, and also of their identity and action. Examination of condition may distinguish between 'market' and 'work' situations (after Lockwood's (1958) classic study). The former includes the structure and conditions of rewards and place in the labour market. The latter stresses work content, organisation and control, along with relations with other groups in the workplace. In each case, although some of the questions explored overlap with those considered by the structural or abstracted approach, the emphasis is on empirical research to bring out the actual state of affairs rather than prejudging or over-generalising from predefined categories.

An important aspect of this research also emphasises employees' experience of their objective conditions and relations. From this follows the need to examine the identity and actions of particular groups, and the relationship of this to their condition. In many aspects, it is this apprehension and interpretation of behaviour which forms the ultimate point of such research, since it is the texture and direction of class struggle which acts upon and changes the material world. The logic of the emphasis on investigation of condition, attitudes and behaviour is that these cannot be deduced a priori from abstracted analysis.

However the attempts by these writers to classify various groups of white-collar workers on the basis of their condition, experience and behaviour, have produced results which are as equally complex, varied and contradictory. Some writers, taking departure from at least the initial classification of the structural theorists, begin by analysing the status of non-manual groups within a 'new middle class'. Others seek to develop the related notion of a distinct 'service class' (Goldthorpe, 1982, Gould, 1980; Abercrombie and Urry, 1983), in some cases in deliberate opposition to any Marxist explanation invoking a convergence of manual and routine non-manual work. Finally, taking their inspiration from the optimism of Mallet (1975), still other writers set out to chart the contours and limits of the 'new working class' (cf. Hyman and Price, 1983).

More recent contributions have taken the view that to abandon structural analysis because of irritation with some of the mechanical classifications that have followed from its abstracted application is to throw the baby out with the bathwater. It remains useful to begin with the Marxist concept of surplus value production, and the attendant conflict between capital and labour, they argue, since these objective structural factors define certain crucial limits and constraints on the experience and actions of particular groups. The particular configuration and perception of these can only be deciphered through a concrete examination of the historical formation of a given set of 'employees' circumstances, and of the detailed manifestation of constraints as conditions of their interpretations and responses.

Thus where Goldthorpe (1982) emphasises the key role of 'trust' between employer and service class employee, maintaining their distance from manual workers, Crompton and Jones counter that this relies on the presumption of a 'spurious homogeneity' of the category. In fact they suggest the service class includes a continuum from deskilled routine non-manual workers, who are effectively proletarianised, to senior routine non-manual workers, who in effect perform the functions of capital with little qualification. Between the two poles Crompton and Jones re-establish the notion of 'structurally ambiguous' class locations, covering much of the service class, whose responses will be shaped by a series of contingencies and alternative labour and management strategies in the labour market and labour process. In the process, it should be added, it is our judgement that the ground for referring to a service class quo *class* at all are dismantled.

Smith (1987) has argued in similar vein to Crompton and Jones that

the structural factors affecting the role of technicians are not translated into class position in some 'linear determination'. Rather they are mediated, *inter alia*, by the development of collective organisation and the strategies adopted, and by the precise 'form of association' with manual labour. We think this approach – seeking to identify and employ structural relations of production, but as constraints and tendencies within a less deterministic and more textured analysis, derived from careful empirical examination of condition and identity – is the most fruitful available. The problems of applying it remain large however, and in some respects are particularly well illustrated by an examination of local government staff, to which we now turn.

CLASS ANALYSIS AND LABOUR PROCESS: THE DEBATE ON STATE EMPLOYEES

The analysis of employees of the local state sits uneasily in all the approaches considered thus far, as difficult ambiguities arise around all of the key criteria typically employed: the level and determination of rewards; the nature of the work; the functional or experiential relation of those concerned to the exercise of power on behalf of 'capital'; the 'productive' or 'unproductive' status of their labour; and the identity, attitudes and organisation of such employees themselves.

In particular, three dichotomies commonly implicit in classificatory discussions appear to blur and stumble across one another here: the private sector–public sector distinction; that between productive and service work; and that between manual and white-collar employees. Moreover any pursuit of these issues dauntingly forces the invocation of still more arenas of complex debate, including those on the sexual division of labour and on the nature of the state under capitalism.

Our own research, it should be said at the start, was not designed to resolve such problems of analysis, since it was designed with the far less ambitious aim of charting the effects of the introduction of new technology on work organisation and experience – that is, on a fairly restricted element of employee condition in the terms of the earlier discussion. In the course of that research, nonetheless, we gathered other material which at least allows us to pose certain questions and hopefully cast a little further light on some of the issues raised above, if not to provide any definitive answers. At the same time, we hope

thereby to set the specific processes on technological change in their appropriate wider context.

White-collar workers in the public sector form a major segment of the working population, and one which is notable by its apparent differences from most other white-collar groups. Unionisation is very high for example, where it remains meagre for private sector white-collar employees. Indeed as NALGO, the British local government clerical union, is the largest white-collar union in the world (Blyton and Ursell, 1982), we are hardly dealing with a quirkish fragment of the labour force or labour movement. Nor is it necessarily a conservative sector, as the periodic success of the left in the civil service unions examplifies.

For the particular groups with which we are concerned, Administrative, Professional, Technical & Clerical staff (APT & C), it seems evident that a service is being provided rather than 'production' being undertaken, though any close interrogation of the notion of what activities are required to produce value can question the validity of this distinction.

Leaving this particularly tedious debate to one side, let us ride with the structuralist argument. Since APT & C staff in local government do not produce surplus, they live off those who do, paid out of monies raised through taxation, and so may be seen as tied to 'petty bourgeois' interests. Yet this could also be said of private sector shipyard workers building Trident submarines, who are similarly not rewarded according to putative exchange value produced but from tax revenues. These issues are partly acknowledged by Carchedi in a specific discussion of state employees, whom he divides between capitalist and non-capitalist activities, the latter distinguished, he argues, by producing use-values with an end goal of service provision itself rather than accumulation.

This lures us on to look instead at the distinction between public and private sector *per se*. It might be possible to argue that by being detached from working for private capital, and so from being directly pumped for surplus value, public sector employees are in some ways protected from the rigours of capitalism. Their levels of pay become detached from the market for their services, and are determined through analogous mechanism such as comparability or 'equivalence'. Quite whether the implications of this are that they are privileged, as the non-productive criterion implies, or potentially more progressive and collectivist, as certain left-reformist views of

the State as a nexus of 'prefigurative socialist forms' might imply (see Ramsay and Haworth, 1984 for discussion) is not immediately clear from this. But for such questions to be properly considered, another must be addressed. This involves the presuppositions concerning the nature of the state as an employer. Again within Marxism one encounters opposed views; at one extreme, in economistic analyses which view all aspects of the system as superstructures of a 'base' defined by class property relations, the state is the 'executive committee of the bourgeoisie', performing tasks for capital and functionally locked into the heart of capitalism. If this view is accepted, working for the state (and the argument logically extends to the local state) is no different to working in the private sector, and the same analytical criteria therefore apply. Thus Poulantzas asserts that all administrative workers in private and public bureaucracies may be classified as a proletarian-polarising fraction of the new petty bourgeoisie; 'it is immaterial', he avers, whether they work in private or state organisations.

At the other extreme, the state is represented as 'relatively autonomous', and as a prefiguration of collectivised and socialised relations within capitalism, a contradiction of its core, which in key respects may be an oasis of non-capitalist relations. In some respects this is Carchedi's eventual line. Only if some variant of this latter view is adopted are the other questions about the likely responses and affiliations of any group of state employees as such worth asking.

Our own view is that these issues are indeterminate to an important degree, and can only be ascertained through a concrete analysis of the actual relations and experience prevalent in a given part of the public sector. In other words, the questions cannot be answered *a priori* any more than those about class already discussed. It would appear that when the chips are down (so to speak, in more sense than one for our discussion), even those advocating function and place as the basis of analysis are forced to shift ground. In the end class analysis is driven back to a detailed knowledge of the nature and direction of change in the labour process, as one key aspect of condition at least, and given the insolubility of such 'structural' questions as the particular nature of work for the state on an *a priori* basis, even the constraints or conditions of action which these functional questions impose have to a large extent to be ascertained empirically.

MANAGEMENT AND ORGANISED LABOUR IN THE LOCAL STATE

It is true that even a cursory examination of the public sector suggests that in some respects it is a relative haven of labourist practices – namely the scope for union activity noted already – but that it is not invulnerable to efforts to transform the face it presents to employees. Apart from the grotesque exaggerations of private sector 'macho management' epitomised by Sir Michael Edwardes and Sir Ian MacGregor, a far more broad-fronted effort to introduce market-equivalent criteria into traditional public sector work has been seen in the form of privatisation and the emphasis on payments by results and 'managerialism', even into enclaves such as the Health Service and local authority work.

As in the NHS, Prices & Incomes Board reports in the 1960s proved important in setting managerialist processes in motion, by criticising poor management expertise and lack of adequate cost consciousness among local government officers (Somerton, 1977). Following the Bains Report (1972), principal officers such as the Town Clerk became Chief Executives 'in the accepted business sense; the most senior manager, to whom all other managers were subordinate and over whose work he had the authority of direction and co-ordination' (Fowler, 1975, p. 55). The intensification of this process since 1979 has been propelled by the mechanism of cash limits and rate-capping, and reinforced by direct instruction where this inducement was resisted. In consequence specific government policies towards local government, and the exigencies of their implementation, play a major role in the actual shaping of the local government labour process in a way that abstracted analyses are entirely unable to grasp.

Moreover the typical characterisation of local government workers as 'town hall bureaucrats' and their subordinates administering the rates, obscures a remarkably complex and disparate collection of services and associated labour processes. APT & C staffs can cover as many as 60 distinct job groups, each group containing several different occupations. It is impossible to speak of local government staff in the same way as one does of other specific categories such as 'engineers', 'technicians' or 'teachers'; indeed, all of these occupations can be found within local government.

This occupational heterogeneity is largely a result of the changing political wisdom concerning which services should be seen as appropriate for local public provision over the last 150 years. During that

time, local government has retained traditional areas such as housing, schools and highways, has gained expanding areas such as social work, and has lost such tasks as the provision of gas supplies. In short it has no innate or functional logic – a lesson which Conservative policies questioning traditional British assumptions concerning public provision should have already made clear.

Despite this heterogeneity, there are at least two major factors for local authority white collar staff which have provided some sense of unified identity, and have distinguished their status and work situations from those of other occupational groups. One of these, and so by no means to be treated merely as a dependent variable (that is, as an outcome of class position), is the trade union, NALGO. The other is the ethos of public service.

The Union

The National and Local Government Officers' Association organises all APT & C staff, 'from office junior to Chief Executive'. Indeed its origins lie in the formation of a professional association for senior local government officers whose primary aim was to secure adequate pensions.

Blackburn's indices of 'unionateness' have been criticised for their inappropriateness for white collar unions, taking the traditional manual union as the archetype of union consciousness (Crompton and Gubbay, 1977). Yet intriguingly NALGO's development fits remarkably well with the notion of a cumulative acquisition of 'unionate' characteristics. From its initial stance, represented by the much-quoted statement of General Secretary Hill in 1910 that 'Anything savouring of trade unionism is nausea to the local government officer and his Association', NALGO moved through the stages of certification in the 1920s, the development of collective bargaining machinery, a hotly-debated affiliation to the TUC in 1964 (Volker, 1966), to taking industrial action for the first time in 1970 (Newman, 1982, p. 423). At the time of writing this has been extended, partly as a reaction in combination with changing national government policy towards local government services, to a further controversial debate about the establishment of a political fund.

The early goals of NALGO between the wars were to fight to secure national grades of pay and conditions. This was only achieved, however, with the setting up of Whitley-type structures by a wartime government anxious to create flexibility in transferring staff between

different parts of the country. The choice of national level Whitleyism to fix wages and conditions secured a high level of union membership, to satisfy Whitley encouragement of adequate representation for all groups, and in the process secured the dominance of NALGO, as the most representative organisation, against the encroachments of new public sector and other white collar unions. At the same time the Whitley emphasis on consensus minimised confrontation for the post-war period, and more importantly separated negotiation from local level activities. The role of the union at local level was mainly restricted to 'consultation', which in turn may be seen as a marginal prop for the management definition of 'what was best for the service' (Winchester, 1983). This solution did have the advantage for those most involved that it avoided a role clash for those staff wearing both management and union hats. Reorganisation, 'managerial' and financial stringencies have put increasing pressure on this configuration however.

The post-war expansion of local government services, and the potential threat from APEX, ASTMS and other white collar unions, prompted NALGO to recruit downwards to include clerical and secretarial staff. One justification for this lay in the view that local government service had its own special identity and requirements, so that organisations with their power-base elsewhere in the public sector would be inappropriate bargaining agencies. This vertical extension of recruitment changed the class composition of the union markedly, if we regard the service as internally stratified. In response there have been occasional pressures for secession by particular professional groupings, but the fragmentation which an abstracted analysis might predict has not in fact occurred.

The reason for this seems to lie chiefly in the way the union operates to accommodate greatly increased heterogeneity. Our own observations confirm those of other studies of local government unionism (Terry, 1982; Kessler, 1986; Nicholson et al., 1981) that the higher local government grades are still disproportionately represented among union officers and shop stewards, and that this seemed to be a matter of conscious choice by lower grades. The possession of managerial skills, equal status with many employer-side negotiators, and perhaps access to insider information, are seen as important assets at the bargaining table.

At the same time this left the problem, particularly at workplace level, of lower grades often being represented by their own supervisors. The distinction between managers and managed has traditionally

been blurred, easing role-conflict by emphasising the administrative rather than managerial responsibility of senior grades. This was aided by the expectation of career progression, lending substance to the notion still enshrined in the union title, of 'local government *officers*'. Managerial changes have begun to pressurise this identity, into which must also be introduced the role of gender divisions (see below and Crompton and Jones, 1984), but it is sustained at the same time by the unifying sense of working in public service.

The Service Ethos

It remains reasonable to characterise local government white-collar work as non-commercial and largely insulated from market defini-tions of success, notwithstanding the changes in process already noted. This is combined with a sense of providing essential, and in many cases caring services for the general public. The ethos of the 'public servant' has been remarked by several observers (Blyton and Ursell 1982; Winchester 1983) among all grades of local government staff. The immediate visibility of the effects of local authority work enhances this perception further by comparison with, for example, many civil servants, as does the fact that most local authority staff are also consumers of their employing authority's services.

This service ethos was given more overt expression still by NALGO. In its early days, the principle of 'harmonistic collectivism' (Price, 1980, p. 161), with its weak sense of employer-employee conflict and strong vein of individualistic career advancement, was cemented with this ideology of public service. Indeed the union historian, Spoor (1967), goes so far as to suggest that NAGLO was the originator of the whole concept of public service through its early campaigns against the nepotism and jobbery which riddled the early town and country councils.[1] One of the union's early academic advisors de-scribed this as:

A special kind of trade unionism, possessing a sense of public service, of noblesse oblige towards the community which gives it a distinguishing quality of its own (quoted in Spoor, 1967, p. 576).

Despite the evident sharpening of the sense of divergence of interest between employer and employee in local government over the past two decades, the public service ethos has survived as a continuous thread running through the way local government staff and their union define their problems and legitimate their responses. Moreover there is

still evidence that management also accepts this vocabulary of objectives, even though current contingencies place this prioritisation under tightening siege. Thus a commitment to the extension of service quality emerged in our own studies (in both Scotland and Australia)[2] as the claimed priority of management in local government. This phenomenon is augmented by a recognised responsibility for meeting certain staff obligations which marked them out from private sector employers, as reported in Crompton and Jones' study across public and private sector organisations.[3] It might be expected that this approach would be reinforced where the official ultimate decision-makers are an elected council comprising a Labour majority, although we found this to be seen by management as at most a background factor, encouraging them not to act too precipitously or in an over-draconian manner, since the level of interference with their expert management role was otherwise very limited.

While this shared ethos affords a degree of mutual reinforcement and alliance between even top management and unions in local government, both our study in Strathclyde and the linked study in Brisbane, Australia confirmed that the strongest commitment is on the union side, while management seem increasingly to pay only lip service to the improvement of service quality as first priority. This has one interesting paradox, in that it enables the union to occupy the higher moral ground in terms of an officially shared ideology between themselves and their employers, and that in support of a defence of jobs where their more immediate membership interests also lie.

The Gender Question

The focus thus far in the analysis of 'class', trade unionism and the service ethos has been presented in terms which allow only for homogeneity. This neglects a further dimension which recent studies have shown may have major independent relevance to the trajectory of technical change. In particular most of the conventional approaches to class analysis have unfortunately conformed to Dex's observations 'Ignoring women was a fairly standard sociological technique ...' (Dex, 1985, p. 143).

In our assessment it has been convincingly demonstrated that the gender composition and roles of a workplace are crucially important contingent factors in the social structuring and organisation of the labour process in that workplace. Definitions of skill, exercise of

power, capacity for union involvement (particularly in the context of domestic restrictions on time), attachment to work, workplace involvement (for example via the distribution of part-time employment particularly to female staff; and through chances of promotion) and numerous other interrelated and mutually reinforcing dimensions, have been catalogued in some detail in recent years. It is therefore necessary to consider the effects of gender on the aspects of local government employment relations already considered, and directly or indirectly upon the impact and experience of technological change at the present time.

Despite much valuable help from agencies collecting data on employment in local government in both Scotland and England and Wales, we were unable to locate any detailed figures on the gender breakdown of the various occupations within APT & C staff. Thus although Crompton and Jones report a far greater concern by 'Cohall' management than their counterparts in the private sector to apply equitable rules to the promotion of women, there are no collations of information enabling local authorities to monitor their progress (or lack of it) in this respect. Since Crompton and Jones also report that it is the factors blocking women from fulfilling the criteria for promotion rather than direct prejudice which forms the main factor sustaining inequality, this lack of data may be a comfort to equality of opportunity employers in the municipal sector.

The latest aggregate (Manpower Watch) figures at the time of writing provide some idea of the potential importance of gender, however, since it can be calculated from them that in Scotland 55 per cent of non manual local government staff are female.[4] Part-time employment is still not a prominent feature of most non-manual work in local government, but while just 10 per cent of all employees in this category are classified thus, this conceals a variation from 1.8 per cent of male staff to 16.4 per cent of female staff.[5]

The impact of gender divisions on technological change has been chartered by several writers in recent work. Responding in part to the generalisations concerning 'deskilling' in Braverman's thesis, the way in which skill is defined has been explored. It has been shown that there are major social inputs to such definition, rather than simply the description of objective dexterity, training or whatever, and that many jobs carried out by women and whether they are seen as 'skilled' are classified not by any 'objective' evaluation of the task but by the very fact that women carry them out (Phillips and Taylor, 1980; Coyle, 1982; Armstrong, 1982; Cavendish, 1982).

This naturally creates a vicious circle – women's jobs are defined by both management and (male-dominated) unions as typically low in skill and thus rewards, and the definition of women as best suited to semi-skilled tasks is reinforced. This labelling takes on an added dimension when work roles are being restructured and jobs reallocated and shaped in the course of restructuring and technical change (Cockburn, 1983, 1985, 1986).

For white-collar employees, some confirmation of the way in which male-dominated occupations (and male individuals within given occupations) are able to influence the implementation of new technology, and the consequent allocations and definitions of the work tasks, is provided by Crompton and Jones (1984). They take the view, also adopted here, that computerisation of office tasks is not inherently deskilling in the nature of the technology itself, but that the new labour process and the stratification of tasks associated with it is a matter of some degree of choice by management, and therefore of management's value-laden perception of the options and their relative desirability. It may thus also be subject to negotiation by those with the capacity to exert influence on management's decisions. In practice they report finding that these influences had resulted in increased central control, objective deskilling of most jobs in the dominant routine clerical category, and an increased stratification of employees which further sharpened the gender inequalities in the labour process. Their findings do not report any marked differences, in this respect between the two private sector organisations and the local government establishment in which their research was conducted.

INFORMATION TECHNOLOGY WITHIN LOCAL AUTHORITIES

It has been evident over the last decade that local government has come under increasing financial pressure from central government, and that the bottleneck of 'efficiency' (as commercially-defined) in its operation is the labour-intensive office-based nature of much of local government employment. Both a market-based and a labour process approach would lead us to suspect therefore that local authority management would welcome information technology (IT) in order to make labour cost savings and to tighten the processes of managerial control in the administration of local government.

However, following the now familiar distinction between process and product innovation, Quintas (1986) points out that IT in local government can be used for either:

- Rationalisation and increased labour productivity, that is, cutting staff and increasing managerial control, *or*
- The enhancement of the service. The choice will depend he suggests, on a combination of management strategy, economic factors and political choice.

For in addition to our previously noted characteristics, local government is unique in that ultimate decisions on policy rest not with the 'management' but with a political body – the Council. In industrial relations terms this provides an extra dimension, a means of exacerbating or abating the power relationship between union and management in the workplace according to the political complexion of the council.

There is therefore a possibility that such characteristics as a political context and an internal service ethos may mediate between the technology and the organisation and militate against the over adoption of policies of rationalisation. Firstly, due to the political sensitivity associated with direct redundancy, the choice of either cutting costs or improving services will in many cases depend on the political complexion of the council. As Barras and Swann (1985) noted in their survey of different types of local authority, Labour councils were more likely to bear in mind the idea that their local policies of job creation should not be contradicted by reduction in local government employment, while Conservative-dominated councils were more ready to resist union demands for job security and go for immediate cost-reductions.

Secondly the recession has progressively increased the demands made of local government services such as social work, careers, and housing and this has contributed to the maintenance and even expansion of employment levels in local government administrative, professional, technical and clerical (APT & C or white-collar) staff. Computerisation may seem to offer a solution to the fundamental problem of coping with these increasing demands with a restricted budget, and here the local government ethos of being essentially a public service can serve to direct the application of computer technology. When the LAMSAC survey of local government

chief officers in 1981 (LAMSAC, 1981) asked the respondents to rank potential major benefits from the expansion of microcomputing 88 per cent selected 'improvement of services' and on 12 per cent 'reduction of costs'.

However we must distinguish here between the administration processes that go to produce the service, and the actual end-user service the public get. A review of public sector IT usage in 1984 found that most IT applications in local and central government were to be found in the internal management function rather than in changing the service provided to the public (Zmroczek et al., 1984).

CALEDONIA REGIONAL COUNCIL: THE RESEARCH PROJECT

'Caledonia Regional Council' is a large Scottish local authority created by the reorganisation of local government in Scotland in 1974. It has been Labour-controlled throughout its existence. Unionisation in the Region was extremely high, with NALGO enjoying what amounts to a closed shop for APT & C staff. At the start of our study, employee costs (wages, salaries and deductions) accounted for 53 per cent of the Region's current expenditure; of these employee costs, 24 per cent represented the employment costs of APT & C staff (for instance white-collar, excluding teachers).

Scottish Regional Councils are 'first-tier' authorities similar to the now defunct English metropolitan counties, and so provide a range of municipal services. APT & C employees in Caledonia Region are found particularly in such areas as Social Work (roughly one third of all APT & C staff) and Education (25 per cent), with significant numbers in Police and Fire administration and in the Roads Department. In addition several Regions, including Caledonia, cover large geographical areas which include both urban centres with a high population density and sparsely populated rural and island communities. Employment locations are thus very diverse, with large concentrations of staff at sub-regional offices (which correspond to the old county councils that preceded reorganisation) and a large number of small, sometimes even individually-staffed offices.

The Bains Committee Report of 1972 led Scottish local government down the path pursued south of the border, entailing the

establishment of a new corporate management structure under a Chief Executive and a management team of departmental Chief Officers. An important role was given to central support departments such as Manpower Services, Management Services and Finance. To this was added a Computer Services Department with the establishment of the first mainframe processing of payrolls, rents and rates, and the demand for large-scale calculation and standardisation brought about by the reorganisation itself.

In January 1983, a New Technology Agreement was signed between the Region and the local branch of NALGO. We then commenced a two-year survey of the process of technical change in the authority, both to monitor the working of the NTA and to assess the implications on the work, employment and bargaining situations of APT & C staff. The main source of data was a postal questionnaire sent out to NALGO workplace representatives three times over the lifespan of the project, supported by interviews with staff and management in selected locations.

We have already indicated that local government employment is heterogeneous and so, as Quintas (1986) points out, generalisations across the range of multifunctional departments within one authority (let alone across different authorities varying in size, political complexion and industrial relations structure) are problematical. While both Roads and Social Work provide a public service in Caledonia Region, therefore, there are obviously likely to be major differences in work content and organisation which could also be highly significant for the nature and consequences of IT introduction, as might be the case with different employment locations even within the same department.[6] Rather than this being a problem, it provides an excellent opportunity to study variations in the processes and outcomes with which we are concerned and to begin to examine the part played by the social factors addressed earlier. Previous studies of IT in white-collar locations have commonly had the shortfall that they have given little indication of whether the office investigated was typical of the organisation as a whole, or whether the effects in that location were encountered elsewhere, so tending to over-generalise and simplify the processes involved. To extend our own analysis of differences in the results of introducing IT, for each location within a department we asked whether the work of the majority of members was professional, technical, administrative or clerical, allowing us the possibility of a two-dimensional variation in the experience of computerisation, by function and by type of work, and enabling us to

consider some aspects of the effects of internal stratification on outcomes both across and within departments.

After our first survey, we provisionally classified the different Departments of the authority into three major groupings:

- 'Central Support' departments (such as Finance, Manpower Services, Chief Executive's Office).
- 'Social' departments providing face-to-face services to the public (such as Social Work, Education and Careers).
- 'Technical' (such as Roads, Architects, Surveyors).

Given the 'innovation trajectory' in local government discussed later, it could be predicted that of the three categories, the second – 'social' departments – would have had the least prior experience of IT. 'Central support' departments like Finance and 'technical' departments such as Roads, in contrast, had long experience of the use of mainframes for batch processing of complex data and calculations.

Barras and Swann suggest an additional distinguishing feature marking out from others the departments we have labelled 'technical' in that they rely for much of their findings on capital expenditure, while the preponderance of funds for areas like Social Work and Education are labour costs funded from revenue expenditure. As the main initial effect of central government restrictions has been virtually to freeze the level of capital spending, it is suggested that it is the technical departments which have come under particular pressure to improve their cost-effectiveness through productivity improvement. In many cases this has accelerated computerisation and directed its use.

In practice, the results from the survey showed the clearest differences to be between those work locations which were 'technical–professional' and those which were 'non-technical' (mainly clerical and administrative workers in central and social departments), as defined by the combination of departmental function and self-classification. This dichotomy was so marked that it formed the major focus of our analysis.

Types of Equipment

The trajectory of technological development in Caledonia Region follows the path described by both Quintas and Barras and Swann. Thus the first stage involved the use of a mainframe as described

earlier. At the time of our study, the Region had two mainframes, 70 per cent of the capacity of which was taken up solely by the Roads Department. The second stage saw the introduction of micro and mini stand-alone computers, to be followed in the third by office automation (such as word processors and electronic mailing). Caledonia's NTA was signed roughly at the start of stage two, with the result that some departments were already quite used to the idea of computerisation, though largely through use of the services of Computer Services on a remote batch-processing basis. Other departments and locations were almost completely untouched by any form of computerised technology.

In the three years subsequent to its signing, the NTA seems to have facilitated three chief types of development:

- It hastened the rate of expansion and use of mainframe-related equipment and the facilities offered to particular departments by Computer Services with a move from batch processing to more on-line terminals.
- It prompted a growth in the use of mini and micro computers, especially in departments previously untouched by computerisation.
- It formally allowed an Office Automation Pilot Project to be established in the Chief Executive's Department.

The few studies of the results of IT introduction for white-collar workers to date have tended to concentrate on the word processor as the key item of office technology. This has the disadvantage that the effects of computerisation *per se*, and its differential pattern across all staff groups within APT & C, have been somewhat neglected. A decision in Caledonian Regional Council to freeze the introduction of all word processors pending the evaluation of the Office Automation Pilot made it easier for us to identify the changes in work experience concomitant with the introduction of other forms of computerisation, and to differentiate between the uses of mainframe-based and stand-alone equipment both within and between different types of work location.

Crompton and Reid (1982) had reported on the use of batch processing in a local authority finance department, finding that it had produced a significant degree of deskilling of clerks in the department, associated with loss of control of decisions on the conduct of the job and feelings of being an appendage to the computer. They

suggest that the onset of on-line systems might work to reverse this trend and reintroduce elements of control to the jobs. As most of the terminals in our survey were now on-line, we were interested to see whether there was any evidence for this.

Terminals

Easily the most common item found was the mainframe terminal. There proved to be clear differences in the effect of terminal use on the work experience of the two categories of staff. After weighting the response from each work location to allow for the number of items of equipment in use, it was found that while 31 per cent of 'non-technical' locations felt that the volume of work handled by their office had increased following the introduction of the equipment, for 'technical' locations, this was reported by only 15 per cent. Similarly 86 per cent of 'non-technical' locations were reported by their representatives to have experienced an increased workrate, compared to only 9 per cent of technical locations. For both technical and non-technical groups, about a third felt that the work had become easier, but non-technical locations had a greater tendency (14 per cent) to say the work had become harder.

This result may be partly explained by familiarity, since 76 per cent of terminals in non-technical departments had been installed for less than a year, while 91 per cent of those in technical departments had been in use for more than two years. On the other hand, where the systems had been in operation for some time, it may be that changes in the volume and rate of work directly attributable to, or at least facilitated by, technical change were simply less immediately evident as such to those involved.

These differences in perception were also associated with differences in the pattern of use of IT among staff. Thus terminals in 62 per cent of technical locations were used by 'all or most' of the staff, while in 90 per cent of non-technical locations the terminals were used only by a few regular operators. This may indicate a higher degree of specialisation and intensive use by a few in clerical and administrative locations, while technical staff used such equipment more as a 'tool of the trade'. However it also hints at possible patterns of internal stratification within and between departments and locations, a question to which we shall return.

The differences between technical and non-technical staff reappear in the response to a question on general job satisfaction. Over half of

the non-technical responses claimed that work was now 'less satisfying' than it had been prior to computerisation, whereas just under half the technical responses indicated the satisfaction had actually increased. In this question, and in one asking about work difficulty, non-technical staff were more likely to give a definite answer (either positive *or* negative) whereas the predominant response from technical locations was that IT had made 'no change'. This would seem to confirm that for the former group technical change was having a more definite and perhaps fundamental impact on their work experience than was the case with technical workers. The non-technical staff reported favourably on the increased speed and accuracy of the new equipment, but a majority also reported an increase in supervision, and a decrease in the ability to pace their work and choose the order in which the tasks were performed. All these variables in their original status had been listed among the most important positive features of their tasks prior to computerisation.

Micros

The pattern of responses concerning the introduction of micro computers[7] resembled that reported above for terminals in many respects, especially those highlighting the differences between technical and non-technical departments. However the differences were less marked, which may possibly be attributed to the more limited experience of such equipment even in technical locations; in over 80 per cent of both types of department, micros had been in operation for less than one year. The lesser contrast is more likely to reflect different patterns of use however. Again, non-technical departments were more likely to report an increase in both the range and volume of tasks, while technical departments were more likely to cite increased job satisfaction, and to report a greater proportion of staff working such equipment. This last proportion was a little lower than that for terminals however, while in the non-technical departments use was instead slightly broader based.

The reasons for this narrowing of the contrast are complex. Within technical departments the terminals tended to be older and the functions relatively straightforward, and so all employees could normally operate the equipment. Conversely, the micros ran more sophisticated and specialised programmes in these departments, and since the drive to introduce such equipment typically came from those interested in its capabilities, usage was more restricted than for

terminals. Within non-technical departments, to the contrary, the aim of micros was to make possible a widening of the range of tasks carried out and to undertake different operation to those performed by the mainframe system. Hence in non-technical departments, while particular employees might be dedicated to terminal work, this was less likely to be the case for micro work, and introduction of micros was thus reported to be more likely to lead to other tasks being performed in these locations.

Both categories of respondents reported more of an increase in the volume of work with micros than with terminals, but less of an increase in the work rate. For technical departments, work volume increases were reported in 15 per cent of cases following the introduction of terminals, but in 42 per cent of cases where terminals were introduced. However, while a third felt their workrate had increased with terminals, the comparable figure for micros was 25 per cent. Within non-technical departments, 31 per cent associated an increase in the volume of work with new terminals, but 66 per cent reported an increase following the introduction of micros. Yet while 86 per cent associated an increase in the workrate with terminals, only 33 per cent saw the effect of micros in this way.

This contrast between the experienced effects of micros and terminals seems to arise from a number of connected factors, a combination of economic, social and technical influences. Firstly, it seems that micros were introduced to perform different tasks than terminals, as was indicated earlier. Terminals were found either handling high volume routine number crunching or in bureaucratic administrative centres, in each case appearing to facilitate intensifying work pressure. The association of micros with the widening of the range of work provided a smaller pull in this direction.

However this simple interpretation must be regarded with some caution. For example, as we have suggested, the difference between centrally planned and individually motivated acquisitions of equipment may play a significant role. Terminals are typically far more expensive than micros, and so were more subject to budgeting scrutiny and planned use. For micros, respondents from both technical and non-technical departments highlighted the apparent 'absence of any clear plan or purpose as to optimum use'. Employees were 'left to do their own thing on it', and in many departments 'no expert help on programmes' was provided. Discussions with representatives and advisers for the central inter-departmental committee which vetted the introduction of computer systems confirmed the

impression that the pattern of introduction of micros had reflected more the accidents of managerial and individual interest in computers rather than the more coherent plan and logical patterns which were the hallmark of the setting up of mainframe links. It may be that future efforts will be made to codify the introduction and application of micros, altering some of the patterns we have observed, so again these should not be regarded as fixed or in any way inherent in the equipment.

DIVISIONS OF LABOUR AND IT

The contrasts in enthusiasm for new IT equipment in technical and non-technical departments remain to be properly explained. It certainly seems true that the long term training and experience of work with IT has equipped employees in technical departments to accept new technologies more readily than their colleagues in non-technical departments. This leads to the comforting expectation for management that as other staff grow more used to the application of IT, and it becomes a normal and accepted feature of their jobs, so they too will become more adaptable and receptive to future changes. There may be some grains of truth in this, since people do become inured to change. As Crompton and Jones report for all three of their organisations, where highly routinised computer-related work was the norm, computers had been around long enough for them to have come to be seen as a natural and inevitable part of the labour process.

Yet this obscures other differences between departments and groups of employees which may invalidate or at least markedly qualify such a simplistic conclusion. We have already shown the danger of making blanket statements or any description about 'new technology and white-collar staff'. Our method of gathering data, which relies on reports from representatives for a particular location, makes possible only preliminary investigations of some of these issues, since it provides a blanket response for the most part for a section or office. Where there are important divisions within that location, we have to rely on a combination of inference from interview case studies and other sources, and to an extent on conjecture from the limited data available and from comparisons across different types of location. At the least, however, this marks out areas for future investigation.

The first avenue of enquiry concerns the internal stratification and

differentiation among local government staff, and the implications of this for responses to IT (and vice versa). Thus far we have addressed differentiation only through the seemingly narrowly functional division between 'technical' and 'non-technical' staff, further aggregated by departmental locations. Yet in order to comprehend these differences, to talk only of familiarity with IT and its use in disparate ways is to gloss over the differences of control and other aspects of condition, status, the organisational purpose and position of tasks, and other possible social divisions.

In particular it is necessary to look at the patterns and experience of use, in terms of the possible effects on status and control for different groups of staff. These may affect their access to IT, their ability to define the purpose of use and shape its pattern, the extent to which being a user is a privilage or a sentence to routinisation, and may in turn be affected by them. It is possible IT recasts stratification by redefining jobs, but a social choice perspective suggests that the differential capacity for control of different groups may simply reinforce and sharpen existing stratification. In practice a combination of these seems likely, manifested as constraint and possibility for action, both across and within departments for different groups.[8]

Many of the differences discussed so far in terms of stratification can quickly be recognised to overlap heavily with gender differences. In particular, clerical and to a large extent administrative work is predominantly female, while technical work is male; some of our returns from representatives acknowledge this explicitly, for example reporting a location with female-only clerical and male-only technical staff. If we concentrate on the more aggregate differences between types of department, at which level our data is largely pitched, we can examine aspects of this division a little more fully.

Our survey information confirms the importance of this gender dimension to internal stratification and differences in the experienced nature and effects of IT. Looking first specifically at locations with a concentration of primary administration and clerical staff, and so predominantly female also, we find that in three-quarters of these 'few' staff use terminals. (The exceptional cases where all use them are exceptional in their work also; one is a small three-person section recording all policing incidents, the other is an inquiries section of a pay office.) Here terminal use is predominantly female – solely so in two-thirds of locations, including all those with more than two terminals.

The implication is that terminal work is low in attractions and

status in these departments, this being tied to predominate female use. This is confirmed by examining data on those locations with all-female operators, where a high proportion report reduced control over work pace, over work method, and especially a decline in freedom from supervision and an increase in work rate. There was no clear pattern in the reporting of the work as either easier or harder, but responses on its experience as more or less satisfying indicated less satisfaction was associated with locations working *only* with terminals and also more generally applied to those whose work had already been the most routine, that is it confirmed the reinforcement of pre-existing inequalities.

For technical departments, the population was more likely to be male-dominated, and it appeared that this phrase holds true in more senses than one. In half the departments, terminals were used by 'most', and in a third by 'few', but the use in all was entirely by males, in complete contrast to administration. This related directly to distinguishing features discussed earlier: the individual control over obtaining, training for and using new equipment, and its specialist role. Use by few seemed to indicate the equipment carried out too specialised a task to be other than peripheral to the work of the department.

These technically trained males wanted more equipment, and found it nothing new. Though all locations reported increased speed of work, over half reported increased work volume, and nearly half thought work rate had increased, this was under their control and to their liking for the most part. About half of these male technical workers' representatives thought their ability to pace their work had increased, and four-fifths believed the work was more satisfying. This seems to stem from an identification with the task and the quality– challenge of control over performance, tied to qualification, job security (at least as they perceived it in relation to the IT and what it did), status etcetera. Females in these locations were almost entirely secretaries or other clerical–administrative staff in subordinate servicing roles.

Thus the data we have, though it needs greater depth and texture within departments where there are both male and female staff, shows that male-gendered work is closely associated with the ability to control and enhance work experience via IT that goes with particular organisational positions and tasks. It also confirms the vicious circle effect – the powerless get more powerless and routin-ised if anything by IT, as Crompton and Jones discovered. But the

effect on 'white-collar work' cannot be generalised as degradation or deskilling so readily, at least (and this may prove an important remark) in what are still relatively early stages in the development of computerised work.

CONCLUSIONS

We conclude that the way the introduction of IT is experienced by local government staff will depend on a multiplicity of factors which mediate between the economic objectives of technical change and the subjective dimensions of the labour process. On the one hand there are homogenising factors which have been shown to include, the political context of the local authority, the effect of a single union which both encompasses and blurs the distinctions between members in objectively very different status (and arguably class) positions, and the widely shared internal service ethos which rationalised technical innovations as a contribution to the improvement in public service.

On the other hand there are sources of diversity in the form of external financial pressures from central government upon local authority management, the multifunctional nature of the authority, and the internal stratification of departments in terms of both gender and the ability to control resources.

We have argued in this paper for the value of the insights provided by an analysis of workplace changes associated with computerisation in terms of class- and gender-based employee experience and responses. At the same time, we have suggested that a consideration of a category of employees such as local government ATP & C staff demonstrates the limitations of *a priori* approaches which characterise many structuralist accounts of class in particular.

Thus our analysis of the particular configurations of management and union methods, both influenced by the ideology we described as the 'service ethos', demonstrates the importance of specific and historically shaped contingencies. Further, our analysis of our data on Caledonia Regional Council has shown the importance of detecting and exploring internal stratification and division of labour.

Our research data remains deficient as a detailed means of dissecting relationships and processes of change over the longer term, within as well as between departments. Hopefully, it nonetheless provides sufficient illumination to suggest avenues for more definitive investigation.

Notes

1. Spoor counts it 'their greatest single achievement' (p 569).
2. While the main study, from which data are reported here, took place in Scotland, a separate and linked investigation was carried out in Brisbane, Australia, covering both municipal and Queensland State service. Initially one of the UK researchers carried out exploratory interviews, but subsequently a team of researchers at Griffith University have carried out a parallel survey study. There are strong similarities in the findings of the two studies emerging from the analysis to date.
3. Crompton and Jones, 1984, where the issue is discussed only in passing, but elaborated and confirmed in personal communication with Rosemary Crompton.
4. The category of 'non-manual staff' includes teachers as well as APT & C groups, which tends to increase the overall proportion of female employees in the total.
5. The overall figures (provided by LACSAB) for Britain do not provide an equivalent breakdown, but it is noteworthy that total employment figures for local authorities offer three categories: 'male' (11.6 million, at the end of 1986), 'female full-time' (4.9 million) and 'female part-time' (4.5 million).
6. It should be noted that we use the term 'department' throughout in its local government usage of a functional division of the authority or specific area of service, rather than in its more customary usage as 'workplace' or 'location'. Thus the Roads Department will have a great many geographically separate locations, each of which was sent a questionnaire in our survey.
7. This term is used to refer to all small-desk-top or stand-alone computers.
8. Unfortunately due to the necessity to survey every location, the nature of our data made it easier to compare across locations and departments than within specific locations.

References

Abercrombie, N. and J. Urry (1983) *Capital, Labour and the Middle Classes* (London: Allen & Unwin).

Armstrong, P. (1982) 'If Its Only Women It Doesn't Matter So Much', in J. West (ed.), *Women, Work and the Labour Market* (London: Routledge & Kegan Paul).

Armstrong, P. J., Carter, C. Smith and T. Nichols (1986) *White Collar Workers, Trade Unions and Class*, (London: Croom Helm).

Barras, R. and J. Swann (1985) *The Adaption and Impact of Information Technology in UK Local Government*, (London: Technical Change Centre).

Blyton, P. and G. Ursell (1982) 'Vertical Recruitment in White Collar Trade Unions: Some Causes and Consequences;, *BJIR*, vol. xx(2).

Carchedi, G. (1977) *On the Economic Identification of Social Classes* (London: RKP).

Cavendish, R. (1982) *Women on the Line* (London: Routledge & Kegan Paul).
Cockburn, C. (1983) *Brothers: Male Dominance and Technological Change* (London: Pluto Press).
Cockburn, C. (1986) *Machinery of Dominance: Women, Men and Technical Knowledge* (London: Pluto Press).
Coyle, A. (1982) 'Sex and Skill in the Organisation of the Clothing Industry', in J. West (ed.), *Work, Women and the Labour Market* (London: Routledge & Kegan Paul).
Crompton, R. and J. Gubbay (1977) *Economy and Class Structure* (London: Macmillan).
Crompton, R. and S. Reid (1982) 'The Deskilling of Clerical Work' in S. Wood (ed.) (1982) *The Degradation of Work* (London: Hutchinson).
Crompton, R. and G. Jones (1984) *White Collar Proletariat: Deskilling and Gender in Clerical Work* (London: Macmillan).
Dex, S. (1985) *The Sexual Division of Work* (Brighton: Wheatsheaf).
Fowler, A. (1975) *Personnel Management in Local Government*, (London: IPM).
Goldthorpe, J. (1975) 'On the Service Class, its Formation and Future' in A. Giddens and G. Mackenzie (eds) *Social Class and the Division of Labour*, (Cambridge: CUP).
Gould, A. (1980) 'The Salaried Middle Class in the Welfare State', *Policy & Politics*, vol. 9.
Hyman, R. and R. Price (eds) *The New Working Class? White-Collar Workers and Their Organisations* (London: Macmillan).
Kessler, I. (1986) 'Shop Stewards in Local Government Revisited', *BJIR*, xxiv(3).
LAMSAC (1981) 'Potential Demand, Input and Implications of Micro-computer Applications', *Micro computing in local government Element 3* (London: LAMSAC).
Lockwood, D. (1958) *The Blackcoated Workers* (London: Allen Unwin).
Mallet, S. (1975) *The New Working Class* (Nottingham: Spokesman).
Newman, G. (1982) *Path to Maturity*, (Manchester: Cooperative Press).
Nicholson, N., G. Ursell and P. Blyton (1981) *The Dynamics of White Collar Unionism*, Academic Press.
Phillips, A. and Taylor, B. (1980) 'Sex and Skill: Notes Towards a Feminist Econimics', *Feminist Review*, no. 6: pp. 79–88.
Poulantzas, N. (1975) *Classes in Contemporary Capitalism* (London: New Left Books).
Price, R. (1980) 'White-Collar Unions; Growth Character and Attitude in the 1970s', reprinted in R. Hyman and R. Price (1983) *The New Working Class? White Collar Workers & Their Organisations* (London: Macmillan).
Quintas, P. (1986) 'Information Technology and Employment in Local Government', *New Technology, Work and Employment*, I(ii).
Ramsay, H. and N. Haworth (1984) 'Prefigurative Socialism and the Strategies of Transition', *Discussion Paper No. 12* (Glasgow: CRIDP, University of Glasgow).
Somerton, M. (1977) 'Trade Unions and Industrial Relations in Local Government', *Studies for Trade Unionists 3(11)*.

Smith, C. (1987) *Technical Workers: Class, Labour and Trade Unionism* (London: Macmillan).

Spoor, A. (1967) *White-Collar Union: Sixty Years of NALGO* (London: Heinemann).

Terry, M. (1982) 'Organising a Fragmented Workforce: Shop Stewards in Local Government', *BJIR*, xx(1).

Volker, D. (1966) 'NALGO's Affiliation to the TUC', *BJIR*, iv(1).

Winchester, D. (1983) 'Industrial Relations in the Public Sector', in G. S. Bain (ed.) *Industrial Relations in Britain* (Oxford: Blackwell).

Wright, E. O. and J. Singlemann (1982) 'Proletarianization in the Changing American Class Structure', in M. Burawoy and T. Skocpol (eds) *Marxist Inquiries: Studies in Labor, Class and States* (University of Chicago Press).

Wright, E. O. (1985) *Classes* (London: Verso).

Zmroczek, C. et al. (1984) *Technological Development and the Public Sector* (Brighton: SPRU).

4 Autonomy and the Medical profession: Medical Audit and Management Control*

Mike Dent

INTRODUCTION

There have been several challenges to the autonomy of the medical profession during the recent history of hospital medicine. The biggest challenge has proven to be the issue of clinical efficiency, particularly with regard to costs. Doctors both individually and collectively are now being pressurised into being more cost conscious and for consultants to become *resource managers*, responsible for the costs of running their particular clinics (Royal Commission, 1979; Griffiths Report, 1983). Medical audit constituted the focus of negotiations (both explicit and implicit) between the medical professional and the state during the sixties and seventies. On the one hand, the 'managerial strategy' at the Department of Health (the state) was to directly involve doctors in the controlling of clinical costs and generally improve efficiencies. While on the other, the medical profession responded by attempting to develop their own system of 'audit' which was concerned with the quality, rather than the cost, of care and entirely under their own collegiate control. Utilising Friedman's terms, the situation is analogous to skilled workers who exercise 'craft control' being confronted with a managerial strategy aimed at introducing 'responsible autonomy' (rather than 'direct control') as a means of extending control over the labour process (Friedman, 1977).

This paper examines the role of the two competing control strategies in shaping the organisational changes within the recent history of the health service. The first part consists of a short discussion on management strategies and labour process analysis and

---

* I am grateful to Rod Coombes and Chris Smith for their comments on an earlier draft of this chapter.

their applicability to the work of the medical profession in health service. The longer second part is concerned with the development of medical audit within British hospital medicine. This second part is intended to illustrate the applicability of labour process analysis to medical work in the health service. The evidence relating to the responses of the organised medical profession to the issue of medical audit is based on a survey of the British Medical Journal between 1965 and 1981.

PART I: MANAGEMENT STRATEGIES, LABOUR PROCESS ANALYSIS AND HOSPITAL MEDICINE MANAGEMENT STRATEGIES

Following Child (1985), managerial strategies can be seen as the conceptual linkage between structure, action and outcome as played out within the arena of the work organisation. This is not to assert, however, that management strategies *determine* outcomes, rather that they constitute a *mediation* between the imperatives of 'capitalism', the corporate intentions of the organisation and the labour process outcomes. There is no implication that the strategies in practice will always be coherent, nor that the implementation of the policies will reflect precisely the intentions of management (which are rarely unitary in their organisation). Nor is it to assume that the labour process is necessarily the major focus of management strategies. But what can be asserted is that the organisation of the labour process will be primarily affected (but not necessarily determined) by managerial strategies. The primary orientation of the managerial strategies are towards the objectives of cost reduction, increasing flexibility, improvements in quality and the enhancement of management control (*ibid.*, p. 113). This model explicitly relates to 'the organisation of the labour process in enterprises funded by private capital, excluding those of a professional and–or cooperative character' (*ibid.*, p. 108), which clearly does not include NHS hospitals.

This exclusion of public sector organisations is not however, wholly warranted, for as Coombs and Jonsson have suggested, managerial strategies are visible within hospital clinics even in relation to the organisation of medical and nursing work (therefore work of a professional character) and furthermore the visibility of these strategies will increase the continued introduction of budgetary mechanisms which act as an alternative to the market mechanism (1986,

p. 20). Their analysis is based on case studies carried out in Sweden but there are parallels to be found in the British case. It can in fact be argued that the organisation and control of the medical labour process within the NHS hospital service has been subject to a managerial strategy, emanating from the DHSS, at least since the early 1960s. The general strategy has had the aim of bringing about the general rationalisation of the hospital service through the control of costs, effecting greater flexibility and enhancing managerial control through the incorporation of the hospital consultants within an integrated organisation structure.

This overall strategy of organisational rationalisation can be dated from the implementation of the Hospital Plan in 1962, with its commitment to concentrating resources on developing one large district general hospital within each health district (at least with regard to acute and maternity care) (Klein, 1983). This policy, which in itself was not directly concerned with the role of consultants in hospital management, was followed by one which did attempt to do so; this was the introduction of the divisional system which followed the publication of the 'Cogwheel' Reports (1967a and b), a process further reinforced by the 1974 reorganisation of the health service.

None of the policies, however, resulted in the kind of fundamental changes in the organisation and control of the work of hospital doctors that the *rationalisers* were looking for (more on the details in a moment). By the 1980s their concerns had been overtaken by the issue of escalating healthcare costs and the ideology of the market reformers, which has come to dominate current debates surrounding the NHS and is currently encapsulated in the report of the Griffiths enquiry into health service management (1983).

The medical professional was not unaffected by the organisational innovations that followed the implementation of the Hospital Plan, the 'Cogwheel' reports and the 1974 NHS Reorganisation, and responded with the introduction of a strategy of its own intended to ensure that hospital consultants remained independant and autonomous of hospital management. The aim of this *professional strategy* was to ensure that doctors would remain the ones to organise and control the clinic work processes of diagnosis, treatment and care of patients with no (or minimal) concern for the resource implications of this work. The resulting interplay and conflict between the two strategies (managerial and professional) is the subject matter of this paper. But before going on to present the details of the politics of these managerial and professional strategies it is necessary to say a

little more about labour process analysis and its applicability to medical work.

LABOUR PROCESS ANALYSIS AND HOSPITAL MEDICINE

Wood has suggested that we have seen three waves of reaction to Braverman's *Labor and Monopoly Capitalism*; the enthusiastic, the critical and what might be termed the 'reappraisal', for it

> stresses the importance of subjectivity and workers' knowledge in the labour process; the variety and uneven ways in which Taylorism has been adopted; and the 'joint creation' of the labour process (Wood, 1983, p. 16)

While the reappraisal of the labour process, contained in the studies of researchers such as Friedman (1977), Burawoy (1979) and Littler (1982), have moved the analysis beyond the limitations of Braverman's original formulation, little attention has been paid to the labour processes within the *public sector*. In terms of marxist economics, labour processes in the public sector are *unproductive* of surplus value unless they are directly involved in providing goods and services for the market – it is strictly speaking the non-market organisations only that are being referred to here (Gough, 1979). But while these organisations do not contribute directly to capital accumulation they do provide the social and political conditions necessary for the accumulation process to take place (O'Connor, 1973; Gough, 1979). The relationship between non-market public sector activities and capital accumulation is a complex one, of which space prohibits any greater exposition here, but complexity is not a sufficient reason for excluding the public sector from labour process analysis. Indeed this sector is in many ways a critical case for labour process analysis, if only because of its historically necessary role within all capitalist societies, and to ignore it leaves labour process analysis seriously weakened.

There is rather more literature on the question of the putative proletarianisation of professionals which has been an abiding concern of those involved in the New Middle Class debates (cf. Abercrombie and Urry, 1983). Those involved in this debate have been less reluctant to study work outside the manufacturing and commercial sectors of the economy. To adopt the position proposed by Larson

(1980) and further developed by Derber (1983) proletarianisation in this context is analagous but not identical to that experienced by manual workers. It is not deskilling as such but 'The transformation of professionalisation strategies into generalised credentialism' that leads to a general loss of occupational status that may be experienced as 'proletarianisation' (Larson, 1980, pp. 44 and 45). Proletarianisation here is viewed as an *ideological* phenomena whereby a profession loses, to some degree, its autonomy in return for what Derber refers to as *sponsorship* which is a concept very similar to that of *responsible autonomy* but specifically applicable to professional employees (1983).

In the case of the medical profession, however, their status, power and autonomy predates and has formed the very basis of healthcare provided by the state which has meant that the profession has been particularly resistant to attempts to encroach upon its traditional autonomy (cf. Johnson, 1972; Larson, 1977). This is not to say that the autonomy of hospital consultants goes unchallenged. Godber, as Chief Medical Officer at the Department of Health from 1960–73, was to argue over a long period of time that the traditional assumptions about the medical autonomy of doctors required revision, the reasons given being that of changing patterns of diseases coupled with increased medical specialisation and application of high technology to medicine necessitated a more 'collective' interpretation to medical autonomy. Chronic illness, he argued, increasingly required the coordination of the services of different health professions and support staff over a long period. Similarly, specialisation and the use of high technology in medicine necessitates extensive cooperation between the hospital specialist and a whole range of other skilled and professional personnel (Godber, 1975). These were the primary reasons behind the rationalising trend of the 1960s and 70s referred to earlier. In the event, while the organised profession had to respond to these developments, the result was that medical autonomy of consultants *within* the institutions of healthcare was undiminished. But this is not the same as saying that the autonomy had been unaffected, for the nature of the relationship between the doctors and the state administration has been a changing one.

As a way of clarifying the relationship between the medical profession, hospital consultants and state it will be useful to adopt certain key terms to distinguish between the two forms of control that impinge upon the organisation of hospital doctors and their clinics. The first is *intitutional* control which refers to the profession's control

of the health services labour processes of diagnoses, treatment and care of patients, the second is *organisational* control which refers to the management arrangements within the health service as preferred by the state (that is emanating out of the DHSS) and which impinge upon the doctors' professional autonomy (see figure 1). Both *institutional* and *organisational* controls refer to formal arrangements and not simply to value orientations, or socialisation, and in this key respect differs from Ouchi's conceptualisation of *professional control* (a variant of clan control) (1981, p. 837). This is why the medical executive committee and divisions are located under the heading of Institutional Control, for while the arrangement was sponsored by the DHSS ('Cogwheel', 1967a and b) the system typically operates wholly under the control of the consultants (for example Forsyth et al. 1971). Figure 1 does not make reference to nursing, nor to other professions within the health service, but focuses solely on the institutional and organisational controls relating to doctors. Hospitals in reality possess a polyarchic structure, within which hospital consultants have historically enjoyed a position of dominance legimated by reference to their right to clinical autonomy (Freidson, 1970). It is the doctors role as diagnostician and coordinaor of the treatment of the patient's disease (injuries or condition) that puts him, or her, in this position of ascendancy within the organisation, for it is the clinical work on patients that is the *raison d'être*, of the hospital service.

Medical dominance does not however, derive solely from technical necessity, the *politics* of professionalism plays a considerable role in the matter and since the mid-nineteenth century the state in Britain has generally protected the interests of doctors. On the one hand doctors have been released from the domination of insurance companies, friendly societies and trade unions, while on the other the state has protected them from their patients' inability to pay for their treatment. The 1911 National Insurance Act can be viewed in this light, as can the 1948 nationalisation of the health service (cf. Eckstein, 1958; Klein, 1983). At the same time the British state was itself unable to develop its own effective system of controls over the doctors, with the result that the medical profession was able to exercise a suzerain power to counter government policy if it judged the matter to be against its interests as a profession. The issue of medical audit is a recent example of where the state (in the form of government and Department of Health) had wished hospital consultants to be both more integrated within the hospital organisational structures and more accountable for the resources they used.

71

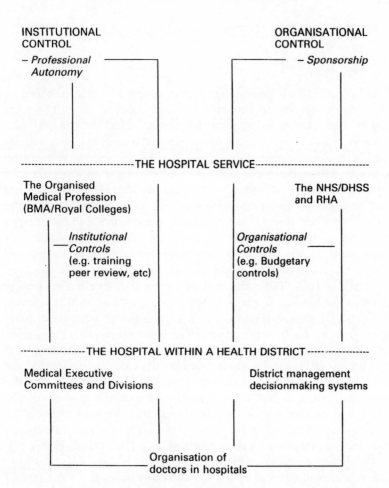

INSTITUTIONAL
CONTROL
– *Professional*
Autonomy

ORGANISATIONAL
CONTROL
– *Sponsorship*

---------------------------------THE HOSPITAL SERVICE---------------------------------

The Organised
Medical Profession
(BMA/Royal Colleges)

The NHS/DHSS
and RHA

Institutional
Controls
(e.g. training
peer review, etc)

Organisational
Controls
(e.g. Budgetary
controls)

-------------------THE HOSPITAL WITHIN A HEALTH DISTRICT-----------------

Medical Executive
Committees and Divisions

District management
decisionmaking systems

Organisation of
doctors in hospitals

Work in hospital clinics as a *labour process in*
which consultants exercise clinical autonomy within
a division of labour that also includes nurses,
paramedical, clerical/secretarial workers and patients.

Figure 1   Hospital doctors and labour process analysis

PART II: MEDICAL AUDIT AND MANAGEMENT CONTROL

MEDICAL AUDIT

Medical audit is a general term that covers a whole plethora of techniques relating to the evaluation of medical care. The term 'audit' has been seen by some advocates within the medical profession to have connotations of an external assessment in a manner paralleling the practice of accountants. This has led to the common practice within the profession of using the more anodyne term of 'quality assurance' (Duncan, 1980; Shaw, 1980a). Here *medical audit* will be used as a generic term to cover all forms of evaluation of the quality of medical work. Medical audit as a practice is in fact fraught with difficulties both definitional and, more particularly, *political*. It originated in the United States with the American College of Surgeons (ACS) national standardisation programme for hospitals as far back as 1919. The roots of the movement can be traced directly back to the Flexner Report on medical education of 1910 (Maynard, 1978) and reflected a real concern regarding the often inadequate arrangements for both the quality of patient care and the organisation of doctors within American hospitals at that time (Roemer and Friedman, 1971, pp. 36–7). It was also the case, however, that the ACS programme was one of self interest, being the response of the private interest of the doctors to the competitive anarchy of the market in medical care in the US at that time. By implementing the national standardisation programme the ACS was able to enhance the status and income levels of its members (cf. Maynard, 1978, p. 7).

Originally medical audits were little more than case meetings where the management of the patient was discussed. In the case of surgical specialties mortality and morbidity meetings would be organised, sometimes known as the 'Death Round'. In practice these meetings appeared to function less as an audit and more as a cathartic exercise for those involved (Arluke, 1977; Millman, 1977). While these meetings still take place, medical audit methodology in the United States has become more sophisticated. Instead of reviewing individual cases, explicit, written criteria for judging the adequacy of the care provided is established beforehand by the senior medical staff for the medical audit committee. The medical records staff have the responsibility for monitoring the clinical records and when discrepancies are found bringing them to the attention of the medical audit committee (Sanazaro, 1974; Shaw, 1980b). The formal require-

ment is that doctors found to be consistently substandard in their work are recommended for remedial education (Sanazaro, 1974).

This more sophisticated *criteria* method of audit is premised on a systems model developed initially by Donabedian (1966). The model comprises of three key elements, *structure, process* and *outcome* which together define the components of medical audit within modern medicine (see figure 2).

STRUCTURE >>>	PROCESS >>>	OUTCOME
The hospital facilities and equipment, skill and qualifications of staff (etc)	The clinic Work processes directly under the consultants control	The patient's condition after treatment (i.e. morbidity, mortality and quality of life)

Figure 2 The medical audit model

The methods of medical audit generally preferred by the profession (including criteria audit) are those concerned solely with the process element, which refers only to the clinical care directly under the doctors' control. In contrast to process, structure refers to the setting in which the clinical care takes place, the facilities and equipment, qualifications of staff, administrative and technical support and suchlike (*ibid.*, pp. 169–70). Outcome, as the name suggests, refers to whether and how well the patient or patients recovered. This compartmentalisation of the major components of health care means, however, that the medical care (process) is viewed as being central to the whole system and structure, including the work of nursing and paramedical staff, as well as outcome can only be treated as residual factors.

There have been and continue to be debates around the issue of outcome and its measurement that has threatened the ascendancy of process evaluation (for example Cochrane, 1971; Illsley, 1980). But the problem, which is a practical one, is that outcome studies are notoriously difficult to carry out. Tracing ex-patients, for example, is difficult and usually expensive. Furthermore in cases of chronic illnesses the outcome may be more a matter of the alleviation of suffering rather than whether the disease has been cured or not, and the alleviation of suffering is very difficult to measure objectively (Cochrane, 1971; Illsley, 1980; Butler & Vaile, 1984). It is also the case, however, as Cochrane in the British context has clearly shown, that many outcome studies indicate that some medical procedures are

less effective than might be supposed (*op. cit*). Similarly the Scottish Home and Health Department has reported that more than one third of all patients were dead within two years of leaving hospital, and if they were not dead the medical condition in over a half of the discharged patients was unimproved (quoted in Garner, 1979, p. 114). It is hardly surprising therefore that those in the medical profession who favour medical audit tend to favour the process varieties (including Donebedian, 1966, p. 168) for these are not overtly concerned with outcome. Clinical work is 'intervention' in the disease process, and focusing on the adequacy and expertise involved at this point of intersection between the disease and the healthcare systems draws attention to the clinician's work and away from the condition of the patient (that is, outcome). The doctors define the rules of performance themselves, an example of the institutionalisation of the 'vocabularies of realism' identified by Stelling and Bucher (1973).

MEDICAL ORGANISATION AND AUDIT IN BRITAIN

Prior to the publication in 1967 of the two reports later known as 'Cogwheel' (1967a and b) there was little obvious interest among the medical profession for medical audit. At the same time the Department of Health was committed to challenging the profession on the issue of the cost and effectiveness of medical work. The challenge first became public with the 'Cogwheel' recommendations concerning the organisation of medical work in England and Wales (1967a) and Scotland (1967b). Both reports recommended the introduction into the NHS of a '*divisional* system of staffing similar to that widely used in North America . . .' (BMJ., Leading Article, 1967), although it was only the Scottish report that contained any specific reference to medical audit (*ibid.*). Nevertheless even the 'Cogwheel' report for England and Wales (1967a) made specific reference to

the review of hospital bed usage against the background of community needs, the organisation of outpatient and inpatient services [and], *the review of clinical practice*,'. (Quoted in Forsyth, et al., 1971, p. 5. emphasis added).

It is hardly surprising that the BMJ's leading articles on the week of the report's publication expressed concern that whilst the divisional system[1] might well promote the

more efficient use of beds, staff and equipment. The danger is that a doctor's freedom to treat his patients as he sees fit (clinical autonomy) may be eroded by the adoption of *uniform* regiments of management (*op cit.*).

In short the essential ingredients of an institutionalised system of medical audit (the review of clinical practice) was introduced with the reorganisation of hospital doctors along the divisional lines recommended by 'Cogwheel'.

In practice the divisional system recommended by the 'Cogwheel' reports was often no more than groupings of the traditional consultant led 'firms'. This led one hospital doctor at least to comment in a letter to the BMJ:

> One has been encouraged . . . to find as expected, that there are many ways of playing Cogwheel – by various paper schemes . . . designed to satisfy the administrators . . .
> (*BMJ*, 30 January 1971, p. 29)

In rather less cynical terms, Forsyth came to a parallel view that the reorganisation of hospital doctors into divisions has not necessarily led to the development of better control over costs and quality of medical care. This he argued was because the doctors and others involved did not always fully accept their new responsibilities (1971, pp. 41–3).

THE PROFESSION'S STRATEGY

Neither the BMA nor the Royal Colleges recommended or accepted the kind of medical audit contained within the 'Cogwheel' Reports. Any development of medical audit during the latter half of the sixties was entirely at a local and voluntary kind (with the exception of the various 'confidential enquiries' which have been excluded from this account being very much a separate development). Medical audit did not emerge as a major issue for the organised medical profession until 1971, and it did so because the profession was becoming disquieted by the lack of discussion between themselves and the Department of Health over the then proposed reorganisation of the NHS. In the words of a leader writer in the BMJ,

> there is . . . serious concern among doctors about the virtual exclusion of the health professions from the management in the

reformed NHS. They are concerned less *clinical care* will take second place and patients will suffer . . . Medicine is not the same as business

And further on,

> If the Consultative Document ['Grey Book', 1971] is translated into legislation, then the Health Service is destined to have management based on *cost effectiveness*. . . . It is not the way to provide good medical care (*BMJ.*, Leading Article, 1971a emphasis added).

It was in this pre-reorganisation period (1971–4) that the organised profession, or at least its leadership at the British Medical Association (BMA), began to recognise the potentiality of medical audit as the basis of a strategy to thwart what it considered to be the unwarranted encroachment of the state and health service administration into the area of the organisation and control of medical work. This was no doubt in part because it was becoming concerned that if the profession did not take the initiative the Department of Health would. For example the profession had to be reassured by the Permanent Secretary to the DHSS that the term 'monitoring' which is used in the 'Grey Book' (1972) (the consultative document relating to the NHS reorganisation) 'did not entail the right to give orders [to doctors] (*BMJ Supplement* 16 December 1972, p. 97) and later the BMA was able to tell its members that the new specialism of Community Medicine would not be used to operate as a system of clinical audit (*BMJ Supplement*, 3 February 1973, p. 29).

If one traces the development of medical audit strategy in the pages of the *BMJ*, and in particular its supplements where the proceedings and deliberations of the association's various committees, conferences etcetera are reported, one can clearly trace the rise and fall of the medical audit strategy of the profession. On 20 November 1971 the *BMJ* published a leader article and the first of a series of three articles which *directly* linked the then proposed reorganisation of the NHS with the issue of medical audit. The 'leader' was concerned with a book of essays, edited by G. McLachlan and entitled 'Challenge for Change'. Whereas previously the leaders had tended to emphasise the perceived excesses of the reorganisation proposal (for example *BMJ*, 1971a quoted above) this one asked, 'But is what the Government has proposed . . . enough?' and with reference to the

introduction of the book argued for the then proposed reorganisation to become more than simply a reordering of management structures and functions. The leader writer clearly wanted the agenda of the book's authors brought to general notice within the profession,

> In their introduction . . . [the editors] put forward four proposals which specially merit the profession's attention:
> 1) to develop a philosophy of health services . . . without political or professional bombast;
> 2) to develop series of objectives for the NHS . . . ;
> 3) *the monitoring of the quality of health care*; . .
> 4) the development of a coherent manpower policy (*BMJ* Leader Article 1971b, p. 443. emphasis added)

Here we have in the pages of the *BMJ*, for the first time, medical audit being advocated as the means of defending the interests of doctors. The argument developed in the article was that if the profession could make 'their concerted views, based on thorough research . . . continuously available to local and central health authorites' they were more likely to be able to 'claim . . . a bigger share of national resources for the NHS . . .' (*ibid.*). In other words medical audit was being promoted within the profession as a means of defending their interests and not as a means *per se* of improving the efficacy of medical diagnosis and treatment, although improvements in medical care might follow. A primary reason for this proposal was that doctors were being criticised by the Department of Health for the problems clinical freedom gave rise to in relation to forecasting the annual budget of the NHS (*ibid.*). The leader writer's response to this claim was to argue for a system of medical audit controlled by the profession, for it was, the doctors '*collective duty* to suggest improvements in health care, *within* resources likely to be available . . .' (*ibid.* Some emphasis added). This notion of professional responsibility, which relates to concern for the interests of the institution rather than the individual patient is a point doctors do not often make.

The actual strategy adopted by the BMA was not, however, always a coherent one. The problem, which was not specific only to the issue of medical audit, was a lack of organisational unity within the BMA. This difficulty the Association's leadership attempted to overcome by instigating a reorganisation of the BMA. The problem for the leadership was that the Assocation's Council had few executive powers and was considerably constrained by the Representative

Body (of the membership) in its negotiations with the government, particularly during the period of reorganisation of the NHS. The BMA attempted to remedy this by instigating its own reorganisation. Sir Paul Chambers was asked to investigate and make recommendations. This he did and the resulting report appeared in the *BMJ* Supplement (6 May 1972, pp. 45–67). The changes in the balance of power between the Council and the Representative Body no doubt had some effect on the efficacy of the organisation of the BMA, but with regards to the issue of 'audit' the results were not apparent. The problem was that while the leadership (the Council) of the organised profession were willing to accept medical audit in a number of forms (so long as it was totally under medical control) the membership were less convinced. From 1972 onwards the issue was discussed in one form or another at the Annual Representatives Meetings of the BMA, specifically from 1977, but not until 1981 was the policy of medical audit organised and administered by the medical profession finally accepted,[2] despite the leadership's known preference on the matter over a number of years. This lack of firm policy and commitment gave rise to criticisms within the report of the Royal Commission (1979).

OTHER PRESSURES

At the beginning of the 1970s the organised profession was also being made aware that there was considerable public and political pressure for doctors to be more answerable to the state administration (ultimately the government minister and parliament) for the quality of medical care delivered, particularly in the cases where mistakes were believed to have been made. Between 1971 and 1975 three government reports were published, that in different ways were concerned with 'medical mistakes', these were,

— The committee of enquiry into Farleigh Hospital (1971).
— The 'Report of the Committee on Hospital Complaints procedure' (Davies Report, London, HMSO, 1973).
— The Committee of Inquiry into the Regulation of the Medical Profession (Merrison, 1975).

These three reports were in varying degrees evidence of the concern of the administration and other interested parties that doctors were too

well protected against the complaints of patients and others. To explain, the 'Farleigh Enquiry' recommended the appointment of a Health Service Commissioner (Ombudsman). The recommendation was implemented towards the end of 1972. Although the powers of the Ombudsman did not extend initially to matters of clinical judgement (autonomy) this did eventually change in 1981 when, in Klein's words, a 'compromise was cobbled up' (1983, p. 163) which permitted complaints into the quality of medical treatment to be investigated, although only in a form totally controlled by the medical profession (*ibid* pp. 84 and 163). The BMA, at the time of the report of the original enquiry, experienced a sense of

> 'grave disquiet' over many of the details. [and] did not believe that any convincing case had been made in favour of appointing a commissioner . . . (*BMJ Supplement*, 29 January 1972, pp. 29–30).

Nevertheless the Ombudsman fared better than the recommendations of the 'Davies Report' which called for internal reforms. This report was an attempt

> [T]o provide the hospital service with practical guidance in the form of a code of principles and practice . . . [relating to] matters affecting patients which go wrong in hospitals (p. 3, para. 1.1)

This guidance principally concerned the 'overhaul' of the system of handling complaints from patients and their possibly litigious consequences. In addition, and pertinent to the issue of medical audit, the report also recommended that the system of external checks available through the services of the Health Service Commissioner, the Community Health Councils and the Hospital (now Health) Advisory Service should have their 'functions, powers and constitutional status . . . reviewed and . . . reformed or supplemented as necessary' (*ibid* p. 104, para 60). This report, despite being nominally accepted by the government, was never implemented for not only did the BMA oppose it but apparently no major group within the NHS lobbied for its implementation (Martin, 1984, pp. 151–4).

Initially the organised profession was concerned that the Merrison Committee (1975) might recommend a system of medical audit not fully under medical control (cf. *BMJ Supplement*, 23 June 1972, p. 133). For this reason the BMA called a Special Annual Representatives Meeting (ARM) that year to consider its evidence to the committee of enquiry. The problem for the BMA was that if it simply said that there were already sufficient safeguards to maintain the

professional competence of doctors the committee might not believe it. Yet if it said that outside regulations were unnecessary because the profession was already dealing with the matter and was in the process of setting up its own committee of enquiry (the Alment Committee which reported in 1976) then that might also be seen as an admission that new forms of regulation and monitoring were required in the profession. The BMA was clearly pessimistic regarding its powers to convince. The dilemma for the profession however was not a very real one. By the December of that year (1973) Dr Merrison was seeking the advice of the BMA on the question of 'competence to practice' (one aspect of medical audit). The BMA chose to respond by telling Dr Merrison, possibly in less tortuous prose, that,

> an advanced stage was being reached in preliminary arrangements for setting up the profession's inquiry into the subject. Dr Merrison would be advised as to its progress (*BMJ Supplement*, 22 December 1973, p. 86)

This the Merrison Committee found satisfactory and was quite prepared to leave the matter of the 'surveillance of doctors competence' (*BMJ*, 26 April 1975, p. 156) wholly in the hands of the organised profession. The Committee touched upon this matter in terms of 'relicensure'[3] commenting only that,

> We do not wish to prejudice the consideration of schemes of relicensure, especially because the medical profession is in fact mounting its own inquiry in this field . . . (Merrison, 1975)

This internal committee of enquiry into 'Competance to Practice' of the organised medical profession was chaired by E. A. J. Alment (Consultant Obstetrician and Gynaecologist) and had 19 members; seven were from the BMA., seven from the Royal Colleges plus four more representing medical education and postgraduate training (Alment, 1976, Appendix 1; *BMJ Supplement* 27 April 1974, p. 30).

TOO LITTLE TOO LATE

The Alment Report can only be described as anodyne. On the specific issue of medical audit the committee found 'peer-group reviews' and 'self assessments' acceptable so long as they were solely for educational purposes and no sanctions were 'deployed against those who

appear to do less well than their colleagues' (*ibid.*, p. 55, para. 9.12). The reason being that medical audit was thought to be 'threatening to a professional', for the establishment of 'norms' of good practice might be interpreted as rules for doctors to obey. Furthermore these 'norms' might be used by 'employers and others to serve their own purposes . . .' (*ibid.*, p. 37, para. 6.9). It was recommended that peer reviews should be encouraged by the Royal Colleges and their faculties, who should also carry out such activities (p. 39, para. 6.14). This the 'Colleges' did and the results were subsequently reviewed in 'Reviewing practice in Medical Care' (McLachlan, ed., 1981). In the prologue Alment indicated that the major reason for the cautious tone of report was that the committee was concerned to avoid internal polarisation and antagonism within the wider profession. The committee had also been at pains to point out that a high standard of care was dependent on the 'level of resource availability' (*ibid.*, p. 55, para. 9.8) which was not seen as being the responsibility of the doctor. They argued instead that 'there is a level of resource availability below which doctors are not able to provide reasonable standards of care' (*ibid.*, p. 30, para. 5.20). Baulking at this issue weakened the organised profession's influence in determining the future of the NHS, as the subsequent Royal Commission (Merrison, 1979) and the more recent organisational restructuring (Griffiths Report, 1983) have indicated. In short, the organised profession had great difficulty in 'cobbling together' a workable consensus and was in a state of some disarray on this issue even after publication of the report.

This inability to develop and sustain a coherent policy on this issue was to have its implications for the profession when it again came under public scrutiny in the form of the Royal Commission, which reported in 1979 (Merrison, 1979). The British Medical Association was unable to gain formal membership support until the appropriate motion was passed at the ARM in 1981 (*BMJ Supplement*, 1981). This only added to the leadership's problems, and in its evidence to the Royal Commission the BMA was forced to equivocate over the issue of medical audit, commenting that 'its place . . . in health care is still controversial' but if it was to be inevitable it should be carried out by the profession as a whole (*BMJ Supplement*, 1977). The BMA also regretted 'any suggestion that there should be "medical audit" by the state' (*ibid.*). The Royal Commission had reservations about the medical profession's will, if not its ability, to implement medical audit, for they commented,

... [W]e are not convinced that the professions generally regard the introduction of audit or peer review . . . with a proper sense of urgency (Merrison, 1979, p. 176, para. 12.56)

and recommended that,

... [A] planned programme for the introduction of audit or peer review . . . should be set up for the health professions by their professional bodies and progress monitored by the *health departments* (*ibid.*, p. 370. para 63, emphasis added)

The report also favoured doctors becoming their own resource managers and holding their own budgets, a proposal currently being implemented as part of the Griffiths reorganisation (1983). The overall tenor of the commission's report was for doctors to come under greater *organisational* control, or sponsorship.

CONCLUSIONS

The medical audit strategy of the leadership of the medical profession was intended to bring about the introduction of an effective system, or systems, of peer review with the objective of ensuring the maintenance and improvement of the *quality* of clinical care within hospitals without reference to costs. There were those in the profession who supported this development as desirable in itself, but the principle aim of the strategy was to prevent, or make unnecessary, the introduction of externally designed control systems aimed at making hospital consultants more accountable to third parties (including the state) than previously, either for resource management or medical *mistakes*. As we have seen, this strategy never wholly cohered, largely because the membership were unconvinced of the merits of medical audit, either as practise or policy, as evidenced by the fate of the recommendations of the Alment Report and the BMA's inability to get formal support in time to counter criticism from the Royal Commission into the NHS of 1979. Even so the strategy of the profession's leadership did postpone for over a decade any serious negotiations between themselves and the state administration over the matter of controlling clinical costs (and the issue of medical mistakes still remains to be fully resolved).

In contrast, the long term managerial strategy of the state administration has been to attempt to incorporate hospital consultants more fully within the system of organisational control and relatedly to take

responsibility for their clinical budgets. The earlier attempts to introduce a measure of cost effectiveness into clinical care, associated with the introduction of the divisional system of medical organisation and the NHS reorganisation of 1974, were unsuccessful because no way could be found to breach the profession's legitimate monopoly control of medical work. It has only been the adoption of the Thatcherite policies of rejecting managerialism and attempting instead to introduce market mechanisms within the NHS that has begun to erode the profession's resistance to clinical budgeting. The Department of Health (the state), and others that Klein (1983) has referred to as the *paternalistic rationalisers*, wanted – and had wanted at least since the early sixties – that hospital consultants should become explicit resource managers (cf. 'Cogwheel' Reports, 1967 (a) & (b), 1972, 1974; Royal Commission, 1979). But it has been the *market reformers*, to adopt Alford's term (1972), who have brought about the changes in the NHS aimed at limiting the autonomy of hospital consultants by insisting they take responsibility for their clinic budgets,

> Doctors should be closely involved in local management through the development of management budgets for which they would be accountable . . . (Statement on the NHS Management Inquiry ('Griffiths'): Tuesday 25th October, 1983, p. 2 Secretary of State to Parliament).

Doctors collectively, however, never wanted the formal responsibility of allocating possibly scarce and life sustaining resources according to *financial criteria*, and it remains to be seen whether the formal requirements to adopt this new arrangement will be carried through into practice, or whether the doctors will again prevaricate long enough for the circumstances that brought about the reforms to have changed and made them, from the organised professions' point of view, unnecessary.

In terms of 'managerial strategies' and labour process analysis the discussion on medical audit has demonstrated that managerial strategies are discernible within the NHS hospital service (that is, a non-market public sector organisation), and that they are orientated to the same types of objectives found in the private sector, at least as identified by Child (1985, p. 113), although these strategies are policy rather than market driven. Within the health service, management's ability to attain objectives has been attenuated by the presence of the organised medical profession, which has a legitimate ability to implement strategies of its own, or to reinterpret management

policies with regard to the organisation of medical work in a way commensurate with the members' professional concerns, as demonstrated by the discussion of medical audit. Nevertheless major organisational changes were brought about broadly in line with the original policies, despite the reservations of the medical profession. In the health service, as in the private sector, management strategies do set the parameters on the organisation and control of the labour processes, including those involving clinicians, which have not been inconsequential despite substantial attenuation between policy formulation and implementation (cf. Child, 1985, p. 111). The argument is not whether management strategies are functionally effective, but whether the concept is of any use in analysing organisational change involving hospital doctors. In this context management strategies can be seen to need major qualifications, given the institutional controls the doctors can draw on to oppose the strategies if they believe it necessary. The discussion of medical audit, however, indicates the usefulness of the concept of *managerial strategies*, for it is only by being aware of the competing strategies (of the profession and mangement) that the development and outcome of the medical audit issue be understood.

Notes

1. The divisional system of medical organisation advocated by the 'Cog-wheel' reports (1967a and b) entailed the organisation of hospital doctors into 'divisions'. These divisions would normally be according to medical specialties, or clinical areas. The chairpersons of the divisions within a hospital, or group of hospitals, would form the medical membership of the medical executive committee.
2. See *BMJ Supplement*, 24 June 1972, p. 168, Motion 284. *Ibid.*, p. 133. 'Competance to Practice', and *BMJ Supplement*, 29 July 1972 'ARM Professional Standards'. The motions and debates 1973–6 subsumed medical audit under other issues, notably the Merrison Inquiry. See for example 'From the ARM: Competence to Practice', 23 June 1973, p. 133, and more generally, 'BMA Special Representatives Meeting', 16 June 1973. *BMJ Supplement*, 13 August 1977, p. 474 'From the ARM: Competance to Practice'. *BMJ Supplement*, 17 June 1978 'ARM Agenda'. *BMJ Supplement* 14 July, p. 143, 'From the ARM: Medical Audit'. *BMJ Supplement*, 14 June 1980, p. 1467 'ARM Agenda'. *BMJ Supplement*, July 1980, pp. 243–4. *BMJ Supplement*, 18 July 1981, 'From the ARM: Medical Audit'.
3. 'Relicensure' refers to a system of retraining or reeducation whereby

doctors have their medical knowledge, and perhaps skills, updated at intervals. If a doctor failed such a course he or she could lose their license to practice medicine. However no such system exists in this country and in the USA relicensure appears only to apply to the 'impaired physician' (Stimson, 1985) despite earlier pronouncements that relicensure would apply to all physicans (Sanazaro, 1974, p. 274).

References

Abercrombie, N. and J. Urry, (1983) *Capital, Labour and the Middle Classes* (London: Allen & Unwin).

Alford, R. R. (1972) 'The Political Economy of Health Care: Dynamics Without Change', *Politics and Society* (Winter).

Arluke, A. (1977) 'Social Control Rituals in Medicine', in R. Dingwall et al. (eds), *Health Care & Health Knowledge* (London: Croom Helm).

Armstrong, P. (1984) 'Competition Between the Organisational Professions and the Evolution of Management Control Strategies' in K. Thompson (ed) *Work, Unemployment and Unemployment* (Milton Keynes: Open University Press).

Braverman, H. (1974) *Labor and Monopoly Capital* (New York: Monthly Review Press).

Burawoy, M. (1979) *Manufacturing Consent* (Chicago University Press).

Butler, J. R. and M. S. B. Vaile (1984) *Health and Health Services* (London: RKP).

Child, J. (1985) 'Management Strategies, New Technology and the Labour Process', in D. Knights et al. (eds) *Job Redesign* (Aldershot: Gower).

Cochrane, A. (1971) *Effectiveness and Efficiency* (London: NPHT).

Coles, J. et al. (1974) 'Control of Resources', *Health and Social Services Journal*, p. 2654–5, 16 November.

Coombs, R. and O. Jonsson (1986) 'New Technology and Hybrid Control Systems: a Case Study of Hospital Outpatient Clinics'. Paper presented to the UNIST–ASTON Organisation and Control of the Labour Process, Fourth Annual Conference.

Cousins, C. (1984) 'Labour Process in the State Service Sector', paper presented at the Second UMIST/ASTON Organisation and Control of the Labour Process Conference, Birmingham.

Derber, C. (1983) 'Sponsorship and the Control of Physicians' *Theory and Society*, vol. 12, no. 5.

Donabedian, A. (1966) 'Evaluating the Quality of Medical Care', *Millbank Fund Quarterley*, vol. XLIV, no. 3, part 2.

Eckstein, H. (1958) *The English Health Service* (Boston: Harvard University Press).

Forsyth, G. et al. (1971) *In Low Gear?* (London: NPHT).

Freidson, E. (1970) *Professional Dominance* (Chicago: Aldine).

Friedman, A. L. (1977) *Industry and Labour* (London: MacMillan).

Garner, L. (1979) *The NHS: Your Money or Your Life* (Harmondsworth: Penguin).

Godber, G. (1975) *Change in Medicine* (London: MPHT).

Godber, G. (1976) 'The Confidential Enquiry into Maternal Deaths. A Limited Study of Clinical Results', in MacLachlan (ed.) *A Question of Quality?* (London: NPHT).

Gough, I. (1979) *The Political Economy of the Welfare State* (London: Macmillan).

Illsley, R. (1980) *Professional or Public Health?* (London: MPHT).

Johnson, T. (1972) *Professions and Power* (London: Macmillan).

Klein, R. (1983) *The Politics of the National Health Service* (London: Longman).

Larson, M. S. (1977) The Rise of Professionalism (London: University of California Press).

Larson, M. S. (1980) 'Proletarianisation & Educated Labor' *Theory & Society*, vol. 9 no. 1, Jan.

Littler, C. R. (1982) *The Development of the Labour Process in Capitalist Societies* (London: HEB).

McLachlan, G. (ed.) (1971) *Challenge for Change* (London: NPHT).

McLachlan, G. (ed.) (1976) *A Question of Quality?* (London: NPHT/OUP).

McLachlan, G., (ed.) (1981) *Reviewing Practice in Medical Care* (London: NPHT).

Martin, J. P. (with D. Evans) (1984) *Hospitals in Trouble* (Oxford: Basil Blackwell).

Maynard, A. (1978) 'The Medical Profession and the Efficiency and Equity of Health Services', *Social & Economic Administration*, vol. 12 no. 1, Spring.

Millman, M. (1977) *The Unkindest Cut* (USA: Wm. Morrow & Co.).

O'Connor, J. (1973) *The Fiscal Crisis of the State* (New York: St Martin's Press).

Ouchi, W. (1981) Theory Z: How American Business Can Meet The Japanese Challenge (Reading, Mass.: Addisson-Wesley).

Roemer, M. I. and J. W. Friedman (1971) *Doctors in Hospitals* (Baltimore: John Hopkins Press).

Stimson, G. V. (1985) 'Recent Developments in Professional Control: the Impaired Physician Movement in the USA', *Sociology of Health & Illness*, vol. 7, no. 2, July, pp. 141–66.

Stelling, J. and R. Bucher, (1973) 'Vocabularies of Realism in Professional Socialisation', *Social Science & Medicine*, vol. 7, pp. 661–75.

Wood, S. (1983) book review of *The Development of the Labour Process in Capitalist Society* (C. R. Littler) and *The Unequal Struggle?* (J. Tomlinson) in *Network*, no. 25, Jan., pp. 16–17.

Reports

Alment, E. A. J. (Chairperson) (1976) Compeance to Practice: the report of a committee of enquiry set up for the medical profession in the UK (London).

'Cogwheel' Report (1967a). First Report of the Joint Working Party on the Organisation of Medical Work in Hospitals (Chairperson: Godber, G. E.) London: HMSO).

'Cogwheel' report (1967b). Organisation of Medical Work in the Hospital Services in Scotland (Chairperson: Brotherstone) (Edinburgh: HMSO).

'Cogwheel' Report (1972). Second Report of the Joint Working Party on the Organisation of Medical Work in Hospitals (Chairperson: Godber, G. E.) (London: HMSO).

'Cogwheel' Report (1974). Information for Action, O. Goldsmith & A. Mason (eds) (London: DHSS).

'Davies Report' (1973). Report of the Committee on Hospital Complaints Procedure (Chairperson: Sir M. Davies) DHAA/Welsh Office (London: HMSO).

Farleigh Hospital Report, NHS (1971). Report of the Farleigh Hospital Committee of Inquiry, Cmnd. 4557 (London: HMSO).

'Grey Book' (1972) *Management Arrangements for the Reorganised NHS* (London: DHSS).

Griffiths Report (1983). National Health Service Management Enquiry, dated 6 October.

Merrison, A. W. (Chairperson) (1975). Report on the Committee of Inquiry into the Regulation of the Medical Profession (London: HMSO).

Merrison, A. W. (1979). Royal Commission on the NHS (London: HMSO).

Royal Commission on the NHS (1979), *see* Merrison.

Medical Journal Articles

(Where full reference does not appear in the text.)

British Medical Journal (BMJ), leading Article 1967 'Modernising Hospital Medicine', 4 Nov.

BMJ., Leading Article (1971a) 'Difficult Decisions' 3 July.

BMJ., Leading Article (1971b) 'Challenge to Change', 20 Nov., p. 443.

BMJ Supplement (1977) 'Submission of Evidence', 29 Jan., p. 301, para. 2.5, and p. 303, para. 3.12.

BMJ Supplement (1981) 'From the ARM: Medical Audit' 18 July.

Chambers, Sir Paul (1972) BMA Report of an Inquiry into the Association's Constitution and Organisation, *BMJ Supplement*, 30 Mar., pp. 45–67.

Duncan, A. (1980) 'Quality Assurance . . .', *BMJ*, 2 Feb.

Sanazaro, P. J. 'Medical Audit: Experience in the U.S.A.', *BMJ*, 16 Feb., p. 271.

Shaw, C. D. (1980a) 'Aspects of Audit: 1. The Background', *BMJ*, 24 May, pp. 1256–7).

Shaw, C. D. (1980b) 'Aspects of Audit: 5. Looking Forward to Audit', *BMJ*, 21 June, p. 1510.

5 New Technology and Management in a Non-Market Environment: A Case Study of Office Automation in Swedish Hospitals

Rod Coombs and Ola Jonsson

INTRODUCTION

Office automation is a convenient label for those applications of 'New Technology' in which clerical activities are in some way automated, or their degree of automation increased. The common feature of the majority of instances of office automation is the ubiquitous VDU and keyboard, which convey a superficial similarity to the appearance of office automation, despite the widely varying contexts. In reality, the clerical processes experiencing change as a result of office automation vary enormously with respect to complexity, scale, range of functions, centrality to the organisation, connections to physical processes and so on. Clearly they merit individual examination, and we should expect substantial variations in associated changes in work organisation. Furthermore, there is an additional aspect of office automation which differentiates its significance from that of manufacturing automation. Systems which increase the degree of automation of routine information transactions also create data-bases from which more elaborate analyses of the performance of an organisation can be calculated. This is a potential management motivation for office automation. Thus it may change the scope, nature and pattern of availability of management control information within an organisation, and thereby have direct consequences for management practices, as well as for the people performing individual clerical tasks.

This paper reports the results of a case study of office automation in hospital out-patient clinics. The technology concerned will be discussed more fully in later sections. Briefly however it can be described as a network of approximately 150 VDU terminals connected through a number of central mini computers. Nurses and secretaries use the terminals to make patient appointments, schedule admissions, collect fees and for various other administrative procedures. Since these operations were formerly carried out using paper forms, telephone conversations and intermittent computer batch processing, the technology achieves a considerable increase in the degree of automation of these procedures. It also forms part of a series of wider changes to the Management Information Systems of the hospitals studied. The effects of these changes on the management structure and managerial motivations are reported in other papers (Coombs 1987). This paper focuses on the changes in functioning of outpatient clinics, the work of the nurses and secretaries who carry out administrative tasks using the terminals, and on the circumstances surrounding the introduction of the technology. We are concerned with the question of what managerial strategy, if any, accompanied the introduction of the technology, whether it had any specific component addressed to the organisation of the work of nurses and secretaries, whether this work did change and how it changed, and whether the changes have any broader significance for the relationships of control and authority between the various occupational groups involved. The two hospitals where the study was conducted are in the southern part of Sweden. One hospital has completed the introduction of the technology over a five-year period, and the other started the process during 1985. The study is a continuing longitudinal one and this paper reports interim results.

THEORETICAL ISSUES

Before examining the case-study in detail, it is worth considering some theoretical issues raised in the study of the relationship between new technology, managerial motivations and work organisation, concentrating in particular on the special circumstances of a publicly-funded healthcare organisation. The *locus classicus* of most discussions of the labour-process has been manufacturing industry and marketed service industries. Many of the recent advances in theoretical and empirical specifications of variations in labour-process change

have made use of variations in the *market* environments of the organisations being studied (Kelly 1985, Rose and Jones 1985). Although these advances have not explicitly addressed the question of the theory of firm behaviour, they have made assumptions about the pressures exerted on managements by product markets and input markets, which are more consistent with a profit maximising model than with any articulated managerial theory of the firm. Market pressures have, to be sure, been finely differentiated and their various possible effects discussed, but little attention has been given to instances of labour-process change in organisations where market pressures are *not* a proximate influence on managerial behaviour. This is however an important case to discuss, since non-market services form an important sector of the economy, (Gershuny 1983).

Hospital services in the UK, and in Sweden where this case-study took place, fall predominantly into this non-marketed category (although the marketed sector in the UK is growing, and is beginning to exert some influences on the NHS). Although some inputs are purchased in (relatively imperfect) markets, the quantity of *output* is not determined by price (explicit or shadow) since none is perceived by the consumer. Furthermore until recently management's knowledge of the relative costs of different medical services was non-existent and their internal accounting procedures incapable of permitting any calculation of efficiency remotely resembling those considered normal or desirable in organisations whose output is marketed. In this situation, external budgetary limitations are the primary financial discipline on the organisation. The extent to which these budgetary limitations exercise a direct influence on managerial attitudes to technology of production and work organisation therefore depends on the stringency of the budget in relation to expected levels of service and past patterns of resource utilisation. It further depends on the extent to which aggregate budgets are passed down the line to unit managers as restraints on their local freedom of action. These matters therefore need analysis in any study of technology and work organisation change in a hospital.

In fact there has been significant change on both these counts in recent years. After the expansion in health care budgets in the 1950s and 60s, the late 1970s and 80s have witnessed increasing pressure on health care expenditure as a component of the pressure on public expenditure in general. Abel-Smith (1984) reports that cost-containment programmes are proliferating in the health systems of all European countries. In addition, a feature of many cost-containment

strategies is indeed the implementation of more disaggregated systems of budgetary control in which smaller units are made into cost-
centres, and even clinicians are required to be budget holders. (This
phenomena is discussed in the Swedish context at some length in
Coombs 1987). The Griffiths Report on the NHS in the UK has this
recommendation at its core. These changes might therefore be
expected to have increased the sensitivity of managers introducing
new technology in health services to the possibilities for cost-saving,
as compared to earlier periods. To summarise this point then, a study
of new technology and work organisation in a hospital must take into
account changes in the nature of the budgetary system (and other
performance-measuring and behaviour-controlling devices).

The second theoretical issue to address in the hospital context is
the ambiguous role of the medical profession in the management of
the organisation. Doctors' clinical decisions are the immediate source
of influence on consumption of resources, but in general it is
administrators rather than doctors who have responsibility for the
resources and who attempt to control them. This makes for a dual
system of authority and control in the organisation with hazy divisions between the roles of the two groups. The basis of the division is
of course the ability of doctors to use their status as a profession to
maintain autonomy in clinical decision-making, and to use this as a
platform from which to influence all management decisions which
affect clinical activity. Indeed Becker and Neuhauser (1975) argue
that the specification of work procedures by management in a
hospital is only possible and only efficient in the non-medical areas of
the hospital, such as general services and administration. They regard
managerial attempts to intervene in the doctors' areas of autonomy as
likely to be dysfunctional for the organisation. Nevertheless recent
trends in budgetary mechanisms, mentioned earlier, go against this
principle. Elsewhere (Coombs 1987) we have argued that some
'doctor-managers' are embracing managerial innovations for a variety
of reasons, and that their direct influence on the details of management could increase. In any event, it is clearly important in the
context of this case-study to examine the relative influences of
doctors and managers on the introduction of the administrative
technology in question, and on the organisation of work of those
using it since their respective motivations may differ.

A third issue, which is partly related to the first two issues,
concerns the goal uncertainty of hospital organisations. The nature of

the patient population to be treated, the prevalence of disease, the identification and implementation of treatment, the assessment of effectivness and efficiency, and changes in these variables, are all matters of interpretation and even dispute within the organisation. This is not to suggest that there are no similar goal disputes in market-based organisations, but in general it should be accepted that there is a relatively high goal uncertainty in hospitals. This phenomenon, coupled with significant task uncertainty, makes the environment for the introduction of new technology less straightforward from a managerial point of view.

There is little theoretical analysis of management motivation in introducing office automation in non-market environments. In a recent review of the links between management strategies and new technology in market environments, Child (1985) identifies four principal management objectives and four principal techniques which form a 'repertoire' of strategies. The four objectives are reduction in costs, increases in quality, increases in flexibility, and increases in managerial control. The four techniques for achieving these objectives are elimination of labour, contracting arrangements, polyvalent labour, and de-skilling of labour (see also Coombs 1985 on some of these points). However, since the context of his review is one of organisations facing markets for their output, with management structures which are not in competition with a strong internal professional group, and who are likely to at least be able to agree on the goal of a surplus of revenue over expenditure in the long run, it is not clear whether these motives and techniques will apply in nonmarket situations. It is therefore interesting to consider to what extent Child's objectives and techniques are evident and significant in this hospital case-study, or to what extent they are in need of modification.

THE CASE STUDY

The account of the case-study is divided into four parts: a description of data-sources and methods; a description of the work of an outpatient clinic and the role of the computer technology; an analysis of the origins of the technology and the motivations behind its introduction; and a discussion of changes in work organisation and the reasons behind them.

Data Sources and Methods

Two surgical out-patient clinics were studied. The first clinic, in hospital A, has been operating the computer technology for some years, as had the rest of the clinics in the hospital. The second clinic, in hospital B, was the first clinic in that hospital to use the technology, and the implementation took place during the study period. Data were collected by observation, interview and analysis of documentation. In both clinics the researchers spent several weeks observing the work of all of the staff carrying out administrative tasks. Lists of tasks for each work role were compiled and validated with the staff. Note was taken of any formal or informal task-sharing, job rotation etcetera. Maps of the information flows generated by the administrative tasks were developed and checked with staff to ensure that they were accurate. Staff were interviewed at the place of work to cross-check the accuracy of our observations of the division of labour, and to elucidate some of their attitudes to the work. The relevant forms, diaries, files, computer material and other records were also examined. The result was a complete description of the administrative processes associated with the flow of patients, records, cash and information through the two organisations. In the case of the clinic which implemented the technology during the study, this was done before and after the implementation. Thus there is a comparative and a longitudinal dimension to the study. The attitudes and reason which lay behind the introduction of the technology were examined through another programme of interviews conducted with managers, doctors and EDP professionals in the various levels of hospital management. These interviews were part of the larger project on changes to management information systems mentioned earlier (Coombs 1987).

The Functioning of a Clinic and the Role of Computer Technology

The clinic is the basic organisational unit in the Swedish hospital. It consists of a number of doctors with a common clinical specialism, a staff of nurses, secretaries and associated staff, and physical facilities such as wards, treatment rooms etcetera. The clinic is a cost-centre with a management structure led by a senior doctor. Unlike the UK NHS, the nurses and facilities are under the direct control of the doctors, rather than nurses having their own hospital-wide management structure. The two surgical clinics studied were therefore large, relatively self contained organisations each employing over 100

persons, but relying on the hospital services for laboratory facilities, laundry, meals, supplies etcetera. Our work concentrated on out-patient activities, though the interface between out-patient and in-patient work was also examined. The functioning of the out-patient clinic can be briefly described as follows.

The clinic receives a continuous flow of requests for appointments to be made for patients at the clinic. These come from a number of sources; patients themselves may ring or call, doctors outside the clinic may write a letter of referral, doctors within the clinic may decide that a patient needs to be seen again at some interval in the future, in-patient departments discharging patients may require their treatment to be continued in the form of a series of out-patient consultations, accident and emergency clinics may refer patients for follow-up treatment at an appropriate specialist clinic. These requests arrive on paper, by telephone, and in person. The heart of the administrtive system is therefore a set of appointment diaries for the doctors or teams of doctors, and a system of priorities and evaluation mechanisms to allocate the demand for appointments to the appro-priate doctors. In the Swedish context, the actual appointments have to be registered at the time of patient arrival for two purposes, firstly to ensure that the patient has arrived and that the time slot is not vacant, and secondly because the patient is required to pay a small standard fee and receive a receipt, and if they are from outside the tax-base area of the hospital their home county will be charged a larger fee.

Associated routines which have to be integrated with the main routine are: the coordinated booking of appointments at diagnostic service departments such as X-ray, blood testing etcetera, and the provision of the results of these tests at the appropriate time; placing patients on waiting lists for in-patient treatment; up-dating and archiving of medical records (patient notes) following treatment, and provision of records to the doctor at the time of appointment; recording of diagnostic information for statistical purposes and transmission to central data-collection agencies; correspondence with patients on appointments and other matters.

It is clear therefore that there is a considerable burden of adminis-tration surrounding the operation of the out-patient clinic. Some aspects of the work are necessary simply to operate the clinic itself, some are necessary to achieve efficient coordination with the other parts of the hospital and other clinics, and other aspects reflect the need for aggregate statistical information on the flows of patients and

resources consumed in the clinic for the purposes of managerial surveillance and control. Some of this work is performed by secretaries, medical and non-medical, some is performed by nurses, alongside more recognisable nursing functions, and a small part of the work may be performed by doctors.

In a paper-based system for the performance of the above functions, the main components are folders or books used as doctor diaries, multiple-copy-forms for recording of visits, test requests, waiting list placements, diagnosis records etcetera. Without pre-empting the later analysis, it is clear that there are a number of physical limitations on data-availability imposed by this system. Access to the appointment possibilities is limited by access to the diary, and access to data on visits and other topics dealt with through multiple copy forms is dependent on the transmission and processing of the form copies.

The computer based system is call 'TPAS' (Terminal-Based Patient Administration System). On this system, the doctor diaries for several weeks or months ahead are stored in the computer memory, thus becoming available to any other system user with a terminal and the appropriate security code. Some other limited information on purpose of appointment can also be entered at this stage. The registration of visits and fees paid, as well as waiting list placement and several of the other routines which are form-based in the manual system, are also achieved through direct data entry on the terminals. In a large out-patient clinic there may be as many as 15 terminals with access to this information and in use as points of entry of such information to the system. Some are used by secretaries, some by nurses, and some by medical records archivists.

Given that the clinic is one of several clinics in the hospital, the system is developed in such a way that the specialised administrative departments outside the clinics also have terminals and printers attached to the system, and use them to receive and process information on such issues as billing of other authorities for treatment of external patients, billing of non-attenders, centralised computer printing of appointment letters to patients, and printing of special statistical summaries of the clinic's activities both for clinic management and for hospital management. At present the incorporation of diagnostic service departments into the system is incomplete. Thus while it is possible for some clinics to make direct X-ray bookings on the terminals, it is not possible to make other test bookings, and so multiple copy forms are still in use for some of these functions, in

conjunction with telephone contact. These and other aspects of the system are subject to continual development and integration as the system is implemented throughout the hospital. This evolutionary character of the system will eventually change the system into something much more substantial than the original conception, with all-embracing management information purposes. This is partly a consequence of the enormous potential of the technology itself.

The Origins and Development of TPAS

TPAS was not purchased as a complete system from an outside supplier. It was developed internally by the computer staff of hospital A in the late 1970s using hardware components available on the open market, but with software produced entirely within the organisation. It has continued to grow in terms of range of functions as well as in terms of numbers of clinics and workers using the system. Hospital A then agreed in the mid-1980s to sell the software package and the expertise to Hospital B (which is financially separate and in a different county and tax-base). Hospital B is making its own substantial alterations and extensions and thereby contributing to the evolution of the system. Thus the context of managerial motivations is slightly different in the two cases. Hospital A was engaging in an internal technological innovation process, whereas hospital B was deciding to adopt and improve a reltively established technology. We can expect this difference to have some impact on expectations and intentions of those concerned.

Taking the innovating hospital first, it is useful to distinguish external and internal sources of influence on the decision to develop the technology. There were two external influences. Firstly, during the late 1960s and early 70s there were a number of government instructions to hospitals to increase the complexity of the statistical information generated on incidence of certain diagnoses, and on length of waiting lists. This increased the need for administrative procedures, and in particular it triggered the need for accurate data on bed-occupancy on a day to day basis. Secondly, in 1972 hospital doctors were finally placed on a formal salaried basis as hospital employees. They no longer collected their own fees for out-patient appointments and made their own administrative arrangements, instead it became the responsibility for the hospital administration to perform these tasks. This was the final eradication of the fee-for-service principle in Swedish medicine. These demands on

administration resulted in the development of substantial EDP departments carrying out batch processing of the data provided by clinics on machine-readable paper forms.

The internal sources of influence were three-fold. First and most important were the EDP–Computer staff. They experienced the pressing problems of organising the collections of large volumes of paper forms from around the hospital site, getting the information coded, running the batch processing, and returning the data to users in a short time-span. The logistics of the problem became progressively unmanageable, and so they sought a solution in which the data were captured remotely, as a direct result of the work of the people in the clinics. The technology of distributed on-line computing was by then the state-of-the-art for these professionals. It was therefore both the solution to their problem and desirable as a professional aspiration and as an increase in the size and significance of the computing function in the organisation. They set about establishing a coalition of forces in the organisation to support the considerable investment and upheaval necessary to develop the system. This called into play the two other internal sources of influence; the doctors and the administrators.

Doctors in some of the clinics at the hospital were interested in collection of more accurate data on numbers of patients with specific diagnoses for the purposes of clinical research. The suggestion of on-line data capture of patients administrative data appealed to them. There was also pressure on doctors to increase the continuity of patient-doctor interactions, so that patients could hope to see the same doctor on successive visits. The paper-based systems resulted in many mistakes in the appointment schedules, with double-bookings, gaps, fluctuating work-loads etcetera. Therefore there was some expectation that the on-line system would improve this situation. A small group of doctors therefore supported the project and offered their clinic as a test-bed for the development work.

Finally, the administrators were involved when the computer staff asked them to help in the systems analysis required to design the system. Their contribution to this task alerted them to the long-term potential of the system, and they realised that immediate decisions on altering designs of new buildings were implied. They undertook the task of producing detailed plans for a fullscale TPAS for the hospital, costings, and arguments to convince the county council (the source of fiannce), that the investment was worthwhile. Their motivating arguments concentrated on the improvement in service quality which would result from the system. A subsidiary argument was a reduction

in the rate of growth of administrative employment; there were no planned reductions in employment, nor have there been. The administrators did not have a clear view of *how* increased managerial control might also result from the system, though some of them suspected it might be an extra pay-off in the longer term. For the most part, the administrators saw themselves as promoting a technological solution to the problem of a creaking batch systems of data-processing, which would bring added spin-offs in the area of service quality. The financial climate in Sweden at the time was not as stringent as it is now, and the technology appeared to be a prestigious and modern thing to develop, which would reflect well on the organisation's image.

In hospital B, a number of things combined to make managerial intentions rather different. Firstly, the initiative came from the administrators at the top level, as well as computer professionals; doctors were not centrally involved. Secondly, the hospital had had the opportunity to observe the system in the first hospital, to witness growing wareness of more elaborate functions and long-term potential, and to contemplate how the system could be used in their hospital. Thirdly, hospital B was very concerned with other changes to administration and management procedure, and had for some time been operating highly disaggregated budgets which were designed to increase financial discipline at clinic level. Therefore it was predisposed to pursue any possible means of strengthening the management information systems of the hospital. Fourthly, it decided to implement TPAS at a time when the financial climate had changed dramatically, with overall budget cuts for healthcare in three successive years, and great pressure to increase efficiency and cut costs.

In terms of Child's objectives then, there was some significant change in the period between hospital A's development of TPAS, and hospital B's decision to adopt. For hospital A, quality improvement was the most clearly visible objective, with cost reduction and increased managerial control only faintly visible. For hospital B, all three objectives of quality, efficiency and control were prominent. (Hospital B went so far as to calculate interest savings from the ability to use TPAS to chase unpaid bills more effectively).

Child's objective of flexibility does not translate so directly into this environment. In the manufacturing context it refers to more frequent changes to products and production schedules, and to flexible work-roles. There are some similar consequences of TPAS for the clerical workers, but they were not anticipated by managers. The more relevant way to interpret the flexibility concept in this context is

perhaps the degree of permissiveness of the TPAS technology which allows other data, such as budget data, to be transmitted on the same terminals. Thus TPAS becomes the information technology 'core network' for the hospital. This possibility was only dimly perceived by hospital A, but is seen as a definite benefit by hospital B, which is already conducting experiments in this area. Thus TPAS confers 'system flexibility' on the information system of the hospital.

There was therefore a substantial difference in the factors leading to the use of the technology in the two hospitals. The second hospital perceived more benefits than the first, despite the first hospital being the innovator. This is not out of line with other analyses of the changing nature of incentives during diffusion of innovations, (see for example Metcalfe 1981). If the same technology can be associated with differing managerial intentions in two closely related organisations, then we can expect implementation and techniques to vary also. These issues are discussed in the next section.

Changes in the Work of the Clinics Associated with TPAS

The description and analysis in this section start by examining the changes in each of the two clinics, and then proceeds to broader issues. In the case of hospital A's surgical clinic the data is based on observations on the present situation, and reconstruction of the preceding developments through interviews and study of documentation. In the case of hospital B's surgical clinic, the data is based on observation of the situation both before and shortly after the introduction of TPAS.

Hospital A

Before TPAS was introduced, the normal division of labour was for medical secretaries to do almost all administrative work, and nurses almost none. The clinic was divided between three sites with a different pool of doctors on each site. On two of the sites some secretaries dealt exclusively with typing and handling patient notes, while others dealt solely with making appointments and related tasks. On the third site the principle was a one doctor to one secretary system in which the secretary did both typing and booking. When TPAS terminals were introduced there was no immediate change. Secretaries used the terminals only in the modes and tasks which

related to their pre-existing role, even though all terminals had the same potential, and so task reorganisation could have been contemplated.

One interesting change did take place at this stage. A new role was created called the 'advice nurse'. She dealt with incoming fresh patient enquiries (self-referrals) on the telephone by counselling them on whether they really needed to make an appointment and making the appoinment with a doctor of her choice if she saw fit. This role had been suggested earlier, but was difficult to implement without the multiple access to the doctors' schedules afforded by the TPAS terminals. The technology therefore facilitated a work organisation change already sought by the staff themselves (this was not a managerial suggestion).

Some time after the introduction of TPAS the clinic was rationalised from its three sites into one new building. This resulted in a perceived imbalance between the work-loads of various secretaries because of the differing practices inherited from the three previous sites. The senior clinic secretary, who has some administrative responsibility, together with the deputy senior doctor, decided to implement the one-doctor–one-secretary principle as standard throughout the clinic, with the exception of a general office to handle registration of arriving patients, and other clinic-wide tasks such as telephone requests for changed appointments etcetera. Furthermore a job-rotation scheme was agreed amongst the secretaries working for the doctors, though this did not include personnel in the general office. This situation entailed purchasing more TPAS terminals. It was certainly facilitated by a relative over-manning of the clinic due to the concentration of staff from the different sites and the failure to exploit scale economies in the new unified clinics. There was no attempt to reduce manning.

The secretaries working for the doctors now had what they perceived as 'enlarged' jobs, since they did all the administrative tasks associated with one patient: tests ordering, booking, note-typing, filing etcetera. In the general office, although secretaries dealt with a flow of patients, they had other responsibilities resulting from the extra administrative procedures made possible by TPAS, and so also perceived a more varied job, even if less so than that of their colleagues who worked for one doctor. Nurses were still doing relatively little administration, though they sometimes came to look at the terminals to get information needed to conduct some interaction with a patient or to deal with test or X-ray results.

A comparison of the functioning of this clinic, with TPAS in a mature state, with the paper-based administration we witnessed in hospital B (or in residual areas in hospital A) reveals a number of important changes in procedure. Firstly, the multiple access to the data-base yields very evident reductions in time spent on some tasks and in time spent on the internal telephone. Secondly, routine production of printed material such as appointment letters saves typing time. Thirdly, a rudimentary electronic mail function in TPAS speeds up interactions with the medical records department. Fourthly, new functions have been created, such as computer-based taxi ordering for invalid patients and automatic flagging of patients who need to be called in for long-term follow-up appointments. In general, it is clear that these operational changes represent a considerable increase in the *capacity* of the administrative system, both in terms of quantity of functions performed, and range of functions. Indeed, during the period since TPAS was installed, patient thoughput has increased considerably but staff numbers have remained constant. In the areas where TPAS terminals provide a new way of performing existing tasks, it appeared to the researchers and to the secretaries that task uncertainty was reduced. The secretaries felt more in control of the situation and had to hold less information in their heads. This facilitated the capacity increases in the system but, as we have seen, did not result in a concentration of roles on smaller task repertoires. In fact the opposite occurred. Furthermore the increases in service quality which had been hoped for did occur, in terms of fewer appointment errors, more regular work schedules for doctors, and dramatic increases in patient-doctor continuity.

In terms of Child's four 'techniques' for achieving work-organisation benefits from new technology: labour reduction, contracting, polyvalence, and de-skilling, the following tentative conclusions can be drawn. Labour reduction occurred only in the specific sense of increasing the productivity of existing labour, and avoiding extra recruitment. Polyvalence did appear to some extent, but at the instigation of the secretaries themselves, not the hospital management. Contracting and de-skilling did not occur to any significant effect. This apparent absence of explicit interventions in work organisation by management is consistent with the loose and ill-defined motive of increasing quality. The technology was essentially left to have 'its own' effects which meant, in practice, giving responsibility to the users.

Hospital B

The pre-TPAS organisation in this clinic was quite different to that in the hospital A clinic. Firstly, all booking of appointments, placing on waiting lists and similar tasks is done by under-nurses, who also do the low-level nursing tasks of getting the patient and notes into the right rooms, helping them to undress etcetera. This administrative work was done by secretaries in hospital A. The note-typing is done by secretaries 'borrowed' from the wards for several hours a day. Amongst these under-nurses and secretaries in the consulting rooms there is no rotation, they are there every day; but the doctors change on a daily basis. Secondly, in the clinic's general office, which performs similar functions to that of the other clinic, there is some job rotation around the more repetitious roles such as patient registration. This was not the case in the first hospital. The most striking difference between the two clinics is in their staffing levels. The second clinic has only half the combined nurse and secretary staff per patient as the first clinic. The economy appears to result from the historical particularity of having a sizeable part of the administrative work done by the under-nurses *interspersed between their nursing tasks*. Even so there are fewer nurses per patient in this clinic, despite their wider roles.

These differences in organisation and staffing result from the peculiar local traditions and received patterns. Our interviews revealed that no-one, either at hospital management or clinical management level, knew that such wide differences existed. The most knowledgeable organisations concerning the differences were the various unions representing the different types of staff. These variations illustrate, if nothing else, the wide range of *possible* work organisation patterns which can be imagined for these clinics. The staff at the surgical clinic in hospital B, both nursing and secretarial, certainly feel under pressure and over-worked; the researchers formed the opinion that the pace of work was indeed more hectic than in hospital A. The staff hoped for benefits from TPAS, but also showed some suspicion towards it and resented the disruption surrounding its introduction.

At the time of writing, over a year after the installation of the TPAS terminals in hospital B's clinic, no changes in the division of labour have taken place. All roles have the same basic task repertoire, though some have new tasks resulting from the extra

administrative functions permitted by TPAS. However this is not really surprising. No change to work-organisation was almost a *condition* of implementation as far as the staff were concerned, and the staff have simply accepted the technology as an aid to speedy information transactions and have not even discussed any need to change work-roles.

What is interesting is that in this case there is considerable pressure on the functioning of the clinic's administration and on quality of work, yet the new technology is not associated with any *intentions* to change work organisation. In hospital A, slack resources *facilitated* some re-organisation, but by the staff themselves, rather than from above. This hospital (B) is the one which we identified as having more elaborate and cost-related objectives in its decision to implement TPAS. Yet, as has been shown, this has *not* been manifested as a more articulated and detailed strategy for extracting the benefits of TPAS. So far the technology has simply been superimposed on an existing organisational structure, without changing it. At the time of writing however, there is some evidence that some of the *doctors* in the clinic may be thinking about possible benefits or re-organisation. The reason for this slow rate of change are discussed next.

MANAGEMENT STRATEGY AND WORK ORGANISATION

An issue which emerges from both clinics in the case study is that the management of both hospitals, while having objectives for the TPAS which have some limited similarity to those mentioned by Child, have almost no views on, let alone strategy toward, the actual organisational context in which TPAS is used. Indeed the specially created hospital-based 'expert' teams who coordinate the implementation of TPAS take it as an article of faith that the clinic staff themselves should decide on organisational matters, and the teams simply provide the technology, explain it, and put it in the appropriate places. This important attitude on the part of the implementation teams stems from a mixture of three factors. Firstly, some of the personnel articulated the view that the staff have a right to determine how they will use the technology. This appears to be an important feature of the ideological climate toward work quality in Scandinavia. The notion that workers have a right to 'hands-on' control of the introduction of new technology appears deeply rooted in the contem-

porary Swedish culture, such that explicit management interventions are considerably attenuated.

Insofar as the senior managers are aware that their implementation staff take this non-interventionist stance, they do not appear to challenge it. Secondly, the implementation teams do not want to alienate the clinic staff by suggesting organisational changes. Thirdly, especially in the case of hospital B where experience is lacking, the implementation teams simply have not formed any personal opinions on whether any organisational changes are desirable, let alone what they might be. Thus the balance of initiative rests entirely with clinic staff to respond as they see fit to the opportunity afforded by TPAS to change their mode of operation.

Why is this? The answer lies in the relative roles of doctors and administrators in running the hospital and the clinic, as mentioned at the beginning of this paper. Management is divided between administrators and doctors. The administrators concentrate on hospital-wide matters, and leave the management of individual clinics to their senior doctors. In fact the new budget systems give the doctors even more managerial responsibility. The doctors in their turn, practice a laissez-faire, reactive approach to the management of the administrative work in the clinic. Their culture, ethos and concerns are framed in medical terms and not in managerial or administrative terms. They do not see the organisation of secretarial work or nursing work as a problem unless it either inconveniences their own work through not meshing with their needs, or else is forced to their attention by discontent amongst the administrative staff.

Thus, over the years, arrangements develop in an atmosphere in which the administrative tasks can be organised by the staff themselves, as long as the *outputs* to doctors and to hospital accounting departments are seen as adequate by those recipients. In other words the hospital managers and the clinic doctors see clinic administration as a black box which has inputs and outputs. So long as the outputs are produced they do not look inside the black box. Thus the wide variation in practices, manning levels, and responses to technical change can be seen as explicable in terms of the local circumstances. The dual control system of an administrative hierarchy and a professional hierarchy which is characteristic of a hospital appears to be capable of exerting only a weak influence on the way in which administrative personnel use new technology. The close integration of the administrative work with the patient flow, which is at the heart of the *doctors'* work content, further insulates it from outside

managerial intervention. Furthermore the hospital management are at full stretch reacting to and extracting the management information potential of TPAS to generate benefits in the higher-level management tasks of long-term planning, and cost analysis.

However it is precisely these more elaborate changes in management practice which may eventually bring pressure on clinic management (senior doctors) to open up the work-organisation 'black box'. The trend to create detailed budgets, output targets, and performance indicators for clinics is accelerating. Systems such as TPAS contribute to the hospital administrator's ability to do this. Their strategy is to place clinics under a more severe regime of incentives and penalties to be cost-effective. As this continues, senior clinic doctors will have to look more carefully at all aspects of their organisation in order to achieve increments of performance along the administrator's chosen dimensions of performance. This may result in more scrutiny of work organisation, uncovering of 'irrational' variations, and tendencies to suggest 'norms' of best-practice. This may be more evident in hospital B than hospital A, where awareness is already greater, and the early stage of TPAS implementation offers more opportunity for intervention. Again, this will be monitored by future research. A related issue for further research is the attitudes of the secretaries and nurses unions to the possibility of greater intervention, and to the expression of some managerial preference as to whether nurses or secretaries should be primarily responsible for operating TPAS.

CONCLUSIONS

We have argued that the presence of a budgetary mechanism, whether loosely or tightly imposed, as an alternative to a market for output has resulted in this case in a relative *dilution* of the immediacy of Child's four managerial objectives of cost reduction, quality improvement, control increase and flexibility increase. Nevertheless the objectives are visible, and they are more manifest now than five years ago because of the change in financial climate. Indeed they are more manifest in the second hospital than the first, because of the change in climate during the time lag between the two decisions to implement TPAS. Publicly funded organisations can therefore exhibit similar managerial motivations to market-based organisations with respect to introducing new technology, but with differing degrees of intensity.

But, the will, knowledge, and instruments to intervene in the way in which the new technology is implemented are also low in these two hospitals, because of the peculiar management structure described in earlier sections of the paper. The dual authority system, and the traditional pattern of doctors being 'absentee supervisors' of clinic-based clerical work, is a major obstacle to the existence of management strategies of the type seen in other organisations and discussed in the literature. Set against this however, if the new tendency to make senior doctors more responsible for performance continues, they could begin to take their supervisory responsibilities more seriously. The consequences for the organisation, for the clerical work, and for the medical profession, will be interesting to observe.

References

Abel-Smith, B. (1984) 'Cost-containment in healthcare', Occasional papers in Social Administration, n. 73 (London School of Economics).

Becker, S and D. Neuhauser (1975) *The Efficient Organisation*, (Amsterdam: North Holland).

Child, J. (1985) 'Managerial Strategy, New Technology, and the Labour Process' in Knights et al. (1985).

Coombs, R. (1985) 'Automation, Management Strategies, and Labour-Process Change' in Knights et al. (1985).

Coombs, R. (1987) 'Accounting for the Control of Doctors: Management Informaion Systems in Hospitals', *Accounting, Organisations and Society* (in Press).

Gershuny, J. (1983) *'Social Innovation and the Division of Labour'* (Oxford University Press).

Kelly, J. (1985) 'Management's Redesign of Work. Labour Process, Labour Markets, and Product Markets', in Knights et al. (1985).

Knights, D. et al. (eds) (1985) *Job Redesign* (Gower Press).

Metcalfe, S. (1981) 'Impulse and Diffusion in Technical Change' *Futures*, vol. 13, no. 5, pp. 347–60.

Rose, M. and Jones, B. (1985) 'Managerial Strategy and Trade Union Responses in Work Reorganisation Schemes at Establishment Level' in Knights et al. (1985).

6 Academics and their Labour Process

Henry Miller

The U.G.C. can rest assured that Aston will unprompted seek academic excellence against a background of improved cost effectiveness, enhanced efficiency, better plant utilisation, devolved accountability and last but not least an unwavering corporate commitment to clearly articulated academic objectives.

'Planning for the Late 1980s',
Response to the U.G.C. from Aston University
1985, p. 67.

The most disturbing aspect of the current debate which reduced everything to competing styles of relative emphasis was a slow but certain erosion of academic freedom, the proliferation of bureaucratic control, the hasty and almost opportunistic assertion of spurious standards for measuring performance and quality and the mounting burden of meaningless attempts to prove this or that to the powers that be.

Dr I. G. Patel, Director of the London School of Economics,
THES, 21.3.86, p. 7.

This chapter attempts to discuss some aspects of the situation of academics as cultural workers in higher education in relation to questions of their labour process. The above contrasting quotations illustrate different stances which academic management in universities have taken in the current situation. At the level of the ordinary academic we also find a range of responses, which may include co-operation and defiance as well as a routine or ritualised performance of tasks. Some concentrate on specific academic work which insulates them from and facilitates movement out of particularly hostile or unsatisfactory work environments. Many have already left academic institutions, taking enhanced mobility payments or early retirement.

This is in an economic and political context in which throughout the 1980s government has underfunded universities and been critical of academics. It is not surprising that many have sought posts in

109

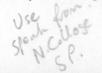

universities abroad or in the private sector, where rewards and recognition are more assured. A joint survey by the Committee of Vice Chancellors and the Association of University Teachers showed that in 1988 one in eight posts fell vacant (West 1989).

There are many paradoxes about trying to write about the work of academics from a broad labour process perspective. Firstly, the writer and many of the readers know at least their own work situation and that of immediate colleagues, but that does not mean that academics have been particularly forward in analysing their own situation in any rigorous way, let alone from a Marxist labour process position. That is hardly surprising in that the focus of labour process theory has been on the division of labour around the production of goods for profit in the private sector rather than the provision of services in the public sector.

There is the further oddity that the very process of writing the chapter is seen by many as part of the academic work process we are attempting to analyse. We could all be seen in one sense as participant observers of the labour process of academics, although we are not of course simply participant observers. The work is part of our life so that the freedoms and constraints are real. We live with the work, so that re-working a paper originally presented with a colleague from Malta, Reno Samut, to the Fourth UMIST–Aston Labour Process Conference, presents to the writer in a reflexive form the stresses, satisfactions, pressures and opportunities of academic life! The topic of the academic labour process does not attract a large audience at sociology, education or political economy conferences; it gains more attention at meetings of the managers and administrators of universities and polytechnics. Nevertheless the topic is endlessly discussed informally over coffee or in the bar, particularly when established routines are under threat. I am writing this piece influenced by my own experience as an academic at Aston University and draw on Aston as an example of changes in the management of the academic labour process.

In one sense Aston could be seen as a deviant case; most universities are not as predominantly technological as Aston nor have they been subjected to the same degree of contraction and restructuring. On the other hand, perhaps we can see Aston as an extreme case which other universities may increasingly resemble, not only experiencing considerable external economic and political pressure, but also in the developers style and structure of management with the

Vice-Chancellor acting like a chief executive. This seems to be gaining some external recognition, including a knighthood for the Vice-Chancellor, Professor Crawford, after only 4 years in office, a subvention of a quarter of a million pounds from the UGC, and only average cuts in the 'second round' in 1986 as compared to a cut of 31 per cent in July 1981. Some have seen close connections with Conservative party policy and personnel, the Personnel Officer in the early 1980s being Norman Tebbitt's brother and the University being favoured with a string of ministerial visits.

There have been considerable changes at Aston. For example, between 1980 and 1989 the University has changed from an institution with four faculties (including one of Humanities and Social Sciences) with twenty-four departments and groups and nearly 540 full-time academic staff to one of three faculties (Science, Engineering and Management and Modern Languages) with only nine departments and under 250 academic staff. While there has been a very substantial reduction in student population the staff–student ratio has increased from 1:10.3 in 1980 to 1:12.9 in 1985–6 and 1:15 in 1988–9. As the November 1985 response from the University to the UGC *Planning for the Late 1980s* put it:

> The restructuring that has occurred in the University over the last five years in its academic programme, staffing, student body and physical facilities is probably more profound than anywhere else in the UK university system. (pp. 6–7, Aston University 1985).

At the same time, for many of the remaining staff the academic labour process remains in its core activities remarkably constant. Little of the activity of teaching, research, scholarship, counselling and administration has changed in five or ten or even fifteen years. What has changed are the context and the pressures on these activities and these in their turn may change the experiences and their meaning.

In order to attempt to analyse academic work as part of labour process and in its other dimensions, I believe we need a number of perspectives and approaches, not least of which is reflection on one's own situation and activity. I intend to do the following. A brief discussion of general features of the labour process debate as it does and does not relate to the situation of academics is followed by some discussion of some education theorists as they discuss academic work. I then return to a Marxist labour process perspective to describe the

work of academics. I attempt to do this by using a description of the day-to-day routines of teaching, administration and research, while considering variation and difference within them. This approach leads to a more general discussion of the labour market and how the managerial strategies of universities and the state affects control of the labour process. This will involve consideration of the use of contracts, the relations between qualification, legitimation and control, and the ways in which parts of the state and capital have been restructuring the work of academics over recent years. Finally, there is some consideration of academics' actual and potential response to these pressures.

THE LABOUR PROCESS DEBATE AND ACADEMICS

Thompson (1983) commenting on the labour process debate in *The Nature of Work*, says

> A labour process perspective locates the basic activity of transforming raw materials into products through human labour within a given technology, within the specific dynamics of a mode of production and antagonistic class relations. (p. 4, intro.)

His argument is focused centrally on the 'transformation of raw materials' and while a wide analysis of the dynamics of a capitalist or indeed socialist system of production can include the relation of academic work to that process of transforming nature into products with a market and–or use value, the labour process perspective has not as yet dealt directly with this sort of service work.

Thompson (1983) argues that the question of 'how do workers control themselves in the context of practices deeply embedded in the capitalist labour process' is important, and that 'this means taking up issues of ideology and culture and how they influence the relations between consent, control and resistance at work'. Certainly questions of ideology and culture are central to an understanding of the work of academics in universities, polytechnics and colleges and indeed the work of teachers in schools. Perhaps these are more easily considered from perspectives concerned centrally with the processes of reproduction of labour and labour power and the legitimation of state and the social order.

Littler and Salaman (1982), in their critique of Braverman and

discussion of recent theories of the Labour Process, identify the way in which *Labor and Monopoly Capitalism* (1974) has

1. Rejuvenated the sociological study of the workplace and the labour process, by re-assessing the inherently class-based nature of work organisation.
2. Has advanced class theory and work analysis by insisting on the connection between the two.
3. Served to restore the sociology of the labour process to its central place within sociological debate and theorising.

They show some of the weaknesses of Braverman's analysis in terms of the restrictions of his theory of class conflict, relating this to what they see as an inadequate conception of control in the labour process. They note the extensions and revisions of Braverman's work by authors such as Offe (1976), Burawoy (1978) and Edwards (1979), particularly in their emphasis on the importance of dependence in employment relationships and the variety of modes of managerial control, but they conclude '... a more useful theory of labour processes cannot be restricted to the specification of work activities at the point of production itself but must take account of the control implications of decisions taken elsewhere in the organisation and, indeed, outside it. The subordination of labour, real or otherwise, cannot be understood at the level of labour process' (*Sociology*, Vol. 16, No. 2., p. 266, May 1982).

We can recognise the utility of raising these central questions for an analysis of the work situation in terms of its relation to the general dynamics of class forces. We can accept that the debates have become increasingly sophisticated in terms of identifying different forms of control. What is more difficult to accept is that a labour process analysis which still starts and focuses on industrial labour within the private sector of a capitalist society can easily be extended to deal with the public sector, or specifically a higher education in capitalist or socialist societies. It may be that links can be made if the analysis encompasses ideologies of collegiality, professionalism and service. Certainly the attention to forms of control which connect the appropriation, planning and organising work to the higher reaches of management (academic in this case) and the place of technology within this is useful. Conventional non-Marxist accounts of academic work and institutions seem to miss crucial dimensions of the ways in which crises within the economy and policy translate themselves into

the problems facing us in universities now. What is needed is a location of labour process theory within a broader political economy approach which itself does not neglect to pay attention to specifics of work and work organisation within this sector, but we shall return to this.

ACADEMICS WITHIN HIGHER EDUCATION SYSTEMS

Let us now turn to Burton Clark (1983), one of the foremost analysts of comparative higher education systems, and identify the central elements of his analysis of the work of academics in relation to the broader social system. Burton Clark's work is concerned with the academic labour process. Like Weber he focuses on power and politics in his analysis of education systems and their relation to society. He also argues that the distinctive processes of academic work, teaching and research (but particularly research) form the most important features of the academic profession and that each education system will have distinctive features related to the history and politics of the society in which its exists.

Trow (1983) in focusing on the finance of higher education identifies in Clark four analytically, if not practically, distinct ways or modes, which organise and decide the size, shape, character and funding of higher education systems. These ways of organising and managing the institutions of higher education are characterised as firstly, a professional guild system where academic norms and values are defined and applied by more or less eminent members of the academy through their contact or colonisation of high administrative office. Secondly, the political system, whether it be by minister, cabinet, legislature, president or junta, may decisively control and shape higher education. Thirdly, the bureaucracy and its rules and regulations and civil servants can be crucial in determining what happens in and to higher education. Fourthly, the influence of the market, not planned, where the decisions of many actors competing for goods, money or power, students, teachers or graduates, influence the shape, structure and processes of higher education. These formulations are of some use in analysing particular cases, but the analysis has to be placed in the broader context of the influence of economic and production relations. This emphasis, present in labour process theory, needs to be retained, and in turn to be related to the role of the State as it responds to and regulates both the economy and higher education.

ACADEMICS AS WORKERS, INTELLECTUALS, PROFESSIONALS

Academics in Britain, whether in universities or polytechnics, share some of the characteristics of a broader group of lecturers and teachers working throughout the education system. The great majority are state employees, although of course amongst academics there are the few working at the small private university of Buckingham, and amongst teachers a much bigger and more significant group working in independent (public–private) schools. Most are primarily dependent on wages in the form of a monthly salary, usually on scales with incremental points. Some are able to supplement this income from consultancy fees and others with royalties from books, and earnings from journalism in various media.

In common with other cultural workers (for example journalists, discussed in Chapter 6), the position of academics can be analysed not only in terms of their labour process and their broad class position, but also through their location and categorisation within the discourses of professionalism and the intellectual.

Through the classic debates on the work of Marx (1973), Gramsci (1971) and Mannheim (1956) and more recently in Britain in the work of Anderson (1968, 1983), Thompson (1965), Williams (1979) and Hickox (1986), there has been an ongoing attention to the relationship of intellectuals to class structure and action. Debray (1981) formulates a wide-ranging and comparative analysis of intellectuals which seeks to relate them to different bases, institutions and sets of productive cultural relations. Thus the education system, publishing and modern electronic media, although interlinked are different bases from within which different types of intellectuals, teachers, writers and celebrities work. He distinguishes between the different political and cultural traditions and their associated institutions, the different cultural apparatuses which distinguish, for example, France, Great Britain and the United States. Mulhern (1981) argues that in the United States the development of mass markets through the applications of research and development occurs earlier than in Britain or France so that, for example, in the 1930s the French educational elite was roughly half the size of that in Britain, and the United States had more institutions of higher education than France did academic personnel.

Not only differences in size but also configuration are important. Thus there is significant centralisation in Paris of intellectual life,

academic publishing, media and political institutions. In Britain certainly there is a dominant Oxford–Cambridge–London nexus and in the United States, New York, Boston and Washington still form somewhat separate but linked centres of control. In the United States and United Kingdom the Ivy League colleges and those of Oxford and Cambridge may still retain an important degree of intellectual dominance, but the expansion of higher education from the late nineteenth century has occurred largely in provincial institutions like the huge state and private universities in America or the British civic universities.

The different relations between state politics and the institutions have already been alluded to in the work of Clark (1983). Clearly in the French case there has been a close association between the political and intellectual establishment since at least the Third Republic. One could argue that from the revolution to the Fifth Republic, the intellectual and political scene in France has been in the main at least formally meritocratic and universalistic, so that intellectuals (including academics) are seen to comprise a distinct stratum or milieu, not simply a network of family connections dependent on a dominant class. This description might apply more easily to the English scene. The question of the existence, never mind the nature, of English intellectuals remains on the agenda, see Hickox's (1986) recent article, 'Has there been a British Intelligentsia?'. It may be too much to deny its existence but clearly intellectuals do have a specific, almost residual character within the British social scene. Many – including academics who in other cultures would describe themselves as intellectual – refuse to do so.

The notion of the professional seems to sit more easily on English academics than that of the intellectual. Indeed Fores and Glover (1981) and Child (1983) see it as a peculiarly Anglo-Saxon phenomenon and Lawn (1981), Larson (1977), Ginsberg et al. (1980) and Meiksins (1986) have all recognised the deeply ideological (yet nevertheless still potent) nature of professionalism, which limits the possibilities of alliance with sections of the working class. The consciousness of status in professionalism is expressed, as Meiksins (1986) has noted:

> a powerful sense of distinctiveness, of entitlement to special privilege and respect and its success may also rest on its ability to provide at least temporary protection from the worst effects of wage-labour by legitimising the professions 'right' to autonomy and high social reward although 'deprofessionalisation' remains a constant danger.
>
> (*New Left Review*, 157, p. 115)

This seems opposite to the situation of academics threatened (amongst other things) with the abolition of 'tenure'. Certainly in the vocabulary of academics and teachers 'profession' is as frequently mentioned as 'union' (Ginsberg, 1980).

Larson (1977) points out distinct differences in the ways in which professionalism has been formed and is articulated in the United States and Britain by the different roles of and relations between the universities, ruling elites and professions. Furthermore within universities the different professional cultures of Law, Medicine, Engineering and Accounting will all have their impact on the self-image, power and prospects of academics working within these institutions and who may see themselves as members of two overlapping professional groups.

ACADEMICS' LABOUR PROCESS

Let us now turn to the core labour processes of the 'typical' academic, keeping in mind the variations in culture, professional history and institutional setting already discussed. I will identify analytically at least the major components of academic work and then explore further variations established by discipline and market situation before discussing the central problem, which is the impact of various forms of control emanating from university management, which itself mediates state and market pressures.

Most academics other than professors, readers and those with a specific research label, carry the title 'Lecturer'. Lecturing and other forms of teaching are the main parts of the academic labour process. These may include the formal lecture, the seminar, class, or laboratory session or individual or small group supervision. Within them the range, social relations, hours and intensity of work can be very various. Usually the activity is solitary and not directly supervised, although there are some instances of laboratory classes which often involve work with and supervision by technicians, and of team teaching. Usually the teaching is part of some larger course or degree programme, which requires agreed syllabi, patterns of teaching, assessment and examination. Thus, while in the immediate context of teaching the lecturer could be seen as similar to a lone craftsperson, in the wider context he or she works as part of a team, often with both leadership and constraints. She or he may be subject to collegial control and not immune to pressure from the institution, the market,

a professional body or the state on course content, mode of teaching, or even the very existence of the course itself.

Let me illustrate by my own case. Until 1982 I was teaching a range of courses in an education department, which included the Sociology of Education, to relatively small numbers on an undergraduate and masters degree programme. At undergraduate level this had to be coordinated with other education teaching from a psychology and philosophy discipline base, and similarly on the MSc course with an awareness of the need for relevance of the course in market and professional terms to the potential students, who were mid-career teachers. I was also engaged in teaching a Development of Social Thought course in a Behavioural Science degree and a course on Media on a Human Communications degree. With both these latter courses I had a high degree of control over course content and the method of teaching (being able to bring outside experts in or use TV and video as additional teaching aids for example), but again they were subject to loose overall control from a course committee.

Since 1982 all these courses have been discontinued as a direct result of the UGC cuts and their specific implementation by Aston management. I now teach Elements of Social Science, Industrial Sociology, and Problems of Management in a Changing Environment on an undergraduate management course, and a Social Context course on a masters personnel management programme. There are clear differences (although not as many as one might imagine) in the course content and curriculum. The professional and market pressures are stronger than before, but much of the activity remains the same; lecturing to students in rather larger numbers now, trying to stimulate seminar discussion, some attention to problems and possibilities for individual students and, of course, the routines of setting, invigilating and marking examinations. The plant and technology remain largely the same – the lecture hall, seminar room and office. The overhead projector, Xerox handout and the use of video and computer interactive programmes have become more widespread over the last decade, but it is difficult to see these increasing uses of technology as themselves fundamentally changing the teaching relationship.

Perhaps more significant is the steady massification of the student–lecturer relation. As the staff–student ration worsens through financial pressure and a determination to preserve research time, the quality of lecturer–student relations may be changing. There is a difference in my experience between teaching to 40 and to 140, and

the student may feel that more acutely. An anecdote may illustrate: on meeting a student, who was obviously seeking help, walking along in the corridor, I invited her into my office. She (a first year student in her second term) admitted she had not been in a lecturer's office before and indeed had not realised that lecturers had offices!

This story illustrates not only changes in teaching relations but also the intermixing with another feature of most academics' labour, the pastoral-counselling function, which is sometimes a formal one with personal tutees, but more usually an informal, amorphous, ambiguous activity, difficult to quantify and currently one of the casualties of increased pressure on time, resources and administration.

Administration itself, of courses, resources or research contracts, will also involve many academics in a supervisory relationship with secretaries, technicians and administrative assistants. Depending on seniority and size of research resources, this may involve the managerial control of several people and substantial amounts of money and equipment, but for most academics the interaction with other university or college employees is limited to a small group and even here the managerial control exercised by the academic is often not clear, as secretarial and administrative staff are subject to administrative as well as academic staff control. Nevertheless can we regard academics as managers of people and resources, as well as particular forms of symbolic expression? On this matter, it is interesting to note that a recent Federal Labor Board ruling in the United States prevents academics in private colleges being represented by labour unions on the grounds that they are effectively managers of their institutions.

ACADEMIC WORK, RESEARCH AND THE STATE

If the form of teaching varies by discipline, so even more does the research enterprise. Despite variations, involvement in research is often taken to be the distinctive feature of the University academic in Britain. While many university managements emphasise the importance of teaching, and efficient and humane administrative and pastoral practice, it is research productivity and quality which is taken as the hallmark of the successful academic, department, or university. Recent events have emphasised this.

The UGC seemed to use, if clumsily and ambiguously, criteria relating to research productivity and quality (placing particular

emphasis on research supported by the Research Councils) in implementing the 1981 government cuts. Since then there have been
decisions by the Economic and Social Research Council to penalise
institutions with low PhD completion rates, and the Science and
Engineering Council in 1987 applied sanctions to 41 departments with
low submission rates by removing a studentship from their quota.

Monitoring and selective support of PhD students in particular
institutions or departments is part of more general moves at national
and even international level involving closer scrutiny of research
productivity and relevance. There is an increasing tendency to concentrate resources in those areas deemed to be already strong.

This process can be seen as the result of three forces. Firstly there
is the increasing power and cost of research, particularly scientific,
technological, and medical, which is well above general inflation
levels. Lyotard (1984, p. 44) puts this in a general and historical
context when he writes:

> The need for proof becomes increasingly strong as the pragmatics
> of scientific knowledge replaces traditional knowledge or know-
> ledge based on revelation. By the end of the *Discourse on Method*
> Descartes is already asking for laboratory funds. A new problem
> appears: devices that optimise the performance of the human body
> for the purpose of producing proof require additional expenditures
> – no money, no proof – and that means no verification of state-
> ments and no truth. The games of scientific language become the
> games of the rich, in which whoever is wealthiest has the best
> chance of being right. An equation between wealth, efficiency and
> truth is thus established.

Secondly, in the British context the state is driven by a Thatcherite
programme of the reduction of public expenditure (except perhaps
immediately before an election). This is confusingly masked by a free
market rhetoric but results in increased attempts to direct and control
research. Again Lyotard catches something of the complex of forces
which affect research activity and its funding. 'The prevailing corporate norms of work management spread to the applied science
laboratory: hierarchy, centralised decision making, teamwork, calculation of individual and collective returns, the development of
saleable programmes, market research and so on. Centres dedicated
to "pure" research suffer from this less but also receive less funding'.
(Lyotard 1984 p. 45). And again he presents the core of the matter
(*ibid.*, p. 47):

Research funds are allocated by states, corporations and national-ised companies in accordance with this logic of power growth. Research sectors that are unable to argue that they contribute even indirectly to the optimization of the system's performance are abandoned by the flow of capital and doomed to senescence. The criterion of performance is explicitly invoked by the authorities to justify their refusal to sustain certain research centres.

These are prophetic words if we look at current developments in British Universities, such as the UGC and UFC research selectivity exercises of 1986 and 1989. The previous convention was that univer-sities received roughly 70 per cent of their UGC funding for teaching and 30 per cent for research, but individual academic departments, facilities or even institutions did not necessarily approximate to this in terms of their research activity or productivity. The UGC and UFC exercises attempt to assess, however crudely, research activity, to rank cost centres (a significant appelation in itself). The UGC in 1986 designated departments and disciplines, as starred, above average, average or below average and the UFC in 1989 used a five point rating as a basis for differential allocation of funds within the overall funding devoted to research support (30 per cent in 1986 and 40 per cent in 1989). The UGC judgements seem to have taken into account staff and research student numbers, income from Research Councils and charitable bodies, contract research income and peer evaluation of publications. These criteria were much debated and criticised but nevertheless were those the UGC and its successor the UFC and the cost centre advisory bodies have used.

In 1987 there was a further development which reinforced this trend of selective support for research in certain institutions and departments. The Oxborough report on the Earth Sciences proposed a three tier division of departments, concentrating research in the top tier with the bottom tier having no research, just scholarship and teaching, and the intermediate tier having limited research. The Advisory Board for the Research Councils follows this logic but the ABRC strategy for UK research called for universities *as a whole* to be placed in three categories. The top 15 centres designated 'R2' would be funded fully for leading-edge research. Roughly the same number would be designated 'X' doing some high-level research in less costly areas. The rest would be classified as 'T' centres conduct-ing teaching at undergraduate and masters level with associated scholarship but little real research (THES 10 June 1987).

Other features of the ABRC proposals emphasised a shift of

funding from the UGC to the Research Councils, more exploitation of academic research and stronger external representation of non-academics from industry and commerce on research councils. They argued that research councils should provide data on the 'take-up' by industry of the work they support. Although Vice Chancellors, the UGC and the AUT were certainly unhappy and critical of these proposals, particularly the rigidity of a three division structure, it seems likely that in effect a similar structure will emerge through the research rating exercises as funds are differentially distributed. Certainly the general trend of increased monitoring and selectivity of research funding, and emphasis on the need for relevance to the market economy, are powerfully present, and as we shall see have their impact on the internal management of academic institutions and the labour process of academics.

THE CONDITIONS OF ACADEMIC WORK

When looking at the factors affecting academics in general – salaries, promotion, tenure provision, working conditions and managerial control – it must always be remembered that different disciplines and departments (and even apparently similar ones) have their own ideologies, discourses and set of social relations amongst staff and with students. So that for example Thomas (1990) has shown that there are not only obvious differences between Physics and, say, English but also between Physics and Physical Science and English and English and Communication studies. These differences extend to the conception of the discipline, the varying practices of teaching and research and, at a fairly fundamental level, the different market situations of academics as lecturers, consultants and researchers as well as the differing career prospects of the students they reach. Thus in a management school it may be very difficult to attract lecturers at current university salaries in areas like law, accountancy or marketing where much more can be earned outside the university. This of course affects the power position and bargaining strength of academics in these areas.

The report by the PA (1986) international management and consulting group, commissioned jointly by the CVCP and AUT on behalf of Committee A (dealing with salary negotiations) to examine factors affecting the recruitment and retention of staff, shows some of these differences but it also reveals a remarkable uniformity in the

expectation held by most staff interviewed of worsening conditions of salary, promotion opportunities, job security and tenure, overall workload, status, administrative work, working conditions and environment, and teaching duties and research facilities. Only opportunities for consultancy were seen to be improving. While PA found that in 1986 minimum starting salaries paid to new graduate entries in universities were broadly in line with practice in the 192 organisations they surveyed, salary progression on university scales is limited so that the median salary for a 32 year old lecturer was some 44 per cent behind that of counterparts and if she or he was an above average performer his or her salary would be some 63 per cent behind counterparts in industry. While some university staff do have opportunities for additional earnings, the average from consultancy in 1986 being approximately £1500, academics cannot benefit from the additional earnings which are common for management in industry, through bonuses and profit-sharing or share-option schemes. The twenty fourth Report of Committee A (1989) on salaries – recording an agreement reached between the CVCP and the AUT after protracted and bitter industrial action on examinations – in its preamble notes 'it leaves salaries of academics and related staff at a very depressed and uncompetitive level. This has serious consequences for staff morale and is affecting recruitment and retention'.

Also in the 1989 salary award we can see the pressure of state and market and how it reinforces managerial authority. One seventh of the pay award from October 1989 was 'to be made at the discretion of local management for market reasons and to reward exceptional performance' but 'To qualify for funding a university must commit itself to the introduction of selective payments in each of the professor and lecturer grades' (DES 1989). While management may consult with the Union the ultimate decision about these discretionary rewards – whose distribution can be seen as decisive and controlling – rests with management.

If we turn now from general managerial, monetary and market factors and look at the related question of contractual relations and tenure, we see developments which parallel the changes in the market situation of academics, but which also signal a perhaps more fundamental change in their position. The introduction of ever larger numbers of short-term contracts for lecturing as well as for research staff affects not only the staff so employed but also the relationship to tenured staff and the overall cohesiveness of the academic body. Moves towards more flexible short-term contracts and weakening of

124   *Academics and their Labour Process*

tenure bring universities and their workers more into line with
current industrial and commercial practice. Their contracts of employment and work conditions become less distinctive in precisely
those aspects most valued by academics and which attracted them to
the work in the first place, that is a freedom to pursue research and
excellence in conditions of security (PA, 1986).

One could argue, as Lyotard does, that the temporary contract is
part of a very general development in social interactions well beyond
the bounds of the work contract, extending to professional, emotional, sexual, cultural, familial and political domains. Certainly:

> The temporary contract is favoured by the system due to its greater
> flexibility, lower cost, and the creative turmoil of its accompanying
> motivation – all these factors contribute to increased operability.
> (Lyotard, 1984, p. 50)

In the case of academics this means that universities are able to
employ younger people at the bottom end of the lecturer scale, the
renewal of the contract or move to a tenured position being dependent on proven performance, particularly in the research area,
and unless that performance is outstanding can mean his or her
replacement by another young, keen and cheap academic labourer.
There may of course be costs, as the emphasis on short-term research
productivity may inhibit long-term scholarship and is certainly a
pressure against time-consuming commitments to teaching, administration or pastoral duties for students. This is one of the areas which
may cause conflict between tenured and non-tenured staff, tenured staff
feeling that those on short-term contracts are too obsessed by their
research and publication performance, while those on short-term contracts may see tenured staff as less efficient, more complacent, and not
contributing to current scholarship or research. Certainly this is a potential if not actual division over and above existing divisions (by gender,
status or discipline) and one which enhances managerial control.

The question of managerial control or, as it has often been put
recently, 'the right to manage' is clearly at the centre of the State's
moves to limit tenure, but this also can be related to a more general
move within the commercial–industrial sphere, of which recent
examples might include the strategies pursued by Michael Edwardes at
BL or Rupert Murdoch at the News International plant at Wapping.
In university work this has become a particular issue due to the highly
labour intensive nature of academic work and the pressure of

government cuts from the early 1980s onward, which has meant that because of financial exigency and the need to rationalise teaching, managements in universities have been compelled (more or less willingly) to attempt to break existing tenure arrangements in order to dismiss staff for reasons other than 'good cause'. This means that at least some university managements welcomed proposals in July 1987, prior to the 1988 Education Reform Act from the government, which threatened to 'ensure that the institutions concerned (universities) have the power to terminate the appointments of their academics and academic-related staff for reasons of redundancy of financial exingency' thus limiting tenure arrangements. The DES also intended 'to add inefficiency to the category of "good cause" for dismissal' and to appoint commissioners to review and change relevant statutes of universities. It was proposed that existing procedures for dismissal (which usually are the prerogative of Councils or even, on appeal, of the Senate and Council acting together) would be replaced by a procedure whereby 'the Vice Chancellor or Principal would decide on the dismissal or other penalty to be imposed on the member of staff'. There would be a right of appeal to a small board, chaired by a Lawyer and consisting of persons appointed by Council and persons nominated by representative staff. There would be no internal appeals procedure beyond this. These proposals would substantially weaken tenure conditions for staff. They would also strengthen managerial prerogative by including 'inefficiency' as a ground for dismissal. How will that be defined? They would further increase the chief executive's power over dismissal and reduce the collective collegial authority of Councils and Senates as final appeal bodies.

These proposals and their enactment in the 1988 Education Reform Act produced considerable debate and criticism. The 1988 Act preserved existing arrangements for tenure for academic staff appointed before November 1987. This was tested in a case at Aston University where the visitor ruled that the Council of the University could not breach its own Statutes and Charter, and that the implied but unwritten power which the University's lawyers argued applied to make staff redundant at a time of financial need in terms of the managerial interest did not apply. Although the position of existing, tenured unpromoted staff has been protected, university managements are increasingly appointing staff on short-term contracts and their position is not protected. Also the University Commissioners, appointed as a result of the 1988 Reform Act, have powers to change

University Charters so that any academic staff appointed or promoted after November 1987 may be dismissed on the grounds of
redundancy. Lord Justice Dillon, making one of the judgements in
the Aston case, caught one aspect of the change of climate in attitude
towards academics' security of employment; referring to the statute
protecting academic tenure established at Aston in 1968 he said:

> These adopted the then view of academic independence. It was
> easy then to remember how academic staff had been treated in
> Nazi Germany . . . in the changed political climate and the changed
> financial policy towards the funding of the Universities, the
> fashionable watch cries now are 'economy and the managerial
> interest'. (Perce et al., 1989).

I have looked at features of the academic labours process, their
configuration and dynamic, particularly the interplay of trends,
movements, and pressures emanating from state institutions, and the
reactions and accommodations of academics at local level. Next I
focus on the ways in which institutional management has responded
to state pressure and market situation, and in turn pressured and
attempted to control and guide academics' activities at the departmental and individual level.

UNIVERSITY MANAGEMENT AND ACADEMIC WORK

There are now several detailed accounts of how the Conservative
government, committed to reducing government expenditure and
faced by the demographic decline of the number of 18 year olds by
1994 to two-thirds of the peak of 1983, imposed drastic cuts in 1981
(Kogan and Kogan 1983; Scott, 1984). These accounts also deal with
how these cuts were implemented by the UGC following the directive
from the DES to be selective and directive.

Aston University was one of the universities selected by the UGC
to suffer fundamental change, losing one third of its funding and one
fifth of its students. Walford (1987) gives a detailed case study
account, using a sophisticated model of political decision making, to
chart the dynamic of management changes at Aston. I shall draw on
that account, but seek to focus on the impact of changes in managerial practice and strategy on the academic labour process.

It might be argued that to focus on managerial impact at the level

of the institution is somewhat arbitrary, as academics are constrained by wider market and professional pressures and are affected directly by the imperatives of the central state. Nevertheless as Fielden and Lockwood (1973) point out, in legal and organisational terms:

> Universities are organisations which have corporate responsibilities, and which possess power to manage the activities of their members in order to carry out those responsibilities. Members of the academic staff collectively constitute the major element in the government of a university, but individually they are employees by contract. Members of academic staff may be influenced by, and give their prime loyalty to, the national and sometimes international professional groups which cut across all universities. However in terms of organisation and management, the existence of the University creates a firm boundary. Faculties, colleges, departments and other units are not autonomous units within a guild structure, they are interdependent parts of a unitary organisation (Fielden and Lockwood, 1973, p. 22).

Certainly as far as senior management is concerned, it seems reasonable to assume that in the short term at least most will be concerned primarily about the survival of their own institution as a separate entity and their own status, UFC research rankings and knighthoods.

We largely accept the development and critique of Braverman's thesis, developed by Brewster (1986) and Storey (1982), that emphasises the varieties of managerial control over and above the Taylorist direct supervision analysed by Braverman. That analysis seems peculiarly appropriate to universities where control over recruitment and promotion and the attempt to maintain involvement and motivation is likely to be as or more important than the monitoring and supervision (when it is possible) of day-to-day teaching and research.

Analysis of University management and its impact on the staff labour process can therefore look at the varieties and efficacy of different forms of control in terms of the type, if any, of overall strategy adopted and the style and practice of the implementation of that strategy through the formal and informal social relations which surround the activity of academics.

The government cuts in funding, implemented by the UGC from 1981, forced University managements to consider alternatives in terms of their overall strategy. In some cases this seems to have

consisted of varieties of inaction or rhetorical resistance, particularly where initially the cuts were not too severe. Even in cases like Keele or Cardiff where that was not the case, Vice Chancellors' strategies have not necessarily involved compliance with UGC directives, but either short-term accommodation (Samut, 1986) in the case of Keele or outright defiance in the case of Cardiff with, in the end, dramatic results.

In the cases of Aston and Salford, which were both heavily hit in terms of cuts (Aston 32 per cent and Salford 43 per cent), there have been somewhat different strategies adopted by their new Vice Chancellors, Professors Frederick Crawford and John Ashford. At Salford the main preoccupation has been the generation of new income over and above UGC sources and the strengthening and extending of links with industry. So Recruitment University Income, excluding UGC grant and home fees of students, at Aston increased from 20.1 per cent in 1980 to 26 per cent in 1985, while at Salford it increased from a somewhat lower percentage, 16 per cent in 1980 and 1981 to 39 per cent in 1985. Links with industry have not been neglected at Aston, with the establishment jointly with the City Council and Lloyds Bank of a Science Park, and with the West Midlands Enterprise Board of a Technology Transfer Unit, but the connections have been perhaps less integral than that at Salford, where Integrated Chairs jointly funded from the University and Industry and the CAMPUS organisation developed a very close connection to industry.

We shall look in more detail at the Aston management strategy and compare it in passing with that of Salford, Bath and Keele, using data gathered by Samut (1986). At Aston, information-gathering, analysis and strategic decision making were established centrally, primarily in the Vice Chancellor's hands soon after his appointment in 1980 and increased following the 1981 cuts. Walford (1987) gives a good account of that process, whereby the Vice Chancellor's superior information base on courses, student characteristics, and staff enabled him to use one-to-one negotiations with heads of departments to present to Senate a package of course reduction which was difficult to resist. At the same time the establishment of the Vice Chancellor's advisory group on Budget adjustment, including the Vice Chancellor as chair, the Senior Pro Vice Chancellor, the Deans of Faculty and, significantly, three administrative officers including the Finance Officer, provided a small centrally placed well-informed committee which could effectively analyse the situation, take decisions and

make recommendations to Senate and Council with considerable authority.

This gives something of the process and apparatus at Aston, but what was the policy and what of the implications for ordinary academics? The policy could be summarised as a commitment to academic excellence and strict financial probity. In practice these rather general aims meant a sustained effort to improve the quality of the undergraduate entry by insisting on A level scores above the national average in each subject area, a policy on staff recruitment that insisted in almost all cases that candidates should possess a first class undergraduate degree, and various efforts to improve research productivity and quality. The financial probity aspect translated into a plan to balance the books on a year-by-year basis; somewhat remarkably this has been achieved. Together with these major aims there has been an attention to public relations and image management which has found its expression in extensive campus improvement – tree planting, fountains, and entrance complete with Beaubourg-like lifts – and the employment of PR Consultants, Wolfe Olins, who developed a new corporate identity style, logo and so forth around the symbol of a triangle.

STUDENT, STAFF AND RESEARCH CONTROL

If we look in more detail at three areas mentioned already – student recruitment, staff recruitment and mobility and research – we can see how Aston management's objectives affect the autonomy, discretion and working conditions of academics.

It was assumed by many that the pattern of the 1981 UGC cuts was informed by the relative strength of different departments' courses as measured by the A level grades they were able to ask of students, so it was hardly surprising that measures to respond to the cuts and improve Aston's standing in case of continuing cuts should include measures to raise A level scores for all courses. However A level grades were not only to be improved because this was expected to lead to more favourable treatment by the UGC, but also because they could be used as a way of restructuring departments and putting pressure on some staff to leave. Even before the 1981 cuts the Vice Chancellor had gathered comparative figures on these scores, including information on overseas and non-traditional entry for each subject for all universities. Data was also collected on student

drop-out rates and on degree results. As explained earlier, and in Walford (1987) in detail, the Vice Chancellor persuaded Senate to discontinue many of the University's courses within a week of the UGC announcement in 1981.

In 1982 Senate adopted a policy to improve entry grades so that the average was to become higher than the national average in *each* subject for student entry in October 1983. This drastic shift in policy has had several implications. Admission tutors' discretion was severely limited, with 10 per cent quotas imposed for overseas and non-traditional entry, and the required A level grades (using the points system) became the determining criterion in admissions policy. If numbers of students on courses which had previously accepted low A level scores, and which were now not able to attract above-average scoring students, dropped below the minimum acceptable to the University the courses were speedily axed with consequent pressure on staff in those areas to move and retrain or to leave the institution. So decisions on A level entry were instrumental in the wider reshaping, restructuring and redeployment of staff. In areas which were popular, recruitment was allowed to expand and this brought its own pressures on staff, who were expected to teach larger groups of students. This became particularly acute in subject areas such as marketing where it was difficult to attract staff, particularly of the high academic standard demanded by the Vice Chancellor.

We have already indicated the obvious connection between student numbers and the deployment of staff, but staff control policy was equally influenced by the need to balance the budget and improve the quality of staff, particularly because costs are some 70 per cent of total budget in a university, and management perception seemed to be that many staff (some inherited from Aston's previous status as a College of Advanced Technology) were too old or mediocre to contribute to Aston's future as a 'quality-driven institution'.

The detail of the processes by which Aston staff has been reduced by over a half since 1981 are documented in Walford (1987) and Miller et al (1987). The main points are that the process has been centrally directed; policy largely emanating from the Vice Chancellor and the Advisory Committee on Budget Adjustment has been accepted by Senate and Council, except that Senate has consistently refused to condone compulsory redundancy. The process has involved the setting of public targets for overall staff reduction – 350 in 1982, 300 in August 1984, 260 in 1987 and 250 in 1989 – with staff ranges being established for each department based mainly on

student numbers. A variety of pressures and incentives have been applied to encourage staff to transfer, retrain or leave. The process has been remarkably effective in that Aston management reduced staff from 543 in 1980 to 276 in 1985. We can compare Keele University with staff at 291 in 1980 and 246 in 1985, or Salford with 491 in 1980 and 339 in 1985.

The question of reduction of staff in its most crude form, compulsory dismissal, found expression at Aston. The nationally significant court cases (Pearce et al., 1989), eventually resulted in the Visitor to Aston University ruling that the University Council had to abide by the University Charter and Statutes and could not dismiss tenured academic staff except for 'good cause'. The issue at stake, although presented by the University Administrations lawyers as about financial exigency and the need for redundancy, in reality went deeper than that, to the core issues of managerial power and authority. The Registrar at Aston is quoted in the Birmingham Post: 'the judgement appeared to remove Aston's right to manage, with implications for universities across the country' (Morris, 1989). Although in this instance management received some check, the fact that the issue was raised again at Aston in the late 1980s when the immediate financial pressures of the early 1980s were not present in a symbol of law, meant the issue of managerial control in both crude and sophisticated form has become central to the academic labour process.

MANAGEMENT AND NUMBERS

The emphasis on numerical criteria at Aston has been clear in the organisation of teaching, and in particular class size. It has had dramatic consequences for example for the teaching of masters level students. Before 1981, because of its pre-history as a College of Advanced Technology, there was a pattern at Aston of high student class contact hours and consequently heavy staff teaching load. The Academic Planning Committee, in attempting to leave staff more time for research, proposed a reduction in contact hours for students and an increase in the average number of students per class. Calculations proceeded on the assumption that academics should only teach six or seven hours a week and that students should have 18 or less contact hours. This indicated that average numbers of undergraduate per class should be 28, and 20 per class for postgraduate levels.

In November 1983, some 20 diploma and MSc graduate courses suspended their entry for 1984. This usually meant closure of the course. The question of the quality of the courses was not considered, nor their relation to research effort or focus. Simple numerical criteria were applied with no exceptions. Courses in Welding Technology and Management, Industrial Mathematics, Chemistry and Technology of Polymers were all discontinued.

One particular MSc casualty illustrates possible implications for research. A new MSc in Ethnic Relations had started in 1981, mainly taught by staff from the then SSRC-financed Research Unit in Ethnic Relations which was attached to Aston University. The loss of the course increased the uncertainty about the future of the Unit and in the end the Unit was transferred to Warwick University, so that the strange result of moves intended to increase academic research at Aston was that a major research unit was lost.

The loss to the University of active researchers has been considerable and this can be expected to have some consequences on the morale of those staff remaining who are active in research. On the surface it appeared as if per-capita research output increased, improving from 1.30 publications per member of staff in 1980 to 2.56 in 1983 (compared with 2.12 at Salford, 2.49 at Keele and 2.11 at Bath) but the historial base, and long gestation time of many publications, together with the difficulty of establishing comparative measures, should make us deal with these figures with caution.

At Aston, from the establishment of the University Research Committee and Faculty Research Committee in 1983, there has been an attempt to identify key researchers and research strengths within the University and channel resources into these areas. Of course, given limited resources, this inevitably means a reduction of resources in less-favoured areas and to those staff not undertaking research. The characteristics identified in the Aston response to UGC planning for the late 1980s document as a basis for selective funding are:

- Existing internationally-recognised strengths in the area, and a sustained record of high quality publications.
- A research focus which allows the group to address significant research problems.
- A substantial nucleus of staff and associated doctoral students actively pursuing work in the area so as to allow economies of scale in allocating resources to the work.
- A substantial level of research income by November 1985.

On this basis some 69 separate research groups have been reduced to 25 active research groups. Currently the University management has developed a research allocation of resources policy which rewards strong and flourishing areas and removes resources from weaker areas while allowing a degree of discretion at University and Faculty level, largely vested in the Deans and Research Committees for extra awards.

In the research areas the pressures on the academic to perform have been increased, but at the same time it is probably true that at Aston as elsewhere there is increasing recognition and resources for those actively engaged in research, particularly in these cost centres receiving high ratings. The difficulties are firstly that those not researching or in low rated cost centres will find their resources reduced and teaching and administrative duties increased, and secondly that there may be attempts to mislead the monitoring central authorities about what research is being undertaken and the extent of publications.

The establishment of a points system in the Aston Business School, giving scores for different types of publications and for student load and administrative duties, has been developed over the last five years. The scores of individual members of staff have been recorded, ranked, published and divided in quartiles (four divisions appear). While it was initially claimed that this was not being used to allocate duties, clearly a public expression of monitored work performance like this lays individual academics open to peer as well as management pressure in terms of their workload. The publication of this points monitoring system, perhaps as much as anything, epitomises how management action on student recruitment, class size, research policy and staff control come together in at least symbolic pressure on the individual academic's labour process.

CONCLUSION

My thesis and conclusion is that, very broadly, similar processes are happening to the academic labour process as Braverman asserts has been happening to skilled craft labour in his analysis of capitalism in the twentieth century. A crucial function of academic labour – the conception and management of academic work itself – is being alienated from the practitioner. These functions are being concentrated in the hands of a relatively new and expanding strata of

academic managers. Consequently academics are losing some control over their day-to-day work processes. The pressures guiding this process operate both at the level of the state and that of the institution, and the dynamics of the capitalist labour market contribute to this process, albeit largely indirectly.

This is not to say the process is uniform, unresisted or inevitable. The varieties of academic work and managerial strategies, as well as institutional, disciplinary and national cultures, ensure that there are opportunities for effective resistance to autocratic management, and a chance of preserving or even extending democratic control. That task remains a political and ideological task for academics concerned for their craft and democratic values and practices. Changes in technology, particularly information processing, may at the moment seem to favour centralised management and control, but neither the technology, nor the social relations surrounding it, are predetermined in their development or outcome. The conditions for effective intervention include a knowledge of what processes are already underway, but also a will and capacity to resist, agitate, organise and educate, which are surely appropriate activities in universities and other institutions of higher education. Higher education has as a core activity the discovery and dissemination of knowledge, at least sometimes in a critical mode. Working on culture and the shaping of symbolic forms is at the core of our endeavours. This gives hope for a radical project.

However I believe that that hope can only be realised if it is founded on an effective understanding of and alliance with those workers who presently stand outside the walls of academia. Can currently isolated academics, assailed by limiting managerial practices from institutional directors or state ministries, break through to show the relevance of their research and teaching to the improvement of the lives of the mass of the population? If they can they may put knowledge under the control of the people instead of being used to serve the interests of those who are already powerful.

Note

I have used my own experience at Aston, where I was initially appointed in 1972 to the Department of Education, and subsequently transferred to the Management Centre in 1983 after the dissolution of Education. I was on

Senate in 1981–3, representing staff in the now defunct Faculty of Humanities and Social Sciences and am a local executive member of the AUT. The origins of the chapter lie in work done with Geoff Walford (Miller and Walford, 1983–86) on Aston's response to government cuts, and on the M.Phil dissertation of Reno Samut (1986) comparing different managerial responses to government political and financial pressure in Britain and Malta. Chris Smith made useful critical comments on early drafts and I have benefited greatly from discussions with John Bowen from Keele, and with Hugh Willmott, now at UMIST, and Peter Clark from Aston Business School. Concurrently with writing this chapter I was working with Geoff Walford and Steve Warburton (from the Vice Chancellor's office) on a paper on Information and Management in Universities (Miller et al., 1987) and that has certainly informed the writing. Typically crucial for me in the academic labour process has been secretarial support. Myra Wheeldon from the OSAP division typed early drafts, which were subsequently redrafted by Shirley Wilkes and extended with useful critical comments by Janet Beardmore and Pat Newman, and finally revised by Rita McNamara. Thanks to all these.

References

Anderson, P. (1968) 'Components of the National Culture', *New Left Review* (London).

Anderson, P. (1983) *In the Tracks of Historical Materialism* (London: Verso).

Aston University (1985) *Planning for the late 1980's* (Birmingham: Aston University).

Braverman, H. (1974) *Labor and Monopoly Capital* (New York: Monthly Review Press).

Brewster, C. J. (1986) *A Typology of Management Controls.* Paper to 4th Annual Labour Process Conference. (Birmingham: Aston University).

Burawoy, M. (1978) *Manufacturing Consent* (University of Chicago Press).

— Child, J., et al. (1983) 'A Price to Pay: Professionalism and Work Organisation', *Sociology*, vol. 17, no. 1.

Clark, B. (1983) *The Higher Education System.* (Berkeley: University of California Press).

Debray, R. (1981) *Teachers, Writers, Celebrities* (introduction F. Mulhern) (London: Verso NLB).

Department of Education and Science (1985) *The Development of Higher Education into the 1990's* (London: HMSO).

Department of Education and Science (1987). Letter to CVC&P. *Academic Tenure and Related Matters: Outline of Proposed Legislation* (London: DES).

Department of Education and Science (1988) Education Reform Act (London: HMSO).

Department of Education and Science (1989) Letter to Sir Pat Lowrie and *The Twenty-Fourth Report of Committee A* (London: DES).

Edwards, R. (1979) *Contested Terrain* (New York: Basic Books).

Fielden, J. and G. Lockwood (1973) *Planning and Management in Universities* (London: Sussex University Press).

Foucault, M. (1980) In C. Jordon (ed.) *Power/Knowledge* (Brighton: Harvester).

Fores, M. and I. Glover (1981) 'The British Disease: Professionalism', *Times Higher Education Supplement*, 24 Feb.

Ginsberg, M. et al. (1980) 'Teachers' Conception of Professionalism and Trades Unionism: An Ideological Analysis'. in P. Woods (ed.) *Teachers Strategies, Explorations in the Sociology of the School* (London: Croom Helm).

Gramsci, A. 1971) *Selections from Prison Notebooks*. (London: Lawrence and Wishart).

Hickox, M. S. (1986) 'Has there been a British Intelligentsia?', *British Journal of Sociology*, vol. xxxvii, no. 2.

Jacques, M. (1975) 'Universities and Capitalism: The Present Crisis', *Marxism Today*, July 1975, London.

Kogan, M. and Kogan, D. (1983) *The Attack on Higher Education* (London: Kogan Page).

Larson, M., (1977) *The Rise of Professionalism* (Berkeley: University of California Press).

Lawn, M. and J. Osga (1981) *Teachers, Professionalism and Class* (Brighton: Falmer).

Littler, C. and G. Salaman (1982) 'Bravermania and Beyond: Recent Theories of the Labour Process', *Sociology*, vol. 16, no. 2.

Lyotard, J. F. (1984) *The post modern condition: A report on knowledge* (Manchester University).

Mannheim, K. (1956) *Essays on the Sociology of Culture* (London: Routledge).

Marx, K. (1973) The Eighteenth Brumaire of Louis Bonaparte, in D. Fernbach (ed.) *Surveys from Exile* (London: Allen Lane).

Meiksins, R. (1985) 'Beyond the Boundary Question', *New Left Review*, 157.

Miller, H. and R. Samut (1986) *Universities and the Labour Process*, Paper to the 4th Annual Labour Process Conference, Aston University, Birmingham.

Miller, H. and G. Walford (1983) 'University Cut and Thrust', in G. Walford *Schooling in Turmoil* (London: Croom Helm).

Miller, H. and G. Walford (1986) *A Case Study of Financial Constraints in British Universities*, IHECL Monograph (University of Houston).

Miller, H. G. Walford and S. Warburton (1987) *Information and Power in University Management*. Paper to the 9th Association for Institutional Research European Forum on The Changing Relationship between Government and Higher Education: The Management Challenge (University of Twente, Centre for Higher Education Policy Studies, Enschede: The Netherlands).

Morris, N. (1989) 'Union Claims Victory on Aston Staff Cuts', *Birmingham Post*, 3 Aug.

Mulhern, F. (1981) introduction to R. Debray, *Teachers, Writers, Celebrities* (London: Verso/NLB).

Offe, C. (1976) 'The Theory of the Capitalist State and the Problem of Policy Formulation', in Lindberg et al. (eds) *Stress and Contradiction in Modern Capitalism* (New York: D. C. Heath).

Perce, G. et al., Aston University (1989) Court of Appeal, 23 June, London.

P. A. Personnel Services (1986) *Report on Factors Affecting Recruitment and Retention of Non-Clinical Academic Staff* (London: University Academic Salary Committee A).

Samut, R. (1986) *The Management of Universities in a Period of Rapid Change*, unpublished M.Phil thesis, Aston University.

Scott, P. (1984) *The Crisis of the University* (Bechenham: Open University Press, Croom Helm).

Storey, J. (1982) *The Challenge to Management Control* (London: Kogan Page).

Thomas, K. (1987) *Gender and Subject*, (Buckingham).

Thompson, D. (1983) *The Nature of Work* (London: Macmillan).

Thompson, E. P. (1965) 'The Peculiarities of the English', in *The Socialist Register* (London: Merlin).

Trow, M. (1983) 'Defining the Issues in University–Government Relations', *Studies in Higher Education*, vol. 8, no. 2.

Walford, G. (1987) *Restructuring Universities: Politics and Power in the Management of Change* (London: Croom Helm).

West, C. (1989) 'Staff Turnover hits Universities', *The Guardian*, 11 Sep.

Williams, R. (1979) *Politics and Letters: Interviews with New Left Review* (London: Verso).

Williams, R. (1985) *Towards 2000* (London: Penguin).

7 Journalists and the Labour Process: White-Collar Production Workers

David Murphy

INTRODUCTION

This paper is concerned with the empirical study of how three groups of workers attempted to gain control over the organisation of and rewards from their own labour. By examining their experiences it may be possible to show how, even without bureaucratic or other management constraints, workers' choices are still limited by the markets for the goods and services they produce as well as for their labour, and that by organising together in co-operative enterprises they do not escape the contradictory tendencies towards individualism as a form of motivation and social co-operation as a necessary precondition for organised production. In attempting to answer why this is the case we are obliged to examine the plight of any co-operative organisation or similar attempt at collective worker autonomy in the context of a monopolistic market economy.

The workers under consideration are journalists. Although white-collar workers their occupation shows many of the characteristics of skilled manual work. They constitute a highly unionised workforce.[1] They participate directly in the process of production; they are paid by a variety of different methods approximating to pro-rata payment for work or time, rather than for status and length of career; in large companies the job is broken down by division of labour; they are a variable cost rather than a fixed cost, and if they withdraw their labour they can instantly stop a production process.

They are different from manual workers in a number of ways. The system of control over journalistic work is only partly concerned with the volume or speed of their output. An equal and major concern is

to do with the content of what they produce. The co-operatives I have observed at work have been instituted specifically in order to bring this aspect of decision making within the collective and individual power of workers.

A series of studies of journalistic work have concentrated on the issue of how management obtains the compliance of workers in promulgating management aims.[2] In general these have been functionalist or broadly interactionist in their assumption and have not looked at the market context of journalism. They have tended to take the social organism of the newspaper office and ask how social order is achieved and maintained. This has been done by addressing the question of how the individual journalist comes to accept the policy, slant or bias of the management in writing news. The answers tend to concentrate on the social control processes of the office and often rely heavily on status hierarchical models as explanatory devices.

This is posited on the ideas of norm conformity and role playing as if the individual simply fits into a space in the social system, which is non-problematically evident, by a process of obeying its necessities.[3] This is a simple model of worker behaviour which does not address the issue of how the journalistic labour process is controlled in terms of day-to-day work routines and management practices. It also fails to take account of the wider social economic and political context within which this work takes place and of which it is a part.

Numerous radical critiques of what journalists do in maintaining and producing capitalism through ideological production on the other hand attend precisely to this question. Where they are Marxist they attempt to relate the state, the force of the market and private capital and ideological hegemony[4] to what is produced by journalists. In this approach, writers such as Hall[5] have generated an analysis of the mass media, fulfilling a function in the maintenance of the power of the state and corporate capitalism, following a similar line of argument to that of Miliband[6] and Althusser[7].

In this analysis the work of journalists is seen from the point of view of its 'objective consequences' for the system. In such large scale explanations the politics of the life of workers engaged in the processes tend to be ignored. This is undoubtedly an inevitable consequence of the enterprise of attempts to locate empirical particulars in general theoretical schemes. There may also be another factor in this dislocation between the activities of individual toilers and the collective outcomes in the 'ideological-hegemony' analysis of the mass

media. This is the tendency to stress structures – the state, the corporation – at the expense of market processes. This is the same lack as the functionalists manifest. This is not to argue that the market is completely ignored, but that its power as a means of control over workers' behaviour is marginalised because of concentration on structural-ideological factors.

There is also however a compendious literature which offers a critique of journalistic work (Marxist and radical). Much of it locates the output of the mass media in the successful macroscopic control of the labour process by management in the sense that detailed empirical work is used to attempt to highlight two broad themes:

— That there is a constant anti-labour, pro-capital bias in the production of news.
— That the products of the mass media, especially those aimed at manual workers and other low status groups, are trivialised and diversionary.

The Glasgow Media Group[8] and the Birmingham Centre for Contemporary Cultural Studies[9] have produced a stream of concentrated work in this area, as have individuals and groups elsewhere. An encyclopaedic literature also offers a feminist critique showing how the news media produce and reinforce sexual stereotypes, often used as part of a systematic manipulation of the self-images of the consumers of mass culture in the furtherance of their exploitation as consumers of the other durable products of corporate capital[10].

Other writers, it must be acknowledged, have attempted to employ an analysis of the output of journalists in which the effort has been primarily an empirical account of the nature and extent of bias, usually in relation to industrial relations[11]. As the writers themselves often recognise, such issues are often more complex than common sense suggests because the idea of bias is inherently ideological and cannot rigorously be used as an empirical measure.

Concentration however has been on the analysis of what journalists produce rather than how they produce it. The functionalist's analysis of journalistic work has thus looked at the control of journalists in terms of pliable individuals fitting into a discoverable social structure, defined in terms of order, hierarchy, role and status. This adaptation is a process of learning: it is not a negotiated order and the individual's collective life is defined simply by this structure, to which he learns to conform. Functionalist social scientists nevertheless

were the first to pose the question of why and how workers in newspapers produced versions of events which were in conformity with the ethos of their paper and the demands of editors and proprietors. They ignored, or regarded as analytically marginal, the processes of negotiating order in the office (these would simply be seen as part of the socialisation process).

Marxist and critical analysis propose no such simple model of the mass media and journalistic work, or of any other. Conflict becomes a central issue and the nature of dominance a focus of attention. The social economic and political context of the enterprise is of primary relevance since it determines the scope of the analysis. There is however a tendency to dwell on structure rather than process and to limit significance of individual workers' (journalists') responses, motives and initiatives.

A more sophisticated analysis of the labour process of journalists has been produced by a number of writers taking a broadly inter-activist perspective[12]. They have attempted to show how work practices of journalists lead to consequences in terms of output of newspaper stores and broadcast programmes. Usually however, these accounts posit the idea that journalistic work culture results in the production of pro-establishment news. And although it seems that these studies regard organisations as negotiated orders, in effect they explain social order in terms of individual compliance with a social code, rather than in terms of interactional process.

JOURNALISM: TECHNOLOGY AND THE MARKET

What I hope to present here is a brief account of the division of labour among journalists, related to the dominant technology and corporate form of their industry with the consequent separation of execution and control, and attempts by groups of journalists to assert their own control over their labour in the context of new forms of technology and ownership.

The development of the newspaper as an industrial process is of recent origin, although many of the crafts involved have developed in an unbroken train since the late middle ages. But the industrialisation of journalistic work has altered the relationship between execution and control in three ways. First, the journalist was brought into the 'factory' system from working mainly as a freelance or in small offices. Secondly he (and 'he' has been predominantly 'he') has been

subjected to Taylorite management processes attendant on mechanical engineering giantism. Thirdly, the industrialisation of journalism has followed the normal development of corporate capitalism with an increasing focus of concern on the marketing of goods, and this has accelerated the division of journalistic labour as new jobs and new techniques have been devised to take account of this marketing function[13].

The movement of newspaper production into the factory system was not simply a technological issue. It was the outcome of two processes: first the development of a technology capable of producing large print runs quickly and a transport system capable of putting such papers on the streets over a wide area in a matter of hours; secondly the combined social cultural changes of rapid urban growth and the spread of near-literacy to the majority of the population. In Britain there was also the particular political change brought about by the abolition of the Stamp Duty, which immediately effected drastic reduction in newspaper prices. This changed the nature of the newspaper from a small scale operation, often written by free-lance hacks and sold at prices which restricted it to the well-off literate, to a large scale commercial enterprise, sold cheaply enough to be afforded by the poor and written increasingly by staff writers working in increasingly large workshop-like offices on a production line.

Quite how the Grub Street hacks were brought under managerial control was never a subject of sociological analysis. What we do know is that many publications were concerned with political debate, often of an intemperate nature involving the frequent libelling (by present day standards) of individuals. And within the range of accepted opinion of the time a hack could probably find a paper which suited his own view of things. Even local newspapers were of this type. But these debates were for an educated literati. When the scale of newspapers became a mass phenomenon the nature of their content changed. The change worked in two directions. One was towards entertainment, the other towards 'professionalism' based on the idea of views as a factual comment and account of events. The notion of value-free news is of course unsustainable. What occurred was that the explicit strident distortion of news was replaced by *apparent* neutrality on the basis of unstated and therefore unacknowledged assumptions.

The content of journalistic work therefore changed towards a standardised product. Writing was geared to a certain audience,

which was conceived of as less intelligent and–or educated than the writer, and was to be entertained and informed. This work was, and is, done by reference to a formula. The work involved in writing a news story was subjected to a Taylorite form of production analysis. A news story written for a mass produced newspaper has to meet two sorts of demands: the demands of production and those of marketability.

Production demands are focused around the structure of the story. All of the salient points have to be summarized in the first paragraph. Subsequent paragraphs then come in declining order of importance. This means that at any point in the production process of the newspaper the story can be cut 'upwards from the bottom', and as a result time does not have to be wasted in a busy production schedule in deciding which paragraph is best left out.

The marketability of news is measured in terms of its 'angle'.[14] The introduction has to be 'nosed' on a certain aspect of the story in order to attract the journalists' perception of the typical reader. For instance in the late 1950s and early 1960s one of the favourite industrial relations stories was the strike-over-nothing. This depicted the striker as a mindless mulish member of the 'awkward squad'. He would typically be striking over a demarcation dispute 'Who makes the chalk mark?' or 'Who drills the hole?' or because of some worker's over-sensitive reaction to 'legitimate' authority – the foreman who did not say please. In 1984 a favourite was the 'video nasty' story which showed that 100 per cent of two-year-olds had seen films depicting sexual assaults on old age pensioners. At the height of the Greenham Common protest it would have been a story depicting a lesbian living with another woman at the peace camp while the husband cared for their deserted children in Nuneaton. By the mid 1980s it was the bobby who gives the kiss-of-life to remand home padre and contracts aids ('policeman slain by Gay Plague!').

Part of the skill of the newspaper reporter is therefore to devise an angle which is seen as marketable, and in order to do this he has to have a sense of the market in news at any given time. This is an important factor in the social control of journalists. Prior to the industrialisation of the newspaper industry when the reporter was predominantly a freelance, survival depended on his meeting the demands of the market for news. Now the freelance news reporter remains a significant element in the newspaper labour market. Not only do news agencies provide much of the routine reporting of matters such as court cases, but the mode of organisation of newspapers

remains geared to a culture of selling and buying news. Most staff reporters on local papers engage in freelance news reporting or 'tipping off' national newspapers to supplement their incomes. There is also a system of casual working among the national press wherein a reporter, often a freelance, will work casual shifts as a sub-editor or as a duty reporter. This enables the mangement to increase or decrease its labour force on an ad hoc basis without lay-off costs.

More important however is the way in which the form of news production organisation is geared to what we might call market routines or rituals. The occupational structure of a typical newspaper will consist of an editor-in-chief and a deputy editor, who make decisions about the overall distribution and display of material throughout the paper, specialist editors dealing with, say, features, news or sport, their deputies – sub-editors – in each section, and finally (and least) reporters. In a big national daily, day-shift editors are replicated by night editors. In each section, but especially in the news desk, the sub-editors (subs) are the mainstay of the journalistic office workforce. The news subs are the men of the cinematic cliche in their shirt sleeves, sitting at their long desks in a haze of cigarette smoke, a telephone to each ear, a pencil in one hand and a piece of copy in the other. The job of the sub-editor is to correct grammar, rewrite unclear parts of stories or completely reconstruct them (as the case may be), to decide the paragraphing, the shape of the story, its position, page, typeface, headlines and crossheads.

On a paper such as the *Daily Mail* subs take news from staff men, freelance agencies, enterprising individual freelances and render it all into the house style of the *Daily Mail* . In the Express empire in Manchester, a news sub may be directed on one shift to work on the *Star* on another on the *Express*. In each case he, or occasionally she, will work according to the appropriate formula of the relevant establishment. Sometimes a sub will decide a story has the wrong angle and will persuade the reporter to look again at his notebook or go back to a party involved for other facts or quotes to prop up some other angle. The skills of the sub-editor are the skills of marketing the product – news – of manufacturing it so that it will appeal to the demands of the readers, as perceived by the editor or the proprietor. But in this type of production the maketing of the product and the product are all the same thing. The skill of the journalist in mass circulation newspapers is to create a version of reality encapsualted in an account of some event which is angled to meet the needs of the news market.

The subs' skills are a necessary precondition for the work of the newspaper executive, the editors, deputy editors and chief subs. These are skills to do with the presentation and marketing of news as a product, and in the bigger circulation newspapers these are the dominant forms of work. In the *Daily Express* in Manchester for instance about two thirds of journalists are subs, executives and 'copy tasters'. The form of management control implicit in this system is then implicit in the mode of production and organisation. Where a story is accepted as acceptable this confirms for the reporter his or her skills as a reporter. And compliance comes from the reporter's desire to meet the requirements of the job. The sanction is the positive acceptance into the social world of competence. All industries based on casual work have this element in the mangement control of workers. In journalism it has been developed to the extent that it is at the same time the mode of control and the mode of production, and there are more people engaged in maintaining the qualitative presentation of the work than in its original production. On average, the reporters say, a staffman will get three quarters of a story in each issue of the *Daily Mirror* and therefore regard a decent showing of one of their efforts with the pleasure derived from success. Whether or not the three-quarters-of-a-stay story is accurate, it illustrates the preoccupation which journalists have with their own identities as competent professionals. In this their reputation is only as good as their last 'good story'.

Thus the formularisation of story telling is a form of conceptual technology necessary to the mass production of news, which contains control over workers in its processes in just the same way as does machine production. Machine production in newspapers also implies controls. Newspapers are produced frenetically over a short space of time. Loss of a given day's production can never be made up. A number of editions run off the rotary presses at 50 000 an hour, which means that news pages have to be re-arranged and rewritten several times a night. In order to achieve this, newspaper production process of editorial material is undertaken according to a regular system of layout and an intricate system of deadlines. This system of Taylorite rationalisation, as Braverman argues, gives the management control over workers by depriving them of their freedom of decision making since its essence is its circumscription of performance.[15] On the other hand, before the introduction of new technology, it gave the newspaper workers a power of resistance. This did not relate to control over the pace of production or the content of production but (by use

of the strike weapon or the threat of it) to wages and manning levels. The new methods of production have now eliminated so many production workers that this sort of resistance is now a piece of industrial archeology.

Summary

Control by management over journalistic work is achieved primarily through the permeation of the work relationship by a market ethos. And the desire of the journalist to succeed in this context leads to control as the result of a self denying ordinance implicit in the journalist's desire to succeed within the system. The stress on marketing and presentation of news is the outcome of the mass sales of newspapers, just as the Taylorite work methods are the outcome of the mechanised industrial production system. They are both sides of the same coin and both produce a workforce based on the division of labour in which the operative is primarily concerned with short term technicist problems which are generally of the kind: 'How do I present this piece of journalism so that it is acceptable as competent, professional journalism?'

THE CO-OPERATIVE ALTERNATIVE

By the beginning of the 1970s the new print technology, successfully resisted by the print unions in Fleet Street and in the big provincial evening papers, was being introduced in smaller firms and by jobbing printers. Some writers predicted that this would result in lower printing costs and enable a wider range of views to be represented among newspapers, as groups previously excluded by production and capital costs came into market.

I have examined two such attempts by jouranlists at the production of radical news magazines, and a freelance news agency intended to provide news to 'alternative' outlets. The formation of such news magazines has been a national phenomenon over the past decade and a half. They have acquired a certain similarity in their style of content and layout as they distribute copies among each other. They are a combination of entertainment news and features, primarily aimed at the young, and 'alternative' news about their locality: that is news which discredits and undermines established institutions of Government, order, business, education and so on. The aim of the co-operatives

who run these papers is to take control of the content of the journalism they engage in, as well as the pace, system and financial organisation of their work.

The first of such magazines I examined was an early entrant into the field, *The New Manchester Review*. It was founded by a group of young academics in the mid 1970s. As time passed they invited journalists from national newspapers to improve the professionalism of the magazine, and after its first two years all but one of the active members of the co-operative running the magazine were journalists. The production of the publication was undertaken by a combination of origination and layout done on the premises with the printing undertaken elsewhere. This arrangement was the outcome of a decision by the co-operative to buy secondhand computerised machinery for originating copy. Further costs for providing a darkroom and compositor's studio were relatively minor by comparison. The co-operative was run by journalists but the employees were three production workers, two clerks and an advertising representative.

As in almost all forms of production, changes in methods do not simply constitute ways of producing the same thing but involve changing the definition of what is produced. In controlling the nature of what was produced the journalists worked to a model of what constituted news, which contests the dominant version of unproblematic factual accounts of communal life. It was a version of news in which the institutions and spokesmen normally used routinely by reporters to validate versions of events become the objects of suspicion. Accounts of events publicly promulgated by such institutional, established forms were rejected in favour of the 'truth' which lay behind them. How did the Labour Housing Chairman arrange a lease exchange for his daughter? How did the Tory group leader make his money from lucrative property speculation combined with some fortunate planning decisions? Why did the Iranian consul donate the Chief Constable a crate of Crawford five star single malt whiskey? In other words, the taken-for-granted assumptions made by normal journalism in verifying stories are made problematic and the truthfulness of institutional sources of 'fact' is made the subject of inquiry. Thus this form of journalism constitutes a subversive project.

The traditional commercial press manufacture news by routine acceptance of the bona fides of public spokesmen and the validity of institutions. They need the co-operation of such institutions. This is nowhere made clearer than in the lobby system and in the denigration of individuals such as Clive Ponting and Sarah Tisdall, who breach

the normal relations between the news producers and the social world they profess to investigate and describe. The necessity to keep 'sweet' the official sources of news is one of the chief aspects of Government control over journalists, since in order to gain the approval of Government the journalist requires the co-operation of such sources in generating a supply of 'good stories'. And the relationship is symbiotic: the stories done by reporters often sustain and enhance the authority of their sources.[16]

For the radical, subversive 'investigating' reporter no such constraints apply. He–she does not want anything that the official spokesman has to offer. In this mode of work it is the 'mole' who has to be assiduously courted and encouraged. Such moles also have interests which they promulgate: the destruction of individuals in high office or the system itself. To maintain the relationship, the journalist has to be able to draw blood: an enforced official enquiry; criminal charges against corrupt individuals; premature resignations; public embarrassment.

Whereas the symbiosis between news production imperatives, managerial imperatives and business imperatives tend to coincide in the traditional press, in the radical version there are fundamental conflicts. The nature of the news content tends not to attract large audiences. Therefore a sufficient income for survival requires advertising revenue on as large a scale as possible. Radical news about the police, politicians and businessmen does not attract business advertising. Pop music coverage, film critiques, what's on guides, food and wine columns, books pages all do attract advertising since they are seen as attracting customers.

This implicit conflict of interest between the journalist attempting to define his own work as a reporter of news and the advertisement reps constantly bedevilled the *Review*, and there were frequent conflicts between the interests of profitability and the interests of maintaining an output of radical news. One of the ways this manifested itself was in the organisation of rock concerts to prop up the finances of the magazine. One of the entrepreneurial members of the co-operative who undertook this enterprise eventually began to see it as more rewarding in its own right and took up the impressario's role on his own account. This caused great antagonism among the other members of the co-operative. He was considered to have betrayed the co-op by taking away business, and was characterised as a variety of forms of life ranging from a snake-in-the-grass downwards.

In this, the market in which the co-operatives operated provided

opportunities for individuals to better themselves economically, either directly at the expense of the co-op or at least in a way which bore no collective fruit. In the *Review* the news editor was able to use the offices and facilities of the co-op to generate business for himself as a freelance journalist. This also provided news for the magazine and in turn a shop window for him as a journalist. Given that after an initial period on a very low wage, he abandoned payment from the co-op because of its straitened circumstances and lived on his freelance earnings, this arrangement advantaged the collective.

Nonetheless after he had done two investigations for BBC television the multitude began to murmur and said verily he was only interested in making his way up the rubber ladder. One such incident arose from a film made by the BBC called 'The Whistle Blowers' about investigative journalism. The producer contacted me as an appropriate academic and said he wanted to film such an office at work. This he did. He paid the news editor a fee for appearing, me a smaller fee for my help and the co-op a facility fee for the use of the premises. The news editor handed his fee over to the co-op. But he also received another fee from the BBC for a different and unrelated Newsnight investigative film. Numerous and repeated allegations were made against the news editor, partly based on the proposition that he should hand over all monies made and partly under the misapprehension that the second and much larger sum was also for the 'Whistle Blowers' film. There was also much 'aggro' from another source – the unpaid contributors who accused him of insufficient dedication to socialism in his pursuit of news. Eventually he left to work for Radio 4 and then for BBC TV.

The day after he left, a member of the co-op told me 'He was nobody when he came here. He had no contacts, no job, nothing. Everything he got he got from us'. Factually this was not so. He had previously worked for the *Daily Express*, for Thomson's newspapers as a news editor and had run a freelance news business. It demonstrated the antagonisms which constantly rose to the surface when an individual seemed to prosper by selling some expertise, gained in the co-op, in the market to the highest bidder.

This also manifested itself, but in a different way, in the second co-operative, the freelance news agency. Here four journalists, two women reporters, a male reporter and a male photographer formed themselves into a co-operative to dig dirt about the mighty and provide coverage sympathetic to 'progressive' causes. In the weeks prior to the inauguration of the co-op there were long and detailed

discussions about the way in which they should pay themselves: an equal amount each out of what was left after they had paid their bills or set aside some funds for future needs. They opted for the latter on the basis that the idea of a co-operative meant that one of the central purposes should be that workers should support one another both financially and emotionally. In the end, so long as everyone pulled their weight, it would even out, they decided.

They worked together in a small office obtained rent free from the county council, but their work tended to follow lines inherited from their own previous careers. Both women worked in the newspaper market – one had developed the health field as a special market and did work for specialist publications such as the Nursing Times, the second was a female old style foot-in-the-door-man. They both produced a comparatively high rate of return. The male reporter, who had previously been, amongst many other things, the news editor of *The Morning Star* cashed in on his contacts with the trades union and Labour movement and worked almost on a retainer for the *Labour Weekly* as well as *Tribune, The New Statesman* and *The Morning Star*. This also produced a steady return. Only the photographer posed a problem. He was a polytechnic trained photographer whose work was of a quality rarely seen in a news room. Every job he was sent on he produced impeccable photographs. *The New Statesman* used his picture of Manchester Chief Constable James Anderton as their full title page for an issue on the police. Another picture of his published by *The New Statesman* showed police photographers with zoom lenses taking pictures of pickets. The police claimed these were for training aids in lectures on crowd control. His pictures showed that they were photographing individuals. But although his craftsmanship was never in doubt, his professionalism as a journalist was. The two women expressed doubts about his ability and willingness to drum up business. He saw his job as doing the work the reporters needed, not as finding work for himself or offering work to newspapers. A growing ill-will between the two women and the photographer eventually led to a row in a co-op meeting, at which the photographer's inability to tout for work was identified as a personal failing – he was driven into a sullen silence.

After only six months in operation the co-operative was about to collapse. The women brought in a woman photographer to do a job at a theatrical event. Her camera would not work and she did not have a stand-by camera, as the male photographer always did. Relationships then fell apart. The two women left, the one to work

for a company doing work for Channel Four, the other to work as a freelance for BBC TV and then to have a baby. The men struggled on primarily on the work drummed up by the male reporter, now hobbled by demands from the women for back pay for the period they had worked. The two who stayed on had not yet received all the payments due to them from customers. The two women demanded that the books should be brought up to date. After a further meeting, they were paid but remained dissatisfied about the books. After a further six months the male reporter left also; to work for the press office of the GLC. The photographer returned to his home town. Two years later letters were flying among the participants full of recrimination and blame. The £400 ex-BBC Uher taperecorder, all the photographic equipment and the books have all been lost in the mists of time. The Registrar of Friendly Societies is still awaiting properly prepared books and records.

During the short life of this venture, the journalists never ceased to calculate their own and their colleagues' contribution to the collective purse. At any time they were only as viable as their ability to find stories and to persuade buyers to take them at a reasonable rate. The market model of control over the journalist in the industrialised news organisation operates even more vigorously on journalists in the freelance market. Even more so, since their aim and the aim of the *Review* news editor was to work at the sort of stories they thought were valid journalism and not simply market orientated products. This meant that selling stories was more difficult, both because fewer buyers were available and because regular interests such as the *New Statesman* and *Labour Weekly* were not able to pay large fees, and now no longer exist. Thus the attempt to escape the market control of the 'straight' industrialised newspaper organisation actually puts the journalist under a greater market pressure. The market model of managerial control in the newspaper industry reflects the way the visibility of journalistic output makes calculation of the market value of an individual worker's effort a relatively easy undertaking.

One of the aims of the freelance co-op was to launch a news magazine. But from the outset the members were engaged in a day-to-day struggle to survive. *The Review* on the other hand began as a magazine and then survived because the major news of journalistic input was by a member who was able to make a living by his freelance earnings. In the end however his position was severely disadvantaged by working for the co-op and the price of his skills in the labour market, combined with expensive needs such as mortgages and single malt

whiskey, drew him back into the sector of the labour market dominated by the industrialised–bureaucratic news producing organisations.

This is not in my judgement an atypical individual instance. The *Review* co-op as an entity experienced the same fundamental schism. All the time it produced the magazine it did so at a loss. The co-operative sustained it with the two other sources of capital and income. The first was the injection of redundancy money from two journalists who put considerable efforts as writers, and in one case management, into the enterprise while still working full time as journalists on national newspapers. Due to the Byzantine processes of logic employed by the national newspaper business management, they had each had the following experience. They were redunded as full time members of staff and each received around a year's salary in compensation for this shock to their systems. They were both immediately reinstated to work on a casual shift basis, and both continued to work permanently full time for the same employer and the same salary. One eventually moved to another paper, the second remains at the same newspaper as he began. Since the *Review* was in difficult straits they contributed £3000 each into its capital to save it from bankruptcy. This then meant that they had a proprietorial stake in the magazine. And one of the two who was derided behind his back as a 'wanker', commanded large space in the magazine for his articles which the others regarded as 'crap'. When asked why, they always referred to the £3000 he had donated. The second source of capital came from the news editor, who put up his house as a security and guaranteed a further £3000. This produced a sort of two class co-operative where varying amounts of money invested created a class of proprietors and a class of workers in embryo.

This tendency was exemplified in the final decision to close down the publishing part of the co-operative. Because they wished to take advantage of the new cheap equipment in the printing industry, and because of the deskilling consequence upon this technological innovation, the co-operative was able to train typesetters and do their own origination work. But the photosetting machinery, darkroom facilities and the increasingly capable man and woman power they had trained in their composing room provided an origination capacity beyond the needs of the magazine. This gave them a potential income to offset the losses incurred by the magazine. As time passed the origination and layout studio became a stable and profitable element in the business. An accountant with socialistic principles examined their books free of charge and concluded that the long term survival

of the co-operative lay in dropping the publishing part of the business in favour of the design services.

Eventually, faced with a bank overdraft of £2700 in 1980, after four years of publication the co-operative ceased to publish the magazine and concentrated on the layout design part of the business. After six months they had paid off the overdraft. After a further year they paid off the £3,000 put into the business by one of the redunded journalists. They subsequently merged with another co-operative, *The Free Press*, who had also previously published a news magazine and had abandoned the effort to go into origination and graphic design work also. Now the newly merged co-op employs twelve workers and operates at a profit. In the end the decision to abandon the publication of the news magazine was taken in the light of the large inputs of capital by some members.

The third co-operative news produces another magazine, *City Life*, based very closely on the style of content and layout of the *Review*. Over four years they have been able to make a profit by paying themselves very low wages, by organising rock concerts, and increasingly through layout studio work. As the journalists grow older they will need to find alternative sources of income to supplement their incomes. Whether or not they close down will depend on whether the Labour market for journalists draws them away, or whether inequality among different reporters' ability to pull in freelance money produces stresses which shatter their common purpose. They also have to produce income from advertising, which in turn requires a decent level of sales – at least 5000. In selling space generally, the advertising representatives refer to *City Life* as an entertainments magazine, since this is seen as an indictor that advertisements in the magazine give access to entertainment and consumer goods orientated readers. If they were to say 'we're the magazine that slags off the fuzz and local businessmen and treats gays sympathetically', selling ads would not be so easy.

Such a source of tension between advertising and radical news coverage is central to such co-operative news enterprises. A letter in the London magazine *City Limits* from a disgruntled animal-rights orientated reader illustrates the point:

> The whole of *City Limits* reeks of 'do what we say, not what we do.' Articles and reviews align themselves with 'action' and anti-bourgeois views.
>
> The rapidly increasing space given to features on wine bars, flash

restaurants, expensive holidays, and furniture is overt encouragement to be bourgeois; not only that but it could only affect the
bourgeois, who can afford such waste and make dammed sure they
stay that way.

Much of your magazine is excellent and forms an important link
between people and art. Why then the two conflicting faces to the
magazine – art and consumerism? The latter only seems to take
money from *Time Out* [the competition] and then turn such readers
into hypocrites, by letting them play at 'radical' politics at the same
time as frequenting wine bars[17]'

This reflects the poignant conflict which affects all such magazines. In
order to promulgate a leftist version of news they must survive by
selling advertisements. To sell advertisements, and through an
intrinsic interest anyway, they include their 'entertainments' section –
rock music reviews, interviews with famous film stars who are giving
the *Guardian* lecture. In the minds of advertisers this identifies with a
certain readership – predominantly the 20–30 year old *Guardian*
readers, largely in professional work, and therefore relatively affluent
and willing to spend their money on haute cuisine nut cutlets. To
encourage further advertisements, it is therefore politic to include
eating out articles. During recent years a number of such magazines
have abandoned the radical news input and have become the what's
on entertainment guides beloved to the advertisers.

But the conflict between the demands of the market in advertising
and consequent pressure to court the consumerism of a sort of
nouveau radical chic is not the only contradiction faced by the co-
operative news magazine operating in present day Britain. The
individualism of the labour market in journalism permeates the
consciousness of those involved. They consequently seek success in
terms of this competitive arena. Though they may not be engaged in
the exercise primarily for money – they certainly are not – the idea of
work being rewarded by personal success is deeply ingrained in the
process. None of the journalists in the co-operatives were willing to
share their contacts with others. Reporters of national stature show
an even greater reluctance to share their contacts or exclusives with
one another. Take for instance two such reporters who have collabor-
ated on an investigation in the past, who have been on holiday together,
who are drinking companions. One was subsequently working on a
police corruption story in Manchester. But the other did not know.
As a result the local 'alternative' news magazine *City Life* was able to

sell the story to the one who did not know. To take another example, the same police officer is the contact for a number of journalists: one, a freelance, sells information to another, a staff man on national newspaper. The police contact and the freelance know; the contact is willing to go along with the secrecy and allow the freelance to make money for two reasons: (a) It is useful to have another outlet for the stories he wishes to see published for his own reasons (he is an enemy within). By giving the freelance the means to obtain income he is bolstering a resource of his own; (b) It means he can maximise the output of information with the minimum of risk in terms of meetings and phone calls.

The 'ownership' of contacts and exclusives is part of the journalists' capital and the proof of his competence. Through this means he establishes his identity and repeatedly demonstrates his ability to find and get published investigative stories which prove the fundamental institutional delinquency of capitalism. But the contradiction of the activity is that the deed is done through the exercise of the most extreme form of occupational possessive individualism. And this individualism generates a constant fissiparous tension in attempts at collective production of news and news publications.

A further difficulty for such organisations is the simple working through of price levels in factors of production. The argument that cheap capital would of itself enable the development of long term tendency towards greater ideological variety in news publication was always naïve. This is simply because the same cheap technology is available to all and big companies are able to combine economies of scale in production, distribution and the purchase of raw materials with the cheap technology. They can therefore force down the price of the product and of the service, advertising.

What we now see therefore is a new phenomenon in the local newspaper industry: the domination of the market by 'free-sheets'. As they spread, older traditional commercial papers are collapsing and their owners are moving into free-sheet businesses. The estimate by the newspaper proprietors is that the free-sheets are now distributed to about 56 per cent of local weekly newspaper readers.

At this level proprietors can take advantage of jobbing printers and thus avoid the closed shop power of Fleet Street Unions or big established regional newspapers. Or, as in the case of Eddy Shah, they can set up their presses with non-union labour. Even the 'straight' traditional press can sometimes succeed in such endeavours. ' The Nottingham Evening Post cut back its numbers of printing

workers from 210 to 37 with the introduction of new technology and beat the unions into submission.

Co-operative news publications have to fight constantly to keep down such costs. They seek the cheapest printers, they pay themselves low wages which in turn causes them to seek individualistic solution and market solutions to their own subsistence problems in the freelance news market. Sometimes this predicament produces particular ironies. Before it developed its own facilities for layout, *City Life* was embarrassed because it was using an origination studio which was in dispute with the print unions. This was because the studio is cheap. Other workers' co-operatives in the area discovered this and the *City Life* co-op was condemned at the bar of international working class opinion, or more precisely by those other co-ops in the origination trades who could do with the business!

CONCLUSION

In examining these attempts by journalists to devise a means of organising their own work and taking over the control of such organisation, we are brought face-to-face with certain fundamental issues to do with the predicament of workers in relation to the distribution of goods and money and power.

As I indicated earlier, the method of control over workers employed in industrialised newspaper corporations can be seen emanating from a market model. An ideology of 'marketing' one's work and oneself is built into an ideology of the job. 'Selling' comes to have two meanings: the straightforward notion of an exchange for money, and the idea of convincing someone in power of the validity of a story or of the efficacy of the worker. A journalist for instance may 'sell' a story to his editor who will then be 'sold' on the idea. This has the consequence of individualising the worker who competes with his or her colleagues in a contest to show the highest level of competence, that is the greatest sensitivity to 'market' demands for news; the greatest sensitivity for management definitions of news. In this sense the definition of *competence* comes to include the correct understanding of the *necessary conditions of compliance of labour*. I see no reason to believe that, say, in the world of selling this same system of internalised control does not operate. In this context the debate between the primacy of managements' competing aims of profit or control is seen to depend on a false dichotomy. With any

production system employing large numbers of workers, profit and control are two sides of the same coin. The crucial skill of management is to expose workers directly to the rigours of the market and, as in the case of the journalist, eliminate the need for bureaucratic control.

We see such a tendency again in CBI policies, which favour moving from the large manufacturing enterprises with staff employees to the use by such enterprises of small competing firms of specialist contractors wherever a 'putting out' system can be employed.

In such a context co-operative enterprises can only 'work' if they conform to the conditions of the market. And these conditions are determined by the large corporations who dominate the buying side of factor markets and the selling side for goods. In this case the market for journalistic services always provides a threat to the social nature of the co-op by providing rewards for individualism. Even within the context of the co-op, the skill at 'selling' and the 'will' to sell is seen as a necessary part of the skill of the journalist, even to the extent that failure to sell oneself is seen as shortchanging the socialist principles of the co-operative.

Similarly the new cheap, computerised technology means that small co-ops can move into business where previously the large scale expensive mechanical engineering technology and a rigid union structure kept out such small scale enterprises. But the low capital costs and the deskilling of origination provides the same advantages for the big firms, along with the economies of scale. The co-ops therefore move in on the terms laid down by the corporations. They are like a third world economy within an advanced corporate economy. They depend for their technology on the products of big international companies and they operate in a low wage economy. They either provide their own services at low rates of pay or they contract out to other small firms which pay low wages.

In this area of the economy at least it is possible to argue that the co-operative enterprise poses no threat at all to the market economy. Those elements in the socialisation of workers into a market ideology, which obviates the need for bureaucratic control, remain integral to the practise of journalism whether or not the content of the journalism is radical. In order to keep publications viable, the sale of advertisements and the promulgation of consumerism become necesary preconditions of existence. Therefore one of the ironies of the radical co-operative press is that it has to participate in moving the focus of control from production to consumption[18] which Knights

and others have identified as part of the development of the labour process in advanced capitalism. Thus the fundamental aspects of advanced capitalism which place such co-operatives in a subordinate position can be seen to be:

1. That goods are distributed through the price mechanism in the context of fashion, changing patterns of consumption etcetera, which are heavily influenced by the manipulation of consumer taste.
2. That big corporations determine the development of technology and dominate factor markets (especially the labour markets).
3. That (1) and (2) are interdependent.

These fundamental issues of distribution of goods and decisions about the direction of investment means that changing internal relationships among workers, or between management and workers, cannot change the underlying pre-condition of work: compliance with the demand for corporate profit.

Notes and References

1. See Harry Christian, 'Journalist', Occupational ideologies and Press Commercialisation', in Sociological *Review Monograph 29, The Sociology of Journalism and the Press*, Harry Christian (ed.), University of Keele (1980) pp. 259–306. This provides a detailed account of trade unionism among journalists and concentrates on their rejection of the ideology of 'professionalism' proffered by the Institute of Journalists in favour of the trades union values of The National Union of Journalists.
2. See, for instance, 'Social Control in the Newsroom', *Social Forces*, 33 (1955) pp. 326–35; Aleksander Matejko, 'Newspaper Staff as a Social System', in *Media Sociology*, Jeremy Tunstall (ed.) Constable (1970) pp. 168–181 (reprinted from *The Polish Sociological Bulletin*, 1 (1967) pp. 58–68; David Manning White 'The Gatekeeper'': A Case Study in the Selection of News', in *People, Society and Mass Communication*, Lewis A. Dexter and David Manning White (eds), New York Free Press (1963) p. 160–73; Harvey Molotch and Marylin Lester, 'News as Purposive Behavior, On the Strategic Use of Routine Events, Accidents and Scandals', *American Sociological Review*, 39:1 (1973) pp. 101–112; Gaye Tuckman, 'Making News by Doing Work', *American Journal of Sociology*, 79:1 (1973) pp. 111–131; Lee Sigelman, 'Reporting the News, An Organisational Analysis' *American Journal of Sociology*, 79:1 (1973) pp. 132–151.

3.	See Matejko, *op. cit.*
4.	Work such as the *Bad News Book* by the Glasgow Media Group and the work of the Birmingham Centre for Contemporary Cultural Studies exemplify this sort of approach, but it also underlies the analysis of the mass media and ideological dominance in other Marxist literature, such as *The State in Capitalist Society*, Ralph Miliband, Quartet Books (1973) pp. 196–223; *Strikes*, Richard Hyman, Fontana Collins (1972) pp. 151–3; *Industrial Relations: a Marxist Introduction* by the same author, Macmillan (1975); *Strike at Pilkingtons*, Tony Lane and Ken Roberts, Fontana (1971) pp. 75–6.
5.	Stuart Hall, 'Deviance, Politics and the Mass Media', in *Deviance and Social Control* Paul Rock and Mary McIntosh (eds) Tavistock (1974) pp. 261–307; and 'The rediscovery of ideology: return of the repressed in media studies', also by Hall in *Culture, Society and Media*, Michael Gurevitch et al. (eds), Methuen (1982) pp. 56–90.
6.	Ralph Miliband, *op. cit.*
7.	Louis Althusser 'Ideology and Ideological State Apparatuses' in *Lenin and Philosophy and other Essays*, New Left Books (1971).
8.	As well as the group's collective work on industrial relations news coverage, *Bad News* (1976) *More Bad News* (1980) and *Really Bad News*, Routledge and Kegan Paul, see also works by individual members of the group such as *Trades Unions and the Media*, Peter Beharell and Greg Philo (eds), Macmillan (1977).
9.	For instance, Stuart Hall and T. Jefferson (eds), *Resistance Through Rituals*, Hutchinson (1975) and Hall et al. (eds), *Culture, Media Language*, Hutchinson (1980) among many other works.
10.	See Gaye Tuckman et al. (eds) *Hearth and Home: Images of Women in the Mass Media*, Oxford University Press (1980); T. Millum, *Images of Women*, Chatto and Windus (1975); H. Baker, *Women and the Media*, Pergammon (1980).
11.	Guy Cumberbatch, Robin McGregor and John Brown, *Television and the Miners' Strike*, Broadcasting Research Unit (1986).
12.	Among the many works in this vein probably the best are *Putting Reality Together*, Phillip Schlesinger, Constable (1978) and *The Making of a Television Series*, Phillip Elliot, Constable (1973). This also represents the position underlying my own *The Silent Watchdog: The Press in Local Politics*, Constable (1976).
13.	This is well documented in an as yet unpublished MA thesis by a former Daily Star journalist, Susan Bromley, *News Goes to Market: A Case Study of the Star*, University of Wales, Cardiff, 1988. A similar state of affairs is revealed in D. Simpson, *Commercialisation of the Regional Press*, Gower, 1981.
14.	Bromley, *op. cit.*
15.	Harry Braverman, *Labor and Monopoly Capitalism*, New York Monthly Review Press (1974).
16.	The account of the lobby system given by Jeremy Tunstall in *The Westminster Lobby Correspondents*, Routledge and Kegan Paul (1970) shows this group of journalists in a role similar to that of the traditional manual craftsman: that is he has control over the execution of his work

but not with its direction in that the nature of content is circumscribed by social and political conventions embedded in the institutions on which they supposedly report.

17. *City Limits*, Letters (letter from Peter Godfrey of Seven Sisters Road, W7), March 1–7, 1985, p. 90.

18. D. Knights and H. Wilmott (eds) *Managing the Labour Process*, Gower (1986), p. 7.

8 Recruitment Strategies and Managerial Control of Technological Staff

Diane Winstanley

INTRODUCTION

There has been extensive debate in recent years about managerial strategies and new forms of labour control (for example see Littler, 1982; Wood, 1982). Discussion concentrated initially on managerial attempts to control the labour process. It highlighted strategies of deskilling and emphasised the homogenisation of the workforce and different forms of conflict and co-operation at work (see Braverman, 1974 for example). In the early 1980s the focus of debate shifted to discussion over how companies were restructuring to cope with recession and a changed political-economic climate. There has been a growing interest in fragmentation, both the breaking down of companies into smaller profit centres and the rekindling of sub-contract relationships. Relations in the labour market therefore became increasingly relevant to the debates over managerial strategies for the control of white-collar, and in this case, technological workers.

The research presented below is part of the reorientation away from the labour process and production relations and towards the labour market and exchange relations. It concentrates on recruitment as a form of control of technological staff. This change of emphasis is for two reasons. Firstly, although many technological occupations have strong craft traditions with considerable control over labour supply, this study concentrates on high technology industry. Here many occupational groups are emerging with no tradition of collective muscle. They are often working within non-unionised environments and tend to behave in more individualistic ways. In such companies it is only the more traditional technological occupations that exhibit, the more collective forms of resistance and control (draughtspeople for example). Secondly, direct forms of control are less useful in high technology industry where managers want their highly skilled staff to

have high discretion to work 'flexibly' in a dynamic and unstable environment.

In this chapter it will be argued that the allocation of jobs and the structuring of the employment relationship by the use of the recruitment function is a powerful form of managerial control. The main focus will be on two central aspects of the recruitment of technological staff within high technology industry, their subjection to managerial strategies and their response against a background of relatively weak collective organisation and a relatively strong position in the labour market.

The term technological staff broadly covers staff with qualifications, training and–or experience based on one of the 'technical' disciplines and working in engineering, scientific, electronics and computing based occupations. Their jobs are defined as having a high technical content, and posts are normally filled by graduates or, in former days, people who have progressed through the apprenticeship route and gained a technical qualification (such as the HND).

The framework used here for examining the relationship between recruitment and managerial control strategies for technological staff distinguishes between five main sources of control in this area. These are derived from a wider study of recruitment conducted by the author within the New Technology Research Group at the University of Southampton. The material used here is taken from four high technology companies backed up by case study, interview and questionnaire data from personnel and technical staff from 20 companies, 3 unions and 15 technical recruitment agencies in Hampshire.

These aspects of recruitment and the managerial control of technological staff are discussed as patterns or clusters of policies which combine to contribute to a managerial strategy which crosses many areas of managerial decision-making. They are:

– Labour market manipulation.
– Choice of recruitment mechanisms.
– Adoption of selection criteria.
– The contract of employment.
– Duration of employment.

LABOUR MARKET MANIPULATION

There are three main ways in which managers can manipulate the labour market to attempt control: through segmentation, the creation

of dependency via an internal labour market, or through the creation of a 'reserve army of labour'. The theoretical basis for this analysis is derived from radical segmentation theorists such as Edwards (1979). He emphasises stratification in the labour market, determined by the use of different managerial control strategies and the power of different groups of workers to resist.

There are four examples of labour market manipulation in the case study companies. Laboratory A, a computer development laboratory which was part of a large non-union multinational firm, was subject to high growth, and was a market leader with a relatively large market share at the time of the study. This plant operated a dyadic recruitment strategy with a division between 'core' workers, mainly software development engineers, and 'peripheral' contract workers. The development engineers were subject to a no-redundancy policy, with life-time job security and favourable employment conditions and rewards. This was made possible by the attainment of 'numerical flexibility' through a large subcontracting periphery whose size could be changed quickly to reflect their needs (the term 'numerical flexibility' being coined by Atkinson, 1984).

Establishment B, part of a mature, unionised avionics corporation where business was largely conducted on MOD contract, also segmented staff into permanent and contract staff. The bulk of technological staff are project team avionics and electronics engineers, and these are supplemented by contract workers.

Company C was a small–medium sized non-unionised computer company involved in servicing and support functions plus some developmental computer networking. Here the segmentation was combined with a locational strategy which enabled different practices to be employed without resentment. This was facilitated by the geographical separation of the servicing and support functions from the development and applications engineers. The former was conducted from one office, where staff were subjected to direct control, work rationalisation, the setting of objectives, and work monitoring; while the latter were involved in the more innovative work in a building several miles away and were subject to 'responsible autonomy' types of control. The research centre Laboratory A was separated off from the firm's other functions partly for the same reason.

Where the former group at Company C were subjected to a strategy of direct technical and bureaucratic control to limit the negative aspects of the variability of labour power (Braverman,

1974), Friedman's alternative concept of responsible autonomy related to the latter group where employers:

> Harness the adaptability of labour power by giving workers leeway and encouraging them to adapt to changing situations in a manner beneficial to the firm. To do this top managers try to win their loyalty and co-operation, their organisation to the firms ideals ideologically. (Friedman, 1977, p. 78)

This dichotomy of strategies between attempting to limit the particularly harmful effects of labour or alternatively to capture its benefits, can be described simply as the use of direct control or responsible autonomy respectively. A level of investment in each strategy is required and this produces rigidities which prevent vacillations between strategies (*ibid*. 1977). Thus different groups of workers have to be isolated and insulated from each other, and so managers have to segment the labour force and create separate recruitment and utilisation strategies.

Plant D is part of an electronics component subsidiary of a large unionised multi-national corporation. This was a mature organisation undergoing change to keep pace with developments in high technology. As a result, at the time of study it was laying 50 people off via early retirement, and yet at the same time experiencing problems in recruiting graduate electronics engineers (particularly in the fields of circuit design and software development) and semiconductor physicists. The company was highly bureaucratised with a formalised approach to recruitment and career development, although there were moves to increase flexibility in order to combat the mobility of staff and their loss through poaching. In this firm there was two-fold segmentation, one dividing those staff and areas that were being run down (particularly staff who had come up through the traditional apprenticeship route and whose more traditional engineering skills were becoming obsolescent) from the newer graduate level recruits. The second division was in terms of separating the new recruits into 'high flyers' and others. The company was attempting to circumvent nationally agreed standard practices by developing high flyer routes for key staff, and market group supplements to give extra pay to valued staff without upsetting the complex job evaluation scheme and salary structure (based on the HAY/MSL model). The Staff Development Manager said of the 'high flyers':

> Once they get on this list of high flyers they become owned not just by their own manager, but they become owned by the plant

committee, and they are seen in a plantwide category of people who can contribute in the future at a high level not just in the environment in which they are employed. Every graduate who is identified as a high flyer gets a job change after two years and is put into a challenging situation to isolate them and make them realise they are being given some sort of special treatment.... What we are saying clearly is that we now have to focus on a number of groups of people like our sponsored undergraduates, like our high flyers, and we have got to establish an ownership of them and do something special for them.

The latter practices relate to the manipulation of the labour market through bureaucratisation of the employment relationship and career structuring to create a separate internal labour market and dependency for technological staff.

Littler and Salaman (1982) and Littler (1982) have recently drawn attention to ways in which control at work can be located in the employment relationship. A major emphasis here is on the notion of dependency (a concept also mentioned by Weber (1947) as being important for power). Littler defined dependency in terms of the availability of 'alternative sources of need satisfaction' and the 'capacity of subordinates to organise'. He cites Japanese industries and the big British banks as examples of where alternative employment opportunities and vacancies offered on the external labour market are lacking, and there is firm specificity of worker skills. This means that 'once a worker accepts that (s)he can no longer move, (s)he is more likely to accept company policies', because 'resistance in any form is extremely difficult where no alternative employment opportunities exist' (1982, pp. 43–7).

The core workers divided by the segmentation policies of the companies mentioned above were all subjected to some sort of internal labour market policy to create dependency. As many companies were unable to limit the transferability of many technological staff skills, these mainly related to the provision of rewards in pay and careers. In Laboratory A they used a number of attractions to retain these key workers. The company was situated in a beautiful country house, with very high tech equipment and laboratories. There were sports facilities, a plush canteen, and good pay. Technical employees here were dependent by virtue of not being able to get nearly so good salaries and fringe benefits elsewhere. They were also made more dependent by their integration into the social networks of

the company through paternalist socialisation processes, and their being cut off from external links such as trade unions.

In Plant D the 'carrots' provided to the high flyers, such as the market group supplements to their wages and good career progression, have been attempts to create an internal labour market. Managers are not always successful in their attempts at control, and these technological staff, due to their good position in the labour market, were able to resist becoming dependent through retaining transferable skills and thus job mobility. Ironically where dependency was successfully created among those with ageing firm specific skills, the company would have preferred mobility. One manager sums up these problems by saying:

> It is usually the people that you want to keep who are going to leave, and the people who you would quite happily see move on that stay. That is a difficult one to grapple with managerially. If you really wanted to control it you would presumably be much more ruthless. But you have to balance that with the social aspects of employing people, and the industrial relations aspects that could attend to that.

The third way companies can manipulate the labour market in order to achieve control can be through the encouragement of the 'reserve army of labour', or more simply by ensuring a surplus of labour within the labour market. This is not however a feasible option for companies to apply to technological staff because the high level of skills required means that 'shortage' rather than 'surplus' often characterises this labour market. Virtually all the companies interviewed and surveyed complained that the educational system was not producing enough technical graduates. When companies complain of a skill shortage, this can be an indicator of the shift of the balance of power between employer and employee in the labour market in favour of the latter. As a result of this shift, firms such as B, C and D, all reported problems of poaching and a high turnover of key staff.

Relating these points to company strategic objectives, manipulation of the labour market is a managerial strategy used to gain numerical flexibility through segmentation. It is also used to gain operational control and flexibility of labour through the development of the internal labour market for technological staff. In return technological staff have utilised their individual labour market power in terms of their skills and the demand for them to counter this through their ability to be mobile. Where skills become highly

enterprise specific (Doeringer and Piore, 1971) then this individual power becomes eroded and staff become more dependent on the company. When their skills become obsolescent with changing technology, they may then be made redundant as happened for some technological staff in Establishment B and Plant D.

CHOICE OF RECRUITMENT MECHANISMS

The second aspect of control and managerial strategy mentioned relates to the manipulation of recruitment mechanisms. One part of this corresponds to the choice of recruitment channels. In the literature there is much discussion over the growth of informal and internal types of recruitment channel. Firms may use the extended internal labour market (Manwaring, 1984) or informal contact and 'word-of-mouth' recruitment. The extended internal labour market is where recruitment is through the existing employees in a firm, relying on social networks. It ensures that the new recruits will fit in, and be stable and controllable. Maguire (1984, p. 4) shows how in this and other ways firms gain control through reproducing the social relations of the locality in which they are based, and this is one way discrimination can be perpetuated.

This raises the issue of whether formalised or informalised practices are more associated with control. Jewson and Mason (1986) argue that although much work on recruitment and selection criteria have usually associated informal procedures with control, bureaucratised forms of recruitment can have the same effect. This can be via the generation of internal labour markets or segmented labour markets (Rubery, 1978), and by the institutionalisation of the 'imperatives of the capitalist market within the workplace' (see Clegg, 1975 and Clegg and Dunkerley, 1980 for example).

Jenkins et al. (1983) show how the impact of a recession can encourage the use of informal and internal 'word-of-mouth' recruitment channels, due to the large pool of candidates available and the strategic need for managers to reduce uncertainty in the manual labour markets. Control is enhanced by greater knowledge of the candidate and the fact that existing employees have their own reputation at stake in recommending friends or relatives, and they may exert control over the new recruit.

This argument was only born out in modified form in the case studies of technological staff. There was one instance of Company C

having a Staff Referral Scheme where staff were paid a bonus if they recruited people into the firm. This is interesting in that it was the formalisation of an informal extended internal labour market practice and had only happened for the most deskilled and lesser qualified technical workers. The reason why these types of informal and internal recruitment channels were not so much in evidence is that for highly qualified technical staff it is difficult to find sufficient candidates through these channels, and Jenkins et al. and Manwaring were referring to a situation where there is a labour market surplus. The employers of higher qualified non-manual staff were initiating their own adaptations of these models in ways more appropriate for this labour market. Thus for instance the avionics Establishment B were targeting and identifying where pools of candidates were to be found and were tapping the labour market through informal contact in 'hotel walk-ins' on their competitors 'doorsteps'. Others were using informal contact with highly skilled specialists at conferences as another source of candidates. This is only successful where a small group of experts can be isolated.

This leads us to the question of how high technology companies who require highly skilled technical staff can gain predictability and confidence that candidates will be co-operative and have the right attributes, when the 'extended internal labour market' or the 'word of mouth' channels that tell them so much more about a candidate do not provide the technically skilled candidates required. The answer here is that they manipulate the recruitment mechanisms by extension of the recruitment process prior to employer commitment, either into pre-recruitment training on the one hand, or into induction on the other. In the former case companies use sponsorship of university graduates as a way of learning more about candidates. Firms B and D were both increasing their sponsorship of university students. The milkround, used by Laboratory A, Establishment B and Plant D, is a type of screening that makes sure candidates not only have adequate technical qualifications, but also ensures that a candidate is likely to come from a certain type of social background. One manager interviewed would recruit only from four universities which were in a similar setting to that of the company as a way of minimising potential turnover from recruits not fitting into the rural environment of the company. Company C was too small to use the milkround but did use technical recruitment agencies as a form of pre-selection screening, and Establishment B and Plant D also used agencies to supplement their other forms of recruitment.

Extending recruitment into induction occurs where the issue of a permanent contract is delayed until after an initial induction, apprenticeship or trainee period has been undertaken. Company C had a six month probationery period for new staff for example, which was used to check that candidates were suitable before permanent contracts were issued.

Targetting is one technique for controlling the source of applicants and this can also relate to the choice of particular areas in which to recruit. As Littler and Salaman (1982) suggest:

Issues of control become non-issues, irrelevant through geographical relocation in well chosen areas where it is known that, as yet, the workforce will conform to indigenous modes of regulation and motivation.

The links between recruitment, location and control have been discussed elsewhere, (Maguire, 1984; Massey and Meegan, 1982), and in this study companies were often found to consider location in choice of local, regional and national recruitment channels. In addition their own location was often connected to the need to be a part of industrial and employment infrastructures, such as the 'M4' corridor.

Another source of control through the manipulation of recruitment mechanisms is through the choice of rigorous selection procedures. For all case study companies, and in fact for all the other companies surveyed, the interview was the dominant selection procedure used by all companies. This was backed up by references and the application form or curriculum vitae. Even for predominantly technical jobs, procedures which give priority to social selection criteria applied within a social setting were preferred. Detailed participant observation in interviews conducted at Establishment B and Plant D and answers from the survey showed that although some questions asked at interview were technical, most were to judge their problem-solving ability, motivation, co-operativeness, ability to 'fit-in' and so on. The interview record sheets at Establishment B and Plant D stressed social characteristics both in their structure and in the details filled in. The technological staff subjected to the most comprehensive selection procedures were permanent staff, because of the difficulty in dismissal.

Technical criteria are necessary to qualify candidates for jobs, but are not sufficient in themselves. Despite the technical nature of the

work of technological staff, social characteristics are still emphasised partly for work related reasons, but also to ensure operational control and predictability (through recruiting for a low turnover for example). Another reason is the difficulty in directly controlling more skilled conceptual work. The use of procedures that emphasise social characteristics are often associated with the recruitment of 'the controllable worker'.

ADOPTION OF SELECTION CRITERIA

This leads us to the third main area of control through recruitment, that of control through the careful selection of people with social and behavioural characteristics that make them the 'controllable' or the 'flexible' worker. Blackburn and Mann (1979) in their labour market study highlighted the importance of co-operation, responsibility, stability and trustworthiness as social selection criteria used to retain control. When asked for the five most important positive factors desired in a candidate in their own words, the responses of the surveyed companies highlighted the importance placed on disposition and personality, and especially those social aspects which are related to fitting-in with the company and work-group, motivation, enthusiasm and flexibility of attitude.

Likewise Morgan and Sayer (1984) in a study of the electrical engineering industry in South Wales found that more stringent recruitment procedures were being used, with particular emphasis on 'behavioural skills'. They believed there to be a trend towards the dependent flexible worker with technical and behavioural skills becoming more firm specific and less transferable between firms. Oliver and Turton (1982) go further in stating that:

> It is possible that the skill shortages generally complained of are mainly of the behavioural kind. . . . Our claim is that the technicist concept of skill . . . is commonly not sufficient for employability and that, furthermore, the technical attributes can often be easily acquired.

They argue that managers require trainable, reliable, flexible workers with acceptable behaviour, or what they refer to as 'the good bloke syndrome'. Their study was of technician and craft level engineers rather than higher qualified technologists. Friedman and Greenbaum

informal introduction

(1984) have looked at the requirement for computer programmers and state that what companies really require is 'renaissance generalist people' with communication skills and flexible attitudes rather than the pure 'technies'. *Training no Silver Bullet.*

Salaman (1979) stresses the use of self-control and socialisation through organisational culture, plus pre-organisational processes of selection, recruitment, training and induction combined with the provision of good rewards. This involves not just the socialisation into the culture, rules and norms of an organisation but also the screening out of candidates who will not conform to its goals and practices via selection, self-selection and mobility.

Thus there seem to be two aspects of the demand for social attributes as well as technical skills. The first is the 'functionally specific' criteria (Jenkins, 1984) which relate to suitability for a job (such as the ability to communicate with clients), and the second are 'non-functionally specific' criteria for selection which relate to accept-ability to fit into the organisation and its culture and ethos. Control is particularly related to the latter category where social selection criteria are used as a complement to socialisation and ideological control once a candidate has entered the organisation. Take for example a quote which covers both these aspects from Laboratory A, where a manager stressed:

> The graduates we need are inherently versatile, capable of thinking new thoughts and of devising (not simply learning) new skills ... Secondly we need graduates who are inherently sociable, instinc-tively aware of both customers and colleagues. Narrow minded specialists rarely suit our work culture because they rarely appreci-ate our market orientation.

Reducing ... on Folice

He said that candidates must be well motivated, adaptable, flexible, they must work well in a team and want to work for that company, they must have business awareness and the potential to go beyond the initial job, due to their flexible utilisation policy.

The selection policy is related to both the organisational philo-sophy and the type of employment contract used (permanent, temporary or short term contract). The culture of the organisation has to complement the organisational structure and so for Laboratory A 'fitting-in' was important not just for the culture but also because of the 'football team' project group structure. This is more typical of the newer computer and electronics companies than the older more

functionally based organisations such as Plant D. A computer analyst recruited to Laboratory A said about her selection for the job:

> He looked at me and said 'yes, well I think you would probably fit in quite well there, because they don't mind eccentrics there' ... But what the football team basis of organisation means is that your manager has a team he wants you to fit into, so if you are black or a woman then you have got a much smaller chance of really fitting in, because they are all white men. And the man that in fact employed me did have a bias towards the intellectuals, people with academic qualifications, and it was just an odd-ball group.

Establishment B also had a project team based structure and so recruited for 'fitting-in' to the team as well as the company.

THE CONTRACT OF EMPLOYMENT

The fourth main aspect of managerial strategies and control in the area of recruitment relates to all the factors making up the terms and conditions of the contract of employment. This includes the job description, salary and fringe benefits, hours worked, and the protocols for job evaluation and staff performance reviews.

Where a job description is highly rigid there tends to be bureaucratic control, and responsible autonomy where it is flexible. Firms such as Laboratory A, whose managerial strategy required flexible utilisation of staff to enable a 'no redundancy policy', tended to opt for flexibility. The price paid for job security was flexible utilisation. This was supported by the ethos of pride in the company and its achievements. Conflict and unionisation were minimised through many schemes to improve the direct communication of management with the workers, and this was seen as being two-way. Salaries were flexible and performance related, as was career promotion, and there were a number of bonus schemes offered. Most of the non-unionised companies studied had individually negotiated salaries with only broad limits to prevent gross imbalances.

More bureaucratic companies such as Plant D still had remnants of bureaucratic control. The more rigid job descriptions were usually associated with the more formalised forms of recruitment and organisational structure, such as is found in the traditional engineering

sector or as described by Burns and Stalker (1961) as the 'mechanistic' form of organisation. This can be contrasted with the more fluid 'organic' structures found in the smaller establishments and newer electronics and higher technology companies. Increasingly firms such as Plant D were attempting to loosen salary structures and introduce performance related pay. They were copying newer flexible companies in order to maximise productivity as well as to prevent gains won by some workers to spread to other groups.

An example of where bureaucracy and rules and procedures were used for control was in Company C for the less powerful workers, who were also subjected to more direct forms of control. Here the field engineers working in the microproducts area had been considerably deskilled, with one reason being that the reduction of costs was the paramount strategic goal. Being on the less innovative side of the business in a mature area of high technology industry, there was considerable competition and profit margins were being eroded. On the mini-computer systems side of service and maintenance work it had been less possible for the jobs to be so deskilled, as here the repair work had to take place on site, rather than the faulty circuit being replaced and taken back to the workshop for repair (due to the size of the equipment). Here the drive to increase efficiency and productivity was being sustained by performance targets and the setting of objectives with regular performance appraisals and reviews. The company brochure states:

> Our service response times, field service inventory and stores control data are all carefully monitored by computer, and accurate statistics on response, mean time to repair, mean time between failures are made readily available to manufacture clients – on line if required. . . . Once on site, the engineer is supported by a carefully applied system of escalation, which contributes additional technical expertise if required.

Where a level of discretion and creativity is needed and bureaucracy stifles this, then 'responsible autonomy' becomes more appropriate. This applies more where cost-cutting and cost-effectiveness is less important than the quality of work gained by flexibility. So for the development and applications engineers based at the separate R and D facility, there was less direct, technical or bureaucratic control, although time-scales were sometimes set as broad outlines. There was

much less direct supervision, and staff were allowed flexitime to encourage creativity, and one manager said:

> Here we give them flexibility, if they feel fed up they can have an hour or two hour break and walk around in the fresh air – it doesn't matter because you had six hours extra from them the previous day, and they work evenings and take their work home at weekends . . . they are responsible people, and they realise they have been given the opportunity to do what they want, and are paid for it . . . but also you get even more out of them if you give them work that they have got to do, and want to do, and give them a bit of flexibility.

Within the work organisation, division between direct and bureaucratised forms of control and responsible autonomy are based on four factors. One is the relative importance of the different strategic objectives; another is the power of the technological staff on an individual level to gain labour market strength through their skills and scarcity. A third is the level of deskilling possible, and the fourth is the need for conceptual and high discretion work. In all the organisations research, design and development staff were less subjected to bureaucratic control, direct control and deskilling than technicians, manual technical staff, test engineers, draughtspeople and other more non-graduate groups. Where graduates are sometimes subjected to these types of control or work it is often temporary as part of their career ladder (for instance in doing draughting as a precursor to doing more conceptual design and R and D work, or to use Whalley's example of working as a test engineer before going into more analytical development work). Where graduates and other highly qualified technologists, or those in demand, are continually utilised in a demotivating and dehumanised frustrating way then considerable mobility occurs. In Plant D the managers were trying to stop this turnover through better career progression, with the resulting contradictions and problems mentioned above; but in Establishment B, and in fact many aerospace companies, the high turnover was integrated into their personnel strategy and used to enable restructuring of the company through wastage without redundancy.

DURATION OF EMPLOYMENT

The fifth aspect of control and recruitment relates to the nature of the employment contract and work relationship, and whether it is

temporary, fixed-contract, or permanent. This point is particularly pertinent for high technology industry where companies commonly face unstable and fluctuating markets and wish to gain numerical flexibility of staff. One way of dealing with this situation is to have a flexible utilisation policy, as exhibited in Laboratory A where staff were given permanent contracts but were not contracted to do one particular job only, instead being expected to be mobile within the organisation. Staff can then be reallocated away from contracting areas and placed in expanding ones. This policy therefore requires an organisation large enough to spread the risks of fluctuating markets by involvement in many areas.

A second way of dealing with unstable markets is to have a 'hire and fire' strategy where contracts are terminated without warning. Most companies interviewed were reluctant to embark on this where technological staff were concerned because of the industrial relations problems associated with 'laying-off' permanent staff. Thus where Plant D were laying off 50 'obsolescent' staff they had had to separate these from the newer recruits, and undergo extensive negotiation over 'early retirement' and other schemes. Establishment B had achieved restructuring through voluntary wastage and the non-filling of vacancies, which had left inconvenient holes in their organisation and had had a knock-on effect in hastening the departure of colleagues which the company had wished to keep.

A third way of tackling unstable markets and sales was adopted by many of the smaller companies interviewed who were in a situation of unstable expansion. These had issued permanent contracts and had then operated a policy of stretching their existing staff to cover peaks. This understaffing had resulted in high workloads and much over-time. A problem here was that the stress caused by such a policy had in many cases led to staff 'voting with their feet' and leaving, and one company for example had a turnover of 42 per cent in one year.

A fourth approach is to utilise short-term contract staff who are subjected to market control, and so enable a more controlled numerical flexibility of staff. Short-term contract staff can also be used to enable staff assessment as an extension of the selection process where staff are only reissued contracts where they have been judged to have worked well. Such contracts also enable ease of 'laying off'.

All the companies had some contract staff. As a manager from Establishment B put it:

It is to give us flexibility and a buffer. We have only had contract staff for the last 3 or 4 years and it has built up to quite a peak in the last 2 years. . . . We need this flexibility because a lot of the jobs we do are fairly short-term projects . . . although we have got some contract workers who have been here for several years.

Clearly it is very common practice in the military aerospace sector, where there are considerable peaks and troughs in contracts due to the MOD contract orientation of the market. Using subcontract staff is very compatible with a policy of labour market segmentation and for Laboratory A the core of permanent staff were protected by the subcontracting periphery. It is not merely an erosion of control, as it can enable market control to be exerted, and it enables numerical flexibility, and control through labour market segmentation. Thus in this case, flexibility and operational control can be as important as the gaining of direct control over labour.

Braverman (1974, p. 63) and others (Salaman, 1981; Littler, 1982; and in Wood, 1982; Carter, 1985) have seen subcontracting systems as being transitional in form because they only provide incomplete modes of control and are not compatible with direct control. The return to new forms of subcontracting systems, and the continued use of other forms of control, proves this to be an erroneous assumption. The recent expansion in subcontracting is seen as being a crucial development in the 1980s and part of the 'new work organisation forms' (see Smith, 1984 and Brown and Sisson, 1983). Smith (1984) argues that design engineers as well as draughtspeople are being increasingly brought into the subcontracting employment structure with the onset of new technology, the cheapening of fixed capital and the rising of overheads and wages. The case studies and survey conducted in this study confirm this view.

The endurance of subcontracting systems, albeit in different form, has proved to be a considerable problem for the unions hoping to consolidate or increase their membership among technological workers. The use of subcontract and contract staff has historically been a major mode of work organisation in the drawing office for draughtspeople. In the past union strength has forced contract compliance. This means that TASS approved lists of contract labour. These ensure that the contract workers have adequate employment conditions and do not undermine industrial action or trade union strength in plants. However in many new high technology companies

for new types of contract staff, unions lack the strength to impose conditions, and at many companies interviewed unions hadn't even managed to get 'a foot in the door'.

The unionisation of contract staff can cause a dilemma for unions. For example an official from ASTMS said in interview:

> We would argue that employers should be employing permanent staff, as if contracted staff were also members of ASTMS it would cause quite a division of policy in a sense, because they would be expecting us to support them being engaged, and the permanent staff would say 'hey, we don't want contract staff on three month contracts getting better money than us, we want the company to employ permanent staff and provide more jobs.

In this case, unions are worried about the rising trend in both the size of the subcontracting 'periphery' (Yates for the CBI, 1986) and the extension and variation of forms of subcontracting system. Anxieties over dwindling membership in general, and lack of strength in high technology sectors in particular, twinned with often hostile competition for recruits has led to some merger talks between the unions recruiting technological staff (ASTMS and TASS for example – this merger took place in 1988).

Not all technological staff working in a type of subcontracting relationship or in a self-employed capacity can be thought of as being in the secondary labour market, or on the periphery. There is a division between those for whom it is a symbol of their labour market strength through scarce skills (such as software consultants for instance), and those who are less powerful and are on the casualised periphery, (such as some draughtspeople, and those working in the construction industry, Bresnen et al., 1985; Moore, 1981).

The reasons for management using subcontractors or contract workers are not only related to control. There is also the necessity of coping with uncertainties in the production process, and the meeting of the need for flexibility to cover peaks in demand. Subcontract staff may be used to aid industrial fragmentation and change. Subcontracting enables payment to be related to output, and so permits labour to be purchased in discrete and variable amounts. It also allows a firm to increase its range of skills, services or products (Villa, Moore and Rubery and Wilkinson, all in Wilkinson [ed] 1981; Winch, 1985; Bresnen et al., 1985).

SUMMARY OF RECRUITMENT POLICIES AND CONTROL STRATEGIES

From the observations above we can come to three conclusions about the nature of control. Firstly, control cannot be regarded in isolation from other areas of managerial strategy which may at times be more important than the direct control of work. For example operational control or flexibility enhancement through flexible utilisation and numerical control may be more important than the direct control of labour. Strategic choices discussed above relate to the balance of the following objectives perceived to be necessary within different market and organisational environments:

– Cost reduction.
– Cost efficiency and productivity.
– Quality improvement, strengthening specialities and expertise.
– The reduction of risks, or promotion of certainty and predictability.
– Flexibility enhancement.
– Control of labour.
– Operational control.

These factors are clearly highly interdependent and sometimes contradictory.

Secondly, Salaman (1979) points to the variety of forms of control and their use in combination. Control forms do not occur in isolation from each other. To use Storey's analogy (1985) they have to be complementary to each other (if they are to be used together), either by operating at different levels, or through their insulation from each other or by their operation in a circuit, rendering the 'simultaneous application of diverse means of control' possible.

Thirdly, forms of control are not always successful and may be resisted either by individual, or collective and group action. This will be discussed in more detail in the next section.

TECHNOLOGICAL OCCUPATIONS AND MODES OF ORGANISATION

This concluding section explores the link between managerial recruitment policies on the one hand and the structure of the labour market for technological staff on the other. There are two aspects to this:

firstly the way various combinations of recruitment and utilisation policies can contribute to a much divided labour market for technological staff; secondly, the means by which technological staff organisation can limit and counter these managerial strategies.

Managerial strategies and recruitment policies contribute to the segmentation of technological staff at two levels, as shown in figure 1. This is drawn from Mok's model as summarised in Loveridge and Mok (1979).

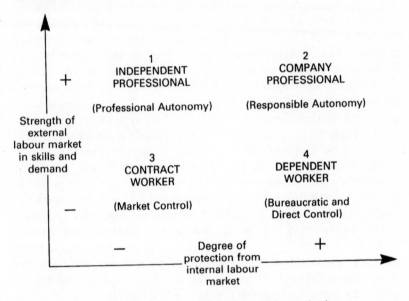

Figure 1 Models of technological staff organisation

Mok also uses a primary, secondary, internal, external matrix. His internal–external axis relates to skills specificity and opportunities for career advancement (bureaucratic–technical axis), and the primary and secondary axis relates to wages, working conditions and job security (industrial relations or social axis). The divisions are here defined differently. Firstly there is the division between technological staff protected by the internal labour market of a company, and those more subjected to market forces on the external labour market. This equates to the division within Laboratory A between the permanent computer staff and the contract staff, and likewise the staff in permanent jobs and on contracts in Establishment B and Plant D. As

Loveridge and Mok (1979) note, external jobs exist on the periphery of an organisation and not just outside of it, and although these are 'marginal' workers they may include highly trained professionals.

The second division here is in terms of an employee's power and skills, and the type of control strategy they are subjected to in labour market terms. On the external market this division can be between those who are powerful autonomous consultants who command high remuneration (such as the small number of software specialists), and the less powerful contract workers subjected to market control (many draughtspeople, and engineers in the petro-chemical industries for example). This division can take place within the company itself between those subjected to a responsible autonomy strategy and those more subject to bureaucratic and direct forms of control. Although the control strategy of dependency may have been attempted for both categories, it is only in the latter case that this has been at all successful. Within Company C this distinction relates to the separation of the applications engineers from the workshop, service and field engineers, or in Plant D between the young high flying graduate electronics engineers and the older engineers who had taken the apprentice and technician route. This division relates to their labour market strength through the level of demand for their skills and their ability to retain valued skills which are not just enterprise specific.

Thus in summary managerial strategies towards the recruitment, utilisation and control of technological staff produce four distinct modes of organisation, the independent professional, the company professional, the contract worker, and the dependent worker. Of the four case study companies presented Laboratory A employs professional–bureaucratic staff (category two), supplemented by contract workers (three); Establishment B employs bureaucratic workers of both the company professional (two) and dependent worker (four) types, supplemented by contract staff (three); Company C uses both company professionals (two) and dependent workers (four) with the former staff being in R and D and applications, and the latter in service and workshop jobs; and Plant D employs predominantly company professionals (two) and dependent workers (four) with a small number of contract staff (three).

In fact most technological staff are in categories two and four within the bureaucratic organisation (depending on their qualifications, experience and skills), and very few are in category one where the professional model of organisation is more applicable (that is independent specialists not incorporated into bureaucratic or

managerial hierarchies). Some insecure contract workers are in category three servicing the large companies without professional or hierarchical status.

The distinction between the independent professional and the company professional type can also be related to the mode of organisation and the types of control applicable. Company professionals are subjected to forms of control which allow for some discretion in the job, and in particular 'responsible autonomy'. This must be distinguished from the 'professional autonomy' of the independent professionals who are not subjected to such managerial strategies, being outside the organisation and having a higher level of professional organisation and self-regulation. Dent (this volume) argues that whereas 'responsible autonomy' is an outcome of managerial strategy in the manner described by Friedman (1977), 'professional autonomy historically predates such arrangements' and 'represents the outcome of competition and conflict between professional and managerial (including administrative) groups'. Due to the incorporation of most technologists into the bureaucratic hierarchy of the firm (and this applies to all the staff with permanent contracts within Laboratory A, Establishment B, Company C and Plant D), they have not had the independence nor the strength of corporate professional representation to have 'professional autonomy'.

Technological staff groups are best defined by the two-fold distinction between their individual labour market status and skills, and their occupational relationship with the capitalist firm. The ultimate reason why the bulk of technological staff in this case were positioned in categories two and four, with growing numbers in three, is the result of their traditional forms of work organisation and their relative lack of collective forms of organisation and resistance in high technology industry.

Their relationship with the modern firm is one of incorporation. Incorporation of technological staff in the British context is two-fold. Firstly with industrialisation and mass production many engineers were brought in to the capitalist mode of production and were incorporated into the large factory style division of labour. This drew engineers into the firm, as company professionals (two) and dependent workers (four) subjected more directly to managerial recruitment and control strategies.

The second level of incorporation has been to wed engineers to the managerial hierarchy rather than to enable them to be technical specialists within the organisation. Very few companies have even a

dual career ladder, enabling high status and pay for technologists to remain as 'incorporated' professionals rather than to gain status through entry into management. Thus even within the organisation engineers are subjected to a bureaucratic organisation of work rather than a professional one (Child, 1982).

The wedding of engineers to the organisational hierarchy and the contradictory nature of their position in the labour process (part managers, part workers) has been one reason for their lacking collective power and consciousness as a group. But there are other sources of their fragmentation and division which have also acted to make technological staff weak as a collective occupational group in the firm. These have been discussed extensively and range from the explanations relating to their lack of professional organisation, mentioning their educational development (Ahlstrom, 1982), or the fragmentation and proliferation of their professional institutions (McLoughlin, 1984). Some relate the lack of collective consciousness to their contradictory position within the capitalist enterprise and wide range of positions held, and this is often discussed in the context of their class position (for instance McLoughlin, 1983). Other explanations relate to their lack of collective union solidarity. The technological staff unions such as TASS, AUEW, ASTMS and the EETPU to mention some of the main ones, have competed for the membership recruitment of technical staff ruthlessly along the M4 corridor, identified as a potential area for union growth. Demarcation and representation disagreements have been rife, and the undermining by one union of industrial action taken by another, as epitomised by the Wapping dispute, has only deepened divisions.

Within the high technology industries there are other, particular reasons for technological groups to have less collective responses to managerial strategies than some other technical groups. One is the immaturity of many of these industries, companies and occupations. Jobs are changing fairly rapidly and so groups have not become clearly identified and established. Unions often find it harder to recruit within small companies, and those with the American style philosophy and approach to employee relations that characterise many of the higher tech companies which articulate 'flexible' practices. There are also ideological movements within the nation as a whole which imply that collectivism is 'bad' and individualistic self-striving is 'good'. Many technologists in high technology industries are highly qualified graduates and feel that their labour market position is strong enough to allow mobility to be the response to

dissatisfaction. Also, collective forms of resistance are not so appropriate where forms of control are less direct, such as where they are embedded in recruitment practices. This discourse has highlighted these more covert less direct strategies and so has emphasised the more fragmentary relationships associated with work.

In conclusion therefore there is little evidence of collective occupational action by technological staff to control recruitment within the high technology industries. Their power within the recruitment process has derived more from their attainment of skills and experience. This has enabled them to be mobile and has forced recognition of their discretion and autonomy at work. These are both symbols of individual control. Technological staff in high technology industry are resisting managerial strategies through more individual forms of action, particularly in the newer companies and for the newer occupational groups. This is because in many of these less established areas collective modes, such as unionisation, have not developed in strength. Collective union action and strength is made more difficult where managers are hostile, companies are small and volatile, and company philosophy is geared towards flexibility with individually negotiated salaries rather than nationally inspired scales. Graduate recruitment can mean a rejection of 'working class' organisations, particularly where their skills are in demand and mobility is an easy option for dissatisfaction in a tight labour market. Collective professional action is also hampered by the lack of independence of many technical occupations, and this is related to the incorporation of technological staff into the capitalist firm and their use of managerial rather than professional career hierarchies.

References

Ahlstrom, G. (1982) *Engineers and Industrial Growth* (London: Croom Helm).

Atkinson, J. (1984) 'Manpower Strategies for Flexible Organisations', *Personnel Management*, August.

Blackburn, R. and M. Mann (1979) *The Working Class in the Labour Market* (London: Macmillan).

Braverman, H. (1974) *Labor and Monopoly Capital*, New York: Monthly Review Press.

Bresnen, M., K. Wray, A. Bryman, A. Beardsworth, J. Ford and T. Keil (1985) 'The Flexibility of Recruitment in the Construction Industry: Formalisation or Re-Casualisation?' *Sociology*, vol. 19, no. 1.

Brown, W. and K. Sisson (1983) 'Industrial Relations: The Next Decade', *Industrial Relations Journal*, Spring.

Burns, T. and G. Stalker (1961) *The Management of Innovation* (London: Tavistock).

Carter, R. (1985) *Capitalism, Class Conflict and the New Middle Class* (London: Routledge & Kegan Paul).

Child, J. (1982) 'Professionals in the Corporate World: Values, Interests and Control', in D. Dunkerley and G. Salaman (eds) *International Yearbook of Organisational Studies 1981* (London: Routledge & Kegan Paul).

Clegg, S. (1975) *Power, Rule and Domination: A Critical and Empirical Understanding of Power in Sociological Theory and Everyday Life* (London: Routledge & Kegan Paul).

Clegg, S. and D. Dunkerley (1980) *Organisation, Class and Control* (London: Routledge & Kegan Paul).

Dent, M. (1986) 'Autonomy and the Medical Profession: Medical Audit and Managerial Control'. Paper presented at 4th Annual *Conference on Organisation and Control of the Labour Process*, Aston.

Doeringer, P. and M. Piore (1971) *Internal Labour Markets and Manpower Analysis* (Lexington: D.C. Heath).

Edwards, R. (1979) *Industry and Labour* (London: Heinemann).

Friedman, A. (1977) *Industry and Labour* (London: Macmillan).

Friedman, A. and J. Greenbaum (1984) 'Wanted: Renaissance People', *Datamation*, 1 Sept.

Jenkins, R. A. Bryman, J. Ford, T. Keil and A. Beardsworth (1983) 'Information in the Labour Market: The Impact of the Recession', *Sociology*, vol. 17, no. 2.

Jenkins, R. (1984) 'Acceptability, Suitability and the Search for the Habituated Worker: How Ethnic Minorities and Women Lose Out', in A. Beardsworth, A. Bryman, J. Ford and T. Keil 'Employers and Recruitment: Exploration in Labour Demand', *International Journal of Social Economics*, vol. 11, no. 7.

Jewson, N. and D. Mason (1986) 'Modes of Discrimination in the Recruitment Process: Formalisation, Fairness and Efficiency', *Sociology*, vol. 20, no. 1.

Littler, C. (1982) *The Development of the Labour Process in Capitalist Societies* (London: Heinemann) and C. Littler (1982) 'Deskilling and Changing Structures of Control', in Wood (ed.) *The Degradation of Work?* (London: Hutchinson).

Littler, C. and G. Salaman (1982) 'Bravermania and Beyond: Recent Theories of the Labour process', *Sociology*, vol. 16.

Loveridge, R. and A. Mok (1979) *Theories of Labour Market Segmentation* (London: Martinus Nijhoff).

Maguire, M. (1984) *Location and Recruitment as a Means of Control: The Case of A Northern Ireland Electronics Factory*, BSA Conference Paper (Bradford University).

Manwaring, M. (1984) 'The Extended Internal Labour Market', *Cambridge Journal of Economics*, vol. 8, no. 2.

Massey, D. and R. Meegan (1982) *The Anatomy of Job Loss: The How, Why and Where of Employment Decline* (London: Methuen).

McLoughlin, I. (1983) *Industrial Engineers and Theories of the New Middle Class*, unpublished Ph.D thesis, Bath University.

McLoughlin, I. (1984) 'Engineering Their Future: Developments in the Organisation of British Professional Engineers', *Industrial Relations Journal*, vol. 15, no. 4.

Moore, R. (1981) 'Aspects of Segmentation in the UK Building Industry Labour Market', in F. Wilkinson (ed.) *The Dynamics of Labour Market Segmentation* (London: Academic Press).

Morgan, K. and A. Sayer (1984) *A Modern Industry in a Mature Region: The Remaking of Management – Labour Relations*, Working Paper No.39 (Urban and Regional Studies, University of Sussex).

Oliver, J. and J. Turton (1982) 'Is there a Shortage of Skilled Labour?', *BJIR*, vol. 20.

Rubery, J. (1978) 'Structured Labour Markets, Worker Organisation and Low Pay', *Cambridge Journal of Economics*, vol. 2.

Rubery, J. and F. Wilkinson (1981), in Wilkinson (ed.) (see below).

Salaman, G. (1979) *Work Organisations: Resistance and Control* (London: Longman).

Salaman, G. (1981) *Class and the Corporation* (London: Fontana).

Smith, C. (1984) 'Managerial Strategies: Capital and Labour', *WORC Working Paper* No. 2.

Storey, J. (1985) 'The Means of Management Control', *Sociology*, vol. 19, no. 2.

Villa, P. (1981) 'Labour Market Segmentation and the Construction Industry in Italy', in Wilkinson (ed.) (see below).

Weber, M. (1947) *The Theory of Social and Economic Organisation* (New York Free Press).

Whalley, P. (1986) *The Social Production of Technical Work* (London: Macmillan).

Wilkinson, F. (ed.) (1981) *The Dynamics of Labour Market Segmentation* (London: Academic Press).

Winch, G. (1985) 'The Labour Process and the Labour Market', in Construction Paper for 3rd Conference on *The Organisation and Control of the Labour Process*, Manchester.

Wood, S. (ed.) (1982) *The Degradation of Work?* (London: Hutchinson).

Yates, D. (1986) 'Is Dual Labour Market Theory Dead?' (London: CBI), paper prepared for 4th Annual Conference on *The Organisation and Control of The Labour Process*, Aston.

9 Engineers and the Labour Process[1]

Chris Smith

INTRODUCTION

This chapter will examine the role of the professional engineer in the labour process. In particular it will compare engineers' perceptions of the relationship between technology and the organisation of work in two contrasting production environments: a mass production food company and a quality production aerospace company. It will assess the perspective engineers in the two settings have towards the division of labour and the role of technology in the work situation. In addition the chapter will examine how engineers' own labour process is affected by technical change and their relationship with management. These latter questions will only be discussed in relationship to engineers in the aerospace company.

ENGINEERS AND LABOUR PROCESS THEORY

Within labour process analysis, white-collar engineers – those responsible for design and planning functions within the industrial firm – have been primarily identified as part of management's technical cadre. Within this hierarchical position, engineers' design production facilities within which other workers are subordinated. They are seen as part of mental labour, responsible for separating direct, production workers from any engagement with formally designing and managing their conditions of production. Engineers' design decisions over the interface between workers and machinery are made without the involvement of the workers themselves, and are informed by criteria of economic efficiency, technological expediency or the needs of the powerful within the firm. Thus, according to Braverman (1974), the management hierarchy of monopoly capitalism possesses an implicit Taylorian ideology, developed by engineers, in which the

189

subordination and deskilling of labour, and fragmentation and control of work, are paramount. Noble (1979) also, following Braverman, views the engineer and engineering as embodying capitalist social relations of production:

> the distrust of human beings by engineers is a manifestation of capital's distrust of labour. The elimination of human error and uncertainty is the engineering expression of capital's attempt to minimize its dependence on labour by increasing its control over production. The ideology of engineering, in short, mirrors the antagonistic social relations of capitalist production. (Noble, 1979, p. 30)

For Braverman (1974, pp. 403–8) white-collar engineering occupations are polarised into routine, proletarianised positions performed by technicians, and bourgeois managerial posts held by qualified senior engineers. For Noble, the professional engineer in monopoly capitalism performs the functions of capital in a non-contradictory way, unlike the 19th century engineering craftsman, and is fully integrated into the managerial apparatus of the firm. Both these views allow little room for ideological or political conflict between engineers and managers over the former's role in perpetuating capitalist social relations. Moreover, within their analysis, differing historical circumstances, national settings or industrial sector conditions are subordinate to the structural or global forces of capitalist production which over-determine engineers' place in the division of labour. Irrespective of context, professional engineers are tied to capital.

An alternative labour process perspective on the role of the engineer in capitalism is presented by the Cooley (1980). His work suggests that there are two competing work organisation ideologies within engineering, not a single capitalist one. These I would define as *craft* and *professional–scientific* perspectives on the division of labour. Cooley is not explicit about the basis of this categorisation, but it is possible to suggest that craft ideologies are a reflection of either of these factors: (i) the historical origins of engineering as a practical craft; (ii) the wage labour condition of engineers and their common bond with other workers and differentiation from management; (iii) the apprenticeship method of training, which supports a definition of engineering as a holistic, integrated labour process, with cooperative manual and mental components that are not easily divorced. Conversely, professional–scientific ideologies reflect: (i) the principles of Taylorism or scientific management pioneered by

American engineers as a strategy for achieving dominance within the managerial hierarchies of large-scale corporations; (ii) the integration of engineers into management and support for capitalism; (iii) the professionalisation of engineers through indirect, university-based training systems, where education divides and filters their relationship with manual and lower technical workers; (iv) the development of technologies such as Computer-Aided Design (CAD), which facilitates the fracturing and compartmentalisation, along Taylorian lines, of the holistic engineering labour process performed by technical labour.

While both Braverman and Noble discuss the importance of the craft tradition within engineering, for them it is as an historical event, not something persisting within monopoly capitalism. This probably reflects their American model of engineering where: (i) corporate capital restructured higher education to provide dependable graduate engineers for its technical hierarchies (Noble, 1977); (ii) the professionalisation of engineers has been more extensive and unionism weak (Meiksins, 1984); (iii) Taylorism was an active part of engineers' bid for a place in corporate, managerial hierarchies (Layton, 1986). Cooley, probably because of his British experience as an engineer, writer on design and active trade unionism, sees the competing ideologies as contemporary alternatives. He is nevertheless pessimistic about the growing dominance of professional–scientific over craft ideologies. Part of Cooley's project is to attack the spread of scientific management in technical work in Britain, and with that has gone critiques of Taylorism entering design through Computer-Aided Design, support for workers' alternative plans for products and the cooperative organisation of production, and championing traditional 'craft' apprenticeship methods of training engineers (Smith, 1987, pp. 41–9). Despite movements towards professional–scientific ideologies in engineering, Cooley maintains that the social interaction between *all* white-collar engineering occupations in Britain is more fluid and less segmented relative to their counterparts in America and France, a conclusion that empirical research supports (Whalley, 1986; Smith, 1987). Cooley's perspective is more sensitive to national variations in engineering training, and more critical of a universal structural determination of engineers' place in the capitalist division of labour. It is also optimistic about the continued potential for interaction between manual and mental labour within the engineering labour process. While at times his analysis is too voluntaristic, I believe we need *both* structural and action dimensions for any assessment of the role of engineers in the labour process.

It is important to understand how national patterns for training engineers institutionalises their role in the division of labour. It is also important to consider, as has Whalley (1986), how differing technological or industrial settings affect the place of engineers within the same national location. Whalley studied different groups of engineers within traditional and high-tech engineering companies, and discovered variations in the methods of integrating them into management, although also a common condition of being disadvantaged within managerial hierarchies and relatively undifferentiated in terms of skill from manual craftsmen. He concluded that different organisational designs suited different production conditions, but engineers in all settings retained an autonomous status of being 'trusted' employees and were part of a new service class. I have elsewhere criticised this element in Whalley's work (Smith, 1989) and want here only to allign my methods with his, and compare the attitudes of engineers towards job design in two contrasting production settings. This approach is based on two suppositons: that the particular circumstances of an industrial sector conditions engineers' perspective towards job design; and secondly, that regardless, of industrial sector, the two alternative engineering ideologies outlined above, exist within engineers' consciousness.

In a recent study of changes in work organisation at Cadbury Ltd I found the design parameters of high-volume, low-skill production shaped the perspectives of engineers, managers and workers alike (Smith, Child and Rowlinson, 1990). In an earlier study of technical workers at British Aerospace (BAe) I found the skill structure, product and production requirements offered more choices over work design than existed at Cadbury Ltd (Smith, 1987). I will briefly examine engineers in these two production settings. In particular I will assess how far engineers involved in process design thought they incorporated conceptions of hierarchy and authority into their designs, and to what extent social considerations entered their consciousness relative to notions of engineering rationality and efficiency. And how far the two engineering ideologies are conditioned by the differing production demands of the two companies.

ENGINEERS AT CADBURY LTD

Cadbury Ltd is part of Cadbury Schweppes, one of the largest confectionery and soft drink companies in Europe. It is a high-

volume producer and has been dominant within the British chocolate bar market for over a century. In the late 1970s the company underwent a major programme of capital investment, and reduced the number of workers, products and smaller production units, concentrating production on large continuous-process plants producing 'core brands' for the global market place. The engineers we examined in our research were responsible for installing these new plants. The production traditions in the company had been Tayloristic, the division of labour between white-collar engineers and production workers very polarised, compounded by a gender-division between male engineers and female operatives. Industrial engineers had traditionally enjoyed considerable power over job design, but they were being increasing displaced by process engineers and R & D engineers involved with introducing the new equipment. We interviewed ten different engineers and I have based the following section on these interviews. However in the interests of comparison with BAe I have exluded interviews with works, methods or industrial engineers who have had a formal Taylorist training, and have rather examined packaging and R & D engineers who lack this explicit job design knowledge. I start by quoting from an R & D engineer's perspective on his role in matching people and technology.

> There are different sorts of people with different ranges of skills, aspirations and motivations. *It's far too complex for a mere engineer to understand*. I personally don't feel that as an engineer I am sufficiently informed about that to design manufacturing systems to in any way take account of [these issues]. All we try and do is – well the process side is easy enough, we try and keep control of the process and the quality, which is the key thing. Re-work is minimised, plant utilisation is maximised and we have as few people around as possible, which I think [are] very primitive objective[s] and it's time we got beyond [them]. (Senior Ṛ & D Engineer in Smith et al., 1990, p. 286)

This engineer neatly expresses the forces of mass production on job design, and the engineer's collusion with this system. All the engineers on the investment projects we interviewed concurred with this basic disparity between people and technology which was projected by this engineer. Nowhere within the project teams was there any attempt to break out of the mass production paradigm of work organisation. Within this paradigm engineers relegated workers

to unskilled roles in which elements of judgement were minimised and the repetitive performance of routine tasks maximised. Work tasks were largely defined through the technology or 'given' by machine designers, which meant labour fitted into the technical shortcomings of machinery, often because of flexibility and variance (Rosenbrock, 1981). Equipment at Bournville was always measured against the efficiency of labour. When three machines at the assembly end of an automatic packing line 'failed' because of 'unsatisfactory performance', this was performance *against* women workers, not due to any integral problem with the machines. Worker's flexibility remained a constant presence in an increasingly mechanised production environment. But it was satisfying marketing and production shortcomings, not contributing independently through its skills to the requirements of production.

The conception of labour central to engineers at Cadburys was of a flexible, efficient and malleable commodity. Some R & D engineers had an absolute commitment to automation, believing workers constantly undermined the potential performance of machinery, and wanting a fully automated factory as the ideal production environment. However most Cadbury engineers responsible for buying equipment for existing lines regarded labour as useful in so far as it was organised and intensified for maximum production. Taylorian practices were strongly embedded in the ideology of the engineers and the design principles of equipment suppliers. Specialisation and the detailed division of labour had historically provided packaging engineers with discrete targets to mechanise. Engineers at Cadburys operated with simplistic and rigid conceptions of labour efficiency and a deterministic belief in technology. Not because of any blind faith in machinery over labour, but rather because of the success of work intensification at Bournville. The historically high efficiency rates reflected the strength, legitimacy and access industrial engineers had to the labour process, something not typical of other sectors for example the car industry (Whipp and Clark, 1986).

Both variable and fixed capital were conceived in 'mechanical' terms, because the division of labour and the piecework environment of Bournville operated successfully to consistently realise the 'efficiency potential' of both labour and capital and therefore reinforce the existing design hierarchy. The engineers at Bournville could not be described as having an *a priori* engineering view of machinery. They did not, despite the above comments, simply 'view technology primarily in its internal connections' Braverman 1974,

p. 84). The strength of industrial engineering meant the labour-machine interface was strongly embedded in the design hierarchy. But, as the engineer who opened this section suggests, interaction was primarily within a low-labour, low-skill perspective.

Despite this narrow efficiency perspective, some engineers embraced certain basic elements of a human relation ideology when considering the 'social' aspects of technology. This typically translated into whether or not equipment facilitated a collective or atomistic working environment, whether operators were isolated or able to talk to each other. One packaging engineer we interviewed differentiated equipment in this way, defining equipment as *sociable* and *unsociable* depending on whether it grouped together or atomised operators. Despite this primitive social categorisation, such distinctions did not determine the choice of equipment and were not noted in engineers' visits to either equipment suppliers or confectionery manufacturers. They remained tacit assumptions that were never formally amplified in applications for capital expediture, evaluations of equipment or the performance of plant in other companies. In sum, Cadbury engineers existed within and helped reproduce a strongly Taylorian work environment, and even when, as in the case of the R & D engineer who opened this section, they thought this a severely limited job design strategy, they could not see any alternative. The conditions of mass production did not offer any alternatives.

ENGINEERS AT BRITISH AEROSPACE

The contrast between Cadbury and the BAe engineers could not, at one level, be greater. The British Aerospace plant at Filton in Bristol, where I conducted my research, had produced Concorde and employed many thousands of white-collar and manual engineering workers, who worked on small-batch production of civil aircraft worth millions of pounds. I interviewed 40 technical workers and an equivalent number of qualified engineers to the Cadbury research, but the focus here is on a small number of interviews with graduate engineers. The full details of this research has been published elsewhere (Smith, 1987), and I concentrate here on the attitudes engineers hold towards design, the technical division of labour and their relationship with management.

I interviewed two young graduate designers with different analyses of the role of the design. Bill Sweeney had worked on the computer-

isation of design and was very keen on technical change. When I interviewed him he had just returned from a union weekend education school on new technology, which I had also attended. The school left me with the impression that the union (then TASS, now merged with ASTMS to form MSF) accepted the necessity of new technology, but wanted to control its introduction. Sweeney was a recent member of the union and had had his faith in the positive importance of new technology unnerved by the school, although he was still convinced of the need for new technology. John Mulvey was the TASS representative in their section and was more cautious about the impact of new technology on work and the role of the engineer in introducing technical change. John was aware that a possible effect of their work as designers could be to deskill draughtsmen and planning engineers who would be side-stepped in the computerised link-ups between the design offices and the shop floor workers. Bill did not agree with the possible deskilling role designers might perform. This is the dialogue they had on these issues.

Bill: The design motive is merely to produce a better product, not to produce something that will deskill the operator and put him in his place. That comes about, but it's not the driving force, at least I hope that's not the driving force. I'm probably being terribly naïve about that.

John: In any interface between a machine and a human being, obviously at one end of that someone has written the instruction 'Do this' somewhere and the bloke has to follow. It is guiding the operator, therefore it must be very difficult in writing the software for that machine not to impose your view of society in someway. Even though it's a very logical process and you're trying to apply it to a whole set of procedures which are very logical. Still in the end you're writing it to control somebody else, making them do what you want them to do.

Bill: I'm sorry but that goes against what engineering is about, certainly in terms of CAD. As far as I saw my job in CAD, and I'm not a draughtsman so I don't see the draughtsman's point of view, but what I wanted to do was give the draughtman a tool. I wanted to give him a tool that he could use and would like using. I didn't want to give him an authoritarian tool that said: 'Do this!' When I design I ask, well 'what does he do naturally? What's easy for him to do? Let the bloke drive the machine the way he wants to! And let the machine be subserviant'.

John: But you're trying to interpret *his* way of thinking.

Bill: Yes, and that's what you should do.

John: The trouble is that some people do like doing the little drawings and things.

Bill: Well, yes I know.

John: [with irony] But that's a disposable skill?

Bill: That's a disposable skill, yes [laughter]

We can see from Bill Sweeney's remarks that at one level he believes he is designing in order to give the draughtsmen greater freedom. He did not want to believe that his designs are used to subordinate other technical workers to the computer. And yet, when pressed, it is clear that the designer will be part of the process of eliminating so-called 'non-essential design work', the 'mechanial' side of draughting. John Mulvey recognised that although the designer denigrates drawing, the draughtsman does not. Sweeney in one sense embodies those features of the 'benevolent technocrat' described by Elliott and Elliott (1976). He wants to aid production, for efficiency's sake, in the interests of 'progress' and does not wish to consider the negative consequences of his job as a designer. Hence he invents a scenario of increased freedom and initiative for the draughtsman, although recognising that this is, in his words, a 'cloud cuckoo land'.

There were pressures on designers to design 'as simply as possible' to account for the productivity of others. But it is also part of engineering practice under commodity production that methods should be standardised and instructions clear, precise and readily understood. Ambiguity in method – that which allowed the use of choice or initiative by draughtsmen – was deemed expensive and unnecessary. Designers did not need to think that they were actively de-skilling other workers, they were simply following engineering practice, itself invested with Taylorian ideology (Cooley, 1980). Their own evaluation of draughting skills allowed them to remove what they considered the non-essential, manual component. This ideology of engineering practice distances them from the real consequences of their actions, although those in non-managerial positions with strong contacts with other technical workers are not unaware of these consequences. The hierarchy of labour within design reproduced the differentiation between mental and manual labour important to the capitalist division of labour. This applied as much to Cadbury engineers as to those at BAe. Using the situation at the latter I will now examine further the social structure of this hierarchy.

HIERARCHY IN TECHNICAL WORK

The hierarchy in design is based on the ranking of engineering knowledge along an abstract-practical continuum. The more abstract the function, the higher up the scale it is placed. However this formal continuum was not 'accepted' as legitimate by those placed in low status positions. Designers at BAe celebrated their work and skill by reference to the non-practical nature of their work, but draughtsmen and planning engineers celebrated the importance of their work by emphasising its utility. Designers concerned with the removal of drawing through CAD, denigrated the status of drawing, and emphasised its routine, non-creative aspects. This allowed them to see the transformation of the draughtsman's role accompanied by CAD in a very positive way. Designers were, in fact, *helping* the draughtsman, making his work easier and more interesting. A designer summed up this view in the following way:

> There's nothing more boring than just pushing a pencil around a piece of paper and making marks. So, as far as CAD is concerned, as long as it gives a man more time to think, it's a good thing. . . . People tend to see the process of drawing as such a magical thing, [but] there's nothing magical in just pushing a pencil around a piece of paper.

This view follows the standard Taylorian practice of dividing a task into its constituent components and then reassembling them through an interaction between the worker and the machine. However draughtsmen tended to see their work in a more holistic way, and had aspirations for an integration of the different moments in the design process. For example, a young draughtsman in tool design told me:

> What I would like to do myself is design the tool, draw it and then go out and make it, you know I think I would get more satisfaction out of that than actually letting someone else make it. I find a great deal of satisfaction when I've done the job, even if I don't make it, just to go out and have a look at it.

Design engineers tended to view design and drawing in polarised terms while the draughtsmen I interviewed saw drawing as a process containing creative and routine elements that were difficult to separate. At least something was lost in the process if disengagement

occurred. Cooley (1981) has strongly attacked the feasibility of disaggregating design into creative and non-creative elements. The designers I interviewed wanted to monopolise the 'creative' elements, whereas Cooley argues that to even talk in these terms is to introduce Taylorian terminology which is inappropriate to design:

> The design activity cannot be separated in this arbitrary way into two disconnected elements (the quantitative and qualitative) which can then be added and combined like some kind of chemical compound. The process by which these two opposites are united by the designer to produce a new whole is a complex and as yet ill defined and researched area. The sequential basis on which the elements interact is of extreme importance . . . [and] depends on the commodity under design considerations. Even where an attempt is made to define the portion of the work that is creative and the portion that is non-creative, what cannot readily be stated is the stage at which the creative element has to be introduced when a certain stage of the non-creative work has been completed (Cooley, 1981, p. 101–2).

Cooley could be accused of mystifying intellectual work to preserve professional autonomy, because he is both a designer and writer on design. But it is probably a stronger expression of radical *craftism*, where the 'mental' and 'manual' components of engineering design cannot be separated and polarised along Taylorian lines.

I asked the two young designers quoted earlier whether they did any drawing, and they replied with an element of humour and indignation:

Bill: We don't do any drawing at all.
John: We draw pretty pictures on scraps of paper
Bill: Yea! Very loose sketches (laughter).

The basis of their differentiation from draughtsmen and other technical workers is revealed here. They are emphasising the flexibility of their work, that design and development are creative, innovative processes. This is counterposed to the inflexible, regimented work of the draughtsman, who must draw or copy with precision and accuracy the information provided to him by the designers who simply do 'pretty pictures' or 'loose sketches' on 'scraps of paper'. There were certain 'design' features performed by some draughtsmen,

although Bill and John were quick to emphasise their dominant intellectual position in the process of design:

John: Now if you take Doug Williams, [a draughtsman] now in terms of racking and basic structural elements which hold our black boxes so to speak, that is a design task which he performs so you can call him a design draughtsman. In terms of wiring, the interfacing wiring *we* tell them [i.e. circuit draughtsmen] what to [do].
Bill: We also tell them which racks to put in, and which boxes to put in.
John: That's right! Basically the overall structural task is ours.

Engineers' confident location at the top of the technical skills hierarchy did not lead to an unproblematical collusion with capitalist values, the aims of business enterprise or the authority structure of the firm as is implied by the writing of Braverman and Noble. As I shall now explain, engineers at BAe frequently experienced major conflict in introducing technical change because their technological zeal has to be filtered through power structures and the economics of the enterprise.

ENGINEERS AND THE MANAGEMENT HIERARCHY

Technical change is not planned under capitalism as a system. It may acquire a certain formal rationality within the firm, but at the macro-level it is relatively chaotic. However writers frequently overstate its rationality within the firm, and ignore the fact that there is no single logical set of criteria for introducing new machinery, but rather a choice of technical alternatives and therefore the potential for disagreement amongst designers, and between designers and managers. Melman (1981, p. 325) has noted this choice:

Designers are always confronted with an array of possible materials and degrees of precision for obtaining desired properties in machine components. . . . Production managers must select from among production methods alternatives that are readily ranked by capital intensity, capital productivity, and total unit cost.

It is often assumed in the literature on new technology and deskilling that managers are unreservedly in favour of change, especially change that enhances their power and control at the expense of

skilled labour. From my research at BAe, although not at Cadburys, I found this model of management-led or inspired technical change unrealistic (Smith, 1987; Smith et al., 1990). Design engineers were frequently at odds with management about the necessity for changes. Managers often stood in the way of new methods and techniques in the interests of peace in their department. Unlike 'conservative' managers, design engineers personified that condition of agitated dynamism central to technological change in capitalism, and this often led to battles with senior management. Much of the conflict designers experienced was with management refusing to authorise technical changes. The requirement of managerial approval for new processes tended to mean designers had to legitimate technology, to sell their ideas or the advantages of buying-in new technologies. The deskilling debate frequently underplays the division between the sellers of new technology and the buyers. The rationale adopted by the sellers of new machinery will frequently be different from the rationale adopted by those who seek to convince a reluctant manage-ment of the necessity for buying such equipment. NC and CAD are usually sold on the strength of their capacity to reduce lead time, save on labour, cheapen labour costs, increase work tempo, and replace skilled operators or draughtsmen by unskilled or less qualified staff. However designers seeking to buy in such equipment may have to emphasise the opposite features, that is, how the machinery enhances skill and gives the draughtsmen greater freedom, in order to justify to local management that such machinery will not upset industrial relations. If a technical manager was dealing with the senior manage-ment, then saving labour may also appear as a rationale. Baldry and Connolly, in their study of Computer Aided Design in seven Scottish engineering companies, found evidence of a variety of rationales used by designers to justify the introduction of CAD. They also noted the disparity between claims made by equipment suppliers on reducing labour, and the fact that none of the firms they examined intended to reduce labour, although one manager said:

> I tell the directors that it'll save on labour costs in order to get the money for the equipment. *That's the only thing the Board under-stands.* But I've no intention of getting rid of any of my people. I need them all (emphasis added; Baldry and Connolly, 1984, p. 13).

Also of importance to capital expenditure are internal company rules over capital expenditure, and the degree of centralisation or autonomy

managers and engineers have over the purchase of machinery. These, together with the dominant company strategy governing variable and fixed capital ratios, provide important contextual parameters which qualify notions of the consequences of the forward march of technology in the capitalist firm.

It follows that if the process of buying technology is not generally informed by a single grand strategy of control, but rather local questions, opportunities and rivalries between different management groups, then the potential for mistakes abound. What I found at Filton was that new machines were frequently introduced on the advice of perhaps one designer and sold off when that designer left the company. In the electrical planning department a mini-computer stood idle for eighteen months because union approval had not been sought before purchase. In other areas draughting equipment stood under-utilised because of changes in demand or because projected demand was never forthcoming. The high rate of obsolescence in high-technology industries means under-utilised machines are an expensive waste. The fact that draughtsmen in a tool design department referred to an automatic draughting machine as the 'white elephant' indicates their scathing assessment of the company's competence to introduce useful technology. It also revealed a gap between the organisation and authority structures for introducing technical change, and the necessity of that change. Engineers were not objecting to the latter, but rather management's inability to 'rationally' introduce change.

ENGINEERS' SOCIAL IDENTITY: CRAFTISM AND CORPORATISM

It was clear from my interviews with design engineers at BAe that their relationship with management was of a different order to that of other technical staff. Designers were not passively reacting to technical change, they were actively promoting it, advising management, and developing new applications for existing systems. The designers were ofen adaptive to technical change because they did not experience it as an external imposition, but as something they had struggled to see developed. Their positions as innovators and their perspective on industrial relations often went together. Their identification was frequently with 'the company' not management or other technical or manual workers. It appeared to them that they were often the *only*

group to be thinking about the interests of 'the company', while management and the unions were merely squabbling between each other. This corporate identity gave them a sense of distance from both sides.

However not all designers expressed this view and a corporate consciousness existed alongside a trade union consciousness. Trade union propaganda could feed into this corporate consciousness by emphasising the need for modernisation, capital investment and a recognition of the status of engineers. A major concern of designers was the lack of investment in BAe and British engineering as a whole. This concern united active union members and anti-union designers, which signifies the corporate nature of the demand. Investment in new technology was considered a corporate goal for the benefit of both unions and management, as this graduate designer explains:

At the moment they're at loggerheads, one group is continually trying to beat the other group down and vice versa . . . [Management] are so bloody backward and sleepy that they ain't woken up to the technological age. I don't go along with the idea of continuing to beat your head against a brick wall. It used to have to be like that, but I don't think it does now. There's too much at stake on both sides.

The logic of this argument is that increased investment would increase wages or 'should do' if management 'woke up to the new technological age'. Therefore workers and managers should be concerned with the corporate goals of increasing investment in plant and putting aside other grievances. There was no sense in which this investment would threaten his position as he saw changes occurring downstream, in the work of the planner and draughtsman, not in his own area. He considered the 'squabbles' between unions and managers to stand in the way of the *real* job of both sides which was making airframes. This argument is a familiar one and not the preserve of designers alone. Mac Smith, another designer, had similar views to Sweeney's:

Mac: I'm glad to see dogma in trade unionism go.
Chris: How do you mean?
Mac: Well the cloth capped unionist. And, for that matter, the pin-striped trousers and black jacketed engineer. We are all part of a whole to produce something. One cannot exist without the other.

The need for unity between management and workers, the need for *better communication* between the shop floor and technical staff, was expressed by management designers in strong human relations terms. John Cockran, one of the 'old school' of designers who had been through the shops, through the drawing office and into design, used the rhetoric of the 'team', and the firm as a 'big family', in his approach to the shop floor.

> It's a partnership that's not emphasised enough. I can go out onto the shop floor and talk to the operators, and I can talk to the supervision and I'm no snob, I enjoy talking to them. Having been through that path myself I know what their world is like. But there are other people who wouldn't talk to a man with a spanner or a screwdriver in his hand and that's wrong.

Cockran's view of the corporate factory meant one skilled group of workers was as functionally important as another:

> A man on the shop floor, the operator of the lathe, if he's an 'A' rate man, he is capable of using his expertise which is of no less an importance than the expertise of the qualified engineer. I see no difference between the skilled worker and the professional engineer.

This craft consciousness produced an egalitarianism that was not unusual in the design engineers I interviewed. However there was also an insistence that the skills of the designer and his expertise were undervalued relative to his counterpart in the US or France or Germany. There was a clear pecking order to this functional interdependence, with the designer at the top and the manual workers at the bottom. With Cockran, functional interdependence assumed a radical craft equality, although behind that ideology Cockran knew where he preferred to work, and was aware of the distance his ideological appeals had to bridge. Most graduate engineers who had entered design engineering after university, applied no moral evaluation to the functional interdependence between designer, draughtsman and operator, as John Cogan, a graduate design manager explains:

> They work in conjunction with each other, they are closely allied, they have two different roles to play and they play them separately,

and they are paid separately of course. A technician has a more practical approach than an engineer, and yet a more academic approach than the man on the shop floor.

In Britain, because of the legacy of craftism and fragmentation of engineering institutes, inter-dependencies between different grades of technical worker persisted as a practice and a strong ideology. Professional elitism, autonomy and the distain for manual labour, while not strong currents, existed more amongst graduate engineers than craft entrants. Professionalism had obtained an organisational expression through engineers-only unions, such as the United Kingdom Association of Professional Engineers (UKAPE), which was concentrated amongst non-managerial, graduate engineers at BAe. UKAPE emerged in the late 1960s in response to this new professionalism amongst the growing number of graduate engineers at the higher end of the technical division of labour. However increasing educational segmentation amongst technical workers did not sustain organisational segmentation. UKAPE failed to establish a national voice, due mainly to union opposition, but also to UKAPE's ambiguous conception of engineers as salaried staff, employers and professionals (Smith, 1986).

It is easy to see how craft consciousness can co-exist with professional elitism, a sense of autonomy and separateness that Cogan outlines. Both managers adopted different styles of management, which again reflected their respective craftism and elitism – Cockran a 'muck-in-with-the-men' style, and Cogan as 'each-to-his-own' style. Both were formally united around improving the wages of design engineers, but there was nothing inconsistent in that. I have discussed elsewhere the competition between the professional engineers' trade union (UKAPE) and TASS for design engineers, and shown that while the dividing line between craft protection and professional elitism is very thin, it is nevertheless crucial for influencing trade union consciousness and industrial action. At present it is a line that influences the potential involvement of higher technical staff in the labour movement and the struggles of other workers.

Alongside changes in the pattern of entry into technical work, developments in new technology have broken the established knowledge bases between the technical department and the shop floor. How this has affected designers themselves is the subject of the next section.

DESIGNERS, COMPUTER AIDED DESIGN AND WORKING CONDITIONS

Britain, as many surveys have revealed, has always had a shortage of technical labour. Writers examining the spread of CAD have interpreted these shortages as either a cause or contextual feature of the introduction of CAD in Britain, (Arnold, 1981; IDS, 1982; Arnold and Senker, 1982). While the majority of writers accept skill shortage as given, most technical workers I interviewed saw this situation in more active terms, pointing to the decline in apprenticeships, poor wages and redundancies in the aerospace industry as creating an artificial scarcity. Cooley claims that the growth of graduate engineers paralleled the decline in 'the traditional 7-year apprenticeship for designers', which in addition to reinforcing the hierarchical divisions, did not actually keep pace with the demand for technical workers (Rader and Wingert, 1981, p. 3). That this growth coincided in Britain with the rise in militancy amongst traditional technical workers may also explain the employers' new-found enthusiasm for indirect channels of training. Although the existence of such a strategy may be difficult to prove, I encountered evidence from Cadburys, Rolls-Royce, BAe, C.A. Parsons and Westland Helicopters of employers encouraging the development of managerial status amongst engineers in an attempt to block union encroachment into higher technical areas. There is also evidence of the strategic use of graduate engineers in sectors of engineering, such as cars. Wrench and Stanley (1984, p. 17) show that at BL in Birmingham, TASS believed 'the company had brought in all these graduates (described as being "very different" from the traditional design staff) to undermine the solidarity of the membership' in resisting shift-working.

Although CAD programmes had been in existence from the 1960s, it was not until the late 1970s that employers began to introduce the technology on any significant scale. This reflects the shortage of engineers created through low pay and the reduction in apprenticeship in the late 1960s, but also the new industrial relations climate that meant employers could introduce the equipment on their terms. In 1970 TASS successfully resisted the imposition of CAD at Rolls-Royce in Bristol on terms that challenged the traditional conditions of technical staff. Fundamental to management's aim was to get the maximum use from the equipment through lengthening the working day of design staff by shift systems. By the early 1980s employers

were pushing through CAD shift working agreements. One study noted that:

> Most employers want either shiftworking or some other means of extending the working hours of those who operate CAD. The main reason for this is to increase the utilisation of the expensive equipment (IDS, 1982, p. 6).

When interviewing engineers at BAe in the early 1980s, CAD was absent on any scale and I was not able to assess the changes the new technology had introduced. However those engaged with experimental equipment, or past users in other companies, offered judgements generally favourable to a widespread increase in CAD. Managerial and non-managerial designers generally highlighted the benefits of further computerisation in the design area. It is not possible to separate the effects of CAD on the designer without examining changes in the work of technical staff intermediate to design and production. Managers typically viewed CAD as speeding up design decisions by increasing the autonomy of the designer, as he interacts with the computer rather than other workers. They had a view of the technology as liberatory. John Cogan, an electrical designer explains:

> With the old system you had a design engineer produce a diagram, and when that diagram was finsihed it was issued to the planning and production engineering departments. . . . Now with the new system these intermediate stages will be eliminated largely, because once the design engineer inputs the original scheme onto the computer, he will have automatically created a data base which will provide him with all the answers he wants.

An electronics manager, who welcomed the elimination of planning and production engineering functions with the application of CAD, was convinced that this would not intensify the labour of designers:

> I don't think that it's a valid argument to say that CAD will increase the work rate. It will bring about a set of conditions, if it's organised properly and administered properly, which allow the interplay of ideas to take place far more freely and therefore it can only be a good thing.

Others also argued against intensification:

> The work pace will increase, the work load will not. Because the
> work will be simpler by the aid of the computer, so that the output
> would be increased. The performance will increase, but the actual
> work load of the individual will not.

Chris: But what about the quality of the working day, the stresses
and strains, do you see them increasing?

> If handled properly, it will enable the design engineer more time to
> think, more time to make good decisions, more time to verify his
> design and that cannot be bad. I'm biased! I'm for the CAD
> system.

Cooley (1972), analysing the role of machinery under capitalist
relations of production, and after discussing the fate of craftsmen
under the impact of NC machines, views the intensification of
designers work as inseparable from the introduction of CAD under
current capitalist conditions:

> The rate at which they (designers) will be required to make
> decisions continues to increase all the time. In the past the freedom
> to walk about to a library to gain reference material was almost a
> therapeutic necessity. The opportunities to discuss design problems
> with one's colleagues often resulted in a useful cross fertilisation of
> ideas and in a resultant better design. As more and more interac-
> tive systems are evolved and software packages built up for them,
> man's knowledge will be absorbed from him at an ever increasing
> rate and stored in the system (Cooley, 1972, p. 32–3).

An illustration of this strain was given to me by one designer,
concerned with CAD and its relationship to numerical control. He
worked in a small unit called the Numerical Geometry Group and
was very much in favour of CAD, as were all the designers.
Nevertheless he supported Cooley's assessment of the computerisation of design intensifying the working day:

> I think there is more mental strain because you don't get the quiet
> periods. If you produce a drawing, there are routine and mediocre
> parts, which you have to do anyway, so there's a quiet time where

the stress is minimal. Now, being specialists, you find that the stress is there, the mental stress is there practically the whole working day.

Rader (1982, p. 173) encountered two managerial strategies for organising CAD in the firm. In the first, the design staff controlled CAD, and in the other, specialist, CAD functions were created. For the individual designer specialisation may change the working day in ways suggested by the above respondent. It could also lead, given a cheapening of fixed capital, to the subcontracting of CAD design out of the firm and a new division between specialist and non-specialist designers. Baldry and Connolly found a definite trend towards specialisation within design offices. Against the desire of technical unions to ensure that specialisation did not occur, their studies revealed that in most firms CAD training was not open to all, and even where it was, certain individuals tended to operate the machinery more than others. They contrasted what they described as the social cohesiveness of the Drawing Office, its light open layout and solidaristic values, with the small, dark computer rooms which housed fewer individuals and were operated by shifts of workers:

> Two thirds said they missed some aspects of the traditional drawing board work, mentioning specialisation among draughtsmen (particularly mentioned by older men), identification with the drawing and the general satisfaction of putting your name on a good piece of work (Baldry and Connolly, 1984, p. 19).

One of the major changes for the draughtsmen they studied was the loss of 'ownership' over his drawing, as CAD permitted groups of draughtsmen to work on more than one drawing. Although their study concentrated on draughtsmen and not design engineers, their findings on the movement towards specialisation and a change in the social arrangements and conditions has parallels with trends at BAe's Filton site. The avionics design room, the NC Geometry group and the computer room adjacent to the NC Programming department, all conformed to their description of small, capital intensive units. However at Filton there was considerable movement between the two environments, and resistence to both shift working and specialisation. This would seem to support more recent research, which emphasises *variety* in managerial utilisation of CAD, rather than a straightforward 'Taylorisation' as predicted and feared by

Cooley. McLoughlin for example, in a study of CAD in four different company settings, found not a single management strategy, but work organisation variation along two dimensions, depending upon 'whether the systems were operated by "dedicated" or "non-dedicated" operators and . . . whether CAD work stations were "centralised" or "decentralised" ' (McLoughlin, 1989, p. 32). In other words, CAD presented management with a *choice* of organisational arrangements, which were mediated by both trade union negotiation strategies and strength, and managerial strategy, which was not uni-directional, but rather, subject to product and labour market pressures.

In his 1972 book on CAD, Cooley argued that the introduction of high capital equipment into the design area would 'proletarianise design staff and increase their strike power' (Cooley, 1972, p. 37). In design staff Cooley includes both draughtsmen and design engineers. This absence of differentiation reflects Cooley's own craftism, as well as the less educationally divided nature of technical work in the late 1960s. At BAe and within British engineering in general, graduate barriers have grown and blocked the flow of draughtsmen into certain design areas. All the young designers at Filton were graduates. I would therefore wish to differentiate where Cooley seeks to integrate. Clearly draughtsmen, as productive wage labourers and active trade unionists, have been members of the industrial proletariat since the 1920s. Designers on the other hand have traditionally resisted union advances. Their employment in small numbers, their professional and mangerial aspirations and autonomous conditions of work, have meant they occupy a position as the technical advance-guard for industrial capital. How can CAD be said to 'proletarianise' them? The obviously mechanical nature of such an equation is surprising, considering Cooley has attacked elsewhere uncritical approaches to science and technology (Cooley, 1980).

The application of high technology to the design function is an attempt by capital to reduce the number of draughtsmen and speed up the time lag between design and production. One effect of this is to reorganise the intermediate technical occupations between the designer and shop floor operator. In assessing the effect of interactive technologies on their autonomy and working conditions, the design engineers at BAe considered CAD would enhance their freedom on the job. It should be stressed however that no CAD system was fully operational in Filton during my interviews, and these were based on the experience of the designers working on experimental systems or their experience in other companies. Those who had worked on

experimental models described increased mental strain arising from an intensification of work, and this has been seen as a feature of design work with CAD (Baldry and Connolly, 1984). But others did not anticipate these changes and welcomed the *independence* the computer would give them. They could call-up information rather than having to go to see a particular technical worker. CAD was not seen as a threat, but a necessity, and a welcome one.

However computerisation has facilitated checks on the performance and cost benefit of the design function, but would this of itself lead to proletarianisation? I asked a design engineer who had worked in the design area of BAe up until 1970, before leaving for NEI Parsons, if new technology would change the class position of designers:

> I don't think it's a matter of new technology as such, I think its more a matter of the scale of technical involvement, the scale of employment of professional engineers. If you've got two hundred graduate engineers scattered in a hundred factories, they're much more likely to be part of management, part of capital. *They would expect to keep things going in a dispute.* But if two hundred graduate engineers are in one plant, then the attitude of management becomes quite different. And with a highly technical product you need engineers, well qualified draughtsmen in bulk, you cannot do it with ones and twos any more. And I think that's the difference between now and the earlier part of the century. . . . You find that your technical staff are being treated as workers. Management adopts exactly the same attitude toward design engineers, they've become a unit of production.

From this perspective, technological change or changes in skill composition in themselves cannot alter workers' class position, a view developed by Smith and Willmott in this volume. Rather the scale of employment, and the particular nature of the product and division of labour between engineers and other workers, are crucial to their experience of wage labour, perspective on production and social relation with other workers.

CONCLUSION: ENGINEERS AND SOCIAL CHOICE IN DESIGN

Designers at BAe demanded more fixed capital and the linking of CAD to NC and CAD-CAM to 'close' the gap between design and

production by eliminating the labour links in production between the two areas. At BAe they did not advocate capital investment and technological change to consciously subordinate and control the labour of other workers. They generally lacked an explicit production orientation. Nevertheless they operated within a professional engineering paradigm in which standardisation, simplification and efficiency of methods had definite implications for the freedom of others. At Cadburys, the mass production ethos meant a dedication to labour elimination and intensification was part of the engineer's working practice. Therefore, although we can at a general level concur with Noble (1977, p. 257) when he says 'technical and capitalist imperatives were blended in the person of the engineer', we must also see industrial contexts as mediating the experience of these imperatives.

The young graduate designers at BAe maintained a strong favourable self-image through the belief that they were 'freeing' others from routine work. Their view of technology reflected both the product and production conditions at BAe, but also the quality of labour in the technical offices they were designing systems for. This was highly skilled, intelligent and therefore in 'need' of a technology to free them from manual labour, give them more time to think and interact with 'liberatory' machines. By contrast, one engineer at Cadburys told me that as the new plant he was installing was operated by women, it not only had to be fool-proof 'but idiot proof' as well (Smith et al., 1990, p. 287). In other words Cadburys encouraged a *control* engineering ideology, closer to Noble's earlier comments on engineers, in which dependable, comprehensible and standardised machines stand in superior contrast to people, who engineers perceive as uncertain, unthinking, stupid and problematical. Whereas at BAe the vision of technology was of an interactive, liberatory tool which did not subordinate workers, but rather offered them an enhanced power over their work.

Some commentators in the 1960s saw technical labour as a new rebellious, advance guard of the working class, aspiring to democratically control production from below and remove athoritarian management and the vagaries of the market, Mallet (1975) and Gorz (1967). More cautious investigations of the stated aspirations of engineers, such as Whalley (1986), found individual career trajectories into management, not collective action out of capitalism, closer to the 'realities' of engineers' ambitions. At BAe engineers held ambivalent feelings towards management, and were not wholeheartedly

wedded to the spirit of capitalism if this meant, as it seemed to in Britain, a short-term orientation to profitability. It is perhaps therefore significant that *alternative* , anti-Taylorian production strategies in the 1970s were pioneered by technical workers seeking to campaign against mass redundancies and rationalisation that destroyed the life chances of skilled workers in the interest of short-term profitability. Moreover, such campaigns were initiated in the areas where white-collar engineers were concentrated, and outside mass production environments. The Lucas Aerospace workers' plan, and its imitations, were spearheaded by technical white-collar trade unionists, and orientated towards democratising strategic planning and enhancing the cooperative elements within the collective labourer of the firm, rather than segmenting these along elitist, professional lines (Smith, 1987, pp. 42–5).

Mike Cooley, who was central to the Lucas initiative, sought to make political capital out of engineers' 'loose' integration into the managerial hierarchy by developing democratically organised 'alternative products' or 'socially useful products', most coherently represented in the Lucas Aerospace Workers' Alternative Plan (Wainwright and Elliott, 1982). Within this trade union strategy it was technical workers who championed a plan to save jobs by proposing a range of products which Lucas should develop to reduce their dependency on military markets. That the engineers' position within the capitalist relations of production permits these radical challenges to the authority structure and design prorities of aerospace companies, is evidence that their class position is not straightforwardly wedded to the interests of unfettered capital accummulation for the benefit of the industrial bourgeoisie. They may serve these interests because they are paid to but also through 'education, habit, ideological blindness to alternatives, social constraints [and] conscious choice' (Noble 1977, p. 257). But choice is also constrained by the production demands of different industries. At Cadburys, alternative perspectives on job design were not considered within the engineers' sphere of competence. The demands of mass production confined the small numbers of engineers to largely maintaining a rigid, Taylorised division of labour. Whereas at BAe highly integrated and fluid relationships between different categories of technical and manual workers encouraged strong support for a cooperative, collective labour process, albeit one possessing corporatist and craftist versions.

At BAe the chief contradiction in engineers' vision of production was between civilian and military products (something at the heart of

the Lucas Plan as well) and not between a proletarian and bourgeois design menu. Without a major assault on the capitalist division of labour and training of engineers and manual workers (Braverman, 1974, p. 443), it is hard to see how this could be any different. Craftism, which had been partially sustained by employers and the state as a barrier to the engineering institutes (Whalley, 1986; Smith, 1987), had maintained a more fluid social relationship between engineers and manual workers in Britain. This has made the class relations between the two groups more ambiguous in Britain than elsewhere. However this situation began to break-up in the 1960s, with the growth of graduate engineers who by-passed the craft route. But, as I have argued here, the two engineering ideologies co-exist, and we can only assess their interaction and relative ranking by introducing such intervening variables as industrial sector, national context or training traditions, which I have argued mediate engineers' relationship to other workers in the division of labour.

Note

1. This chapter draws upon chapter 5 of my *Technical Workers* book, although I have made considerable additions and alterations in the argument presented here.

References

Armstrong, P. (1984) 'Competition between the Organisational Professions and the Evolution of Managerial Control Strategies'. Paper to the Aston/UMIST Conference *Organisation and Control of the Labour Process*, Aston University, March.

Arnold, E. (1981) 'The Manpower Implications of Computer Aided Design in the UK Engineering Industry' paper to the British Computer Society Conference, July.

Arnold, E. and P. Senker, (1982) *Designing the Future – the Implication of CAD Interactive Graphics for Employment and Skills in the British Engineering Industry* (Sussex: Science Policy Research Unit).

Baldry, C. and A. Conolly, (1984) 'Drawing the Line: Computer Aided Design and the Organisation of the Drawing Office', Paper to Aston/UMIST Conference, *Organisation and Control of the Labour Process*, Aston University, March.

Braverman, H. (1984) *Labor and Monopoly Capital* (New York: Monthly Review).

Cooley, M. (1972) *Computer Aided Design: its Nature and Implications* (Richmond, Surrey: TASS).

Cooley, M. (1980) *Architect or Bee: The Human/Technology Relationship* (Slough: Hand and Brain).

Cooley, M. (1981) 'Some Implications of C.A.D.' in J. Mermet (ed.) *CAD in Medium Sized and Small Industries* (Amsterdam: North-Holland Publishing Company).

Elliott, D. A. and R. H. Elliott, (1976) *The Control of Technology* (London: Wykeham).

Gorz, A. (1967) *Strategy for Labour A Radical Proposal* (Boston: Beacon Press).

Incomes Data Services (1982) *CAD Agreements and Pay*, IDS Study 276, October (London: Incomes Data Services).

Layton, E. T. Jr (1986) *The Revolt of the Engineers: Social Responsibility and the American Engineering Profession* (Baltimore: John Hopkins University Press).

Mallet, S. (1975) *The New Working Class* (Nottingham: Spokesman).

McLoughlin, I. (1989) 'CAD – The "Taylorisation" of Drawing Office Work', *New Technology, Work and Employment*, vol. 4, no. 1, pp. 27–39.

Meiksins, P. (1984) 'Scientific Management and Class Relations: A Dissenting View', *Theory and Society*, vol. 13, pp. 177–209.

Melman, S. (1981) 'Alternative criteria for the Design of Means of Production', *Theory and Society*, vol. 10, 3.

Noble, D. (1977) *America by Design* (New York: Knopf).

Noble, D. (1979) 'Social Choice in Machine Design: The case of Automatically Controlled Machine Tools', in A. Zimbalist (ed.) *Case Studies on the Labor Process* (New York: Monthly Review).

Rader, M. (1982) 'The Social Effects of Computer Aided Design: Current trends and Forecasts for the Future', in L. Bannan, U. Barry and O. Host (eds.) *Information Technology: Impact on the Way of Life* (Dublin: Tycooly International Publishing).

Rader, M. and B. Wingert (1981) *Computer Aided Design in Great Britain and the Federal Republic of Germany* (Karlsruhe: Abtelung fur Angwewandte Sysemanalyse, Kernforschungszentrum).

Rosenbrock, H. (1981) 'Engineers and the Work that People Do', *Work Research Unit*, Occasional Paper, No. 21 (London: Work Research Unit).

Smith, C. (1984) 'Design Engineers and the Capitalist Firm', *Work Organisation Research Centre*, Working Paper, no. 7, November, 1984, Aston University.

Smith, C. (1987) *Technical Workers: Class, Labour and Trade Unionism* (London: Macmillan).

Smith, C. (1989) 'Technical Workers: A Class and Organisational Analysis', in S. Clegg (ed.) *Organisational Theory and Class Analysis* (London: De Gruyter).

Smith, C., J. Child and M. Rowlinson (1990) *Reshaping Work: The Cadbury Experience* (Cambridge University Press).

Wainwright, H. and D. Elliott (1982) *The Lucas Plan: A New Trade Unionism in the Making* (London: Allison and Busby).

Whalley, P. (1986) *The Social Production of Technical Work* (London: Macmillan).

Whipp, R. and P. A. Clark (1986) *Innovation in the Auto Industry: Product, Process and Work Organisation* (London: Francis Pinter).

Wrench, J. and N. Stanley (1984) 'Old Problems for New Workers: A Study of the Changing Patterns of Shiftworking in the West Midlands', *British Sociological Association Annual Conference*, April.

10 Selling Oneself: Subjectivity and the Labour Process in Selling Life Insurance

David Knights and Glenn Morgan

INTRODUCTION

Sales work in general but life insurance selling in particular has not been the subject of much research within the labour process literature. Along with other 'unproductive' parts of the economy, it is not clear that selling insurance can be seen as a labour process at all. Where is the product from which surplus value can be extracted? How can production be intensified let alone revolutionised when sales personnel are so free of direct or close supervision? In what way is the sales person exploited, given the 'excessive' earnings for work that requires little by way of formal qualifications? While not professing to answer all of these questions, and indeed not wanting to accept the assumptions underlying some of them, we argue in this chapter that life insurance sales staff are experiencing many of the pressures of labour intensification. But more importantly, we seek to show the way in which these pressures or controls are built into the very sense of what it is to be a salesman or saleswoman. In short, what we focus upon in this chapter is the extent to which selling is an occupation in which the identification with the material and symbolic rewards of success are so reinforced as to transform individuals into subjects who are guaranteed to discipline themselves to a far greater degree than could be established through more direct controls.

Yet even if this form of labour intensification were not in evidence, the prominent role of life insurance institutions in the functioning of a modern capitalist economy would suggest that it is an important area of study. Apart from its sheer size (according to the Association of British Insurers, in 1987 the world wide income of British life insurance was over £21 billion) and growth (50 per cent between 1980 and 1985: see DTI, 1987; Sturdy, 1987), life insurance may be seen as

217

sociologically relevant for a number of other reasons. First, as institutional investors life insurance companies are significant forces in the capital markets, and consequently crucial to the growth and development of the capitalist mode of production. Life insurance companies are in command of massive life funds[1] which invest in markets on a national and international scale. For example, the largest – the Prudential – had a life fund valued in 1986 at £22 billion and all of the top 30 life insurance companies manage assets of £1 billion or more each. Looking at share ownership reveals the influence that these companies wield; they deal in huge sums of money and are frequently among the top shareholders in the major British companies, exercising considerable power especially in relation to takeovers and mergers (Scott, 1986).

Our concern to study the selling labour process, rather than concentrate on the complex web of social and institutional relations that control and reproduce this wealth, is partly because of the crucial role of sales in constructing and sustaining the foundations upon which it is built. For the importance of insurance to capital rests on the ability of the sales staff or agents of these companies to sell pieces of paper and promises about the future to the general public. This takes us to our second reason for considering life insurance an important topic for labour process analysis. For not only is the sales function within life insurance the precarious and flimsy structure upon which this enormous financial edifice stands, but also it involves a labour process that is unique in the way in which it contributes to the realisation of surplus value. There are a number of critics of capitalism (for example Aaronovitch, 1961; Anderson, 1964; Longstreth, 1979; Nairn, 1977) who argue that the financial sector does not create surplus value so much as act as a parasite upon the productive surpluses of the manufacturing sector[2]. However our view is that life insurance indirectly contributes to the realisation of surplus value, either by providing relatively cheap supplies of capital, or by reinforcing the general liquidity of equities and thereby facilitating the efficiency of capital. But even if it did not, the contribution of insurance to the general economy of capitalism and the employment of large groups of employees demand that it be studied in some depth.

Despite the importance of the industry's size and its institutional role in capital markets, this paper focuses on the much narrower sphere of life insurance sales as providing an insight into aspects of work that have frequently been ignored in the labour process literature. For there has been a tendency to see the labour process

exclusively in terms of the economic features of valorisation and realisation (Braverman, 1974; Burawoy, 1979). Within such a perspective, research has concentrated on the intensification of production and the role of new technology in assisting capital in its pursuit of surplus (see Thompson, 1983). This focus has resulted in a serious neglect of the subject and subjectivity in work relations (c.f. Pollert, 1981; Cockburn, 1983; 1985; Wajcman, 1983; Westwood, 1984; Collinson and Knights, 1986) so much so that a number of authors (for example Knights, 1990; Thompson, 1983; Willmott, 1990) have declared this to be the most important area for development in labour process theory. Taking this rhetoric seriously, we seek in the paper to illustrate how, although often a result of the unintended effects of other practices, the sale of life insurance involves the production of certain kinds of identity or subjectivity that are crucial to the control of labour[3].

After providing a brief description of the company within which most of the fieldwork has taken place, the paper examines in the main section how management organises and controls the labour process of selling. This section is divided into three parts, dealing respectively with the discipline to which middle and lower management are subjected, the controls and pressures upon the sales personnel, and the way in which sales staff respond to these controls. In each of these our concern is to focus upon the way that power is exercised to transform individual sales staff into subjects whose meaning and sense of themselves (therefore identity) is contingent on successfully achieving sales targets and winning recognition from the company. What from a labour process point of view is of particular interest is the way in which this mode of self-discipline operates to restrict resistance to individual strategies of employment separation. In considering these mechanisms of power we concentrate primarily on two aspects; firstly, the use of targets and commission-based earnings by management as a form of control, and secondly, management's use of social relations outside of work to shape the subjectivity of the sales force. In the final section we relate these processes to wider issues concerning the creation of financially self-disciplined subjects in the current political and economic climate.

A DESCRIPTIVE ACCOUNT OF LIFE INSURANCE SALES IN HAMLET

Empirical research has taken the form of intensive case study work in a medium-sized life insurance company with the pseudonym Hamlet.

Our principal methods of research were in-depth interviews, non-participant observation and documentary investigations of both an historical and contemporary nature pursued over a period of approximately 18 months. Hamlet was established just over 20 years ago by its parent company, a large financial conglomerate, in order to sell life insurance products to its existing customer base[4]. Well placed in having a large customer base from which to secure its insurance clients, Hamlet has grown dramatically in its short history and has made a significant and increasing contribution to the parent company's overall profits over the last few years.

Sales representatives at Hamlet have a distinct advantage over their counterparts in other parts of the industry in having access to a large 'client bank', and thus not needing to engage in what is termed 'prospecting' and 'cold calling' where securing a sales interview is often more difficult than selling the product. Instead they locate themsleves within the office space of the parent company, which has branches throughout the country, and clients are referred to them wherever the occasion warrants or on the sales person's request. Armed with considerable prior information to qualify the prospect, the Hamlet rep has a much higher completion ratio of sales to interviews than is the industry norm. This more than makes up for the slightly lower than industry average commissions per sale.

Although often working a 12 hour day as a result of evening appointments, the Hamlet sales representatives receive a package of employment benefits which the company claims to be among the best in the industry. Aside from the additional benefits of a company car, a non-contributory pension and a subsidised mortgage, the 400 representatives each earn between £25 000 and £45 000 per year with a few 'superstars', as the company calls them, earning more than that. As in many of the companies, the top half dozen representatives can earn over £100 000 per year and, as one manager put it, 'even as a failure round here you earn £20 000' (RN, Area Sales Manager, Feb. 1989).

Despite these favourable employment conditions, labour turnover of sales representatives in Hamlet is around 25 per cent of the sales force each year, though in some years it has been even higher. This high turnover in relation to other types of staff compares favourably with the industry average of 60 per cent turnover in life insurance direct sales. Senior management declare that they would like to see a reduction in turnover but not at the expense of sales productivity.

This issue of performance takes us conveniently to the subject of management control.

SUBJECTIVITY AND SELF-DISCIPLINE AS MANAGEMENT CONTROL

Although there has been a growing literature on the non-manual labour process in the insurance industry and associated financial services, almost all of it is focused either on new technology and–or gender (Crompton and Jones, 1984; Ashburner, 1986; Rolfe, 1985; Storey, 1986; Knights and Sturdy, 1987, 1989; Murray, 1989) and much of it is peripheral to the theoretical debate on the labour process (DeKadt, 1979; Barras and Swann, 1983; Rajan, 1984; BIFU, 1985). In addition most of the literature also concentrates on office employment, virtually ignoring the sales process which is so important in the life insurance industry (c.f. Collinson and Knights, 1986).[5] In presenting this data on life insurance sales, our principal concern is to demonstrate how the comparatively highly paid and traditionally autonomous occupations of middle management and insurance sales are increasingly subjected to an intensification of labour, but one that stems as much from an internalised self-discipline on the part of employees as from management techniques designed directly to control the workforce.

This internalised self-discipline could be seen as deriving from managerial strategies of 'responsible autonomy' in contrast to 'direct control' (Friedman, 1977) and in that sense not altogether distinct from human and neo-human relations methods of management (McGregor, 1960; Herzberg, 1974; Peters and Waterman, 1982). However we theorise these strategies and techniques as controls that are not simply providing extrinsic or intrinsic rewards which motivate or secure the compliance of individuals. Rather they are mechanisms of power that transform individuals into subjects who secure their very identities, sets of meanings and perceptions of reality through a participation in these practices. From this perspective, power is not imposed or compliance secured through the threat of negative sanctions or the promise of positive rewards that match the so-called needs of individuals. Rather, power involves individuals in practices whose meaning helps to constitute subjectivity. We are not suggesting that management control operates exclusively to constitute subjects as opposed to simply threatening or motivating them. But rather

that mechanisms of power generate identity commitments to the practices they produce, and thus may be seen as both more economical and effective than those that rely on devices to sanction deviance and reward compliance. For, once individuals' identitites are captured or 'caught up' in the successful accomplishment of specific practices, the exercise of power may truly be seen as localised or 'distributed in a capillary-like fashion throughout the interstices' (Foucault, 1980) of an organisation.

What we are suggesting is that control and subjectivity–identity cannot be separated from one another in the way that is assumed in conventional analyses of power (Knights and Willmott, 1989) and in traditional employee motivation schemes within neo-human relations. In our case study managers as well as sales staff are transformed, through the disciplines and mechanisms of power, into subjects whose self-definition or identity demands that they work hard at meeting targets, earning large commissions, competing for prizes so as to secure a sense of themselves as both competent and successful.

Management Control at Hamlet

As in most organisations and occupations, management control at Hamlet begins at the point of recruitment (Collinson et al., 1990) where there is a careful screening of all applicants for sales jobs within the company[6]. Recruitment of sales representatives is in the hands of the area sales managers who are subjected to what are termed 'disciplines' in the company argot. One of these disciplines is occupancy rate (that is the number of actual sales positions filled as a percentage of the number available in a particular area) which has to be maintained as near to 100 per cent as is possible. This is particularly difficult because of the high turnover rate in the sales force. Although various rewards are available to area sales managers who reach the target occupancy rate, and pressure is imposed on those who fail continuously to have a full complement of representatives, as a mechanism of power achieving a high occupancy rate becomes a measure of a manager's subjective competence and thereby a major force of self-discipline.

A key to achieving high occupancy is to manage your team in such a way that people do not leave. This may however go against other disciplines – in particular those relating to producing as much business as possible. The area sales manager has a target set for him by the company in terms of how much business must be produced in

the various categories – regular premium and single premium targets are the main 'disciplines'; these targets are standard throughout the company. He will also agree with the regional sales manager (who is responsible for about 10 area teams) a personal target for his particular team. This will invariably be above the company standard and will reflect the structure and character of the branches, the quality of the sales representatives and the aggressiveness of the area manager in seeking to push his team up the ladder of success. A central mechanism for controlling both area managers and reps is the regular publication of league tables of team and individual performance and the allocation of national and regional prizes to those who are at the top of them. This mechanism works both to 'normalize' and 'individualize' (Foucault; 1980) at one and the same time for it produces a 'norm' or standard of production somewhere between the worst and the best, below which few will want to find themselves. As a moving average this norm will be steadily rising even without the individualising effects of competitive struggles for the scarce material (for example prizes) and symbolic (for example recognition) rewards of success. While the discipline on sales reps is to intensify 'production', managers have to match the often conflicting goals of high performance and full occupancy. So although underperforming reps should be dismissed, managers cannot afford to allow the occupancy rate to fall too far below par, for overall performance is calculated as if there were a full complement of staff.

Managers were under no illusions about the sort of people that were best to recruit. They would not be seeking highly educated individuals, but rather people who were strongly motivated to earn big commissions through their capacity to sell large volumes of business. They tended to employ young men with families[7]. One regional manager said;

The only restriction I put on recruiting were ages and I prefer to employ married people, only because married people in the main tend to have a better responsible attitude towards their employer than single people do in my experience. . . . I don't think I'm a male chauvinist pig but I don't think women generally make long term sales employees – that's not because they go off and get pregnant or want to get married but I think because of the rigours of selling to a very wide cross section of people . . . it can be one of the best jobs in the world; it can be one of the most soul-destroying jobs in the world as well, having to work with certain kinds of

people and I think it affects women more than it does men (ED; Regional Sales Manager, Jan. 1989).

The managers continually emphasised the importance of support for the 'men' by their wives. One manager referred to his own experience;

> I'm divorced and remarried and I'd put that down to this type of job. That's one of the things that you sort out in your own mind – what do I want out of life? – Is my wife prepared to take it? (CK Area sales Manager Jan. 1989)

One salesman spoke about the pressure he got from his wife to do well. He had been achieving good results and was due to win a free trip with the company to Florida for a week if he could keep it up;

> Can you imagine the buzz you get at home when you go in at night and she asks how much have you done today. We bought my wife's airplane seat when we didn't know whether I was actually going – can you imagine the pressure at that stage? (EH; Sales rep; Northtown, Jan. 1989).

Of course prizes such as this are really only the icing on the cake for families, in the sense that the high income earned by Hamlet representatives provides a very comfortable sandard of living, well in advance of anything they have usually experienced. Whilst the previous jobs of the salesforce varied (some had worked for other insurance companies, others in a variety of selling jobs, still others came from 'professional' type careers such as teaching or banking, whilst there were a handful who had moved from manual work), they all came to Hamlet expecting more money than they had previously earned. Whilst a minority failed to achieve this (and left fairly rapidly) for those who could stick it out through the first few months of learning the job, the eventual material rewards more than met their expectations.

By recruiting the right sort of staff then, the area sales manager is able to solve a lot of his problems of control right from the start. However problems do remain and a variety of mechanisms are utilised by the managers in order to, as one manager put it, 'screw' them down. The crucial mechanism is the setting of targets and the way in which the manager monitors performance on targets and seeks continuously to drive sales output beyond existing levels.

The Annualised Target System

At the beginning of each business year, planners at the company's head office assess projected performance levels for each of the main products, in order to achieve profitabiliy targets set by the corporate owner. The result is a calculation for the company as a whole of the annual premium income (api) which must be generated from each product, and this is the basis for company, regional, area and individual targets to be constructed. This mechanism of power depends for its success on individual managers and sales personnel defining their own sense of themselves (that is identities) in terms of achieving or exceeding the targets. In this respect it is a mode of self-discipline that is reproductive of some of the conditions of its own continuous development, though clearly target achievement is also crucially affected by external features. For example, in the aftermath of the 1987 Stock Exchange crash people were more unwilling to purchase unit-linked insurance policies than they were previously. However in order to reinforce its effects or deal with the slippage that may result from imperfections in its operation, an individual appraisal system is administered at three-monthly intervals. This involves an initial meeting between the area manager and each representative to decide the year's targets in the context of the demands of the company, which are reflected in the manager's own targets. The personal target of each representative is usually calculated so as to result in a performance well in excess of the company target, for if an individual and–or the team can make up to 120 per cent of company performance, then there is the reward of regional and possibly national recognition as a welcome symbolic bonus on top of the large commissions resulting from the sales.

Targets and the Divided Self

The company has a reporting system that is capable of keeping an accurate check on all business sold by any individual, and this facilitates the ranking of every representative and sales manager, providing a continuous data bank for staff to engage in a personal self-monitoring of their progress against targets. In addition the information is aggregated for each area and inserted in an area team weekly newsletter, which reports and comments on league table positions. Depending on progress, the newsletter exhorts the 'troops'

either to keep up the good work or pull their socks up. The following extract illustrates the tone:

> Looking at the eight names on the list I am delighted to see that we have the base of an absolutely excellent team. In terms of efficiency this week's average of 407 points per man is equivalent to 150% of target. . . . It's great to see Stewart at the top of the list again. . . . Chas' 439 api shows that he now means business . . . as does Jim's 420 which puts him in 2nd spot MTD, Nice to see the confidence there, Jim . . . Mal's so confident and positive these days I suspect he's secretly decided to go for 'stardom' himself – I'm backing you all the way Mal! . . . We are doing a pretty successful job. It's notable that every man on the team is now pulling his weight (RN; Area Sales Manager, Feb. newsletter).

The targets that are set by the company and by the manager in the individual appraisal can become not just weekly but daily and even hourly targets for the representatives. Representatives find themselves under pressure from Monday morning to start performing; each week is a 'clean sheet', for even if they have done well previously, the discipline of targets shows no mercy or respite. For it not only divides individuals off against one another but also against themselves. The competition for the scarce rewards of 'recognition' from those who monopolise its distribution occurs not only in relation to performing 'better' than one's colleagues but, once having done so, the standard of self-discipline becomes one's past performance. Indeed this attempt to transform discipline into an internal system of self-improvement is what renders the target as a technique of power positive and productive rather than simply negative and constraining. It is also an important accessory to inter-personal competition since self-referential standards can work at any level of achievement and not just for those who are already performing at the top of the range.

Where it becomes particularly significant is in stimulating the sales person to continue working hard even after having reached target in a particular week. This may involve storing up a reserve of completed sales that are then held back to avoid falling below the company target in a lean week. However the system of self-improvement will tend to encourage the use of the reserve only as a 'fall back' and not as a means of work evasion (an issue much explored in the analysis of piecework systems amongst manual

workers; see for example Burawoy, 1979, ch. 4). Apart from building up a reserve or seeking this self-improvement, reaching target early in the week may result in an easing up, but usually only to the extent of finishing early on Thursday evening and perhaps not working on the Friday night. On the other hand, if they get off to a slow start on Monday and fail to make the equivalent of 20 per cent of their weekly target, and preferably more by Monday night, they feel a self-imposed pressure building up that may easily turn into a control from 'above'. Hence the importance of reserve banks of either completed sales or very 'warm' prospects. If a representative fails to achieve company or personal target for a few weeks, then the area manager will take action. One manager described what he would do in these circumstances:

> If they get a minus there in a month [that is fail to achieve personal target], then the following month they phone in to me on a daily basis. First of all, they come in at 9.00 on the first available Monday morning and tell me why they've not done it – we have a comprehensive discussion. Then they phone me in daily for the figures for the following month. I might even take it a step further and get them to phone in in the evening with appointments (CK; area sales manager, Jan. 1989).

Not all managers 'screw' their reps down quite as much; for one thing areas can be as large as 80 miles across and to see a rep can mean losing half a day's business, allowing for travel time. Nevertheless they all have to attend to the statistics, and if a representative consistently underperforms it affects the whole team and the manager has to take action; as one said 'I can't have lame ducks in the area because it's my ass in the sling'.

This does create a problem for the manager in that, after a period of two years in post, representatives cannot be sacked unless they either offend the company's disciplinary code or fail to sell consistently at aporoximately 60 per cent of the company target, which is the Minimum Accepted Selling Level (MASL). Managers however become adept at pressuring people into resigning by, for example, continually phoning them for performance figures, moving them from one branch to another, showing them up in team newsletters and meetings. Thus they are able to sift out those who are not performing close to the company target.

Utilising Social Relations for Control Purposes

Clearly the opportunity to earn large incomes is one of the principal motivators for sales representatives and is both a condition and consequence of the high levels of sales pressure exerted by management. For without the promise of considerable material rewards, it is unlikely that the representative would 'put up' with the pressure that then is partly responsible for their achievement. But there is some recognition among management that material factors are not sufficient in terms of maintaining continuously high levels of productivity. They need cementing with a social glue that the company and the area manager try to provide. The national sales manager takes a truly Herzbergian line on hygiene and motivating factors:

> We never talk about money. The only time we talk about money is when you are advertising for somebody to come and join us. . . . Money is a horrible thing to motivate people by – it's greedy. . . . You'll make a lot of money but we don't talk about it. . . . The sense of pride – nothing to do with money . . . . Herzberg and Maslow were right. . . . It's to do with pride, recognition, being seen (LB; national sales manager, Dec. 1988).

The company instils 'pride' by its continual display of league tables of individual, area and regional performance. At area meetings individuals can be berated for letting the team down, whilst in the weekly newsletters, little homilies can be doled out to those underperforming. The reps are made to feel important by being wined and dined (together with their spouses) by their area managers at regular company weekends. Each region has its prizes, which might include short holidays in Europe. Nationally there is a competition each quarter when the top 50 reps and their spouses are invited on trips with what is called the Presentation Club. This usually involves a trip abroad. On top of this there is the Ambassadors Club for the top 10 performers of the year. This year they are going on a Caribbean cruise, next year they go to India. These clubs are so called because it is not automatic that just because a person finishes in the top 10 or the top 50, he or she will be invited.

> It operates like a club; you can win and still not get invited. If there is any black spot on your character, you won't get on, because you're meeting the senior management as well as company direc-

tors and group senior management (LB; national sales manger, Dec. 1988).

Here can be seen in vivid profile the individualising and normalising effects of this power exercised by management, which stimulates the individual pursuit of sales returns while imposing a standard mode of behaviour, where deviants do not gain entry to the 'club' merely by virtue of sales success. Its effectiveness is in cutting individuals off from one another in such a way that they have little sense of self-worth, except through performing at very high levels of sales production, and then to offer the very social recognition of which they had been deprived through the system of individualised targets and competitive rewards. The normalising force of the targetting system is also strengthened by making admission to the annual sales conference a 'qualifying event'. Sales reps must reach 100 per cent of company target in order to be invited. Thus this year only 250 of the 400 made it:

> We went to Marbella – not one cynic, not one wanker in the audience; everyone there had earned the right to be there . . . this next year we're going to Berlin. . . . Those who didn't go get special counselling from the managers about what they should be doing . . . we made it really special; something that people will really talk about; that's what the philosophy of the sales force is about; it's about recognising excellence (LB; national sales manager, Dec. 1988).

Such dividing practices clearly separate the 'good' from the 'bad' (Foucault, 1982, p. 208) and, as the sales manager makes obvious, prevent the latter contaminating the former while at the same time putting extra pressure upon those excluded to strive for 'normality' so as to be fully accepted the following year. Presumably the cynics and 'wankers' will be ostracised and pressured sufficiently to make them either leave or change. For the very successful rep, the positive side of this normalisation is that five or more trips abroad with a spouse could be expected in the course of a year at the company's expense, as well as a range of other trips within the UK. Success then brings a multiplicity of rewards and the pressure of targets may seem a fair price to pay for the returns.

Burn-out and Turnover

Regardless of the potential rewards from the point of view of the representative, this adds up to a high level of pressure. Each hour of

the day and evening for five days a week the rep is measuring his or
her performance. How well is he or she doing against the company
target, the personal target, the MASL? How well is he or she doing
against other members of the area team, the regional team, the
national sales force? The job of a sales person is, as one manager put
it, 'a lonely one'; they have to be out there selling to people all day
and evening. That means being polite to and friendly with people at
all times and to the point at which it can become increasingly
stressful. It is not surprising then that there is a 25 per cent annual
staff turnover among the sales force. Managers talk of a burn-out
factor among the sales reps. Few make it past four years. If they do it
is usually the case that their performance starts to flatten out; they
have made plenty of money and lack the financial motivation to strain
to improve their figures. In the company's terms, they become lazy.
As a result the area sales manager will start to get on their backs. The
fact that they have been with the company a long time does not save
them. Thus a different set of pressures build up and the long serving
representative may get pushed over the edge as the hopes they had to
move out of sales into management evaporate. One area sales
manager said:

> I haven't got many old stagers – I used to have. One who has been
> with us for 12 years is off through depression – burnt out. Another
> has been a rep for 6 years – she's 90 per cent on the way to a
> nervous breakdown – burnt out. We lose the majority of our long
> serving reps because the pressure on a long term basis is very very
> difficult to keep up – especially reps who don't see themselves
> going anywhere because they haven't managed to get into the
> management pool and are not likely to. If they're in that situation
> long term, to be putting the amount of time in that they need to is
> tough. I don't ease up on them for that reason (CK; Area sales
> Manager, Jan. 1989).

The response to these pressures can be divided into three types –
employment separation, dreams of promotion, internalisation of the
role.

Employment Separation

This is clearly the easiest and most popular means of escaping the
pressure. Large numbers of sales representatives, as previously

pointed out, leave the company each year. It is also worthy of note that employment separation occurs in a mental as well as a physical sense that is the sales representative can withdraw and ignore the pressures of the job. In our view this latter alternative is limited in its availability due to the highly individualised and pressurised form of control operated by the managerial system. Thus in comparison to manual work, where the complex interactive nature of production frequently militates against tight individual target setting, in the sales process the target is for an individual *and* moreover is frequently a moving target – whatever was achieved one year either by the company or the individual is pushed to a further extent the next year. Thus floating along without being challenged is unlikely to last long in such a situation, though we did come across representatives who tried this strategy in the belief that they had either made enough money already or were not going to last much longer before being sacked or leaving.

② *Dreams of Promotion*

Many of the others hope and dream that they can secure promotion. However, despite an exclusively internal sales mangement recruitment scheme, it is generally recognised that because no more than 3 per cent of the 400 strong sales force are promoted in any single year, a necessary if not sufficient condition for upward mobility is to become a star performer. Inevitably then this is a further pressure upon sales staff to perform at a very high level of productivity since, by virtue of the uncertainty as to the standards required to be judged competent for promotion, this particular form of escape intensifies the self-discipline and reinforces the normalising effects of the performance league tables. Thus while entering management may be an ambition of many representatives, few will succeed, a reality that will be inescapable once they have been in the job for three or four years without promotion. At that point the future before them begins to look bleak and the pressure starts to build up and affect staff negatively. Up until this point they are firmly under the control of their area manager. He is continually monitoring their performance, helping them over their bad spells, encouraging them to make more money, hinting at the possibilities for promotion into management. Eventually however that control loses its force; question and doubt enter the sales representative's mind; the 'burn-out' factor is seen to come into play and employment separation has to be seen as the

better alternative to mental breakdown or dismissal for under-performance.

③ *Escape into Work*

One essential area over which the representative maintains control is the actual selling process. While the company sets targets for each person and for each product, the nature of the sales operation itself is left to the representative. Each representative is expected to abide by the company's code of conduct regarding selling as well as ensuring that all proposal forms were properly filled in. However this still leaves space for the salesperson's individual characteristics to be developed. At one level representatives could develop their own style and approach to customers. Most preferred to treat the initial intro-ductions in a conversational manner and only gradually 'warm' the customer up to the point where it became a sales presentation. At another level there is a considerable amount of autonomy regarding the sale itself. In their own personal management of this task, the sales representatives took a great deal of pride. This topic is worthy of detailed consideration.

The Sales Process, Autonomy and the Self

Much of the reason for autonomy in the sales process resides in a combination of the fact that life insurance has to be sold, since consumers rarely purchase it unsolicited, and the difficulty of its sale due to the product having little immediate concrete value to the customer. Although product knowledge and certain selling tech-niques are understood to be capable of being taught, there is a general belief that the 'good' sales person possesses certain unique qualities, and must be given space and autonomy to flourish and realise their potential in business performance. In leaving the sales-person comparatively free of constraints and regulations in respect of the selling act, this autonomy has in the past facilitated productivity through volume sales. The notion of being a good 'salesperson' becomes a way in which the individual escapes from the pressure by internalising management control systems. Targets are not exernal and imposed but become essential to the individual's identity. Thus the external system of rewards (both social and monetary) mesh with the individual's perception of their own identity and worth. The power that sales management exercise (and is simultaneously operated over

them by corporate mangement) is not a constraint; rather it is productive and positive. It produces the sales representatives as subjects, that is active agents, simultaneously producing their own conditions of constraints (the targets and system of management control) and their own conditions of freedom (the sales process and their autonomy within it).

Selling and the Consumer

Finally it is relevant to consider the relationship of these processes to the consumer of life insurance products. The task the sales person is performing and by which he or she is monitored, assessed and rewarded requires that consumers are persuaded of the need to purchase life insurance. Sales representatives utilise a variety of mechanisms to achieve this. They appeal to the consumer's guilt feelings – 'how will your family manage if you die?' They appeal to the greed of the consumer – 'life insurance is a tax efficient form of saving, more productive than putting your money into a bank or a building society'. They appeal to people's perceptions of the inadequacy of public services in general – 'don't you want your children to go to private school? Start saving now'. 'You don't want to have to rely on the state pension–National Health Service.'

The way in which these discourses mesh with contemporary New Right philosophies or 'possessive individualism' (MacPherson, 1962) in general means that the sales process is crucial in subjects acquiring a sense of themselves as individually responsible for their own circumstances and future, thus seeking private rather than collective or communal solutions to the social problems of old age, education, health and security. Because of the bureaucratic and depersonalised character of collective provision through the state, individualised subjects are already conditioned to accept private mechanisms and personal responsibility for their own social security. In effect capital has created and sustained an economy in which the social security of individuals is vulnerable and, through state provision, subjects have become highly sensitive to this vulnerability. Having constituted subjects to be preoccupied with the problems of security, collective solutions through taxation can now be discarded and replaced by individual 'financial self-discipline' promoted by the technologies of private insurance and parallel institutions (Knights 1988). Capitalism has come full circle; having aroused the insecurity and reinforced the isolation of individuals there is a 'natural' market for commodities

that at once sustain yet offer to resolve the social problems of this individualised existence. The exercise of pastoral power, where subjects are protected not only from the vicissitudes of nature but also from themselves, has simply passed from Church through the State and finally to Capital – the culmination of an historical process of continuous expansion in the commodification of social relations.

The spread of this individualised self-discipline and the multiplicity of sites through which it is organised are proliferating such that individuals find themselves increasingly involved with the institutions (for example insurance companies, the stock exchange) that represent it. Under these conditions, collective provision becomes less important, less in need of defence. What becomes more important is the performance of the Stock Exchange, because the individual is buying into the future of capitalism. But these promises of a golden retirement or a large lump sum to fund private education, etcetera can only be delivered if the stock market continues its long term upward movement. For most of the time policy holders may not be conscious of this, but at times such as a stock market crash they can see that a major failure of the system could have catastrophic effects for them. Indirectly then it locks them into compliance with – if not positive support for – the system of private capital upon which their future health, security and welfare is more clearly dependent once public provision is eroded and replaced by market alternatives.

It should not however be thought that management control and financial self-discpline are totalising in their effects; with staff turn-over rates in Hamlet at 25 per cent and much larger elsewhere, and the continuity of consumer scepticism about the life insurance salesperson, there is considerable resistance to the discourses and practices that constitute individuals as subjects preoccupied with success or financial calculation and self-discipline. The power that produces and sustains financially self-disciplined subjects may well be spreading its mechanisms and multiplying its targets, but the process is by no means complete, nor need it necessarily ever be so. However those practices that 'escape disciplinary totalization . . . offer little resistance to its further spreading' (Foucault, 1982, p. 201).

Not least this is because both the resistance and the management control and sales strategies, which are its object, reflect and reinforce individualised preoccupations with the subjectivity of securing material and symbolic success prevalent in modern society (Luckmann and Berger, 1964). They all draw on the wider political ideology that the individual is alone responsible for his or her own current and future

identity, security and welfare. Whether resisting or responding to the discipline of the financial services, there is an implicit assumption that *only* individual solutions (for example resignation) can be found to problems (for example pressure at work) that could equally be managed socially. This all forms part of the general critique of collective provision (for example employment, medical and social security) for the 'ills' of social life on the grounds of their tendency to inflict the moral hazard of reducing individual effort, care and responsibility and that they are open to other forms of abuse. Under the New Right regime, which provides a perfect direct and indirect support for the expansion of financial services, individuals are encouraged or cajoled into managing their insecurities privately by finding the right career and making their own provision for present and future material and symbolic well-being.

CONCLUSION

This chapter has drawn upon, elaborated and extended certain insights from the labour process debate to analyse management control processes in financial services.[8] In particular we have sought to show how the labour process produces not just value but subjective identities on the part of management, sales persons and customers. These subjectivities in turn are constructed from sets of understandings about social relationships which have wider circulation and legitimacy. However, in the act of selling, they are reproduced in a specific context that gives them meaning for individuals in terms of how they understand and run their lives. We would argue that whilst the sale of life insurance has very specific elements to it, this issue is not confined solely to this labour process. Rather we would argue that all labour processes are simultaneously producing value and identity. What we are suggesting is that subjects are constituted through mechanisms and strategies of power that are embodied in social practices within modern societies. Management practices have control effects not just on reduction, but on the very identities and subjectivities of those who have the responsibility to produce *and* on those who consume the product. In short, the truth of what it is to be a sales representative in Hamlet is to aspire, if not to achieve, the social and material recognition that accompanies high levels of productivity. Management do not escape this subjectivity as their own sense of competence is governed by exactly the same success

standards; they may provide workers with targets and a structure of material and symbolic reward which is tied to their attainment, but they depend on the latter for survival as competent managers.

As commodified insurance steadily displaces the collective provision of social security, so private mechanisms and strategies of transforming individuals into insurance producing and consuming subjects will proliferate and expand. Nevertheless there remain material limits and social tensions in these processes that may restrain their individualising and normalising effects. Although they have contributed massively to the re-constitution of the modern subject, it is not beyond the realms of possibility that this subjectivity could become the target of deconstruction. In Foucault's (1982, p. 216) terms we could begin 'to refuse what we are, to get rid of this kind of political "double bind", which is the simultaneous individualization and totalization of modern power structures'.

But what are the conditions for the possibility of this refusal? At minimum it demands that we do more critical analysis of the individualising and normalising effects of social practices and mechanisms of power, which we have a tendency to take for granted. Because of its concern with the intensification and degradation of work, labour process theory has neglected processes of subjectification, or the ways in which the exercise of both managerial power and wage labour transforms individuals into subjects who are tied to their own identities in ways that involve a self-discipline and reification of the objects of their security. However, once we have held up a mirror to ourselves by engaging in an analysis of the objectifying and subjectifying effects of power, we have begun to shatter the illusion that our security can be purchased like a commodity in the market place rather than through the development of a community of social relations. In short we have 'already loosened the grip, the seeming naturalness and necessity' (Foucault, 1982, p. 203) that social practices have for the constitution and control of subjectivity.

Note

* This paper forms part of a research project on regulation, deregulation and corporate strategy in Financial services under the auspices of the Financial Services Research Centre at UMIST. We acknowledge the help and encouragement of our colleagues on the project: Professor David Cooper and Christopher Grey.

Notes

1. The statistics quoted here are drawn from a variety of sources including the Annual Report of the ABI (Association of British Insurers), the Insurance Post Yearbook, Money Management, November, 1988, the Times 1000 and the Annual Abstract of Statistics, published by the HMSO, as well as private company documents. A more detailed breakdown of the industry is also available in Morgan (1988).

2. Despite the finance sector's parasitical role, the theory of finance capital (Hilferding, 1910) to which many of these authors subscribe argues that finance capital has fused with and dominated industrial capital in Britain. Various explantions for this anomaly in capitalist class relations are offered, most of which depend upon some notion of fractions within the dominant class. Although conflicting and competing for political control of the state, the argument is that the financial sector represented by the City has benefited from the 'exceptional' historical circumstances of its association with Britain's aristocratic and imperialistic past. Numerous problems with this mode of analysis exist, not least of which is a failure to understand the distinctively *commercial* role of financial institutions within global capitalism (Ingham, 1984).

3. The production or reproduction of specific subjectivities (for example breadwinner, family responsibility, financial self-discipline) is also crucial to the penetration of product markets, and clearly sales representatives are key figures in creating a reality that sustains them, as we examine briefly later in the paper.

4. Although life insurance companies have invested massively in back office information technology support and, indeed have developed new variations in policies, they deal essentially with the same product as they have done for the last century. The client's dependents are promised a lump sum of money or life assurance in the event of early death and, for what are called endowment or savings plans, a sum of cash at the end of a specified period, or even on request once the 10 year tax qualifying period has expired. The difference between unit-linked and with-profit policies need not concern us here, since it is simply related to how the profits from the savings plan are distributed to the policyholder (see Knights and Willmott, 1987).

5. There are a few unpublished research studies of life insurance sales within the field of occupational sociology (for example Taylor, 1956; Bain, 1959; Knights, 1973).

6. There are no women area sales managers in Hamlet, although there are a handful of women sales representatives. The presumption in life insurance is that women do not make 'good' sales persons, unless, as a result of divorce or single parenting, they have a real need as bread-winners to earn money for dependents (Collinson and Knights, 1986). As a consequence, the presumption of male reps is built into the system – one manager explained that he had just employed his first woman: 'She's a right dolly bird; I don't know how the wives are going to feel about her on company weekends!' Paradoxically, while sexuality is frequently seen as a problem in employing women in sales, in certain

selling jobs (for example finance or hire purchase companies) it is blatantly exploited as part of the woman's sales kit. This is beginning to occur increasingly in life insurance direct selling.

7. In another study we found that 'hungry' and 'greedy' were often the qualities that employers sought in their new recruits, but the sex discriminatory aspects of recruitment in life insurance are much more complicated than this. They are discussed in greater detail in Collinson et al., 1990.

8. The issues concerning the consumer are explored in more depth in Morgan and Knights, 1989; a more detailed analysis of selling practice, and particularly the impact of recent changes in legislation is available in Knights and Morgan, 1989.

References

Aaronovitch, S. (1961) *The Ruling Class* (London: Lawrence Wishart).

ABI (1984) *Life Insurance in the United Kingdom 1980–84* (London: Association of British Insurers).

ABI (1987) *Life Insurance in the United Kingdom* (London: Association of British Insurers).

Anderson, P. (1964) 'Origins of the Present Crisis' *New Left Review*, Jan–Feb.

Ashburner, L. (1986) 'Technology, the Labour Process and Gender Differentiation in the Building Society Industry', paper presented at the 4th Aston/UMIST Conference on *The Organisation and Control of the Labour Process*.

Bain, R. K. (1959) 'The Process of Professionalization: Life Insurance Selling', unpublished Doctorate, University of Chicago.

Barras, R. and J. Swann (1983) *The Adoption and Impact of Information Technology in the UK Insurance Industry* (London: Technical Change Centre).

BIFU (1985) *Jobs for the Girls – The Impact of Automation on Women's Jobs in the Finance Industry* (London: BIFU).

Braverman H. (1974) *Labor and Monopoly Capital* (New York: Monthly Review Press).

Burawoy, M. (1979) *Manufacturing Consent* (University of Chicago Press).

Cockburn, C. (1983) *Brothers: Male Dominance and Technological Change* (London: Pluto Press).

Cockburn, C. (1985) *Machinery of Dominance: Women, Men and Technical Knowledge* (London: Pluto Press).

Collinson, D. and D. Knights (1986) 'Men Only' in D. Knights and H. C. Willmott (eds) *Gender and The Labour Process* (Aldershot: Gower).

Collinson, D. D. Knights and M. Collinson (1990) *Managing to Discriminate* (London: Routledge).

Crompton, R. and G. Jones (1984) *White Collar Proletariat – Deskilling and Gender in Clerical Work* (London: Macmillan).

DeKadt, M. (1979) 'Insurance: a Clerical Work Factory', in A. Zimbalist, (ed.) *Case Studies on the Labour Process* (New York: Monthly Review Press).

DTI (1987) *Insurance Statistics: Annual Returns* (London: HMSO).
Foucault, M. (1980) *Power/Knowledge: Selected Interviews and other Writings* Colin Gordon (ed.) (Brighton: Harvester Press).
Foucault, M. (1982) 'The Subject and Power' in H. L. Dreyfus and P. Rabinow (ed) *Michel Foucault: Beyond Structuralism and Hermeneutics* (Brighton: Harvester).
Friedman, A. (1977) *Industry and Labour* (London: Macmillan).
Herzberg, F. (1974) *Work and the Nature of Man* (London: Crosby, Lockwood Staples).
Herzberg, F., B. Mausner and B. Snyderman (1959) *The Motivation to work* (New York: Wiley).
Hilferding, R. (1910) *Finance Capital* (London: Routledge and Kegan Paul) latest edition 1981.
Ingham G. (1984) *Capitalism Divided* (London: Macmillan).
Knights, D. (1973) 'The Sociology of the Salesman', unpublished Masters thesis, Manchester School of Management, UMIST.
Knights, D. (1988) 'Risk, Financial Self-Discipline and Commodity Relations: An Analysis of the growth and Development of Life Insurance in Contemporary Capitalism', in M. Neimark, (ed.) *Advances in Public Interest Accounting*, vol. 2, pp. 40–56.
Knights, D. (1990) 'Subjectivity, Power and the Labour Process', in D. Knights and H. Willmott (eds.) *Labour Process Theory* (London: Macmillan).
Knights D. and G. Morgan (1989) 'Financial Self-Discipline and Management Control in Sales', mimeo: Financial Services Research Centre, Manchester School of Management, UMIST.
Knights, D. and A. Sturdy (1987) 'Women's Work in Insurance – Information Technology and the Reproduction of Gendered Segregation' in M. J. Davidson and C. L. Cooper (eds) *Women and Information Technology* (London: John Wiley).
Knights, D. and A. Sturdy (1989) 'New Technology, Attitudes and the Intensification of Production in Insurance' in I. Varcoe (ed.) *Deciphering Science and Technology* (London: Macmillan).
Knights, D. and H. Willmott (1987) 'The Executive Fix' in J. McGoldrick (ed.) *Behavioural Studies in Management* (Amsterdam: Van Nostrand).
Knights, D. and H. Willmott (1989) 'Power and Subjectivity at Work: From Degradation to Subjugation', *Sociology*, vol. 23, no. 4, Nov.
Longstreth, F. (1979) 'The City, Industry and the State' in C. Crouch (ed.) *State and Economy in Contemporary Capitalism* (London: Croom Helm).
Luckmann, T. and P. Berger (1964) 'Social Mobility and Personal Identity', *Archives of the European Journal of Sociology*, pp. 3–31.
McGregor, D. (1960) *The Human Side of Enterprise* (New York: McGraw Hill).
MacPherson, C. B. (1962) *The Theory of Possessive Individualism* (London: Heinemann).
Morgan, G. (1988) 'The British Insurance Industry', mimeo: Financial Services Research Centre, Manchester School of Management, UMIST.
Morgan G. and D. Knights (1989) 'Constructing Consumer Protection in

Financial Services', mimeo: Financial Services Research Centre, Manchester School of Management, UMIST.

Murray, F. (1989) 'Organisation Studies and I.T. Strategies. Some Critical Considerations', *Cromtec Working Paper Series*, Manchester School of Management, UMIST.

Nairn, T. (177) 'The Decline of the British State', *New Left Review*, Mar–Apr.

Nairn, T. (1979) 'Britain's Perennial Crisis', *New Left Review*, Jan–Feb.

Peters, T. and B. Waterman (1982) *In Search of Excellence* (Harmondsworth: Penguin).

Pettigrew, A. (1985) *The Awakening Giant* (Oxford: Basil Blackwell).

Pollert, A. (1981) *Girls, Wives, Factory Lives* (London: Macmillan).

Rajan, A. (1984) *New Technology and Employment in Insurance, Banking and Building Societies* (Aldershot: Gower).

Rolfe, H. (1985) 'Skill, deskilling and new technology in the non-manual labour process' presented at the 3rd Annual UMIST/Aston Conference on *The Organisation and Control of the Labour Process*.

Scott, J. (1986) *Capitalist Property and Financial Power* (London: Wheatsheaf).

Storey, J. 1986) 'New Office Technology: Organisation and Control' in D. Knights and H. Willmott (eds) *Managing the Labour Process* (Aldershot: Gower).

Sturdy, A. (1987) 'Coping with the Pressure of Work' paper delivered at the 5th Annual Conference UMIST/ASTON Conference on *The Organisation and Control of the Labour Process*.

Taylor, L. (1956) 'The Life Insurance Man: A Sociological Analysis of the Occupation', Unpublished Phd thesis, Louisiana State University.

Thompson, P. (1983) *The Nature of Work* (London: Macmillan).

Wajcman, J. (1983) *Women in Control* (Milton Keynes: Open Univesity Press).

Westwood, S. (1984) *All Day Every Day* (London: Pluto Press).

Willmott, H. (1990) 'Subjectivity and the Dialectics of Praxis: Opening up the Core of Labour Process Analysis' in D. Knights and H. Willmott *Labour Process Theory* (London: Macmillan).

11 The Divorce of Productive and Unproductive Management

Peter Armstrong

INTRODUCTION: PRODUCTIVE AND UNPRODUCTIVE MANAGEMENT IN CAPITALIST ENTERPRISES

Since, in a capitalist economy, the accumulation of capital is 'Moses and the prophets' (Marx, 1976, p. 742), Marx defined productive labour as that which directly produces surplus value. Beyond the most rudimentary technologies however, there develops a specialisation of function within the 'collective worker', including a tendency for mental and manual labour to become separated. Even so engineering and management – more specifically, that part of management which consists of the coordination and direction necessary within any complex productive process – are, for Marx, explicitly included within the category of productive labour (*ibid*, pp. 1040, 1052–5). This remains true even where the divorce of mental from manual labour can be shown to be primarily a device whereby capitalist employers can enhance their control over the manual labour process for the purpose of increasing its yield of surplus value (cf. Braverman, 1974, p. 126). In such cases managerial control is not simply superimposed, as it were, upon an unchanged labour process in the manner attributed to the first capitalist 'bosses' by Marglin (1974). Rather the intellectual component of the labour process is separated from the manual, incorporated into the capitalist control structure and then used to fragment and simplify the manual component, thereby opening it up to managerial effort controls. This intellectual work nevertheless retains its character as a component of the productive labour process.

But not all management is productive in the Marxian sense. Alongside the division of productive labour, there also develops a differentiation within the 'global function of capital' (Carchedi, 1977)

241

once the scale of the enterprise has reached the point where the employer is no longer able to supervise operations in person. As against productive management[1] as defined above, management within the global function of capital is unproductive, being part of the capital side of the exchange of labour against capital. Marx explicitly criticised those who confused the function of direction which arose out of the communal labour process with that which was made necessary by the antagonistic character of the capitalist social relations of production (Marx 1976, p. 450).

Of course unproductive managerial work is concerned with more than just the extraction of surplus value from the labour process. There is much to be done – equally unproductive but equally vital to the well-being of a capitalist enterprise – in the field of marketing use-values so as to realise surplus value, in the strategic allocation of investment capital and in minimising the leakage of surplus value to creditor capitals and the state's tax collectors, to take just a few examples. Using the terms as Marx intended then, management in capitalist enterprises can be productive or unproductive according to whether or not it forms part of the intellectual component of productive labour.

For Mandel (1975, p. 264) this distinction is mirrored in the emergence of two fairly distinct groups of intellectual worker in the modern capitalist corporation; those 'incorporated into the process of production' and those 'integrated into administrative and superstructural institutions'. In reality these identifications can be difficult since many managers perform both productive *and* unproductive functions. Indeed, since both are necessary to the capitalist process of accumulation, there is no reason in principle why this should not be the case.

This leads into the theme of the present paper. It is first of all argued, as has already been hinted, that the origins of self-aware management in Taylorism lay in just such an interpenetration of productive and unproductive management. Over the next three-quarters of a century, there then occurred in the Anglo-Saxon world (though we are here concerned more specifically with Great Britain), a progressive disengagement of *management* (as defined by management writers, educators, and propagandists of management-as-a-profession) from its anchorage in the productive process. This was a response to growing managerial interest in corporate policy as capitalism progressed from its 'entrepreneurial' into its 'managerial' phase, coupled with an unwavering ideological belief on the part of

all concerned that management at all levels and of all things is essentially the same activity. What from within this last frame of reference appeared to be 'Theoretical Developments Since Taylor' (to quote the subtitle of Rose's (1975) book on managerial conceptions of 'Industrial Behaviour'), were in reality the fruits of a changed focus of attention which involved the *abandonment* with *management* theory of the concerns which had animated Taylorism. Instead of supplementing Taylorite methods of labour process control the new fields of study, whilst ironically claiming universality of application, *supplanted* them. Of course Taylorism did not simply disappear. It remains, as Braverman (1974, p. 87) points out, 'the bedrock of all work design', but it is now relegated to a shadow-zone of non-*management*: to production engineering, work study and the like.

These trends sat well with attempts to establish management education as a going concern and to establish management itself as a free-standing profession (which could, incidentally, lend credibility to the activities of peripatetic management consultants who lacked engineering expertise). Both developments depended upon the establishment of *management* as a body of knowledge independent of the particularities of productive processes, not integrated with them as in Taylorism.

The paper tackles this theme, not by attempting a global survey of changing management thought and practice over the century (a gigantic task) but by examining, in relation to changes in company structure, the shift in meaning of 'scientific management' from Taylor to Urwick. In the British context the justification for this procedure is that Urwick was both representative of and enormously influential within the mode of thinking which prevailed during the formative years of British management education and the emergence of management as a self-conscious occupational group, if not exactly, on some views, a profession.

TAYLORISM: THE INTEGRATION OF PRODUCTIVE AND UNPRODUCTIVE MANAGEMENT

Despite the oppressive nature of Taylor's 'scientific management' – as much rehearsed by managerial writers as Marxists (see for example, Rose, 1975 and Braverman, 1974) – it nevertheless represented more than the superposition of a set of managerial controls, unproductive in themselves, upon the labour process. In fact Taylor's approach to

the eternal problem of capital accumulation was *through* the productive process. The effort controls to be initiated by his 'thinking departments' in the name of a 'scientifically' determined 'fair day's work' and implemented under the surveillance of his 'speed bosses' *depended* upon a prior redesign, fragmentation and deskilling of the labour process. Accordingly that part of the mental labour to be carried out in the 'thinking department' which consisted of the design of tools, products and manual labour processes, lay squarely within the intellectual component of productive labour, however the division of labour may have been distorted in first place in the interests of capital accumulation (see Braverman, 1974, p. 126). The same is true of other aspects of the Taylor system: at least some of the work to be performed by the 'feed bosses' and 'repair bosses' in Taylor's system of functional foremanship must be regarded as part of the productive process.

It is equally clear that other aspects of Taylor's managerial apparatus lay within the province of unproductive management. The 'scientific' determination of effort levels, the selection of 'first class men' for each task, the drive and discipline of the 'speed bosses' and the embryonic management accounting systems – these were all means of carrying out the functions once performed by the individual capitalist himself. They were methods, not of *doing* productive labour, but means of making sure that *other people* did it. The point to stress, however, is that Taylorism approached this problem *through* productive labour. It therefore represented an integration of productive and unproductive management.

TAYLORISM AND THE SHOP MANAGEMENT TRADITION

The second point to note about Taylorism, which was frequently obscured by his own and his followers' extravagant claims of its universal applicability, was that it fell a long way short of what would nowadays be thought of as a comprehensive approach to management problems. This is Taylor in an uncharacteristically ruminative mood:

> We, however, who are primarily interested in the shop, are apt to forget that success, instead of hinging upon shop management, depends in many cases mainly upon other elements, namely, – the location of the company, its financial strength and ability, the

efficiency of its business and sales departments, its engineering ability, the superiority of its plant and equipment, or the protection offered either by patents, combination or other partial monopoly. (Taylor, 1947, p. 19).

The interesting point about this is that Taylor, despite his overall confidence that administrative problems must ultimately yield to the onslaught of engineering rationality, gives no hint that these 'external' factors, so often more crucial to business success than the potential gains from his own system, might also be susceptible to rational management action. And of course these are precisely the concerns of modern strategic management.

It could be of course that Taylor felt most at home on ground with which he had become familiar in his progress from workman to chargehand and thence to factory manager. It is nevertheless significant that the first systematic theory of management was put together by men – and Taylor was not alone – whose concerns stopped some way short of business policy. This suggests that the reason for this early myopia of the scientific management movement is to be sought not in the particularities of individual biography, but in the business context in which these theories evolved.

A clue is to be found in the somewhat later work of Sheldon, a British management thinker who wrote out of his long experience in the Cadbury family's factories:

The function of finance is outside the province of management. The control of finance is a matter for ownership. It is a function of capital, not of management. The latter is concerned only with the *uses* of capital. (Sheldon, 1924, p. 52)

To the modern reader, confronted with a massive literature on financial management, it is apparent that Sheldon inhabited a different world. So did Taylor: Bethlehem Steel, where his work began, was owned by a group of locally-based businessmen whilst Midvale, where he later struggled in vain to install the totality of his system, was owned by a group of financiers more interested in establishing monopolies and trusts than in the internal management of their factory (Rose, 1975). In neither case was Taylor in a position to influence overall policy.

The difference between this and modern capitalism has been much illuminated by Chandler and Daems' (1974) developmental schema,

according to which capitalism passes through personal entrepreneurial and managerial phases. In the personal phase, the owner of the small enterprise not only provides or procures capital and determines overall policy, he also supervises operations in detail. In the succeeding entrepreneurial phase, the scale of operations expands to the point where ownership, normally family or intimates, cedes detailed supervision to managers whilst retaining for themselves the control of key financial decisions. In the final managerial phase, ownership is reduced virtually to its Platonic essence: strategic control of the enterprise, including financial decisions, is taken over by salaried managers.

Accepting that these stages are ideal-typical abstractions from a complex and uneven historical process, it is apparent that Sheldon's modest conception of what management was about was a product of capitalism in its entrepreneurial phase. So, a generation earlier in America, was the 'shop management' tradition exemplified by Taylorism.

FAYOL – THE ASCENDANCY OF UNPRODUCTIVE MANAGEMENT

Though Fayol's career was roughly contemporary with Taylor's, and though he too was an engineer by training, the environment in which his theories were formulated was in fact an early example of managerial capitalism. Thus his long experience as the director of a group of French mines led him to reflect not on how he might interfere with other people's labour processes but on how best to formulate the overall policy of an enterprise and how to translate it into action. Essentially his administrative theory consists of a set of rational and systematic prescriptions for formulating policy and organising a division of labour and a command structure to carry it out. Though Fayol insisted that his recipes were applicable to *all* activities which involved a division of labour, when applied to capitalist enterprises, they imply the systematic imposition of capitalist priorities on the productive process. Note that this is not the same thing as saying that the production of use-values must *necessarily* take a back seat. There may well be circumstances in which the efficient production of use values is precisely the most effective means of pursuing capital accumulation. At other times of course, production may be subordinated to a variety of strategic aims – securing or

exploiting a monopoly market for example. Fayol's administrative prescriptions therefore involve the subordination of productive to unproductive management where other possibilities present themselves and are to be evaluated.

The unproductive character of Fayol's administrative prescriptions in the capitalist context shows itself in certain further aspects of his thought. Most fundamentally, his definition of management is arrived at by a process of abstraction which ignores certain aspects of intellectual productive labour which may be performed by real-life managers. All industrial organisations, he asserts, contain technical, commercial, financial, security, accounting and managerial activities. These are not performed by separate departments or individuals, but are combined in various measures in the tasks which make up the total organisation. In particular, managerial elements (which comprise forecasting, organisation, command, coordination and control) are greater in senior positions than in the more junior tasks (Fayol, 1949, pp. 3, 9, and ch. 5). Having made this point, Fayol then proceeds to discuss the managerial elements without reference to the particular activities to which they are applied or in which they are involved.

This procedure is of profound importance because it has been followed by the vast majority of writers on management since Fayol's day. In the first place the discussion of management prescriptions in *vacuo* fosters the belief that management is always and everywhere the same in essence – and indeed Fayol, as has been indicated above, believed this to be precisely the case. Though now a commonplace, such a view must have been novel at the time. An earlier generation of capitalists, when they thought about management at all, believed it to be mainly a matter of acquaintance with the process to be managed, or even with the particular factory. Management, in the sense of a common body of knowledge and code of behaviour, remained industry-specific (Pollard, 1965, p. 158).

In the second place, even though Fayol starts from a position in which management is seen as an *aspect* of a complex task, the subsequent discussion of management as a thing-in-itself prepares the ground for a point of view in which it is seen as a set of techniques which stand in an additive relationship to the technical elements of real-life managerial work. This is clearly demonstrated in a series of tables in which Fayol estimates the percentage importance of the managerial elements of the work at various hierarchical levels (Fayol, 1949, p. 8). In its severance of the organic link between management

and expertise in the process to be managed Fayolism differs profoundly from Taylorism.

Finally, the supposed universal applicability of management techniques implies that management content of tasks at various levels in an organisation differs not in kind but only in degree. Indeed just such a belief is implied in Fayol's use of the term 'scalar chain' to denote a hierarchical command structure. From the present point of view, the effect is to obscure the difference between a 'scalar chain' designed for the purpose of imposing capitalist priorities *upon* the productive process and any work of forecasting, organisation, command, coordination or control which is a necessary *part* of it. This may not unduly distress the non-Marxist, who may be disinclined to make such distinctions in any case. To these it may be of more interest that it implies that the techniques appropriate for the chargehand are precisely the same as those to be employed by the managing director.

In one respect Fayol failed to follow through the logic of his system. Despite earlier insisting that, at more senior levels in an organisation, the technical elements of the task become progressively less important and the managerial elements more so (Fayol, 1949, p. 11), Fayol was still a mining engineer who had been in charge of mines. Even in the managing director 'lack of competence is inadmissible in the specialised activity characteristic of the business', he wrote (*ibid.*, pp. 72–3), 'technical in industry, commercial in commerce . . .'.

However this is not the Fayol whose influence endures in contemporary British management thought. Despite the wide circulation of his work in his native France, his influence in the English-speaking world depended upon the labours of his great populariser, Lt. Col. Lyndall F. Urwick, in whose hands this last proviso tended to get forgotten.

THE CHANGING CONTEXT OF MANAGEMENT THEORISING

Between the wars, developments in management thinking occurred mainly in the United States of America, where until about the 1930s the Taylorite 'shop management' tradition remained dominant. Taught as 'industrial engineering' in the engineering schools, and later as elective courses in the burgeoning business schools, management at that time was still very much a matter for the engineers. In the American Society of Mechanical Engineers, for example, the

largest section was that concerned with management (Urwick, 1948, p. 5). This indeed was no more than a reflection of what was going on at the time in American Industry. As Noble (1977) put it '... engineers shaped and rationalised the Corporation and in so doing generated modern management'. Alfred P. Sloan, an engineer by training, was only the most prominent example.

However, the context of management theory was changing. In 1923, Sloan had been appointed chief executive of General Motors, typifying the emergent era of managerial capitalism. A few years later he had reorganised the corporation on the then revolutionary multi-divisional pattern which signified, amongst other things, the explicit organisation of senior managers to take over and rationalise key financial and policy decisions which had once been the province of entrepreneurial capitalists. In the interwar years, the multidivisional form gradually spread in the United States and by 1945–50 it had become the normal form of large company organisation (Steer and Cable, 1978). Against this background the American management literature too began to change.

With an appropriate lag of a few years for experience to be chewed over and reproduced in book form, what Pollard (1974) has called a 'practitioner literature' began to hit the American market. A prominent early example was Chester Barnard's 'Functions of the Executive' (1938). This was produced not by Taylorite shop managers but by men who had made it into the senior levels of corporate capitalism before yielding to the altruistic urge to share their accumulated wisdom with those eager to follow in their footsteps. The result, as Wren (1972, p. 360) has put it, was that management thought shifted from a shop-management, production orientation to a 'larger view of the administrating function'. Despite this increased breadth of vision however, these new 'scholars' (as Wren calls them) still had one thing in common with Taylor and Urwick: they 'all saw management as a universal skill applicable to all types of organisation and at all levels in the management hierarchy' (Wren, 1972, p. 408).

In England developments both in corporate structure and management thought were slower and much less impressive. Limited and fragmented markets, together with the determination of English family capitalists to retain control ensured that most firms grew to nothing like the size of their American counterparts. Nevertheless, against the general backdrop of family domination (Hannah, 1980, p. 153), a few salaried managers, mainly accountants, were slipping into positions of strategic control whenever crisis presented the opportunity

(Armstrong, 1985). Where firms did grow large, the dominant English form of organisation was the holding company, partly due to the accounting influence (for example Alford, 1976, p. 61) and partly due to its efficacy as a means of perpetuating entrepreneurial control, albeit in attenuated, exclusively financial form. Not unnaturally this development failed to produce a literature on business strategy since very often there *was* no strategy.

Against this background English managerial education and the efforts to establish managerial professionalism faced an uphill struggle. Apart from the pioneering efforts of Bowie at Manchester Commercial College and Elbourne at Regent Street, Polytechnic, there was little in the way of management education. As for managerial professionalism, the Institute of Industrial Administration struggled through the interwar years with a small, occasionally vanishing, membership before expiring in the arms of the British Institute of Management in 1948. Interestingly the historian of the Institute, TG Rose, has attributed the sorry early history of the IIA partly to the 'shop management' focus of the early teaching syllabus, which failed to appeal to 'senior industrialists' (Rose, 1954, p. 34). However it is also likely that the prevalence of familial control and nepotism in British industry at the time (see Bowie, 1930, p. 131) formed an environment quite hostile to the idea of management education. One could imagine British industrialists thinking of managerial ability as a genetically transmittable characteristic but not as something which could be acquired by education.

Until the end of the Second World War then, the world of the British management movement was a small one. In 1943 for example, the total membership of the Institute of Industrial Administration was only about 1000 (Rose, 1954, p 119). In such a setting the figure of Lyndall F. Urwick became something of a colossus. A tireless enthusiast in the cause of managerial professionalism and education, well acquainted with the American scene through his consultancies, public lectures and publications, he was able from this established position to exert a quite disproportionate influence upon British management thinking and education in the immediate postwar era.

SCIENTIFIC MANAGEMENT ACCORDING TO URWICK: THE ECLIPSE OF PRODUCTIVE MANAGEMENT

Urwick saw himself as lying squarely within the scientific management tradition, the inheritor of both Fayol *and* Taylor. The obvious

differences between the two could, he felt, be explained by their different starting points. Whereas Fayol had analysed the management process from the top down, as it were, Taylor had started from the bottom up, but both represented the same spirit of careful enquiry. The two approaches were destined in Urwick's view to meet in the middle.[2] Taylor's work in particular was 'bound to lead to a new conception of managing any form of organised co-operation, whatever its purpose' (Urwick, 1948, pp. 4–5).

By 1964 at least, Urwick believed that his writings and teachings were representative of just such a unified body of scientific knowledge concerning the administrative process. Like Fayol before him, and to a lesser extent Taylor, Urwick believed that this body of knowledge was applicable to all human activities which involved cooperation, and therefore most certainly to all types of capitalist enterprise and to all levels of management within them (Urwick, 1964, pp. 7–8).

He also believed, like his predecessors, that the body of knowledge which he identified as management theory provided a basis for the teaching of management (provided, as most management writers have provided, that the requisite 'character' was present in the first place). Finally, the universal applicability of management theory provided the foundation upon which mangement could, and indeed had, become established as a profession in its own right (Urwick, 1964).

From the start, Urwick's actual writings claimed a much broader scope for management than Taylor or Sheldon had ever done, even though Urwick had worked under the latter at Rowntrees. The following extract from the 1930 publication *Management of Tomorrow* was admiringly reproduced in *Management Today* on the occasion of Urwick's death in 1984 as evidence of the continuing relevance of his thought:

In the world as it is today, a world in which, on the whole, businessmen have taken to thinking of production first, and distribution afterwards, they have come to regard the main function of distribution as selling what production happens to make. . . . In doing so they have to a large degree lost sight of the main function of those earlier markets – the informational function. The main job of distribution is not to get rid of what production makes, it is to tell production what it ought to make. . . . Market research, while of supreme value to the individual manufacturer, is almost

always undertaken with a view, not to finding out what customer's habits really are, but to selling what some particular manufacturer can make. . . . The first thing to be done is, therefore, the creation in every business of a new and separate main division of responsibilities which may be called the 'marketing division'. . . . This marketing division or department should not be placed 'over' production and sales. It should be a parallel department with its own clearly defined duties and functions of a planning and coordinating type, such as have been indicated. (*Management Today*, April 1984, pp. 50–3)

What was modern about this in the Great Britain of the 1930s is not just that it was moving towards what would nowadays be called strategic management, it is that it is a conception of *management* addressed to the top level of control in capitalist enterprises. Where Taylor struggled to persuade entrepreneurial capitalists to install structures of work control subordinate to themselves, Urwick prescribes a structure of management intended to formulate the policy of the enterprise itself. In that sense it was a product of the coming era of managerial capitalism.

This is confirmed by the different audiences for Taylor's and Urwick's ideas. Where Taylor's views were for the most part disseminated through the American engineering societies and their journals, Urwick's lecture tours were attended by the most senior levels of industrial management. His 1948 series of lectures under the auspices of the Institute of Industrial Administration, for example, was intended for 'managing directors and senior executives'.

In these respects Urwick's work was clearly the descendant of Fayol's – indeed the unkind view would be that it consisted of little more than an elaboration of Fayol – but what about Taylorism? How was the Taylorite machinery for the detailed redesign and supervision of the labour process to be dovetailed into the Fayolite apparatus for determining and implementing overall policy? Within Urwick's writings this question, quite crucial to his claim that the new body of knowledge integrated the Taylorite and Fayolite traditions, receives no answer. His most widely circulated work, *Elements of Industrial Administration* (1947), for example sets out Fayol's administrative prescriptions, asserts that these are of universal validity and leaves it at that.

This suggests that the true relationship between Taylorism and Urwick's conception of management was very different from the

lineal descent which he claimed. In fact Urwick strongly disapproved of the entanglement with engineering which management had inherited from Taylor:

> After, and even before, Taylor's death, a great many people adopted the profession of which he was the first exponent as advisers or counsellors to business undertakings that wished to improve their methods of management. Initially, the majority of these professional men described themselves as *industrial engineers*. Since most of them were engineers by training, they were usually employed in the manufacturing function of business and, most frequently, in the metallurgical industries. This was reasonable enough in the early stages. But as the concept of management has expanded, such counsellors have dealt with all kinds of business problems for which an engineering training is not necessarily the most appropriate discipline and for which, in certain cases, some other and different discipline may be mandatory. To continue to describe as *industrial engineers* firms engaged primarily in introducing psychological concepts into the selection and handling of personnel or statistical refinements into the handling of markets, is an obvious misnomer. The more modern and exact title of *management consultant* is tending to replace *industrial engineer* in these fields (Urwick, 1963, pp. 1–5).

In fact Urwick believed that the interpenetration of management and engineering was an historical accident – it had occurred because engineers had been the only large group of salaried staff on hand at the time when there were new possibilities for logical thinking, as applied to management problems (*ibid*. See also Urwick, 1953, p. 15). However the expansion of the technical aspects of engineering curriculae had created problems for the adequate treatment of management within them. The best solution for all concerned was a parting of the ways:

> The solution of this difficulty depends primarily on a sharper definition by engineers of the boundaries of their function as *engineers* and hence to a clear distinction between those functions in business for which full engineering training is desirable if not essential, and those functions which depend primarily upon some other discipline although making use of engineering skills for the maintenance of equipment and so on. . . . There has from time to

time been a recognisable tendency in some quarters to claim that industrial engineering is synonymous with management. It is not. Management owes an immense debt to engineering, but engineering as practised by the industrial engineer is only a part of the overall work of managing. Engineering as a 'discipline' is concerned with physical forces and physical underlying sciences. Any title which includes the term *engineering* is strictly limited to dealing with things, because engineering knowledge does not include people (Urwick, 1963, pp. 1–6).

It was Urwick's view that the advent in the late 1920s of management training conceptually divorced from engineering had effecitively emancipated management from its origins. Though the syllabus of the Institute of Industrial Administration to which he refers was adopted by the engineering institutions as an educational requirement for some routes to Associate Member status, this signalled that management had become an independent body of knowledge to be 'tacked onto' engineering, as it were, not something which had organically arisen from its practice:

1927 was marked by another significant event, the starting of the lecture courses and examinations for the Diploma of the Institute of Industrial Administration – professing that management was no longer the prerogative of the technically trained engineer however high his personal calibre, and testifying to the existence of a separate profession with its own principles, its own field of study, its own standards, capable of application throughout the length and breadth of industry.

To say that the story of education for management was now complete would be the antithesis of the truth. The story of the movement within the engineering profession was complete – not because the desired end was attained, but because the technical bias had ceased to be overwhelming. The struggle now beginning was that of 'education and training for management' without restriction, the struggle for the recognition of the need for professional training and standards for management *per se*, and for the establishment of approved qualifications which would ensure for British industry a high standard of executive competence in all those to whom was entrusted responsibility for its governance (Urwick and Brech, 1959, p. 129)

Allowing for Urwick's enthusiasms, it is now clear what was to happen to Taylorite labour process controls – and most of productive management – in his vision of the managerial future. Although these would continue, in Braverman's (1974, p. 87) phrase, as 'the bedrock of all work design' they would no longer count as *management*. Instead they would be ghettoised within engineering curricula and practice, notably those of production engineering. Meanwhile Urwick and his followers could claim that 'management – in the past half-century – has developed into a technical skill, a discrete profession.

The body of knowledge on which this profession was to be based, on the evidence of Urwick's own writings, consisted of an endless elaboration of Fayol's administrative prescriptions. Abstract and formal in the sense of relating to no particular productive process, it could, and did, claim applicability to all. 'A valid distinction cannot be drawn between the study of management for one purpose rather than another' wrote Urwick in the report which designed Britain's first national system of management education (Ministry of Education, 1947, p. 7). Unproductive in the sense that the recommended administrative apparatus was dedicated to the determination and superimposition of capitalist priorities upon a labour process designed and largely coordinated outside the regime of *management*. Urwick's 'new' body of knowledge seemed perfectly attuned to the priorities of the emerging era of managerial capitalism in Great Britain. It formed the first convincing foundation for claims that management could be a profession of universal application, for management education divorced from its context of application and for the rationale of the peripatetic management consultant (such as the partners of Urwick Orr and company).

CONCLUSIONS: SOME CONSEQUENCES IN THE POST WORLD WAR TWO ERA

If, prewar, it was possible to regard Urwick as a big fish in a small pond this changed dramatically after World War Two. Official interest in improved methods of management had been stimulated by the drive for production in wartime factories and the Atlee government saw the problems of postwar reconstruction in similar terms. Given Urwick's eminence as an management educationalist, it was natural that he should chair the Ministry of Education Committee

which designed Britain's first national system of management education (Ministry of Education 1947).

In 1947 the Baillieu Committee recommended that a central institution should be formed for the purpose of improving British management, and this eventually became the British Institute of Management, with Urwick as its first chairman. In this capacity he used the platform of the 1950 annual conference to urge the need to establish a residential business school attached to a University (Nind, 1985, p. 8). Earlier, between 1942 and 1944, he had been a member of the committee which was working to establish the administrative staff college (Dictionary of Business Biography, 1986, 5: pp. 599–603).

As a further expression of official interest, 'productivity teams' were packed off to America under the Marshall Aid plan with a brief to report back on the methods by which American industry had achieved its phenomenal output record. Given Urwick's stature as a management thinker and his already wide acquaintance with the American scene, it was natural that he should head the team which reported on the contribution to productivity of American management education. The interpretation of the American success story then was largely Urwick's (Anglo-American Council on Productivity, 1951).

In the postwar context of a much-expanded official interest in management (which he himself did much to stimulate), Urwick was able to build on his previously established eminence in the world of management thought and so exert a decisive formative influence on British management education and the professionalisation movement. Urwick's pamphlet *Is Management a Profession?* (1964) went into seven reprints despite a certain lack of suspense in the story line. His *Elements of Industrial Administration* (1947) was even more influential. By 1967 the two editions had between them clocked up a total of thirteen reprints.

Of course it would be quite wrong to regard Urwick as the only significant influence. Rather he was the leading representative of what Child (1969) has called the 'management principles' approach. Even within this school there were minor differences: Brech's *Principles and Practice of Management* (1953) for example, *does* have a chapter on production, though the actual writing of this was delegated to an engineering 'associate author'. Nevertheless the school generally speaking shared Urwick's conception of management. theory as a set of abstract principles divorced from the elements of productive management in the Taylorite heritage.

On the other hand, it would be equally wrong to ignore the continuing significance of Urwick's approach now that his writings tend to attract only the 'gnawing criticism of the mice'. Later schools of management thought may have reacted against the behavioural and sociological naïvety of the 'principles' approach (see Child, 1969; Rose 1975, for example) but none has sought to restore the Taylorite interpenetration of productive and unproductive management. Today the latter is to be found only in texts and courses intended specifically for engineers or other operational specialists (see, for example, Radford and Richards, 1968). In this respect at least, Urwick's influence endures.

Not that it was established immediately or without opposition. Despite Urwick's chairmanship of the 1947 Committee on Management Education, the syllabus had to take into account the management education rquirements of the engineering institutions, and some of them were represented on the committee itself. To that extent Urwick's vision of a management profession freed from the clutches of engineering remained unfulfilled. The syllabus reflects this compromise. Although the 'management subjects proper' reflected the Fayolite abstractions of *Principles of Industrial Administration*, topics such as Production Methods and Office Organisation were included, albeit as 'tool' subjects in which the budding manager was expected to be literate rather than expert. Though this suggests that the intention was to produce managers with sufficient knowledge of these operations to oversee them rather than to participate in them, the suggested examination topics included Tool Design, Manufacturing, Raw Materials and Design for Production (Ministry of Education, 1947).

By today's standards of course, this represents a substantial involvement in productive functions for a management syllabus. But this did not mean that Urwick's mode of thought had failed in its mission. When the Urwick scheme fell terminally into disrepute (Rose 1970, p. 4), it was replaced in 1961 by the Diploma in Management Studies, in which the divorce of productive and unproductive management was far more fully accomplished. This aspect of the Diploma and later courses will form the topic of a future paper.

Related to its abstraction from productive labour, the claimed universality of management theory, characteristic of most management writers but particularly prominent in Fayol and Urwick, implies that the same management techniques are appropriate at all levels within the management hierarchy. This implication was neatly

illustrated by Urwick himself: his 1948 course of lectures delivered under the auspices of the Institute of Industrial Administration to an audience of 'managing directors and other high executives' was virtually identical to *Principles of Industrial Administration* intended for technical college students. It is at least arguable that some of the eventual disillusion with the Urwick scheme arose from the mismatch between the problems of labour supervision, as confronted by ambitious chargehands, and the techniques of formulating and implementing business strategy which they were learning at night-school.

This disenchantment has its modern counterpart. Conventionally attributed to the tendency of massed academics to commit onanism when insulated from market pressures (Griffiths and Murray, 1985), the fact that Masters in Business Administration should all want to be corporate strategists, and at the same time be unable to actually *do* anything useful when recruited at more junior levels (British Institute of Management, 1970, p 9) is entirely consistent with the logic of Fayolism and its modern descendants.

Apart from its repercussions in the field of management education, a second major consequence of the divorce of productive from unproductive management has been to reinforce the containment of British professional engineers within purely technical functions (Armstrong, 1987). The engineers' traditional remedy for this problem from the early years of this century to the Finniston Report (1980) has been to inject a quantum of 'economics of engineering' or, latterly, 'industrial administration' into engineering curriculae. That this hasn't worked is testimony to the success of the British 'management movement' in establishing *management* as a full-time specialism in its own right and to its refusal to accept as 'real' management that work of direction which arises naturally in the course of operational-ising the intellectual component of productive labour. Despite the fact that professional engineers must necessarily direct the work of others for their intellectual work to have any meaning, they are nevertheless held *qua engineers* to lack credibility as managers. At the individual level, engineers have tackled their career problems by swarming onto the Diploma in Management Studies and, latterly, the Master in Business Administration courses (Whitley et al., 1981, p. 97). Ironically, this only serves to reinforce the ghettoisation of production in British industry: the courses are overwhelmingly used as a route *out of* production and into 'general' management.

In fact the characteristic British isolation of production from the

main lines of management concern and promotion (Fores and Glover, 1978; Gill and Lockyer, 1979) is no more than the practical correlate of the Urwickian conception of *management*, though it would be too much to claim that the latter *caused* the former. In this respect management courses in the Urwick mould can, justifiably if ironically, claim to be very much in touch with the realities of British industry and therefore to play some part in reproducing them. The costs of doing so are not only that this leads to a neglect of the 'engineering dimension' of mangement functions (Finniston, 1980) but also that production, besides being downgraded in importance, is actually *impeded* by the imposition upon it of the requirements of those occupying positions of power within the hierarchies of unproductive management (Child et al., 1983).

Notes

1. Note that productive management on the Marxist definition is in some respects a broader term than produc*tion* management, as conventionally defined. Produc*tive* management includes the coordination and direction of *any* productive activity (design, transport, for example), not just production *per se*. On the other hand, some aspects of the work of produc*tion* managers may be unproductive in the Marxist sense – for example, the design and implementation of incentive payment schemes or other effort control systems, where that is part of their duties.
2. In passing, it is interesting to note how the premise behind Urwick's account of his forbears' work already contained his conclusion: Taylor's and Fayol's work were represented as analyses of different levels of a single administrative process. If both were correct therefore, the result of combining the two *could* only be a unified theory.

References

Alford, B. W. E. (1976) 'The Chandler Thesis – Some General Observations', pp. 53–70, in L. Hannah (ed.) *Management Strategy and Business Development* (London: Macmillan).

Anglo-American Council on Productivity (1951) *Education for Management* (London: Anglo-American Council for Productivity).

Armstrong, P. J. (1985) 'The Rise of Accounting Controls in British Capitalist Enterprises', *Interdisciplinary Perspectives in Accounting Conference* (University of Manchester).

Armstrong, P. J. (1987) *Engineers Managers and Trust*, mimeo, Industrial Relations Research Unit. University of Warwick.

Barnard, C. (1938) *The Functions of the Executive* (Harvard University Press).

Bowie, J. A. (1930) *Education for Business Management* (London: Oxford University Press).

Braverman, H. (1974) *Labor and Monopoly Capital* (New York: Monthly Review Press).

Brech, E. F. L. (1953) *The Principles and Practice of Management* (London: Longmans).

British Institute of Management (1970) *Business School Programmes: the Requirements of British Manufacturing Industry* (London: British Institute of Management).

Carchedi, G. (1977) *On the Economic Identification of Social Classes* (London: Routledge).

Chandler, A. D. and H. Daems (1974) 'Introduction: The Rise of Managerial Capitalism and its impact on Investment Strategy in the Western World and Japan', pp. 1–34, in H. Daems and H. Van der Wee (eds) *The Rise of Managerial Capitalism* (Louvain: Leuven University Press).

Child, J. (1969) *British Management Thought* (London: Allen and Unwin).

Child et al. (1983) 'A Price to Pay? Professionalism and Work Organisation in Britain and West Germany', *Sociology. 17*, 1. pp. 63–78.

Dictionary of Business Biography (1986) Vol. 5 (London: Butterworth).

Fayol, H. (1949) *General and Industrial Administration* (London: Pitman).

Finniston, Sir M. FRS (Chairman) (1980) Cmnd 7794, *Engineering our Future* (London: HMSO).

Fores, M. and I. Glover (1978) 'The British Disease: Professionalism', *Times Higher Educational Supplement*. 24 Feb.

Gill, R. W. T. and K. G. Lockyer (1979) *The Career Development of the Production Manager in British Industry*, British Institute of Management Occasional Paper No. 17 (London: British Institute of Management).

Griffiths, B. and H. Murray (1985) *Whose Business? an analysis of the failure of British Business Schools and a radical proposal for their privatisation* (London: Institute of Economic Affairs).

Hannah, L. (1980) 'Visible and Invisible Hands in Britain', in A. D. Chandler Jr. and H. Daems (eds) *Managerial Hierarchies* (Cambridge Mass.: Harvard University Press).

Management Today, Apr. 1984.

Mandel, E. (1975) *Late Capitalism* (London: NLB).

Marglin, S. (1974) 'What Do Bosses Do?' *Review of Radical Political Economics*, vol. 6, no. 2 pp. 60–112.

Marx, K. (1976) *Capital*, vol. 1 (Harmondsworth: Penguin).

Ministry of Education (1947) *Education of Management* (London: HMSO).

Nind, R. (1985) *A Firm Foundation* (Oxford: The Foundation for Management Education).

Noble, D. F. (1977) *America by Design* (New York: Knopf).

Pollard, S. (1965) *The Genesis of Modern Management* (London: Edward Arnold).

Pollard, H. (1974) *Developments in Management Thought* (London: Heinemann).

Radford, J. D. and D. B. Richards (1968) *The Management of Production* (London: Macmillan).
Rose, M. (1970) *Management Education in the 1970s* (London: National Economic Development Office).
Rose, M. (1975) *Industrial Behaviour* (Harmondsworth: Penguin).
Rose, T. G. (1954) *A History of the Institute of Industrial Administration* (London: The Institute of Industrial Administration).
Sheldon, O. (1924) *The Philosophy of Management*, 1965 Reprint (London: Pitman).
Steer, P. and J. Cable (1978) 'International Organisation and Profit' *Journal of Industrial Economics. 27*, pp. 13–30.
Taylor, F. W. (1947) *Scientific Management* (New York: Harper Bros.)
Urwick, L. F. (1930) *Management of Tomorrow* (London: Nisbet).
Urwick, L. F. (1947) *The Elements of Industrial Administration* (London: Pitman).
Urwick. L. F. (1948) *Business Administration Lecture Course* (London: Institute of Industrial Administration).
Urwick, L. F. (1953) *Management Education in American Business* (New York: American Management Association).
Urwick, L. F. (1963) 'Development of Industrial Engineering'. pp. 1.3–1.16 in H. B. Maynard (ed.) *Industrial Engineering Handbook* (New York: McGraw-Hill).
Urwick, L. F. (1964) *Is Management a Profession?* (London: Urwick Orr and Partners).
Urwick, L. F. and E. F. L. Brech (1959) *The Making of Scientific Management*, vol. 2. *Management in British Industry* (London: Pitman).
Whitley, R., A. Thomas and J. Marceau (1981) *Masters of Business?* (London: Tavistock).
Wren, D. A. (1972) *The Evolution of Management Thought* (New York: Ronald Press Co.).

Index